McLaren

PUBLISHERS INFORMATION
McLAREN – THE CARS

A COTERIE PRESS BOOK

ISBN: 978-1-902351-66-7 (2020 Edition)

2020 British Edition - December 2019
Published in the UK by Coterie Press Limited,
Unit 10 Langley Terrace Industrial Park, Latimer Road, Luton, LU1 3XQ
Tel: 001 303 933 2526 (Head office USA)
coterieltd@aol.com
www.coteriepress.com
www.coterieimages.com

Produced under licence from
McLaren Group Limited,
McLaren Technology Centre,
Chertsey Road, Woking, Surrey GU21 4YH
www.mclaren.com

AUTHOR: William Taylor
ADDITIONAL TEXT: David Long, David Tremayne, Stuart Codling
CREATIVE DIRECTOR: William Taylor
EDITOR: William Taylor
PUBLISHING CONSULTANT: James Bennett
PRODUCTION MANAGEMENT: Jo Taylor
DESIGN & ARTWORK: Violet Cruz - Coterie Press
IMAGE MANIPULATION: Susan Roushey, Violet Cruz
PRINTED & BOUND BY: Codra
ORIGINATION BY: Coterie Press

The author & publisher extend their special thanks to everybody who helped on the concept
and realisation of this project, both on this edition, as well as the first edition published in
2008. Without all of you this publication would never have seen the light of day: Ron Dennis,
Martin Whitmarsh, Zak Brown, Mike Flewitt, Sarah Prickett, Danielle Bottell, Stuart Robinson,
Tim Bampton, Amanda McLaren, Ian Gosling, Harry Mathews, Jan McLaren, David McLaughlin,
Neil Oatley, Diana Kay, John Allert, Harold Dermott, Clare Robertson, Jean-Louis Baldanza,
Tom & Kevin Wheatcroft.

We would also like to thank Emerson Fittipaldi, Alain Prost, Mika Häkkinen, Lewis Hamilton
and Mansour Ojjeh for taking time out of their busy schedules to offer their memories and
thoughts on McLaren. As well of course to the late, great Niki Lauda who sadly passed away
while we were working on this book. In addition, thanks must of course go to the owners of
all the cars. Without their help a book such as this would not have been possible.

Thanks also to everyone who helped on this project: Simon Diffey, John Storr at The Bruce
McLaren Trust, Greg Mathews at The Mathews Collection, David Hobbs, Stuart Leuthner, John
Bolding, John Arnold, Ron Smith, Roy Lane, Zoe Schafer & Emma Shortt at LAT, Jon Day at
MPL, Rick Hall at Hall & Hall, Kerry Adams & Jim Chisman at AM Engineering, David Davidson
at IMS, The Design Museum, Bruce Weiner, Mark Childs, Rick Parent at Prisma Cars, Mike
Longacre at bmc Racing, Dan Davis, Jimmy Aretakis, Peter Reeve at Conrod Cars, Tony
Nicholson & John Steenson at Robin Automotive, Patrick Hogan, Simon Hadfield, Gerry
Kroninger, Pam Shatraw, Garry Rankin & Dave Williams at The Donington Collection, Thor
Thorson & Tom Nuxoll at VRM, Geordie Prodis at Racetrack Legends, Bill Roushey, Tony
Harrison, Tony Roberts, Jeremy Morrison, Christopher Tate at The Masters, Howard Bartrop.

BIBLIOGRAPHY:
Racing Line, Motor Sport, Autosport, Motoring News, Autocourse (Hazleton Publishing/CMG
Publishing), Can-Am (Motorbooks), Driving Ambition (Virgin), McLaren Sports Racing Cars
(Motorbooks), McLaren! (Bond Parkhurst), Marlboro McLaren (Aston), McLaren Honda Turbo
(Haynes), McLaren The Epic Years (Haynes), McLaren, The Grand Prix, Can-Am & Indy Cars
(Hazleton), Can-Am Racing Cars 1966-1974 (Brooklands Books), Indianapolis 500 Chronicle
(Publications International Ltd), Grand Prix Guide (Charles Stewart & Company (Kirkaldy)
Ltd), Le Mans 24 Hours Yearbook (IHM Publishing), the archives of the McLaren Heritage and
Media Departments, Coterie Press, Harry Mathews, Jim Bennett, Jeff Allington, John Arnold.

CONTENTS
McLAREN – THE CARS 1964-2020

FOREWORD & INTRODUCTION

THE 1960s

THE 1970s

THE 1980s

CHAPTER 01

CHAPTER 02

CHAPTER 03

THE 1990s

THE 2000s

THE 2010s

APPENDIX

CHAPTER
04

CHAPTER
05

CHAPTER
06

FOREWORD

ZAK BROWN

Every time I walk through the doors of the McLaren Technology Centre I see the great expanse of our road and race cars lined up on the Boulevard. It's breathtaking, no matter how often you see it. It makes me feel part of a living legacy. And then I pick up this book and am reminded that what we have on display is just a fraction of McLaren's rich heritage.

The title on the cover is 'The Cars'. What I see is a story about people – bright, determined, competitive, ambitious, inventive people, and what they can build and achieve when they unleash those capabilities.

It's a story that begins in a shed with a dirt floor, with a young driver and a hand-picked group of colleagues setting out to prove that they can build better racing cars than anybody else. In the chapter we're up to at the moment the setting is a pair of award-winning, cutting-edge research and manufacturing facilities with clean, shiny surfaces, advanced tools, and a larger but no less select cast of characters crafting world-beating products with passion. The scenery has changed, many of the faces are different, but the core values remain true to those set out by our founder, Bruce McLaren.

Bruce was 25 and at the pinnacle of his racing career when he established the company with a mission to beat the world. Back then, in 1963, Bruce and his friends would sketch the design of a new car or chassis on paper, assemble it with their own hands using the rudimentary tools in the workshop, then race it. Success on track caught the eye of fellow competitors who wanted a slice of the action. Bruce would sell the car and move on to his next, better creation. It was a beautifully pure business.

Motor racing today comes with considerably more gloss attached. It's more professional, whether you're looking at Formula 1, GT racing, IndyCar or even the many club championships across the world. But if you look beyond the presentation, what do you see? The same raw essentials: peerlessly brave drivers at the controls of the slickest, fastest cars, designed by some of the smartest people on the planet.

Of course, we don't draw cars on paper or hammer out chassis frames on jigs any more. Over the past 40 years McLaren have become the leading practitioners of a science-based approach to engineering. We've pioneered the most advanced materials, championed sophisticated electronics, and become adept at using data to understand and drive performance. We measure thousands of parameters on our racing cars in real time, learning and improving continuously, and using those insights both to transform the outcome of races strategically and improve future products.

Big data has become part of the digital transformation of motorsports and the road car space. By itself, though, data is just a bunch of numbers. The skill lies in being able to pick out what's important, and to use that in a powerful way to make smarter decisions and design faster, better, more innovative cars. That skill resides in people, circling us right back to the start of the McLaren story.

Bruce would have known that. And loved it.

Zak Brown
CEO, McLaren Racing

MIKE FLEWITT

In the months immediately before his tragic death in June 1970, Bruce McLaren had begun working on something truly special. Born from the desire to enter his sports racers in European competition, the M6GT was a race car for the road – quite literally.

With Bruce's passing, the McLaren road car project was set aside as the team refocused on continuing the racing legacy he'd started to build. But first with the F1 and later with the formation of McLaren Automotive, we picked up this baton and brought race-bred excellence to the road once again.

Despite introducing our first car less than a decade ago, an innovative and pioneering approach that echoes our founder's spirit has allowed us to take on our long-established competitors; to redefine the supercar experience. And, in the process grow to become the largest part of the McLaren Group with a presence in more than 30 territories around the world.

Fittingly, therefore, one of the defining themes you'll read in this book is progress. Our unwavering principle is that every car we produce should uphold the racing ethos of minimal weight, maximum power and the purest connection with the driver.

We bring these philosophies together with breathtaking style, always with innovation at its heart. The epitome of the McLaren approach can be found in our Ultimate Series –

cars that inspire both our existing customers and those aspiring to McLaren ownership.

As customer tastes change, we too evolve. McLaren Special Operations was created to realise the individual personality of our owners through near-limitless choice and peerless craftsmanship. The Pure McLaren experience programme allows owners to enjoy McLaren road cars in exactly the way Bruce first envisioned – flat-out on the racetrack – while our Pure GT Series takes things a step further still by offering the opportunity of FIA-sanctioned GT4 racing against like-minded enthusiasts.

Teams competing full-time in GT championship racing with McLaren cars are supplied and supported by our Customer Racing division, which is also the home of the McLaren Automotive Driver Development Programme to bring on emerging talent.

From the formative years of the M6GT to the present day, we've never forgotten that the powertrain is integral to what makes a McLaren, a McLaren. And, having created the world's first hybrid hypercar in the McLaren P1™, as we develop the powertrains of the future our motorsport roots continue to inform our belief that weight is the enemy of performance. In fact, the simple reality is that we're no longer engaged in a battle for horsepower supremacy, but a new battle to engineer superlight supercars in the face of heavier, hybrid powertrains.

To pursue this goal, we have opened just our second-ever purpose-built facility – the new £50m McLaren Composites Technology Centre – to innovate the core materials that will form our future models. As a technology incubator, it's also our ambition that the world-class research being undertaken here will be relevant to future mobility demands beyond the luxury supercar world.

I firmly believe there will always be a place for cars that express the passion of extreme performance, the joy of dynamic excellence and the exhilaration of driving in its purest form. It is our single aim that, whenever you return home from a journey in one of our cars – or, indeed, cruise back into the pitlane from a hot lap – we want you to have felt the thrill and sensation that only comes from having driven a McLaren.

I hope you enjoy reading this book. While it may be definitive for now, we're already working on the next chapter – and beyond.

Mike Flewitt
CEO, McLaren Automotive

INTRODUCTION
WILLIAM TAYLOR

Bruce Leslie McLaren's earliest competitive driving experiences came at the wheel of a highly modified 1929 Austin Ulster, an open-topped version of Britain's cheap and ubiquitous Austin Seven. Spurred on by his father, Les, a skilled engineer and a keen motorsports enthusiast, Bruce's initiation into the relatively small community of New Zealand and Australian racing drivers took place at a hillclimb at Muriwai Beach in 1952. It was about 25 miles from the McLaren family home in Auckland, and happened to be part of their holiday home. He had just turned 15.

The Ulster had already been in the family for almost three years, having been acquired by Les, in many pieces, for $110. He planned to fix it up himself, and turn a quick profit. Bruce, however, though just 13 at the time, had other plans for the car and persuaded his father to let him keep it. Several years later, Bruce remembered his first sight of his father's new purchase thus: "*I eyed the dilapidated Ulster on the end of the rope with deep suspicion. Racing car indeed!*"

Soon he was embroiled in literally every stage of the car's painstaking restoration using secondhand Austin Seven parts. Though he could not have been aware of the importance of it at that time, the experience would be a crucial learning process for the future racecar designer and builder. And no sooner had he reassembled the car than Bruce set out to remodel the family garden into a miniature circuit. That was where he first learned to drive.

He passed his driving test shortly after his 15th birthday, albeit opting for a more conservative 1949 side-valve Morris Minor, then soon headed off in the now famous Seven for the gravel hill at Muriwai Beach. Les McLaren was hospitalised with a gallstone, but his son had his paternal warning still ringing in his ears: "*If you damage so much as a mudguard, the Ulster's gone for good.*" As a result, Bruce admitted many years later, "*I forgot to be nervous about my debut. I took things reasonably, with Pop's lecture in mind, as the tail of the little Ulster slid on the loose metal corners and reached the top in one piece. When all the runs were over, I learned with some amazement that I had set the fastest time in the 750cc class.*"

While he was learning how to compete at this level, the Ulster period was of crucial importance to Bruce when it came to gaining an understanding of the mechanical side of the sport. As a result, by the early 1950s he was already a highly capable and ingenious mechanic, something he ably demonstrated when the Ulster's cylinder head eventually cracked. Rescuing a suitable replacement from a humble 1936 Austin Ruby saloon, he filled the combustion chambers with bronze which he then expertly ground to the appropriate shape using a rotary file. Once the engine was reassembled the Ulster proved good for 87mph, a 20 per cent improvement on its official quoted maximum of 72mph.

Thereafter such detail improvements came one after another. Over a three-year period the somewhat skeletal but still highly effective little car gradually metamorphosed into a completely different machine from the one Les had handed over to his teenaged son. New, flatter rear springs dealt with the problem of oversteer, whilst the front set was turned upside down to set the car lower to the ground. 16-inch disc wheels were fitted up front, and with 17s at the rear in place of the original 19s. The short tail was extended, twin SU carburettors replaced the single standard Zenith, and were fitted to a bespoke manifold which Bruce designed and fabricated himself.

Throughout this period he and schoolfriend and fellow Austin pilot Phil Kerr – who had finished second to him at that hillclimb at Muriwai Beach and would go on to become joint Managing Director of Bruce's racing team in England – were fettling their cars in the McLaren family garage. This they did very much on their own terms, Les McLaren reasoning that his son would fare better and learn more if he was left to work out problems for himself. Shop foreman Harold Bardsley was generally on hand to offer advice if it was needed, but mostly the preferred route was to explain to the youngsters how a job was best done and then leave them to get on with it.

When Bruce left for England in 1958, and for many years afterwards, the tired and well-used Ulster languished in

a small museum on New Zealand's South Island. In 1989, however, a deal was made with McLaren Group to buy the car for its collection and, with the help of a friend and close associate of Bruce's called Bruce Sutcliffe, and a lot of detective work, it was finally restored to its present condition. It now takes its rightful pride of place alongside its faster and more illustrious successors on the boulevard at the McLaren Technology Centre in Woking, UK.

Long before he moved to England, Bruce had replaced the Austin with his father's Healey 100-Four and worked hard on that throughout 1957. By then he had amassed some experience of single-seater racing courtesy of a supercharged 3-litre Maserati 8CLT on which he had been working on behalf of the owner. Frank Shuter planned to use this car for record-breaking attempts and was clearly delighted with the whole affair. Bruce was too, and soon after leapt at the opportunity to drive a 1750cc Formula 2 Cooper, which he used in his bid to secure the New Zealand International Grand Prix Association's prestigious 'Driver to Europe' scholarship.

From then on it would be in Coopers that the young Kiwi made his name. Guided by his fellow Antipodean Jack Brabham, who met the McLarens after staying with the family in 1954 during his first overseas trip to drive his famed RedeX Special in the New Zealand Grand Prix, Bruce made rapid progress and won the coveted scholarship for 1958.

In March that year Bruce's Cooper was loaded onto the Orantes for shipping to England. On the 15th he and mechanic Colin Beanland boarded a plane bound for the UK, where Bruce was scheduled to compete in his first European race, for Formula 2 cars, at Aintree near Liverpool on April 15th. He was, he admitted, "20, and a young 20 at that."

He finished only ninth in that race, but what really mattered was that he was in Europe and working on his own car. Later that season, in the German GP at the vaunted Nürburgring, he succeeded in making his mark even more emphatically by overhauling Phil Hill's Ferrari to win the F2 race-within-a-race whilst finishing fifth overall.

Father and son duo Charles and John Cooper assured him of a drive in their works team for 1959, and Bruce was now on his way. Success came quickly. Victory in the US GP at Sebring on December 12th made him, at 22, the youngest driver at the time ever to win a World Championship Grand Prix.

The following season began just as strongly, with victory for Cooper in Argentina, but then came a slump, and over the ensuing years of the 1.5-litre formula, he won only once more, at Monaco in 1962. It was not surprising that his mounting frustration at the lack of development at Cooper encouraged him to form his own team and race his own cars back home, where he took the Cooper as his starting point. Similarly it must by now have been obvious to many that, once Bruce McLaren Motor Racing Limited was up and running, that same Cooper base car would steadily metamorphose just the way the Austin Ulster had, until he created a machine that Bruce could call his own: the first pukka McLaren.

Bruce spent his early teenage years building, modifying and racing the 1929 Austin Seven Ulster that his father had bought intending to restore. 'Pop' McLaren (standing) and Bruce proudly show off the contents of the rapidly expanding family trophy cabinet.

In 1968 the McLaren team moved to new premises in Colnbrook. Here Chief Designer Robin Herd (left) shows his latest designs to Bruce McLaren (centre) and Teddy Mayer.

Inevitably his next step forward had its origins in another Cooper, Roger Penske's somewhat controversial Zerex Special which competed as a sportscar but was in essence a Cooper Grand Prix car with a 2.7-litre Climax engine.

Superseded by similar machines with larger American V8s, the Zerex had been forgotten until two of Bruce's trusted lieutenants – Tyler Alexander and Wally Wilmott – acquired it on his behalf from American magnate John Mecom's team in April 1964. They also acquired an aluminium 4-litre F85 Oldsmobile V8 with eight fairly crude stub exhausts, and this soon replaced the ageing Climax four. Bruce enjoyed success with his new car, but having conducted considerable testing for Ford on its GT Le Mans car he came to appreciate that the Zerex's primitive tubular chassis was flexing too much. It was replaced with a structure of his own design, and in June, on its debut at Mosport in Canada for the

Player's 200, he took the flag first. Ironically, the Chaparral that he beat was driven by Penske. To rub it in, Bruce repeated the feat in the Guards Trophy at Brands Hatch two months later.

The Zerex Special was diplomatically referred to as a Cooper-Oldsmobile to avoid offending the Coopers, and was nicknamed the Jolly Green Giant after its emergency livery was forced upon the team because it was painted on a Sunday and that was the only tin of paint available in the workshop. Its performance was amazing for a two-year old car, especially one in the hands of a very young team, and it earned the outfit its first major wins. But at the new base in Feltham, into which another of Bruce's allies, Teddy Mayer, had moved the team in between the Players 200 and the Guards Trophy, the next chapter was already well underway.....

CHAPTER

01

During the early days of my career in the late-1960s, if you had asked me to drive for McLaren, would I? Of course! It was one of the new teams in Formula 1 but it would have been my dream to race alongside drivers such as Bruce, Denny Hulme and Dan Gurney.

When I first saw the M23 when it appeared in 1973, it was obvious that there was an enormous leap in performance between it and the M19 which it replaced.

When I decided to leave Lotus at the end of 1973 I went to see Brabham, Tyrrell and McLaren. Immediately I liked Teddy Mayer's organisation, which was amongst the best in F1 with an almost American style of business. Marlboro said to me: "Choose whichever you want and we'll take our budget to them," so I tested the M23 at Paul Ricard late that year. It was incredible, very quick on the fast corners, which I liked.

It was more conventional than the Lotus 72, with which I had won my first Grand Prix in 1970 and the World Championship in 1972, without the difficult torsion bar suspension, and straight away I felt I had made a good decision. In Argentina in 1974, my first race, I felt I was in a position to take the lead but then accidentally activated the engine cut-out, so I finished only eighth as Denny won. I went on to win the next race, at home in Brazil, though. That was a wonderful feeling!

That year Teddy and the team were very focused, very committed to winning, and I think the New Zealand mechanics - from Bruce's day - were harder working than their counterparts in some of the other teams. McLaren was very fast to react to any problems, so for example constant improvements were made to the suspension and even a completely new geometry was devised which drastically improved the car throughout the season.

Even so, winning the World Championship with McLaren M23 was much harder than winning my first one in 1972. Clay Regazzoni and I were on equal points, and side by side on the grid, for the last race, in the USA. I think it was the only race where I didn't sleep well the night before. Clay too, probably. With so many good drivers around we needed a real team effort, but I always felt that McLaren was better prepared, and this was the day it really showed.

Emerson Fittipaldi
Drivers' World Champion 1974
McLaren M23

1964 M1A & McLAREN-ELVA M1A (MkI) GROUP 7 SPORTSCAR

Whilst Bruce the racing driver was busy on the track winning trophies, Bruce the astute businessman and hard-working executive was also guiding his small but dedicated crew at Feltham as they laboured flat-out on what was to be the first true McLaren racing car.

Built around a simple spaceframe of Bruce's own design, the new M1A employed round and square-section tubing with light magnesium alloy sheeting bonded and riveted in place to form a strong, stressed undertray. Power for the new, much stiffer car came from what was called the 'Strong Mother', the Traco-built Oldsmobile V8 from its predecessor, mated to a four-speed Hewland HD4 gearbox. Cooper wheels, uprights and steering arms were used. In testing at Goodwood in the summer of 1964, the finished design immediately knocked three whole seconds off the Zerex's best-ever lap time.

The new car made its debut that September at Mosport in Canada. Rather than green of the Zerex, it was now painted in New Zealand's official racing colours of black with a silver stripe. The new car quickly proved to be the fastest on the circuit and Bruce lead the race early on. Unfortunately, failure of the throttle linkage sent him into the pits, and after a long stop he could only finish in third place, three laps down.

At Riverside for the LA Times Grand Prix he qualified second behind Dan Gurney's Lotus 19, but by lap three had built a nine-second lead before a water hose blew off and forced him into the pits, where he lost four laps. He rejoined the race and climbed back into third place only for the same thing to happen again, this time prompting retirement.

The immediate success of the M1A, not to mention its singular design and appearance, quickly created high demand for customer replicas. This was an attractive opportunity to Bruce that was simply too good to miss, but the hard fact was that the payroll at the Feltham factory still amounted to only seven people, just about sufficient to keep the team's own race cars running but certainly not enough for a limited run of production or to service privateers' cars. A partial answer to these financial and logistical difficulties arrived in the person of Frank Nichols of Elva Cars Ltd., a small specialist car maker based in Rye, Sussex. Having the workforce, skills and equipment necessary to do the job, Nichols suggested to Bruce that their two companies co-operate to build customer cars with the McLaren team receiving a royalty on each car sold.

It made plenty of sense to the team and in November 1964 a deal was struck between McLaren and Peter Agg of the bubble-car maker Trojan, Elva's parent company. With the ink barely dry, the M1A went into production with the replica racing cars being branded officially as the McLaren-Elva Mark I. Work began immediately with the intention of having the first customer car ready to display at the 1965 London Racing Car Show in January.

Originally black, for the 1965 Oulton Park Gold Cup where Bruce led before a transmission leak put him out the 'Automatic' M1A was painted red (above).

In early 1964, noted motorsport artist Michael Turner designed a badge for the newly formed 'Bruce McLaren Motor Racing Team' (right).

The most obvious flaw was that the staff there had nothing to work from. No design drawings existed, the M1A having quite literally grown out of the Cooper-Oldsmobile project, driven to completion by some truly inspired guesswork as to how the end might be achieved. At the same time the only M1A which did exist was elsewhere - busy racing in America - leaving very little to go on. The main stumbling block was the bodyshell. The original intention was that the coachwork for the new cars would be formed by moulding glass-fibre copies from the hand-formed and beaten alloy body of the team car. Obviously this was not going to be possible now so, lacking any solid reference material, stylist Tony Hilder and the crew at Elva were instead forced to build the mould from the few photographs they had available.

Not surprisingly the results were not all they might have been and, when he returned from the US, Bruce did not like what he saw. He quickly ordered numerous detail changes to be made, which can be seen in later iterations of the M1A. The cars themselves, however, achieved some success and certainly left their mark. After duly going on display at the Racing Car Show, the first car to be completed (of a production run of 24) was sold to Jaguar dealer John Coombs. Equipped with a 4.5-litre Oldsmobile V8 it was readied for Graham Hill to drive at Silverstone in the forthcoming new season.

Not for the last time perseverance was to pay dividends for McLaren. While Bruce continued to drive for Cooper in F1 fellow New Zealander Chris Amon took the new M1A sportscar to its first victory, at St Jovite in Quebec. A few weeks later, in the Martini International Trophy at Silverstone he took victory again, despite starting from the back.

Silverstone was also to be the venue for what was perhaps the M1A's most memorable outing. This time it was to be in the hands of its creator who went head-to-head with John Surtees' Lola T70, the two gladiators providing race-goers with a truly epic battle in which Bruce and the M1A emerged

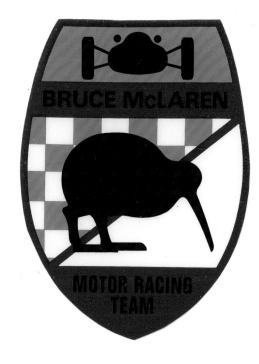

the victors. It was a narrow triumph, however, and before long the team was forced to accept that the ageing Oldsmobile V8 could not hold its own for ever against the Lola's larger-capacity Chevrolet V8. There was an interesting footnote that typified the level of attention to detail and professionalism which continues to characterise the team today: for the first time the M1A bore on its elegant nose a new Bruce McLaren Motor Racing Team badge designed by eminent motorsport artist Michael Turner.

Bruce's ongoing quest for new technical solutions led to the M1A being fitted with a dual-speed Ferguson automatic transmission and in April of 1965 at Oulton Park he led Jim Clark (Lotus 30) and Frank Gardner (Willment Cobra Coupe) in the first heat until a transmission leak forced him out. In the second heat the engine blew, leaving the team to reflect that the cost of developing the auto gearbox was too high in terms of both time and money. The project was shelved.

The aforementioned first production M1A, chassis 20-01, pictured on these pages, proved to be an important marker in the company's illustrious history, not just as McLaren's first production car but also as the first, indeed the only McLaren, ever to have been driven by 'The King' himself. Selling the car to noted Californian racer Jerry Entin after the LA race, Coombs returned to Surrey but was soon to see it again, this time on the big screen, after Hill's old car had landed a part in the movie 'Spinout' starring Elvis Presley.

At the same time several other customer cars were seeing action, sometimes with Bruce himself at the wheel. After some "Five thousand miles of race testing," he reported himself delighted with the quality of the customer cars.

MODEL	McLaren M1A
TYPE/FORMULA	Group 7 Sportscar
YEAR OF PRODUCTION	1964/1965
DESIGNER	Bruce McLaren
EXAMPLES BUILT	2
ENGINE	Oldsmobile V8
CUBIC CAPACITY	3900cc
CARBURATION	Four twin-choke downdraught
POWER OUTPUT	340bhp

TRANSMISSION	Hewland LG400 4-speed or ZF
CHASSIS	Large diameter round & square tubular frame
BODY	Four section polyester resin moulded body
FRONT SUSPENSION	Single top link & radius arm, lower wishbone, outboard coil spring/damper, anti-roll bar
REAR SUSPENSION	Twin radius arms with single top link, reversed lower wishbone, anti-roll bar & coil spring/damper
BRAKES F/R	Dual circuit Girling discs
WHEELS DIAMETER x WIDTH F/R	15x8/15x10in

TYRES F/R	Firestone
LENGTH	164in - 4166mm
WIDTH	64in - 1625mm
HEIGHT OF BODYWORK	30in - 762mm
WHEELBASE	91in - 2311mm
TRACK F/R	51/51in - 1295/1295mm
WEIGHT	1215lb - 551kg
PRINCIPAL DRIVERS	McLaren
IDENTIFYING COLOURS	Black & Silver, Red

1965 M2A
PROTOTYPE SINGLE SEATER

An experimental prototype which was never raced, the Robin Herd designed McLaren M2A was completed in September 1965, just seven months after the first designs had been conceived. Construction on the first single-seater to bear the McLaren name didn't begin until June 1st and took exactly three months.

Showing a degree of inspired thinking which was to become something of a trademark, Herd opted to use an innovative material with which he had become familiar during his time at Farnborough working on various advanced aerospace applications. As senior scientific officer for the National Gas Turbine Establishment, he came upon a product called Mallite, which consisted of a sheet of endgrain balsa wood sandwiched between aluminium panels. According to Herd this was so strong that it could support the weight of a tank over rough territory.

Once working at McLaren he planned to use glued sheets of Mallite for the internal and external skins of an entirely new monocoque chassis, the corner joints being fluid-sealed and the space within the tub employed for fuel storage, thereby negating the need for separate internal rubber bags. Originally the car was designed to accept a de-stroked 4.2-litre Ford V8 Indy engine and to compete in Formula 1, but in the event it was fitted with yet another version of the lightweight 4.5-litre Oldsmobile unit. This was another example of Bruce having to defer politically to the situation with Cooper, for whom he was still driving in F1. He had his sights set on a different horizon, but when the M2A was conceived he was obliged to deny any possible F1 role for it.

After test sessions at both Goodwood and Silverstone, in October of 1965, Bruce was finally caught by the press testing the M2A at a windswept Zandvoort circuit in Holland. Once again strongly denying that Bruce would be driving his own car in next year's Formula One World Championship, team members made every effort to keep details of the car from being released. Bruce's best lap time of 1m 28s compared favourably with Jim Clark's F1 lap record from that year's Grand Prix of 1m 30s. In the event though, after covering nearly 2000 miles of testing, the car never went near a Grand Prix meeting and was instead employed as a high-speed test mule for Firestone.

By March 1967 the car had been fitted with an experimental strut-mounted rear wing which cut lap times by as much

as three seconds at Zandvoort. In Doug Nye's seminal book, 'McLAREN The Grand Prix, Can-Am and Indy Cars', Herd cheerfully admitted to the fact that this device was all but forgotten about until 1968: "*Just put it down to incompetence and short memories... we were fully extended on other ideas.*"

Eventually the chassis was sold to John Ewer, a used car dealer and keen amateur racer. He fitted a 4.7-litre Ford V8 mated to a ZF transaxle in what would be the car's final configuration. With both Ewer and club racer Syd Fox behind the wheel, it made several appearances in British national races, most frequently at Brands Hatch and Snetterton, before being sold to Robert Ashcroft. He prepared it for upcoming racer Peter Gethin before it went on the move again, passing through the hands of talented racer Tony Dean (who won a minor Formula Libre race in it at Rufforth) to reach Welshman Dave McCloy in early 1968.

With only one or two exceptions, the car was now firmly relegated to the club circuit. McCloy crashed it heavily on his third outing, at Oulton Park in 1968, and it disappeared for a year to be rebuilt before resurfacing at Llandow and Castle Combe. An exception to the 'lower league' races was the F5000 International at Koksijde (also known as Coxyde) in Belgium for the Trophee International de la Mer Nord, in August 1969. McCloy qualified 11th for the first heat, more than 18s behind poleman Andrea de Adamich's works Surtees

The M2A was finally caught on camera by the press at Zandvoort in Holland. It put in some seriously quick lap times which compared favourably with the lap record held at that time by Jim Clark's Lotus.

TS5. He finished eighth, four laps behind the winning TS5 of Trevor Taylor. He was 10th in the second heat but was again unclassified after having completed just 19 of the 22 laps by the time Taylor crossed the line. Thereafter a major bearing failure prevented the car making the following weekend's meeting, another round of the European F5000 series at Zandvoort; and in mid-September a gearbox malfunction prevented McCloy appearing for the Hockenheim round.

The car's next appearance was back at Brands Hatch two weeks later, when Peter Gethin qualified on pole with his 'semi-works' Church Farm Racing McLaren M10A. This time the M2A was almost 21 seconds slower, qualifying 13th for the first heat, in which a broken engine mounting put paid to it on the 15th of the 20 laps.

Undeterred, McCloy took the car back to Wales intending to develop it further for the 1970 season. However, fate intervened; in November, chassis M2A-1 was completely destroyed in a garage fire. The likely culprits were a group of children throwing fireworks. There was, however, to be an important further development of the M2A concept, designated M2B.

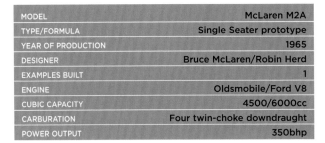

MODEL	McLaren M2A
TYPE/FORMULA	Single Seater prototype
YEAR OF PRODUCTION	1965
DESIGNER	Bruce McLaren/Robin Herd
EXAMPLES BUILT	1
ENGINE	Oldsmobile/Ford V8
CUBIC CAPACITY	4500/6000cc
CARBURATION	Four twin-choke downdraught
POWER OUTPUT	350bhp

TRANSMISSION	ZF 4-speed
CHASSIS	'Mallite' bathtub monocoque, steel bulkheads
BODY	Monocoque sides, GRP nose & cockpit surround
FRONT SUSPENSION	Welded cantilever top arm, lower wishbone, inboard coil spring/damper
REAR SUSPENSION	Reverse lower wishbone, top link, twin radius rods, coil spring/damper, anti-roll bar
BRAKES F/R	Outboard Girling discs
WHEELS DIAMETER x WIDTH F/R	13x8.5/13x12in

TYRES F/R	Firestone
LENGTH	156in - 3962mm
WIDTH OF MONOCOQUE	28.5in - 724mm
HEIGHT	35in - 998mm
WHEELBASE	96in - 2438mm
TRACK F/R	50/52in - 1270/1321mm
WEIGHT	1000lb - 450kg
PRINCIPAL DRIVERS	McLaren
IDENTIFYING COLOURS	Red

1965 M1B
GROUP 7 SPORTSCAR

The M1B was the official McLaren team car for 1965, and subsequently — as the McLaren-Elva M1B Mark II — the new customer car for the following season.

The purposeful design was based on the earlier car with Robin Herd taking the basic frame from a production chassis then extensively revising it to make it 20 per cent stiffer while keeping its weight the same. He achieved this by using a familiar mix of larger diameter round and square mild steel tubes with, once again, sheet alloy riveted and bonded to the frame to form the bulkheads and undertray.

The structure weighed 1300lbs with the twin 25-gallon rubber fuel cells drained, and the much more rigid machine sported the familiar Traco-built 4.5-litre Oldsmobile V8, four-speed Hewland LG gearbox, dual-circuit Girling brakes and a 40:60 rearward weight bias. The external appearance of the M1B, however, was quite different. Artist Michael Turner followed Bruce's strict guidelines with the bluff shape, drawing a blunter nose and more sharply truncated tail. Although it shared the same wheelbase as the M1A, the M1B was over a foot shorter.

McLaren benefited strongly in the genesis of the M1B from the presence of Massachusetts-born Tyler Alexander. Bruce had met Tyler via their mutual friendship with the Mayer brothers: Timmy, the racer, and Teddy, the lawyer who took time off to manage his brother's career until Timmy was killed at Longford, Australia, in 1963. Tyler was trained in aircraft engineering but could turn his hand to anything and had become the mechanic for the Rev-Em team run by upcoming American race driver Peter Revson. After working for John Mecom's team he graduated to a mechanic's role at McLaren when Bruce bought the Zerex Special from Mecom. He already knew Teddy Mayer from their time together on the American circuits and would soon become McLaren's chief mechanic before moving on to special engineering projects. Teddy remained as one of the longest-serving McLaren employees and a true keeper of Bruce's flame until he passed away in 2016.

Alexander's aerospace knowledge was to prove invaluable as he laid out the ducting inside the car's nose and formed the internal structure to secure the radiator. The body sections fitted to the first car were made entirely of aluminium but future M1Bs had glass-fibre bodywork.

Bruce took the first 'alloy' prototype, painted red, to Canada for its inaugural run at St Jovite. Eoin Young was another New Zealander who had come over to England at Bruce's invitation, to act as his secretary and company publicist. He was the first McLaren employee, and would later establish himself as one of the great motorsport writers. When the crankshaft on the M1B broke, Young told the world that it destroyed the engine in "*a most comprehensive manner*". It took the transmission with it, too.

Happily, things went better on the car's 'official' debut at Mosport. With a new engine Bruce took pole and, having led for 96 of the 100 laps, finished a close second to the well-sorted Chaparral 2 of designer/racer Jim Hall. For the next event, at Kent in Washington state, Phil Hill took over the M1B, but having again led for much of the race and set fastest lap he was forced to pit by a sticking throttle.

Bruce was back for the LA Times GP at Riverside, the car now equipped with a new front spoiler and a cockpit cooling duct. After winning his qualifying race and smashing the lap record, a tyre lost pressure in the main race. The resultant pit stop dropped him a lap down. In a superb display he unlapped himself and eventually finished third behind Hap Sharp's victorious Chaparral and Jim Clark's Lotus 40.

Three more M1Bs were built in 1966 before Elva took on the construction of the customer versions: a "*half production*" car for Dan Gurney, as Bruce described it, and two further revised team cars.

Bruce was becoming increasingly aware that the Oldsmobile engines were likely to suffer in the face of Chevrolet's heavier but significantly more powerful 6-litre V8s, and the inauguration of the new Can-Am series for 1966 served only to highlight this. The rules merely called for 'two seater unrestricted sportscars'. There was no upper limit on engine size. This 'big banger' formula was very popular with the race-going public and large crowds made for big purses. The total prize money for the six-race season was $385,000 and the winner at each race received more than $30,000.

Left: Bruce debuted the all-alloy prototype M1B in the Canadian 'Grand Prix' at Mosport in September 1965. In both heats he battled for the lead with Jim Hall but eventually had to give best to the well sorted Chaparral and finished just a few feet behind. The chassis plate attached to the dashboard of the prototype M1B is easily readable and simply identifies the car as a BMMR (Bruce McLaren Motor Racing) 'Test' car.

The M1B was substantially reworked for 1966, primarily to accommodate the Chevrolet engine. This offered an additional 100bhp, albeit at a cost of around 200lbs. Bruce was confident that this could be offset to a greater degree by employing a lighter ZF transmission. The new cars were also now fitted with additional chassis tubes to take account of the heavier burden, wider wheels and a separate rear spoiler.

After being demoted to a role as tyre test car for Firestone and engine test chassis on the Indy V8 destined for Lotus for Ford's KarKraft development department in Detroit, the prototype M1B was rescued from the back lot at KarKraft by a local racer who set about restoring it. He decided to use it on the road and by 1972 it was fully street legal and, to this day is still used once or twice a year for short trips to car shows and exhibitions.

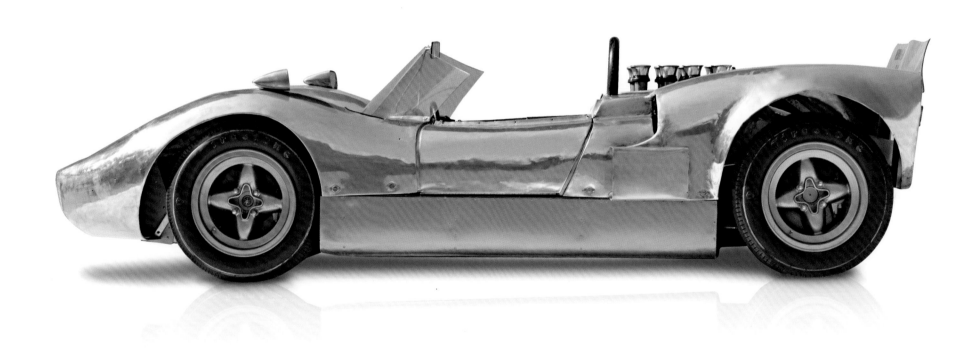

MODEL	McLaren M1B
TYPE/FORMULA	Group 7 Sportscar
YEAR OF PRODUCTION	1965/1966
DESIGNER	Robin Herd/Bruce McLaren
EXAMPLES BUILT	4
ENGINE	Oldsmobile/Chevrolet V8
CUBIC CAPACITY	4700-5400cc
CARBURATION	Four twin-choke downdraught
POWER OUTPUT	340bhp

TRANSMISSION	Hewland LG400 4-speed, ZF
CHASSIS	Large diameter round & square tube frame
BODY	Four section hand made aluminium alloy
FRONT SUSPENSION	Single top link & radius arm, lower wishbone, outboard coil spring/damper, anti-roll bar
REAR SUSPENSION	Twin radius arms with single top link, reversed lower wishbone, anti-roll bar & coil spring/damper
BRAKES F/R	Dual circuit Girling discs, 12.5/11.5 in diameter
WHEELS DIAMETER x WIDTH F/R	15x8.5/15x11.5in

TYRES F/R	Firestone 5.50-15/6.50-15
LENGTH	145in - 3683mm
WIDTH	63in - 1600mm
HEIGHT	31in - 787mm
WHEELBASE	91in - 2311mm
TRACK F/R	52/52in - 1320/1320 mm
WEIGHT	1300lb - 589kg
PRINCIPAL DRIVERS	McLaren, P.Hill, Amon
IDENTIFYING COLOURS	Red

1966 McLAREN-ELVA M1B (MkII) GROUP7 & CAN-AM

"*The fastest car we've ever tested,*" screamed Road & Track in July 1966. Putting racer Charlie Hayes' Chevrolet-engined McLaren-Elva M1B Mk II on the cover, describing it in the opening pages as *"an example of the latest thinking in sports/racing cars,"* the American magazine acknowledged the privilege of such early access to a state-of-the-art machine.

The chassis it took to California's Riverside Raceway was an authentic showstopper, having made its public debut at the Racing Car Show in London. It was chassis 30-01 of the 28 which were to be built at Rye, each to the same basic specification as Bruce's team car which he had campaigned to good effect the previous year. 'Basic', that is, because the $11,500 Elva-built cars were sold without an engine so that the customer could tailor the machine to their own personal requirements with a choice of Oldsmobile, Chevrolet or Ford powerplants.

Hayes had opted for a 5.4-litre Chevrolet V8 prepared by Traco Engineering, together with Airheart disc brakes in place of the standard Girlings. Perhaps mindful of Bruce's multiple water hose disasters with the M1A, Hayes had the car equipped with aircraft-style Aeroquip hardware and Wiggins quick-release units at those points where regular maintenance would require their periodic removal.

Accordingly, R&T's road test team put the price-as-tested closer to $25,000 but even this, it acknowledged, was more than respectable for a race-ready machine which, thanks to four side-draft, double-barrel 58mm Weber carburettors, put out 466bhp at 6,500rpm and developed 445lb ft of torque at 4,500. "Dirt cheap" was its chosen expression, which must have pleased the guys at Rye particularly when Hayes went on to win the first United States Road Racing Championship (USRRC) race at Laguna Seca. No less impressively, the M1B was still winning three seasons later. Expatriate Englishman

John Cannon provided one of the biggest upsets in Can-Am history when wet-weather Firestones handed him a crucial advantage in the sodden 1968 race at Laguna Seca. Driving, as he put it, "like a bloody demon," he lapped the entire field, which included Denny Hulme in the normally dominant works McLaren M8A.

Photographs give little impression of the compact dimensions of the M1B, which is perhaps why Road & Track was at pains to stress just how small it was. With a 91 inch wheelbase and an overall length of just 146, the Mark II in plan was comparable to an MGB or Lotus Elan, although considerably lower at just 31 inches from the track to the top of the minimal, swept-back screen. Its frontal area was some 30 per cent smaller than either roadcar.

The basic structure impressed the testers, who thought it combined "the characteristics of the semi-monocoque

chassis with the multi-tube spaceframe". This they called an *"admirably practical form for a car that is going to be rigorously campaigned by a private entrant."* Exceptionally rigid and durable, the construction also ensured that *"the almost inevitable collision damage of a minor nature can be repaired using hand tools and portable welding kit."*

Besides Cannon, other privateers achieved many excellent results with the M1B, the most notable being Peter Revson who would play a significant role in the ongoing McLaren story. He ran his car with a Ford engine at a support race for the 1966 British Grand Prix at Brands Hatch, as well as at the Nassau Speed Weeks where he led for most of the race

before his brakes gave out. He also took part in the final race of the 1966 Can-Am series, starting ninth and finishing a creditable fourth, two laps down on Bruce in the works M1B. Other drivers to run a McLaren-Elva M1B with the Chevrolet engine that year included Chuck Parsons, Earl Jones, and Masten Gregory. Lothar Motschenbacher ran with an Oldsmobile, whilst Bud Morley, Sam Posey, Skip Scott and Dick Brown all used the less popular Ford unit.

The majority of customer cars run by such drivers used the Hewland LG500 four-speed gearbox fitted to Hayes' car. This unit, with its straight-cut, non-synchronised gears, must have seemed a little crude even in the mid-1960s, particularly

when compared to the full-synchro units which were now making their presence felt. But more than occasionally, simplicity in motorsport scores highly. Just as the essentially straightforward structure of the Mark II made these customer cars easy to work on, owners found their LG500s durable, dependable and far less awkward than many of the more advanced transmissions of the time.

Road & Track magazine concluded that the M1B was: *"A fine machine, beautiful in the intelligent simplicity of what is necessarily a complicated mechanism."* A wonderful resume indeed, for a successful and highly significant design in the McLaren story.

MODEL	McLaren-Elva M1B [MkII]	**TRANSMISSION**	Hewland LG400 or LG500	
TYPE/FORMULA	Group7/Can-Am	**CHASSIS**	Large diameter round & square tube frame	
YEAR OF PRODUCTION	1966	**BODY**	Four section polyester resin moulded body	
DESIGNER	Bruce McLaren/Robin Herd	**FRONT SUSPENSION**	Single top link & radius arm, lower wishbone,	
EXAMPLES BUILT	28		outboard coil spring/damper, anti-roll bar	
ENGINE	Oldsmobile V8 (optional Chevrolet or Ford)	**REAR SUSPENSION**	Twin radius arms with single top link, reversed	
CUBIC CAPACITY	4700-5400cc		lower wishbone, anti-roll bar & coil spring/damper	
CARBURATION	Four twin-choke downdraught	**BRAKES F/R**	Dual circuit Girling discs, 12.5/11.5 in diameter	
POWER OUTPUT	350bhp	**WHEELS F/R**	15x8.5/15x11.5in	

TYRES F/R	Firestone or Goodyear
LENGTH	146in - 3708mm
WIDTH	64in - 1625mm
HEIGHT TO TOP OF SCREEN	31in - 787mm
WHEELBASE	91in - 2311mm
TRACK F/R	52/52in - 1298/1298mm
WEIGHT	1300lb - 590kg
PRINCIPAL DRIVERS	McLaren, Amon, Cannon, Revson
IDENTIFYING COLOURS	n/a

Bruce soon confirmed his intention to field a two-car McLaren Grand Prix team for the new 3-litre Formula 1 in 1966, a relief after all the cloak-and-dagger stuff which had been necessary to reassure his employers at Cooper that the M2A was not a Formula 1 car-in-waiting.

He would drive one car, with fellow Kiwi Chris Amon in the other. It seems probable that just the two cars were built, although contemporary evidence suggests the possible existence of a third tub. Power was to come from an Indianapolis Ford V8, a 4.2-litre, quad-cam unit sleeved down to the appropriate capacity.

It was the construction of the monocoque which attracted most attention, however. Herd described it at the time as "*an inverted top-hat section tub,*" formed from Mallite sheets with outer skins of conventional aluminium sheet providing additional stiffness and crash protection for the driver. Rubber fuel bags were fitted in the spaces between the inner Mallite tub and the outer skins.

Herd's monocoque was further stiffened by four fabricated steel bulkheads, the first and fourth supporting the front and rear suspension respectively, while the two centre units formed a mounting for the dashboard and instruments and the seatback support.

The suspension was conventional. At the front this meant upper rocker arms operating inboard coil spring and damper units, with bottom location courtesy of lower wishbones. Braking stresses were transferred to the tub via a short radius-rod running rearwards from the upper rocker arms' outer ends. At the rear the M2B sported lower wishbones, with a single top link and twin radius rods, and outboard coil springs and dampers.

Bruce took his new McLaren-Ford, and the only engine currently available, to Monaco for its race debut on May 22nd, 1966. Little of the original Ford internals remained, just the original block together with the bottom end and head castings. The rest, including virtually all the moving parts, had been redesigned and remanufactured courtesy of Gary Knutson and Traco in Culver City, California. In theory, driving through a five-speed ZF transaxle, the Hilborn fuel-injected unit should have been good for 335bhp at 9,500rpm. But despite the quite phenomenal noise that the over-ported unit produced, the anticipated power never materialised and with only 303bhp at 8,750rpm Bruce qualified only 10th. He didn't last long in the race, either. An oil pipe union came undone, squirting lubricant into the cockpit, and after 10 laps he retired before the engine suffered damage.

Even in Monaco he had admitted the necessity to "*make some fairly drastic moves in the engine room*", and by the Belgian Grand Prix at Spa-Francorchamps, the Ford was out and a new unit took its place: the Italian Serenissima V8. This

was at least a full 3-litre so didn't require sleeving down or de-stroking, and weighed significantly less than its American predecessor, but it suffered serious oil leaks during practice and soon ran its bearings. Now the team was engineless as there was no spare powerplant, so having qualified 16th with fellow rookie F1 constructor Dan Gurney, Bruce was obliged to miss the race.

He had to pass up the French Grand Prix too, but the Serenissima V8 was rebuilt in time for the British Grand Prix at Brands Hatch on July 16th. He qualified the underpowered and overweight car 13th, but brought it home sixth, two laps behind winner Jack Brabham in his eponymous Brabham Repco, to score the McLaren marque's first World Championship point. It was a fine effort by an F1 newcomer.

Zandvoort was less rewarding, with another non-start due to engine problems after qualifying 14th. McLaren missed both the German and Italian races, as Bruce preferred to concentrate the effort on the more lucrative Can-Am events.

An improved version of the Ford V8 was reinstalled in the M2B for the US and Mexican GPs which completed the F1 season. With power upped to a rumoured 325bhp, Bruce qualified 11th at Watkins Glen and finished fifth, three laps behind Jim Clark's winning BRM H-16 powered Lotus 33 but was forced into retirement in Mexico after qualifying 15th by yet another engine failure. It was to be the last works outing for the M2B. Bruce had lost interest in both the car and the largely abortive Indy Ford engine experiment, but not in Formula 1 itself. McLaren would be back.

The car's swansong came in 1968 as Hertfordshire-based Ken Sheppard Sports Cars reportedly acquired three M2B chassis, planning to fit them with Coventry Climax V8s. M2B-2 appeared at the Silverstone International Trophy meeting, where it struggled around the paddock before being trailered home. At Brands Hatch on Easter Monday, M2B-1 appeared for practice in an F5000 race, fitted with a 4.5-litre Oldsmobile V8.

Below: A McLaren Formula 1 car (powered by a Ford V8) first appeared on the F1 grid at the Monaco Grand Prix. Above: Driving the M2B now fitted with the Serenissima engine, Bruce finished sixth in the 1966 British GP at Brands Hatch, scoring the first World Championship point for a McLaren car.

As the first in the highly distinguished line of Formula 1 cars, the M2B holds a special place in the history of the McLaren. Chassis M2B-1 made its way back to the United States and has lain for many years awaiting restoration, while M2B-2 was acquired by Tom Wheatcroft's Donington Grand Prix Collection. After many years in restoration it finally took its place in the McLaren Hall there during 2008.

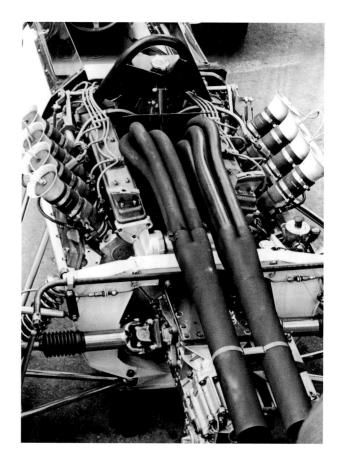

MODEL	McLaren M2B
TYPE/FORMULA	Formula 1
YEAR OF PRODUCTION	1966
DESIGNER	Bruce McLaren/Robin Herd
EXAMPLES BUILT	2
ENGINE	Ford 'Indy' V8/Serenissima V8
CUBIC CAPACITY	3000cc
CARBURATION	Lucas Fuel Injection/4 twin-choke downdraught
POWER OUTPUT	321/260bhp

TRANSMISSION	ZF 4 or 5-speed
CHASSIS	Aluminium 'Mallite' sheet monocoque
BODY	Monocoque sides, GRP nose & cockpit surround
FRONT SUSPENSION	Welded cantilever top arm, lower wishbone,
	inboard coil spring/damper
REAR SUSPENSION	Reverse lower wishbone, top link,
	twin radius rods, coil spring/damper, anti-roll bar
BRAKES F/R	Outboard Girling discs
WHEELS DIAMETER x WIDTH F/R	13x8.5/13x12in

TYRES F/R	Firestone
LENGTH	159in - 4039mm
WIDTH	74in - 1880mm
HEIGHT	36in - 914mm
WHEELBASE	96in - 2438mm
TRACK F/R	50/50in - 1270/1270mm
WEIGHT	1180lb - 535kg
PRINCIPAL DRIVERS	McLaren
IDENTIFYING COLOURS	White/Green

1966 M3A
FORMULA LIBRE

The M3A was another of McLaren's early screen stars, this time with the company providing the car driven by James Garner in the MGM movie 'Grand Prix'. The fabled 'whooshbonk' car - of which just three were built - was another exceptionally neat Robin Herd/Bruce McLaren spaceframe design, this time an open-wheel single seater intended for Formula Libre racing as well as hillclimb and speed events.

With such a broad remit, the trio of cars enjoyed relatively long working lives, appearing first at the Belgian Grand Prix in 1966 - the year Bruce and Chris Amon won Le Mans in the 7-litre Ford Mark IIA - and still clearly highly competitive four years later, when the late Patsy Burt was confirmed as the 1970 RAC British Sprint Champion after several memorable performances in her Traco Oldsmobile V8-powered 4.5-litre version.

That first Grand Prix outing in Belgium was not, of course, as a competitor, but rather as a camera car. Chassis M3A-3 was fitted with a 4.7-litre Ford V8 so that Phil Hill could track the action to provide some highly atmospheric footage - all of it obtained during just one lap of the circuit - for the aforementioned John Frankenheimer Hollywood blockbuster.

Following filming, chassis M3A-3 was then sold to erstwhile M2A owner/driver John Ewer, who in turn passed it on to David Bridges who recruited Lancastrian upcomer Brian Redman to drive it for him in 1967. Driver and car performed admirably during a high-speed encounter in the BRSCC Mallory Park Easter Trophy race meeting, as Redman won and set a new outright fastest lap.

By the end of May the car had changed ownership again and in the hands of Robin Darlington was to score a trio of club victories at Llandow, Silverstone and Snetterton. Unfortunately, a serious road crash prevented him rebuilding the car after it more or less fell apart whilst progressing at speed down the straight at Silverstone. Eventually it fell to David Prophet to gather the pieces together, shipping them off to South Africa where Bob Olthoff planned to join the 1968 South African F1 Championship once the rules were relaxed to allow Formula A cars to compete.

Unfortunately, much less is known about chassis M3A-1. It was bought new by Swiss hillclimb driver Dr Harry Zweifel but disappeared after being raced regularly in Swiss and other European hillclimbs up to the early 1970s. By 1972 M3A-1 was reported as residing somewhere in France and sadly was probably modified beyond all recognition into some sort of hybrid special.

In 1970 Frenchman Pierre Soukry used his M3A to take part in several rounds of the well-supported European Formula 5000 Championship. At the 10th round at Silverstone in June, he qualified last on the 18-car grid, 25s slower than Peter

Gethin's semi-works M10B, and retired from the race on the warm-up lap with an oil leak.

Happily, Burt's well-documented exploits in the second car mean no such mystery attends M3A-2. Now housed in the Donington Collection it is the sole known survivor of the three and thus a uniquely important part of the unfolding McLaren story.

The 1970 RAC British Sprint Championship comprised nine events, with each competitor's six best scores determining the overall winner. Burt won the first six events she entered, breaking the course record at no fewer than four of them, an achievement which will probably never be beaten.

She became the first woman to win a National Speed Championship, something rightly hailed as *"a great personal achievement,"* in her 2001 obituary in the Bruce McLaren Trust newsletter, but it was just one of more than 600 awards she received during a career as a seriously versatile racer. During her four-year campaign with the M3A she took part in both domestic and international events, hitting the headlines several times. She set the course record at the inaugural event held at the Gurston Down hillclimb venue in June 1967, and most notably when in October 1968 she completed a standing kilometre in just 19.84s. At the time that was the fastest time ever recorded in the UK.

Burt deserved the headlines she got, but sadly the car in which she scored so many great triumphs has been all but forgotten. Part of the reason the M3A was overshadowed was the other models McLaren was producing at the time: a glittering family of thundering sportscar racers that would lead to the company's domination of the much more mainstream Can-Am series.

Chassis M3A/2 was ordered by and built specially for Patsy Burt. Fitted with a 4.4-litre 'Traco' Oldsmobile and 5-speed ZF gearbox, the car was hugely successful, winning speed championships and setting records everywhere it went.

Patsy Burt used the M3 to compete in hillclimb events (top: at Great Auclum in 1967) throughout the UK and Europe. In October 1968 her crew once again fitted a high 'streamliner' style screen and nosecone (above) and at RAF Elvington Patsy reset several of the British speed records she had initially set in 1967.

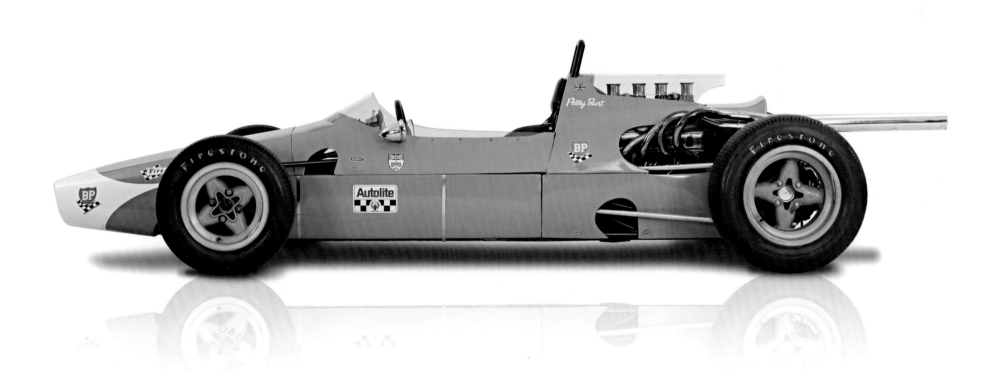

MODEL	McLaren M3A		TRANSMISSION	Hewland LG500 or ZF 5-speed		TYRES F/R	Firestone
TYPE/FORMULA	Formula Libre		CHASSIS	Large diameter tubular spaceframe		LENGTH	148in - 3759mm
YEAR OF PRODUCTION	1966		BODY	GRP nose, cockpit surround & panels to suit		WIDTH	67in -1702mm
DESIGNER	Bruce McLaren/Robin Herd		FRONT SUSPENSION	Unequal length double wishbones,		HEIGHT TO TOP OF WINDSCREEN	29in - 736mm
EXAMPLES BUILT	3			adjustable coil spring/damper, anti-roll bar		WHEELBASE	96in - 2438mm
ENGINE	Oldsmobile/Ford/Chevrolet V8		REAR SUSPENSION	Reverse lower wishbone, top link,		TRACK F/R	51/52in - 1295/1321mm
CUBIC CAPACITY	4500-5400cc			twin radius rods, coil spring/damper, anti-roll bar		WEIGHT	1080lb - 490kg
CARBURATION	Four twin-choke downdraught		BRAKES F/R	Outboard Girling 10.5in discs		PRINCIPAL DRIVERS	P.Hill, Burt, Soukry
POWER OUTPUT	340-380bhp		WHEELS DIAMETER x WIDTH F/R	13x8.5/15x12in		IDENTIFYING COLOURS	Blue

1967 McLAREN-ELVA M1C (MkIII) CAN-AM

The last tubular frame chassis car built by Elva to sell as a McLaren customer car, the M1C was also known as the McLaren-Elva MkIII, particularly in North America where many of the 25 examples built headed. Most of these, unsurprisingly, went on to race in the USRRC but the cars were also campaigned in the higher profile Can-Am championships where lessons learned with the earlier M1A and M1B soon reaped dividends for several privateers.

The M1C was very much the offspring of its two predecessors, a new car but one very closely based on the same spaceframe design. It thus represented the final evolution of the concept, something of a farewell tour for those early cars, since by this time the works McLaren team had moved on to develop the all-conquering monocoque M6A.

The M1C's chassis was constructed using a modified version of the familiar large-diameter round and square tubing, with the structure receiving important additional stiffness and strength from undertrays and bulkheads that were formed using riveted and bonded light-alloy sheets, as well as additional tubes in the front and rear bays. The suspension remained unchanged: an independent set-up at the front using unequal-length, wide-base wishbones designed to facilitate anti-dive and anti-roll, and rear trailing arms with lower wishbones, single top links and fully adjustable coil spring/damper units.

While the spaceframe was even stronger than before, the bodywork was largely similar. Formed from four reinforced polyester resin sections with the twin side sections each housing a 25-gallon rubber fuel cell, externally it gained a separate rear 'spoiler' wing. This distinguishing feature was fitted on the majority of the cars destined for the US and was made adjustable so that the aerodynamics could be tuned to suit the very different characteristics of the circuits there. Fifteen-inch diameter custom-made McLaren-Elva cast magnesium wheels were fitted front and rear.

Once again, the car was engineered to accept a variety of different power units, most commonly Chevrolets, but customers could opt for Ford or Oldsmobile V8s. The Chevrolet V8 came with a choice of a four- or five-speed Hewland gearbox, though a ZF option was still offered.

The M1C pictured here was originally owned and run by Jerry Hansen of Minneapolis. He entered it in the 1967 Can-Am series and it made its debut in the first race of the season on September 3, at Road America in Wisconsin. That race naturally also marked the first outing for Team McLaren's two gleaming new M6As and developed into the first episode of what rapidly became known as the 'Bruce and Denny Show'. A full field of 32 cars started the race, no fewer than 17 of them various different McLarens; the M1C drivers that year included luminaries such as Skip Scott, Peter Revson, Chuck Parsons and Bob Bondurant.

Unsurprisingly, Bruce and Denny's matched pair of M6As came home first and second but production M1Cs finished fifth, sixth, seventh and eighth with Hansen securing a respectable sixth after starting back on the seventh row of the grid. When the USRRC circus came to Riverside in April, Bondurant and Lothar Motschenbacher took their M1Cs to second and third place behind Mark Donohue's Penske Lola T70. The cars were still apparently competitive against the bigger-engined Lolas, and there was plenty more to come from the M1C. Chuck Parsons, for example, arguably the most successful M1C driver of the year, was the first representative of the model on every grid during 1967.

For 1968 it was a case of more of the same. Elkhart Lake saw four M1Cs on the start line, Canadian store magnate George Eaton's being the highest placed in position eight. Having already notched up a 10th place at Edmonton in a car which was certainly becoming outdated, he drove to an impressive third place at Laguna Seca, helped in no small part by torrential downpours. With a tenacious and determined driving style, he had kept going long after the big boys called it a day, to give the M1C its highest placing in a Can-Am fixture.

Incredibly, the M1C was still going strong in 1969, three of them appearing on the grid at Mosport, with John Cordts finishing fourth behind Bruce and Denny in their much more advanced works M8Bs. And then came 1970, when the M1C refused to go away. A trio of customer cars still raced confidently and competitively throughout that final season. The spaceframe era might finally have ended, but at McLaren it certainly enjoyed a long run.

As late as 1971 the M1C chassis was still highly competitive in British sportscar racing. John Jordan (above) in the ex-Ken Wilson, ex-Alistair Cowin, Ford V8-engined M1C heads for another victory at Snetterton.

MODEL	McLaren-Elva M1C [MkIII]
TYPE/FORMULA	Can-Am
YEAR OF PRODUCTION	1967
DESIGNER	Bruce McLaren/Robin Herd
EXAMPLES BUILT	25
ENGINE	Chevrolet, Oldsmobile, Ford V8
CUBIC CAPACITY	4500-6000cc
CARBURATION	Lucas fuel injection
POWER OUTPUT	400-540bhp

TRANSMISSION	Hewland LG400 or LG500, optional ZF
CHASSIS	Large diameter round & square tube frame
BODY	Four section polyester resin moulded body
FRONT SUSPENSION	Single top link & radius arm, lower wishbone,
	outboard coil spring/damper, anti-roll bar
REAR SUSPENSION	Trailing radius arms with single top link, reversed
	lower wishbone, anti-roll bar & coil spring/damper
BRAKES F/R	Dual circuit Girling discs, 12.5/11.5 in diameter
WHEELS DIAMETER x WIDTH F/R	15x8.5/15x11.5in

TYRES F/R	Firestone
LENGTH	146in - 3708mm
WIDTH	66in - 1676mm
HEIGHT TO TOP OF WINDSCREEN	31in - 787mm
WHEELBASE	90.5in - 2298mm
TRACK F/R	52/52in - 1321/1321mm
WEIGHT	1300lb - 590kg
PRINCIPAL DRIVERS	Hulme, Gethin, Revson
IDENTIFYING COLOURS	n/a

1967 M4A & McLAREN-TROJAN M4A/B FORMULA 2

With the decline of Group 7 sportscar racing in the UK, McLaren decided to build a new car to compete in the 1967 1600cc Formula 2 class, 1000cc Formula 3 and even the US Formula B Series. Relatively flush with money from the success of the M1 and its derivatives, Bruce sat down with Robin Herd to create the all-new single-seater which they type-numbered M4A.

Right from the start the plan called for a series of replicas, which would be called M4A/Bs. These would be built off-site at Purley in Surrey, by Lambretta-Trojan. An initial batch of 10 was soon being laid down at Peter Agg's premises and it was hoped they could be sold to new and existing McLaren customers, most probably in North America for Formula B. The price for a rolling chassis was quoted at £2,450.

The M4A was relatively straightforward, based on a constant-section bathtub monocoque. This time Herd ignored the chemically bonded Mallite sandwich which, though immensely strong, posed a number of problems as far as series production was concerned, and opted instead for more conventional aluminium panels. These were bonded and riveted to a quartet of strong steel bulkheads to make up the lower half of the car's structure and were far easier than Mallite to repair after accident damage.

The nose and cockpit surround were in glass-fibre, and the suspension sprang no surprises: double wishbones located by long radius arms front and rear, with conventional outboard springs and dampers. Supplemented by a small, five-gallon seat tank, the bulk of the fuel was held in a matched pair of 10-gallon tanks, one mounted either side of the cockpit. The wheels were cast-magnesium 13-inch diameter items unique to McLaren and Elva, with 7-inch width rims at the front and 10-inch at the rear. The complete car weighed in at 960lbs, just above the F2 series minimum.

The F2 version, which was revealed to the press in January 1967, was designed to accept the brand new Cosworth four-valve A series engine, the FVA. This light and compact four-cylinder unit, built with Ford backing, the design and manufacturing genius of Cosworth founders Keith Duckworth and Mike Costin, and some characteristically far-sighted encouragement from Colin Chapman at Lotus, would spawn the all-conquering Ford Cosworth DFV F1 powerplant that appeared so dramatically later that season. The FVA developed around 230bhp, which was delivered to the rear wheels via a Hewland FT200 gearbox. Bruce immediately took the newly announced car testing at Goodwood, where a lap of under 1m 20s showed the car had good potential.

Early in the season Bruce took part in several Formula 2 Championship rounds in the M4A. There were some potent driver/car combinations in the series that year, and second place at Rouen in July was the best he could manage. His other six races provided consistent if unspectacular results: two thirds, a fourth, two fifths and sixth.

A number of American drivers seemed pleased with the car though, and 25 M4A/Bs were sold in the States where Formula B was proving popular on the ever-expanding North American racing scene. In Europe the M4A/B also appeared in a handful of F3 races, albeit with little success.

Other drivers who competed in these attractive little cars included New Zealander Graeme Lawrence, who campaigned his McLaren in Europe to great effect before taking it home. Old Etonian, Piers Courage, one of Britain's rising stars of the late 1960s, used an M4A while racing in the European F2 series for veteran entrant John Coombs. It was a season dominated by the Brabhams and Matras, and despite taking part in virtually every round the brewery heir more often distinguished himself through his tendency to spin off or commit other embarrassing gaffes. His nickname,

'Porridge', was soon applied to anyone who spun or otherwise came a cropper after losing control of a racing car. This, and his lack of results with the McLaren, left him somewhat despondent by the end of 1967 but the M4A would yet prove crucial to his career. Overlooked by BRM for F1 duties in favour of his smoother and less impetuous fellow countryman Chris Irwin, Courage purchased the car from Coombs and took it Down Under to compete in the 1968 Tasman series as a privateer.

Here, at last, he and the car showed their true potential. Approaching the final race, in Longford, he had achieved a second place and three thirds, fighting the works Lotus-Fords of Jim Clark and Graham Hill, and the works Ferrari of Chris Amon, all of which had 2.5-litre engines. His newfound success would later prompt Colin Chapman to offer him a drive alongside Hill after Clark's death in April. Longford provided Courage with his greatest day thus far in a career that had been in danger of stalling, as he took the McLaren to victory in appalling conditions. It was a wholly apposite swansong for the model.

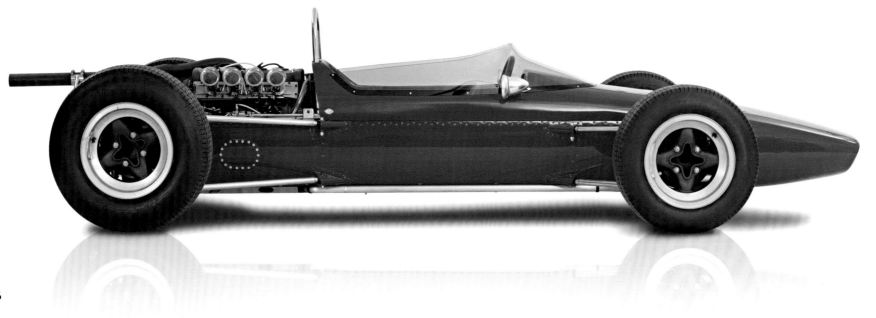

MODEL	McLaren M4A	TRANSMISSION	Hewland HD5 or FT200 5-speed	TYRES F/R	Firestone 5.00-13/6.25-13
TYPE/FORMULA	Formula 2	CHASSIS	20swg aluminium alloy monocoque, steel bulkheads	LENGTH	138in - 3505mm
YEAR OF PRODUCTION	1967	BODY	Monocoque sides, GRP nose & cockpit surround	WIDTH	70in - 1778mm
DESIGNER	Robin Herd	FRONT SUSPENSION	Single top link & radius arm, lower wishbone,	HEIGHT	30in - 762mm
EXAMPLES BUILT	2 + 25 M4A/B Trojan built customer cars		outboard coil spring/damper, anti-roll bar	WHEELBASE	90in - 2286mm
ENGINE	Ford Cosworth FVA	REAR SUSPENSION	Reverse lower wishbone, top link, twin radius	TRACK F/R	54/54in - 1372/1372mm
CUBIC CAPACITY	1598cc		rods, outboard coil spring/damper, anti-roll bar	WEIGHT	960lb - 435kg
CARBURATION	Lucas fuel injection	BRAKES F/R	Outboard 10.5in discs	PRINCIPAL DRIVERS	McLaren, Courage
POWER OUTPUT	230bhp	WHEELS DIAMETER x WIDTH F/R	13x7/13x10in	IDENTIFYING COLOURS	Red

Bruce was confident that the M4A concept had more to deliver than it had so far, and in the continued absence of the BRM V12 one of the factory F2 cars was sidelined for additional development by Herd and his team. It was revamped so that the boss could race it as an 'interim' Formula 1 car. In the way of these things, the resultant machine was somewhat confusingly type-numbered as a McLaren M4B.

Bruce planned to use it in the early races of 1967, until arrival of BRM's V12 would enable completion of the new M5A. It was made at the factory in Colnbrook rather than coming off the 'production line' at Purley, and Herd modified the rear end to accommodate an ex-Tasman Series 2070cc BRM V8 which was said to produce around 280bhp. That was less even than the Indy Ford or Serenissima V8s had managed in 1966, but the M4B was much lighter. It was fitted with long-range pannier tanks either side of the cockpit to provide sufficient fuel for a Grand Prix, but nevertheless had to be ballasted in order to meet the 500kg minimum weight.

The hybrid made its debut at the Race of Champions in March 1967, finished in brick red as Bruce and Teddy Mayer were still undecided on the precise colour the team's livery should be. After breaking a camshaft in practice, Bruce had to race with a borrowed 1,960cc BRM V8 but still did well. Only three 3-litre cars outqualified him: the Eagle Weslake V12s of Dan Gurney and Richie Ginther, and John Surtees' V12 Honda. With only two thirds of their engine capacity, Bruce was still able to finish fourth and sixth in the two heats. Unfortunately, in the ferociously competitive 40-lap final he missed a gear on the opening lap, over-revved the engine, and snapped another camshaft.

The next outing came at Oulton Park for the minor-league Spring Trophy race. With the 2.1-litre BRM engine reinstalled, Bruce qualified sixth. He finished fifth in both heats, and took the same place, a lap down, in the final. At the end of April, in the Daily Express International Trophy at Silverstone, he finished fifth once again on a track rendered slippery with oil.

In a bid to improve reliability for Monaco in May, where it was hoped that the tight street circuit would favour the smaller car, McLaren fitted a heavier-duty Hewland DG gearbox, as well as larger oil and water radiators. The nose was also cut back, as was the custom in those days, to avoid bumping in early-race traffic. Bruce qualified 9th and was running a strong third by the 71st lap when he was forced into the pits by a misfire, which he believed to be caused by lack of fuel. Jack Brabham, who had retired on the opening lap, ran into the McLaren pit as Bruce called for more fuel, shouting: *"It's your battery, it's your battery!"* Bruce was quick to acknowledge the debt to a rival, later writing, *"Good old Jack. It was the battery and we quickly whipped another one on."*

The stop proved costly. Following Lorenzo Bandini's fiery crash, McLaren could have finished second behind fellow Kiwi Denny Hulme, who scored his maiden win in Brabham's second car. As it was he slipped to fourth, separated from Hulme by Graham Hill's Lotus-BRM and Chris Amon who was making his debut for Ferrari. It was, nevertheless, a very respectable performance.

The M4B's final outing came at Zandvoort for a Dutch Grand Prix that saw the arrival of the new Lotus 49 and its Ford Cosworth DFV V8 engine. As the Lotus Fords dominated, Bruce struggled with his horsepower deficit and some electrical difficulties, and qualified only 14th. To compound that, he spun on oil on the second lap and crashed through a fence. Although the car was reportedly badly damaged the monocoque itself was, in Bruce's own words, *"completely unharmed"*. The team nevertheless called it a day, elected not to travel to Spa where the power deficit would have been even more of a handicap, and Bruce thereafter accepted an offer from his old friend Dan Gurney to drive a second Eagle Weslake for the next three races.

The M4B was subsequently repaired, and in the late summer Bruce took it tyre testing at Goodwood. Unfortunately, it caught fire out on the circuit and was completely burnt out. Years later, looking back at the company's success in the 1960s and early 1970s, the respected British motoring writer Leonard Setright was to describe these early machines as having what he called, *"a nicety of construction and an honesty of purpose."* And he noted that, *"much the same could be said about Bruce."*

Top: The pannier tanks fitted to the Formula 2-based M4B were needed to carry the fuel necessary to complete the longer Formula 1 races. The truncated nose was a 'Monaco' speciality which most teams adopted for the race on the narrow streets of Monte Carlo. Above: Bruce heads up the hill at Monaco where the smaller F2-size car (with a specially fitted heavy-duty gearbox) was in its element. He ran in third place for much of the race, only dropping to fourth after a pit stop to change a faulty battery.

Opposite: At the International Trophy race for Formula 1 cars held at Silverstone in April 1967, Bruce made it to the finish in fifth place, a lap down on the Ferrari of winner Mike Parkes.

MODEL	McLaren M4B	TRANSMISSION	Hewland FT200 5-speed	TYRES F/R	Goodyear
TYPE/FORMULA	Formula 1	CHASSIS	20swg aluminium alloy monocoque, steel bulkheads	LENGTH	124in - 3150mm
YEAR OF PRODUCTION	1967	BODY	Monocoque sides, GRP nose & cockpit surround	WIDTH	72in - 1828mm
DESIGNER	Robin Herd	FRONT SUSPENSION	Single top link & radius arm, lower wishbone,	HEIGHT	30in - 762mm
EXAMPLES BUILT	1		outboard coil spring/damper, anti-roll bar	WHEELBASE	93in - 2362mm
ENGINE	BRM V8	REAR SUSPENSION	Reverse lower wishbone, top link, twin radius	TRACK F/R	54/54in - 1372/1372mm
CUBIC CAPACITY	2070cc		rods, outboard coil spring/damper, anti-roll bar	WEIGHT	928lb - 420kg
CARBURATION	Lucas fuel injection	BRAKES F/R	Outboard 10.5in discs	PRINCIPAL DRIVERS	McLaren
POWER OUTPUT	280bhp	WHEELS DIAMETER x WIDTH F/R	13x7/13x10in	IDENTIFYING COLOURS	Red

1967 M5A
FORMULA 1

Bruce's outings as Dan Gurney's partner in the Eagle team, in the French, British and German Grand Prix races, saw him run a little slower than the fleet American, but each time he retired with engine or engine-related maladies. It had been a convenient arrangement that kept him fresh, but doubtless it was a relief finally to be able to climb into Robin Herd's extremely handsome new M5A for the remaining four races of the 1967 season.

The delays with BRM's customer version of its V12 engine effectively rendered the long-finished M5A something of a stop-gap model, and seriously compromised McLaren's second F1 season. But at least the car was a pukka F1 machine. It was a step forward from the smaller car, with its main fuel supplies located within the chassis in tanks fitted both above and beneath the driver's legs, as well as in the extended booms that projected rearwards from the monocoque to support the relatively long engine.

The new combination was finally ready for a 30-lap shakedown at Goodwood in August before being sent out to Mosport for the Canadian Grand Prix. With a little more foresight, its debut could have been sensational.

There were reassuringly few teething troubles in practice, where Bruce qualified a promising sixth just over a second slower than Clark's pole position Lotus. The race began in pouring rain, however, and Bruce spun down to 12th early on before tigering back to fifth after 10 laps. On the 11th he went past Graham Hill, and by the 13th, Jack Brabham. Seven laps later Bruce slipped past Clark to take second place, with only Denny Hulme now ahead. As the rain stopped and the track started to dry, he moved in on the Brabham Repco, but both were repassed by Clark. By lap 59, however, the downpour began again, but instead of Bruce storming after Clark and Hulme again, a bid to save weight started to backfire. As Eoin Young later put it: "For want of a nail this particular McLaren horse lost the race."

The decision had been taken to run the car without an alternator, since the engine had a mechanical fuel pump and, in any case, made low demands on the electrical system. But the battery was losing charge and the engine was beginning to misfire. It may simply have been that the battery was affected by exhaust heat which boiled it dry, but whatever the cause, Bruce was forced to pit to change the unit. He lost three laps and eventually rejoined to finish a disappointed seventh, just out of the points.

Monza too was to end in disappointment. There, for the Italian Grand Prix, he qualified the M5A on the front of the grid, close to Clark and Brabham. Crucially, he was also ahead of Amon's Ferrari, which led to a farcical scene which paints a delightful picture of the occasionally amateurish nature of even topline racing in the 1960s.

The M5A had the same brick red livery as the M4B because, according to chief mechanic Alastair Caldwell, that was all they had in the workshop at the time. The race organisers were displeased since red was Ferrari's colour, and several times ordered the team to paint its car green without delay since it was based in England and green was the British racing colour. It mattered little to them that the car had a vestigial green stripe on the nose. Miffed to be nagged repeatedly about what seemed to him to be a minor point, a busy Caldwell sent someone to buy aerosols containing the most offensive shade of green they could find.

"We were going to paint the whole car bright lime green," Caldwell later told Vintage Racecar. "Wheels, tyres, springs, everything." But then Bruce qualified on the front row, and the organisers suddenly realised that there wasn't a Ferrari alongside him and rushed back to the McLaren pit. "They said, 'The car's still red? Good. Leave it red!'," Caldwell remembered. "Turns out it would have been the first instance, since the dawn of time [actually 1962], when there wasn't a red car on the front row of the Italian Grand Prix!"

Unfortunately, the race story was less amusing. Bruce ran quite strongly after a terribly ragged start that was so typical of Monza at that time, but by the time John Surtees narrowly beat Jack Brabham to the finish line, the M5A had long been gone with a suspected shattered cylinder liner.

In October at Watkins Glen a split hose removed the car from the US GP after just 16 laps. The season ended in Mexico three weeks later, and there Bruce felt that they never got the V12 running cleanly in the thin air at high altitude. He qualified eighth but, lacking the horsepower to be truly competitive, struggled in sixth place before the oil pressure began to drop. Keen to preserve his team's one and only F1 engine, he quit from 13th place after 45 laps and was able to watch Denny Hulme roar on to clinch the World Championship title.

Bruce had dramatic plans for 1968 which centred on a two-car team of Ford Cosworth-powered M7As for himself and new signing Hulme, but the M5A lived to fight another season, initially in the hands of the reigning World Champion. For the first time a single seater McLaren appeared in what had become the team's trademark papaya orange thanks to the successes the previous year of the Can-Am M6As. Running with very limited resources as Bruce stayed at home working on the M7As, Denny put the car ninth on the grid for the South African GP and raced it home to a solid fifth place, marking the only time it ever scored World Championship points in works' hands.

Thereafter it was sold to Swedish racer Jo Bonnier, who was in the twilight of his career. He painted it in his Joakim Bonnier Racing Team livery of yellow, with white and red stripes, and campaigned it as a privateer, with a best placing of sixth in a race of high attrition at Monza.

Back at Brands for the British Grand Prix in July, Bonnier's race was even shorter. On lap seven he pulled into the pits with a suspected dropped valve on the BRM engine.

MODEL	McLaren M5A
TYPE/FORMULA	Formula 1
YEAR OF PRODUCTION	1967
DESIGNER	Robin Herd
EXAMPLES BUILT	1
ENGINE	BRM V12
CUBIC CAPACITY	2998cc
CARBURATION	Lucas fuel injection
POWER OUTPUT	370bhp

TRANSMISSION	Hewland DG500 5-speed
CHASSIS	20swg aluminium alloy monocoque, steel bulkheads
BODY	Monocoque sides, GRP nose & cockpit surround
FRONT SUSPENSION	Single top link & radius arm, lower wishbone, outboard coil spring/damper, anti-roll bar
REAR SUSPENSION	Reverse lower wishbone, top link, twin radius rods, outboard coil spring/damper, anti-roll bar
BRAKES F/R	Outboard Lockheed discs & calipers
WHEELS DIAMETER x WIDTH F/R	13x8.5/15x12in

TYRES F/R	Goodyear
LENGTH	162in - 4115mm
WIDTH	70.5in - 1791mm
HEIGHT	26.5in - 673mm
WHEELBASE	95in - 2413mm
TRACK F/R	58/58in - 1473/1473mm
WEIGHT	1180lb - 535kg
PRINCIPAL DRIVERS	McLaren, Hulme, Bonnier
IDENTIFYING COLOURS	Red, Orange

1967 M6A
CAN-AM

The McLaren M6A was the third major design that Robin Herd prepared for the team in 1967, and the most successful. Working with draughtsman Gordon Coppuck, a colleague from his days at Farnborough, Herd sat down early to work out the parameters of the company's first monocoque Can-Am racer. Using similar chassis technology to that applied earlier to the M5A, and after wind tunnel testing with a modified model of the M1B, the team built three examples of a new sportscar which clearly hit the spot straight out of the box. The M6A was a major turning point in McLaren's fortunes, and was more than to compensate for the late arrival of the BRM F1 engine and its lack of real success thus far in the ultra-lucrative Canadian-American Challenge Cup series.

The M6A also enjoyed the distinction of being the first example of the marque to be painted in the definitive hue that came to be called 'McLaren Orange,' a soft shade of that colour known as papaya. Teddy Mayer had long been unhappy with the team's choice of colour and, having seen a yellow Lola T70 run by British entrant Jackie Epstein, opted for a similar colour which, it was felt *"would show up like a beacon on TV."*

Based around a simple stressed-skin hull, the monocoque was formed via bonded and riveted magnesium and aluminium-alloy panel box structures, welded to a square-section tube frame. Fuel was carried in three rubber tanks - one either side of the driver, a third beneath his knees - these being linked via a series of one-way valves to allow the fuel to run freely through the system even under heavy acceleration. The structure was clad in a simple but distinctive aerodynamic glass-fibre body which featured a sharply raked nose to enhance downforce. Power came from a Bartz-modified, Lucas fuel-injected 6-litre Chevrolet V8 which McLaren built itself in Los Angeles, mated to a five-speed Hewland LG gearbox.

The front suspension comprised outboard coil spring/damper units with lateral links to the top and bottom located by trailing radius rods, and at the rear upper and lower wishbones were employed, with twin radius rods. Once again, the car sported McLaren's own cast magnesium wheels, 15-inch diameter all round, and 8.5-inch wide at the front and 13.25 at the rear. Crucially, Bruce had also negotiated a lucrative tyre deal with Goodyear, so the Firestones of yesteryear made way for American-built rubber on the new Group 7 contender.

The M6A was to be Herd's last car for McLaren before he left to design a four-wheel-drive F1 car for Cosworth. It was uncomplicated, apparently straightforward to maintain and run and met Bruce's initial brief to the letter. Impressively it took just 11 weeks to progress from pen-and-paper to a running prototype, M6A-1 being ready for a test session at the Goodwood circuit on June 19th, a full two and a half months before the first race of the season.

With this unusual luxury, Bruce was keen to put 2000 test miles on the car in order to identify and iron out any possible faults. With a 40:60 weight bias to the rear, the car handled well, and the steep nose seemed to work; to balance the downforce several attempts were made to modify the rear end with small aerodynamic attachments, although none seemed to do much for lap times apart from a small vestigial spoiler on the tail. In hindsight, the effort clearly paid off. The team devoted so much time to fine-tuning an already impressive machine and the M6A was one of the finest handling machines of its era, as well as boasting the greatest success rate in the history of Can-Am.

Its first win came on its debut at Road America, Elkhart Lake, on September 3rd, 1967. It also marked the beginning of the so-called 'Bruce and Denny Show'. The duo dominated proceedings completely in the first of five McLaren victories that year, and they lost only one of the six races as they crushed their opposition in the J-Wax Can-Am Championship.

At Elkhart Lake it was Denny's turn, Bruce qualifying on pole position but being forced to quit when his engine ran a bearing. Hulme qualified second but led the race from start to finish, setting the fastest lap time, and winning by a resounding 93s. Two weeks later in the Chevron GP at Bridgehampton he did it again, romping home ahead of the field despite a mid-race spin. Bruce finished right behind him to give the team its first 1-2. In September the cars were in action again, taking first and second places on the grid for the Players 200 at Mosport Park. Denny was beginning to look unstoppable after scoring a third consecutive victory.

Then Bruce bounced back in the Monterey GP at Laguna Seca on October 15th. He took pole as Denny qualified only third due to ignition and injector trouble. Setting the fastest lap, breaking the course record, and actually lapping Hall's Chaparral 2G, Bruce finished a comfortable first. Hulme however retired on the 81st lap, when his engine blew.

The Penske team took over M6A-1 for 1968 and with the larger 427 block engine, Mark Donohue easily won his second USRRC title as well as taking part in the Can-Am series.

At Riverside the Los Angeles Times GP was altogether tighter. Gurney took pole position, and in the race, Hall in the Chaparral 2G hounded Bruce to the flag. Denny was black-flagged after his M6A sustained bodywork damage thanks to a tyre marker thrown into his path by Parnelli Jones's Lola T70. Thus Bruce now had 30 points and Denny was three shy of him as they headed for the final round; the Stardust GP in Las Vegas.

There a broken rocker left Denny on the third row of the grid. Bruce was on pole, but he started the race knowing his engine was mixing oil and water and was duly forced to retire by the eighth lap. Hulme, despite a bad start and a near-miss in traffic in the first turn, steadily began to fight his way through, knowing a fourth place would be sufficient to hand him the Can-Am Championship to go with the F1 World Championship. He had actually risen to third when his engine self-destructed in front of the grandstands. That left 1966 Can-Am Champion John Surtees to salvage something from his season. Neither McLaren had finished the race, but Bruce was the new Can-Am champion, with Denny those three points behind in second place. It was a fabulous result for a team that, Bruce admitted, had been brought to its knees in the previous three seasons while *"learning how to go motor racing properly."*

For 1968, the Championship-winning M6A-1 passed into the hands of the Penske Racing Team, to be driven by Donohue in the 1968 USRRC series. The team installed a 7-litre aluminium-block Chevrolet V8 and with the 'Sunoco Special' painted in Penske's familiar blue and yellow colours, Donohue became the only driver to win back-to-back USRRC titles, with victories in four of the championship rounds.

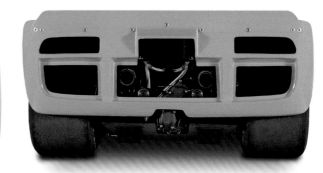

June 19th 1967 and Bruce takes the M6A for its first run at Goodwood. The team was able to put almost 2,000 miles of testing on the car before the first race of the new Can-Am season at Road America in early September.

MODEL	McLaren M6A	TRANSMISSION	Hewland LG600 5-speed	TYRES F/R	Goodyear
TYPE/FORMULA	Can-Am	CHASSIS	Aluminium alloy monocoque, steel bulkheads	LENGTH	153in - 3886mm
YEAR OF PRODUCTION	1967	BODY	Monocoque sides with 4 GRP body sections	WIDTH	68in - 1727mm
DESIGNER	Robin Herd/Gordon Coppuck	FRONT SUSPENSION	Single top link & radius arm, lower wishbone,	HEIGHT TO TOP OF WINDSCREEN	31in - 787mm
EXAMPLES BUILT	3		outboard coil spring/damper, anti-roll bar	WHEELBASE	91.5in - 2324mm
ENGINE	Chevrolet V8	REAR SUSPENSION	Single top link, reverse lower wishbone with twin	TRACK F/R	52/52in - 1321/1321mm
CUBIC CAPACITY	5900cc		radius arms, outboard coil spring/damper, anti-roll bar	WEIGHT	1300lb - 590kg
CARBURATION	Lucas fuel injection	BRAKES F/R	Outboard 12in Girling ventilated discs	PRINCIPAL DRIVERS	McLaren, Hulme, Donohue, Hansen
POWER OUTPUT	527bhp	WHEELS DIAMETER x WIDTH F/R	15x8.5/15x13.25in	IDENTIFYING COLOURS	Papaya

1968 McLAREN-TROJAN M6B CAN-AM

Whatever the original intention had been, the sensational performance of Bruce and Denny's M6As in their first season in North America — and the factory's continuing dominance of Can-Am racing over the next four years — made the production of cash-generating replicas a certainty. The team's partner company was soon building the first of 26 McLaren-Trojan M6B customer cars that would seemingly form the bulk of the cars running in the Can-Am series for the next few seasons.

Demand for a car capable of consistently good performance and of defeating not just the likes of Lola and Chaparral but also Ferrari, was naturally strong, with many privateers both in Europe and the US aspiring to replicate its success for themselves. Here the strength and simplicity of Herd and Coppuck's original design came into its own, the truth being that the majority of privateers had neither the resources of a professional works team, nor the technical know-how required to succeed with some of the doubtless brilliant but otherwise temperamental machines from some rival constructors. In the aerodynamically efficient M6B, with its race-proven and relatively unstressed American V8, they found a car which, priced around a very competitive $36,000, was ready to race and, in the rights hands, to win.

Of all the privateers associated with McLaren at this time, the best known was Daniel Sexton Gurney, the New York-born son of an opera singer. A keen hot-rodder who was later drafted and served in Korea, Gurney made his name in F1 driving for Ferrari in the late 1950s and thereafter BRM, Porsche and Brabham in the early 1960s before, like Bruce, pursuing his goals as a constructor from 1966 onwards with his F1 and Indianapolis Eagles which raced respectively under the Anglo-American Racers and All-American Racers (AAR) auspices. In 1968, in search of a replacement for the Lola T70

that All-American Racers had fielded in 1967, he bought an M6B. He was impressed with the car, and his sound friendship with Bruce led him to drive a third works McLaren M7A in the Canadian, United States and Mexican GPs that year as Bruce reciprocated Dan's generosity in letting him drive the works Eagle the previous season when Bruce had been between the M4B and the M5A.

Dan was always full of ideas for his cars, and the M6B was heavily modified with many parts manufactured in titanium to minimise weight, and revisions to the suspension geometry. The result was the so-called 'McLeagle', a machine that, though outwardly bearing close resemblance to the standard M6B, was nevertheless unique.

The McLeagle rarely appeared twice in the same guise, such was the pace of its development. Gurney tried different wing set-ups and tail sections, particularly as tyre sizes increased for 1969, and championed his own small-block Ford engines with Gurney Weslake cylinder heads. Eventually when a breakdown in supply caused the team to forfeit six races, a switch was made to a Chevrolet big-block for the final three races in 1969.

In performance, even with the gifted Gurney behind the wheel, the car was never a match for the new McLaren M8A or the subsequent M8B; after a long run of non-finishes, however, after running second for much of the race, Dan finished a respectable fourth at his beloved Riverside in 1969. At the conclusion of the season, the car was purchased by Bob Brown who ran it into 1970 and early 1971 more or less unchanged but for the removal of the high suspension-mounted rear wing in accordance with new regulations. He actually enjoyed rather more success than Gurney had, with five top 10 finishes in 1970.

The only man who won an official Can-Am round in an M6B was Mark Donohue, who steered Roger Penske's pristine example to victory at Bridgehampton in September 1968. He fought hard with the M8As and Jim Hall's Chaparral, and when combustion gas blow-by in the M8As' engines pressurised the sump and blew all the oil out, causing them eventually to blow up, and Hall to slow with mechanical difficulties of his own, 'Captain Nice' scooped the spoils.

Since McLaren was always working on its own cars for 'The Bruce and Denny Show', customer cars were always based on the previous year's model. Bruce naturally liked to keep to himself any small detail improvements in terms of both hardware and application. But while they might not have been able to challenge the works car, many customer cars enjoyed a good long run of activity and were competitive with the best of rivals' products.

A fourth place finish in the 1969 Can-Am race at Riverside gave Dan Gurney his best result in the spectacular, high-wing revised 'McLeagle' McLaren M6B-Chevrolet.

Roger McCaig's M6B Chevrolet heads Jim Paul's M1C in the penultimate round of the 1968 Can-Am championship at Riverside in October. Both cars failed to finish.

In the 1968 Riverside Can-Am race Jerry Titus (McLaren M6B-Chevrolet) qualified 10th but pulled into the pits to retire on the 50th of the 62 laps.

MODEL	McLaren-Trojan M6B	TRANSMISSION	Hewland LG600 5-speed	TYRES F/R	Goodyear
TYPE/FORMULA	Can-Am	CHASSIS	Aluminium alloy monocoque, steel bulkheads	LENGTH	155in - 3937mm
YEAR OF PRODUCTION	1968	BODY	Monocoque sides with 4 GRP body sections	WIDTH	68in - 1727mm
DESIGNER	Robin Herd/Gordon Coppuck	FRONT SUSPENSION	Single top link & radius arm, lower wishbone,	HEIGHT	31in - 787mm
EXAMPLES BUILT	26		outboard coil spring/damper, anti-roll bar	WHEELBASE	93.5in - 2375mm
ENGINE	Chevrolet V8	REAR SUSPENSION	Single top link, reverse lower wishbone with twin	TRACK F/R	52/52in - 1321/1321mm
CUBIC CAPACITY	5900cc		radius arms, outboard coil spring/damper, anti-roll bar	WEIGHT	1300lb - 590kg
CARBURATION	Lucas fuel injection	BRAKES F/R	Outboard 12in Girling ventilated discs	PRINCIPAL DRIVERS	Donohue, Elford, Gurney
POWER OUTPUT	527bhp	WHEELS DIAMETER x WIDTH F/R	15x8.5/15x13.25in	IDENTIFYING COLOURS	n/a

The elegant M7A tends to be mistaken as the first single seater McLaren that was designed specifically for Formula 1, doubtless because it was the first to succeed. It was another product of the fruitful Robin Herd/Gordon Coppuck pairing.

Like the M6A, the new car proved a winner not just first time out, but on its first two outings. Bruce won the 1968 Daily Mail Race of Champions at Brands Hatch in March, and the following month Denny fought back from a problem when a stone smashed a lens in his goggles, to win the Daily Express International Trophy race at Silverstone. Both were non-championship events, but the M7A was to make the McLaren marque a Grand Prix winner that season, too.

Herd conceived McLaren's first Ford Cosworth DFV-powered contender around a simple and strong, three-quarter length monocoque, following Lotus's lead in using the V8 as a structural element. Transmission was provided by a standard Hewland DG300 five-speed transaxle.

The chassis was of the so-called bathtub type, open to the top in the fashion of the Lotus 25 and was skinned mainly in 22-gauge L72 aluminium sheet or, in a few places, 20-gauge magnesium sheet, which was riveted and bonded to three internal 20-gauge steel bulkheads. 40 gallons of fuel were distributed between four rubber bag tanks, one each longitudinally on either side of the tub, another behind the driver's seat, and the fourth in the scuttle. Sleek glass-fibre bodywork completed the attractive package. Other notable points were the use of Lockheed brakes, at a time when every other British team opted for Girling.

The suspension was conventional and derived from the M6A's, via outboard coil spring/dampers units at both ends and single lateral links and trailing arms at the front and single lateral top links, reversed lower wishbones and twin radius rods at the rear.

There was a story behind the suspension, for Herd had left McLaren to join Cosworth shortly after drawing the M7A's chassis. Bruce had schooled him in the rigours of applying his impressive aerospace knowledge to the practicalities of motor racing and felt aggrieved when his design protégé upped and left. It was left to Coppuck to do the detail design on the suspension, after Bruce had largely been responsible for the geometry.

McLaren was now reasonably well funded via commercial deals with both Goodyear and Shell, and the two non-championship race successes provided a much-needed boost following Denny's fifth place with the M5A in the opening race in South Africa. Once the Grand Prix season resumed in Spain and Monaco in May, Graham Hill put Lotus back on top. But then came Spa and the Belgian Grand Prix on June 9th, which would prove to be a Red Letter Day for the marque. After early leaders John Surtees in the Honda and Chris

Amon in a Ferrari had dropped out, Denny was embroiled in a battle for the lead with Jackie Stewart's Tyrrell-Matra-Ford. Then Denny retired after 18 laps with a driveshaft failure, leaving Bruce fighting the BRMs of Pedro Rodriguez and Piers Courage, and Jacky Ickx's Ferrari, for second place in Stewart's wake. Gradually Bruce dropped his three challengers and was convinced he had finished as the runner-up as he crossed the line. But Stewart had pitted for fuel on the penultimate lap, leaving Bruce to emulate Jack Brabham as only the second man ever to win a Grand Prix in a car bearing his own name. He discovered this from one of BRM's mechanics, who said: "You've won, didn't you know?" Bruce recalled later: "It was about the nicest thing I'd ever been told."

As Matra and Ferrari, on Dunlop and Firestone tyres respectively, won subsequent races, and Graham Hill and his Firestone-shod Lotus set the pace aerodynamically after full-blown wings had appeared on the Ferraris and Brabhams at Spa, McLaren lost pace. Its wings were less effective, mounted in the middle of the car on the sprung mass rather than, in Lotus style, at the rear on the unsprung suspension uprights, and Goodyear suffered a dip in competitiveness. But its new G9 tyre came as a boost by Monza in September, where Denny scored a great victory in the Italian GP. He repeated the feat in the next race, at St Jovite in Canada, albeit after faster runners Amon, Jochen Rindt and Jo Siffert had all met trouble. Bruce brought his M7A home behind him to record McLaren's first-ever 1-2 in a Grand Prix.

The 1968 Belgian Grand Prix at Spa-Francorchamps gave Bruce McLaren his maiden Grand Prix win as a driver/constructor. Here Bruce in M7A/1 leads Pedro Rodriguez in his works BRM P133. After leader Jackie Stewart's Matra stopped for fuel on the penultimate lap they finished first and second.

Denny Hulme won two Grand Prix races in 1968 (Italy and Canada) and finished the season third in the World Drivers' Championship, ahead of Bruce. For the Constructors' title, McLaren came an impressive second behind Lotus with the all conquering Type 49 that had begun the DFV era.

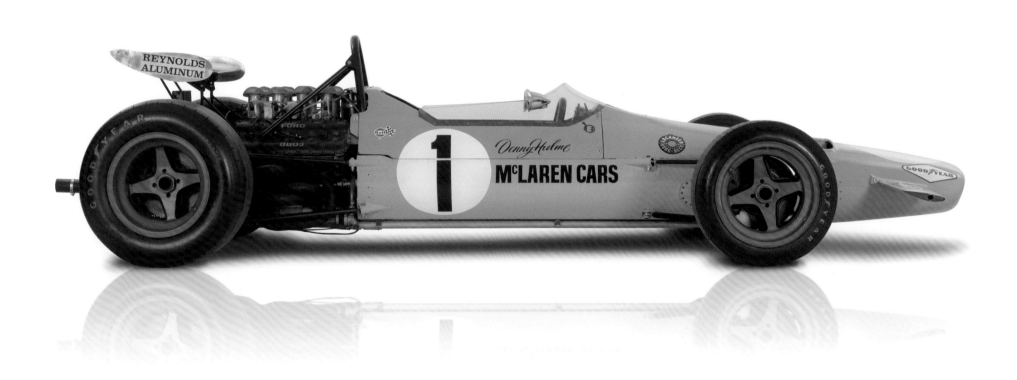

Suddenly the outcome of the World Championship was a three-way fight between Denny, Hill and Stewart, McLaren, Lotus and Matra. The New Zealander and the Englishman had 33 points each, the Scot 27.

Stewart beat Hill in the US GP at Watkins Glen, but Denny unfortunately was forced into retirement while chasing the Lotus driver. First, he damaged a rear brake pipe after sliding off course on oil, and lost ground having repairs effected; then he slid off the road again, badly damaging his car but not himself. Now he trailed Hill (39 points) and Stewart (36) with his 33. The only consolation was Dan Gurney's fourth place in the third M7A.

This time there was to be no New Zealand fairy tale in Mexico. Hill wrapped up the title with victory for Lotus, as a fuel feed problem left Stewart seventh and Denny crashed out after 11 laps with a suspected broken rear damper. He thus had to be content with third place in the World Championship for Drivers as Bruce finished fifth overall, having taken second place in Mexico. Despite the disappointment, their placings were an indication of the growing strength of the young marque. In its first full season with a pukka F1 car, McLaren had won three Grands Prix and two non-championship races, challenged for the title, and finished second (ahead of Matra) in the World Championship for Constructors, just 13 points shy of Lotus.

1969 was less successful and saw Jackie Stewart's Dunlop-shod Matra Ford dominate. Bruce nevertheless repeated Denny's third place in the World Championship for Drivers, mainly through consistency, while Denny had to settle for sixth after a frustrating year of poor reliability. But 'The Bear' bounced back with a crushing victory in the Mexican Grand Prix as he ran away and hid even from the fleet Brabhams of Ickx and Jack Brabham.

Bruce's regular 1968 M7A was sold to South African Basil van Rooyen for 1969 and at that year's Grand Prix at Kyalami he was the fastest local qualifier before brake trouble put him out of the race. He would remain a leading light in South Africa's domestic F1 series with the car and was leading overall after the first three races with 24 points to rival John Love's 15. But then M7A-1 was destroyed late in May, in a spectacular accident during testing for the Republic Festival Trophy race at Kyalami, when a rear tyre deflated at 160mph.

Despite the diversion with the four-wheel-drive M9A, development of the M7 concept continued. M7A-3, which Gurney had raced in 1968, is believed to have been reworked substantially to become the unique M7B, though even today the situation over M7 chassis numbers remains a little unclear.

Pursuing one of his pet themes concerning fuel placement to enhance rear tyre grip, Bruce had Coppuck redesign the chassis with wide pannier tanks skinned into the car's central structure. Coppuck also did a lot of work on the front wings, after making do with just small trim tabs in 1968, and a succession of increasingly large rear wings located on tall struts on the rear suspension uprights.

On the M7B's South African debut, Bruce drove to a steady fifth place. Two weeks later, at Brands Hatch for the Race of Champions, the car had acquired a tall suspension-mounted front wing but it was removed after practice. Bruce ran fifth until a pit stop to replace the spark box, and having rejoined briefly before retiring, he cast the M7B aside and switched his focus to the forthcoming M7C, disappointed that his experimental car had not delivered the performance advantage expected of it.

Classic car enthusiast Colin Crabbe, of Antique Automobiles, had been so excited when his driver Vic Elford took an aged Cooper-Maserati to seventh place at Monaco, that he bought the M7B. It was repainted in his maroon and white colours and Elford qualified it last for the Dutch GP in June before finishing 10th.

The car was subtly modified in time for its next appearance, for the French GP at Clermont-Ferrand early in July, with new anti-roll bars and a downforce generating tea tray-shaped cover over the engine. After a steady run and the retirement of more fancied runners, the former rally star brought the car home fifth, to Crabbe's undisguised delight. Later that month Elford took sixth place at Silverstone in the British GP.

The team headed for the German GP full of optimism, especially as Elford was widely recognised as a 'ring expert and had an extra 300rpm from a revised exhaust system.

In Monte Carlo both team cars featured the customary 'Monaco' style short nose. Having run as high as third,

Denny Hulme finished fifth, scoring points for the third race in a row. Bruce retired on the first lap.

He qualified a brilliant sixth, only two seconds off Denny in his M7A and nearly two seconds faster than Bruce in the M7C. Sadly, the race brought disaster. Elford made a poor start and hit one of the wheels torn off Mario Andretti's four-wheel-drive Lotus 63 when that car bottomed out on the opening lap and crashed. The M7B was completely destroyed as it was launched over a fence and landed upside down. Elford suffered a seriously dislocated right arm. Crabbe's dream was over.

In 1970 Formula 5000 hotshoes Peter Gethin and Reine Wisell had outings in the non-championship races at Brands Hatch and Silverstone respectively in M7A-2, before it was sold to privateer Tony Dean who ran it in Formula 5000 in 1971, with a 5-litre Chevrolet.

After practising M7B-1 (the heavily revised M7A/3) at the 1969 Race of Champions with high wings both front and rear. Bruce chose to run the race with just the tall rear wing. He retired on lap 10.

MODEL	McLaren M7A	TRANSMISSION	Hewland DG300 5-speed	TYRES F/R		Goodyear
TYPE/FORMULA	Formula 1	CHASSIS	Aluminium 'bathtub' monocoque, steel bulkheads	LENGTH		158in - 4013mm
YEAR OF PRODUCTION	1968/1969	BODY	Monocoque sides, GRP nose & cockpit surround	WIDTH AT COCKPIT		28in - 711mm
DESIGNER	Robin Herd/Gordon Coppuck	FRONT SUSPENSION	Single top link & radius arm, lower	HEIGHT AT WING		35in - 889mm
EXAMPLES BUILT	3		wishbone, outboard coil spring/damper	WHEELBASE		94in - 2387mm
ENGINE	Ford Cosworth DFV	REAR SUSPENSION	Reverse lower wishbone, top link, twin radius	TRACK F/R		58/57in - 1473/1447mm
CUBIC CAPACITY	2993cc		rods, outboard coil spring/damper, anti-roll bar	WEIGHT		1140lb - 517kg
CARBURATION	Lucas fuel injection	BRAKES F/R	Outboard 11.66in ventilated discs	PRINCIPAL DRIVERS		McLaren, Hulme
POWER OUTPUT	410bhp	WHEELS DIAMETER x WIDTH F/R	15x10/15x15in	IDENTIFYING COLOURS		Papaya

"McLaren's Mephistophelian M8," Motor Sport once reported, *"fires up like the Battle of Jutland."* It was certainly a monster, in more ways than one. Possessed of immense power and presence, the car that the magazine memorably described as *"the world's fastest slice of Double Gloucester"*, soon built up a formidable reputation for winning, and doing so consistently.

Once again, the design credit for the M8 series goes to Gordon Coppuck, who this time worked closely with new recruit Jo Marquart. Legend has it that since, at 33, neither was quite yet ready to design a complete car, one took the front end and the other the rear. While Marquart tidied up the nose - not dissimilar to the earlier M6A's, and with a huge, flat scoop to keep the brakes cool - and drew the new, wider bathtub monocoque, Coppuck was charged with the more complex task of mounting the engine and hanging the rear suspension on a Hewland LG500 transmission.

Whatever the truth, the results spoke themselves. In various forms - at one point the team was using mammoth, liner-less, 9.3-litre blocks for qualifying. From 1968 onwards the simple but immensely strong M8s were to enjoy a fabulous winning streak until the final victory came courtesy of French Tyrrell Formula 1 star, François Cevert with an M8F at Donnybrooke in 1972.

Inevitably the M8A shared much with Robin Herd's M6A, but to save weight and enhance torsional stiffness the engine was now employed as a fully-stressed member rather than being located between twin pontoons. The concept of using the engine as a stressed chassis member had been pioneered on the Lancia D50 in 1954 and reintroduced on BRM's P83 H16 and the Lotus 43 in 1966, before being repeated on all Ford Cosworth DFV-powered F1 cars since the Lotus 49 in 1967.

It was unusual for a sportscar's engine to be installed thus, but everything on the M8 was done for a reason. The car was four inches wider, the extra width needed to accommodate the larger tyres available from Goodyear; 74-gallon fuel tanks also took up much of the extra space and were necessary to keep up with the thirst of the larger capacity engine – an aluminium-block 7-litre Chevrolet as usual developed in McLaren's Los Angeles facility by Gary Knutson and Bruce's former mechanic from New Zealand, Colin Beanland. These units were not especially lightweight, offering very little advantage in this regard over the previous season's iron-block 6-litre, but they produced some 100bhp more.

The cars also lost a gear as the Hewland gearbox used four rather than five ratios; this was predominantly because Can-Am's rolling starts meant a conventional first was unnecessary, but also because it saved 12lb over the LG600 gearbox and facilitated the use of shorter driveshafts that were less likely to suffer under the immense torque.

What the press referred to as *"the McLaren Magic"* was to earn the team four wins out of the six Can-Am races that season, but it took it until fairly late in the series to get to grips with the engines. Several problems manifested themselves in the new dry-sump lubrication system, which enabled the V8s to sit five inches lower than in the M6A.

The M8A was more conservative than radical, but as Coppuck later observed the plan wasn't to innovate but to win. *"We could have made it lighter, used a bigger engine, fitted a wing,"* he admitted, *"but reliability was a prime function."*

The M6A's flowing, sinuous shape gave way to a dramatic square-shouldered wedge which inspired Motor Sport's cheese reference. Alongside the likes of Jim Hall's 2G Chaparral, with its large overhead rear wing, the brutish M8As certainly looked the part: neat, trim and reassuringly threatening.

The Can-Am Championship had now become a major series and in 1968 massive crowds were on hand to see McLaren cars win all six of the races. Two of the victories went to privateers, Mark Donohue and John Cannon driving an M6B and an M1B respectively, but the other four were down to Bruce and Denny. Bruce won at Riverside and Denny took the honours at Road America, Edmonton and Las Vegas to clinch the championship as Bruce placed second overall. Throughout the year McLaren's performance consistency was reflected as the M8A took pole position for all six races.

At the end of the year the three M8As were rebuilt as M8Bs and used by the team for the 1969 season. In 1970 one of them, M8B-2, which had originally been M8A-2, passed into the hands of privateer Lothar Motschenbacher. After being involved in a crash at Elkhart Lake it was put aside and later turned into an M8D showcar for Goodyear. In 1978 the car was returned to New Zealand to be restored and put on display at the Museum of Transport and Technology in Auckland. After disappearing for several years and nearly being destroyed, the only surviving M8A is now in the hands of the Bruce McLaren Trust.

The M8A design by Gordon Coppuck and Jo Marquart was a clean, simple and logical development of the M6A. Its wide, squat look was the epitome of sportscar design.

For 1968 McLaren finally went over to using the 'big-block' 7-litre Chevrolet engine that some other teams had been testing for nearly two seasons. The tall curved hand crafted 'stack-pipes' were highly distinctive.

More Goodwood testing. Once again Bruce put many miles on the new car in preparation for the forthcoming season. It paid off with the M8A dominating the 1968 Can-Am series.

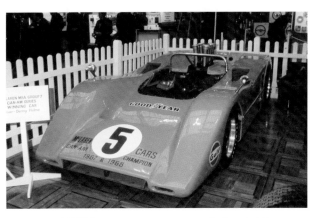

In January of 1969 Denny Hulme's Can-Am Championship-winning M8A from the previous year was displayed at the Racing Car Show held at Olympia in London.

MODEL	McLaren M8A	TRANSMISSION	Hewland LG500 4-speed	TYRES F/R	Goodyear
TYPE/FORMULA	Can-Am	CHASSIS	Aluminium sheet monocoque with steel bulkheads	LENGTH	154in - 3911mm
YEAR OF PRODUCTION	1968	BODY	Monocoque sides, with 4 GRP body sections	WIDTH	72in - 1829mm
DESIGNER	Gordon Coppuck/Jo Marquart	FRONT SUSPENSION	Single top link & radius arm, lower wishbone,	HEIGHT	30in - 762mm
EXAMPLES BUILT	3		outboard coil spring/damper, anti-roll bar	WHEELBASE	94in - 2387mm
ENGINE	Chevrolet V8	REAR SUSPENSION	Reverse lower wishbone, single top link,	TRACK F/R	58/56in - 1473/1422mm
CUBIC CAPACITY	6997cc		twin radius rods, coil spring/damper, anti-roll bar	WEIGHT	1450lb - 658kg
CARBURATION	Lucas fuel injection	BRAKES F/R	Outboard 12in ventilated discs	PRINCIPAL DRIVERS	McLaren, Hulme, Motschenbacher
POWER OUTPUT	620bhp	WHEELS DIAMETER x WIDTH F/R	15x10/15x15in	IDENTIFYING COLOURS	Papaya

An even more remarkable notion than the 26 Can-Am winner replica M6As built by Trojan - and perhaps the best possible expression of the original American 'Win on Sunday, sell on Monday' philosophy - was Bruce's decision to build a short run of roadgoing McLarens.

It was never that straightforward, however. Following the M6A's runaway success in Group 7, McLaren announced its intention to join the lucrative Group 4 GT series for 1969. It was a fast, exciting, and glamorous series with big names including Ferrari, Porsche and Alfa Romeo all fighting for glory, and the plan was to mate the existing M6 chassis to a new coupe body which would be more suitable for endurance racing.

Unfortunately for McLaren, after the initial 'official' paperwork had been completed, the FIA changed the rules governing homologation for the World Championship of Makes, requiring manufacturers to complete a minimum of 50 examples before a car could be considered. Faced with such a requirement McLaren - which had always intended to sell the cars without engines - shelved the project realising that it was simply too big to take on.

Nevertheless, a prototype was completed for Bruce's personal use while evaluating it as a possible McLaren-branded roadcar, which might be licensed to an outside manufacturer such as Trojan. The Can-Am victories had brought funds into the company, and now Bruce - always more than just a driver - was keen to test his skills as an innovator, designer and entrepreneur.

The intention was to build the car, which Bruce designed himself, to the very highest specification possible - something echoed decades later in the awe-inspiring

McLaren F1 project - with as many as 250 units being completed each year. It was a tall order, as were the performance parameters - it was to have the fastest top speed of any roadcar in the world and be the fastest-accelerating - though McLaren hoped to enhance its chances by using an off-the-shelf 7-litre Ford engine. This would save both development time and costs, as well as reduce the need for sophisticated aftersales service and maintenance. As a 'McLaren' it would, needless to say, be based on the latest developments in race engineering, something Bruce recognised would be an immense draw when it came to sales in the large and lucrative US market.

Ultimately no more than three, possibly four, M6GTs were ever built, and only one was built at the McLaren Racing factory. Registered OBH 500H, this was the development car which Bruce used on the roads of South England until his death in June 1970; the other examples were contracted out to Trojan.

Something of a schizophrenic machine, destined always to be a racing car with a new body rather than a convincingly civilised roadcar, the M6GT was surprisingly light and at 1600lb weighed no more than a Mini. It was also phenomenally noisy. Even with the tyres set at the recommended pressures for what the factory referred to as 'quiet driving', the sound of the engine and tyre noise inside the cockpit was nothing less than deafening. At the same time the wider rear wheels made carrying a spare more than a little impractical, as did the need for the driver to get out and raise the headlights manually. Unlike the F1 roadcar of the 1990s, luggage space was virtually non-existent.

The M6GT was also so low at 41 inches that many other road users simply failed to notice it, despite an appearance

The official FIA homologation papers for the M6GT, submitted to the RAC in August 1967, show the M6GT as nothing more than an M6A fitted with lights, a rudimentary roof and crude luggage bags strapped to the tail section.

which could hardly be considered discrete, and the noise it generated. It was nevertheless an intoxicating concept: a genuinely street-legal roadcar based like its Can-Am cousins, on an authentic monocoque chassis with aluminium panelling over steel bulkheads. The 370bhp Bartz-tuned Chevrolet 5.7-litre LT1 engine used in Bruce's car ensured sparkling performance, with a top speed estimated to be in excess of 165mph and a 0-100mph time of eight seconds.

Bruce used the prototype as his daily transport for more than six months, travelling to and from the office as well as attending race meetings that were relatively close to home, as he was keen to discover exactly what it was like as a roadcar. He was intimately involved in the development of what was very much a pet project, and in the final analysis the M6GT is best viewed as a personal testament to his vision for the company.

Perhaps because of this, the project died with him. Denny Hulme bought OBH 500H, chassis BMR6GT-1, with its original engine (No.8932386) from the factory and shipped it home to New Zealand, where it went on display in Auckland at the Museum of Transportation and Technology. The car changed hands a couple of times thereafter, before joining the other McLarens in the Mathews Collection, and is currently in a large collection in Calgary, Alberta. It is still in remarkably original condition - even the fuel and brake lines are unchanged - and with just 1,918 miles on the odometer it still has the same tyres it had when Bruce used it back in 1970.

MODEL	McLaren M6GT	TRANSMISSION	ZF 5DS-26, 5-speed	TYRES F/R	Goodyear
TYPE/FORMULA	Roadcar	CHASSIS	Aluminium alloy sheet monocoque, steel bulkheads	LENGTH	166in - 4216mm
YEAR OF PRODUCTION	1969	BODY	Reinforced polyester resin panelling	WIDTH	75in - 1905mm
DESIGNER	Bruce McLaren/Gordon Coppuck	FRONT SUSPENSION	Single top link & radius arm, lower wishbone,	HEIGHT	39in - 990mm
EXAMPLES BUILT	1 (+3 Trojan built)		outboard coil spring/damper, anti-roll bar	WHEELBASE	93.5in - 2375mm
ENGINE	Chevrolet LT1	REAR SUSPENSION	Reverse lower wishbone, single top link,	TRACK F/R	53.5/56in - 1359/1422mm
CUBIC CAPACITY	5740cc		twin radius rods, coil spring/damper	WEIGHT	1600lb - 725kg
CARBURATION	Quad four-barrel Holley	BRAKES F/R	Outboard Girling 12in ventilated discs	PRINCIPAL DRIVERS	McLaren
POWER OUTPUT	370bhp	WHEELS DIAMETER x WIDTH F/R	12x10/15x14in	IDENTIFYING COLOURS	Red

Another one-off design creation, the M7C was another of Bruce's pet projects that used a monocoque similar to that employed in the recently launched McLaren M10A Formula 5000 car.

Created by Gordon Coppuck for the start of the European leg of the 1969 season, the M7C's chassis differed markedly from the open-topped bathtub-style chassis of the M7As. Now the aluminium skin extended all the way over the driver's legs as well as around the cockpit opening, creating a cigar tube shape more akin to the 1964 BRM P261. From start to finish it was clearly something of a hurried project, as Bruce was concerned that his other 1969 experiment, the wide-panniered M7B, lacked the torsional rigidity and straight-line speed it required to be fully competitive.

Accordingly, the sole M7C to be built was completed only the night before practice for the 1969 International Trophy non-championship F1 race at Silverstone. It was logical to use many M10A components in its construction, since that car was more recent than the now dated M7A and boasted better torsional rigidity and safety. The nose was straight from an M10A, while the monocoque was a clear derivative albeit with the pontoons that were used to support a heavy 5-litre Chevrolet or Ford V8 cut off, so that the Ford Cosworth DFV engine could be used as a stressed chassis member. The suspension components, running gear and fuel tanks were still M7A specification, however.

On that non-championship debut, the car was equipped with a strutted and endplated rear wing mounted on the suspension uprights and braced to the roll-over hoop. Bruce drove to a steady sixth in a race spoiled by rain, a lap down on winner Jack Brabham.

By the time the M7C arrived for the Spanish Grand Prix, it had been equipped with wider front wheels which lightened the steering by allowing reduced offset, and mounting points on the front suspension for another wing, as yet unfitted. Bruce was unhappy with the handling in practice, but this was a general complaint for Goodyear's runners. The race was better, as Bruce steadily worked his way up as both Jochen Rindt and Graham Hill crashed their Lotuses heavily due to wing failures, and Chris Amon's Ferrari blew its engine. From his uninspiring 13th on the grid he climbed to a survivor's second place by the finish, albeit two laps adrift of fortunate winner Jackie Stewart.

At Monaco, in mid-May the bright orange M7C appeared in its most flamboyant form as it now sported high, strutted wings at both ends. McLaren had finally started to catch up with Lotus and Brabham in the aero department. But it was too late. Following the Lotus crashes at Montjuich Park during the Spanish GP, the CSI moved quickly and overnight banned such devices after first practice on the Thursday. That obliged everyone to think again, and the McLarens appeared subsequently with small ducktail lips over their engines. Neither the M7C nor Denny's conventional M7A performed well on the famous street circuit. Bruce finished fifth, one place ahead of his team-mate.

Revised aerodynamic tea tray 'wings' appeared on the cars in Holland, where Denny finished fourth but a stub axle problem sidelined Bruce, who subsequently took the M7C to fourth place in the French GP at Clermont-Ferrand after Denny was delayed by a broken anti-rollbar having started from the front row in his M7A. By the British GP interpretations of the CSI's rules had stabilised around low-mounted aerofoils, and the McLarens were thus equipped for the British GP at Silverstone in July. Denny again started from the front row but succumbed this time to a suspected broken camshaft as Bruce took the M7C to a distant third place. For the German Grand Prix in August Bruce had 13in diameter front wheels of 12in width on the M7C and again took third as Denny retired with transmission failure, and both cars sported extra strap-on fuel tanks for the Italian GP at Monza. Bruce finished fourth as a quartet of drivers lunged for the finish line. He was 0.19s away from the victorious Stewart, with Jochen Rindt and Jean-Pierre Beltoise somehow shoehorned between them.

Denny suffered yet again at Monza with fading brakes and clutch, while poised to fight for the victory, and fell victim to distributor failure in Canada where Bruce took fifth place well behind a Brabham 1-2. Denny started from the front row in the US GP at Watkins Glen but retired with gear selector problems. Bruce failed to start after qualifying sixth only 0.6s off Rindt's pole position, following engine failure on the warming up lap. Exactly the same thing happened to him in Mexico, where a piece of metal jammed the fuel pressure relief valve open, but at least Denny won going away in the M7A to end the season on a high note.

John Surtees had decided to follow the examples of Jack Brabham, Bruce and Dan Gurney and become a Formula 1 constructor in 1970, but until his own Surtees TS7 was ready, he purchased the unique M7C. It was repainted in Surtees red with the distinctive white arrow stripe down the nose, and he participated in the Race of Champions and four Grands Prix. He scored a point for sixth place with it in the Dutch GP, but none of the other outings wer successful. He was sidelined by engine failure in South Africa and Monaco, the gearbox in Spain, and by a sticking throttle in the non-championship race at Brands Hatch.

The TS7 made its debut in the British GP at Brands Hatch in July and the M7C passed into the hands of Jo Bonnier to replace the aged M5A. Racing now as Ecurie Bonnier, he failed to qualify in Italy and burst a water pipe in the USGP at Watkins Glen.

The M7C next appeared at the non-championship Gran Premio de la Republica Argentina in Buenos Aires in January 1971, under the auspices of Ecurie Bonnier YPF, repainted silver and driven by local upcoming Formula 2 racer Carlos Reutemann who was making his F1 debut. He did so in some style, his handling of the ageing car showcasing his innate talent. He qualified fifth for the first heat and finished it in sixth place, then came third in a second heat notable for attrition. That was sufficient for third overall, behind the victorious Chris Amon's Matra and Henri Pescarolo in Frank Williams' March Ford.

Bonnier's F1 swansong came later that season as he failed to qualify in Germany, non-started in Austria and ran without distinction in the South African, Italian and US GPs before switching to sportscar racing in 1972.

MODEL	McLaren M7C
TYPE/FORMULA	Formula 1
YEAR OF PRODUCTION	1969
DESIGNER	Gordon Coppuck
EXAMPLES BUILT	1
ENGINE	Ford Cosworth DFV
CUBIC CAPACITY	2993cc
CARBURATION	Lucas fuel injection
POWER OUTPUT	420bhp

TRANSMISSION	Hewland DG300 5-speed
CHASSIS	360° aluminium monocoque, steel bulkheads
BODY	Monocoque sides, GRP nose & cockpit surround
FRONT SUSPENSION	Single top link & radius arm, lower wishbone,
	outboard coil spring/damper, anti-roll bar
REAR SUSPENSION	Reverse lower wishbone, top link, twin radius
	rods, outboard coil spring/damper, anti-roll bar
BRAKES F/R	Outboard 11.66in ventilated discs
WHEELS DIAMETER x WIDTH F/R	15x10/15x15in

TYRES F/R	Goodyear
LENGTH	158in - 4013mm
WIDTH OF MONOCOQUE	28in - 711mm
HEIGHT OF REAR WING	58in - 1473mm
WHEELBASE	94in - 2387mm
TRACK F/R	58/57in - 1473/1447mm
WEIGHT	1140lb - 517kg
PRINCIPAL DRIVERS	McLaren, Hulme, Bonnier, Surtees
IDENTIFYING COLOURS	Papaya, Red

The M7C was hardly a seminal McLaren, any more than was the M7B which preceded it, but both one-off chassis were testament to Bruce's willingness to experiment, and his canniness in not committing to building more than one chassis until a concept was proven.

The final iteration of the M7 series was another one-off, the M7D, but this one was more than just an experiment. The McLaren Register refers to the construction of the car under 'exploratory use', but the company is believed to have been paid to build it by Alfa Romeo's technical director Carlo Chiti, who often had to resort to subterfuge to avoid the political pressures on his Autodelta racing offshoot, that were a frequent corollary of working for a state-run manufacturer. The M7D would be powered by a modified version of Alfa Romeo's 3-litre V8 which had its roots in sportscar racing and would see duty that season in Autodelta's 33 racers in long distance events. Reportedly it was a brand new chassis numbered M7D/1-5 (to demonstrate it was the fifth car built in the M7 series), built on the old M7A jigs, but a question mark remains over whether the chassis was actually the original M7A-3 whose chassis number had been used on the M7B.

The car first appeared at Jarama for the 1970 Spanish Grand Prix in mid-April. The V8 was said to produce around 425bhp but its trump card, according to Alfa Romeo, would be its healthy torque which should have been perfect for the sinuous Spanish track. Unfortunately, McLaren would soon discover wide discrepancies in performance between individual engines. Autodelta works driver Andrea de Adamich was 14th of the 22 runners in first practice, with a respectable lap of 1m 25.8s compared to pacesetter Denny

Hulme's 1m 24.1s. Curiously, they recorded exactly the same times and occupied exactly the positions in the second session, on Friday afternoon. As Jack Brabham improved the pole position time to 1m 23.9s in the final session, de Adamich cut his time to 1m 25.15s but dropped a place, and in any case the time was recorded in a special qualifying session for non-seeded drivers which did not count for grid positions. Overall, he missed the cut by 0.1s, and after talk of letting the non-qualifiers into the race faded in the face of CSI refusal, did not get to start.

By Monaco the Alfa engine was reportedly producing its 425bhp, and bearing in mind its torque, de Adamich was expected to qualify well. Again, he started well, with 14th fastest time in the first practice session, but ultimately lost out in the non-qualifiers' shoot-out when his 1m 26.1s best left him seventh, after he had brushed a kerb, and therefore just out of the picture. Ironically, had he been a seeded driver with that time, it would have been good enough to make the grid.

The M7D's next appearance was to have been at Spa in June but, together with the two works M14As and John Surtees' private M7C, it was withdrawn in the aftermath of Bruce's death at Goodwood on June 2nd.

De Adamich had a new M14D to try in Holland but reverted to the M7D for the French GP at Clermont-Ferrand on July

5th. There he qualified 15th but finished an unclassified last after a pit stop on the third lap with the engine overheating madly. It was thought that a weak cylinder head seal was pressurising the engine, which was why a water hose had blown off. He continued, made three more pit stops for further attention to the same problem, on laps six, nine and 10, and was nine laps down by the finish.

In the quest for more horsepower Alfa Romeo came up with a half-inch deeper sump for the engine for the British GP at Brands in mid-July, the additional depth requiring the ride height to be set higher to avoid the car bottoming out on the notoriously bumpy track. Even so, the M7D duly did just that and the new sump was damaged. De Adamich was forced to run with the original pan and qualified 19th on 1m 27.1s, but a leaking bag tank was discovered as the car was fuelled just before the race, and since there was no time to change it, he was sidelined yet again.

Thereafter the saga of the M7D Alfa ended as de Adamich reverted to his M14D from the German GP onwards. The M7D never raced again as a works car, but was instead fitted with a Cosworth DFV engine and, together with the experimental M9A, sold to Tom Wheatcroft. In 1973 it went on public display in the Donington Collection, where it can still be seen in this form.

Top left: After John Surtees progressed to his own TS7 car, Jo Bonnier took on the M7C but couldn't get it round the Nürburgring quick enough to qualify for the 1971 German Grand Prix. He was almost a minute slower than polesitter Jackie Stewart's time of 7m 19s in his Tyrrell 003.

Above: During practice for the Monaco Grand Prix in May 1969 the M7C was in its most flamboyant format. With a full complement of 'high wings' Bruce flashes through the tunnel at high speed.

Above: Andrea de Adamich qualified the Alfa-Romeo engined M7D 18th for the 1970 British GP at Brands Hatch but was a non-starter after a fuel tank split during the pre-race warm up.

Opposite page: In the paddock at the 1969 Dutch Grand Prix at Zandvoort, M7C/1 (#6) driven by Bruce and Hulme's car M7A/2, on the left, are fuelled up for the start of the race.

MODEL	McLaren M7D	TRANSMISSION	Hewland DG300 5-speed	TYRES F/R	Goodyear
TYPE/FORMULA	Formula 1	CHASSIS	Aluminium 'bathtub' monocoque, steel bulkheads	LENGTH	160in - 4064mm
YEAR OF PRODUCTION	1970	BODY	Monocoque sides, GRP nose & cockpit surround	WIDTH OF MONOCOQUE	28in - 711mm
DESIGNER	Gordon Coppuck	FRONT SUSPENSION	Single top link & radius arm, lower wishbone,	HEIGHT OF MONOCOQUE	29in - 736mm
EXAMPLES BUILT	1		outboard coil spring/damper, anti-roll bar	WHEELBASE	96in - 2438mm
ENGINE	Alfa Romeo T33 V8	REAR SUSPENSION	Reverse lower wishbone, top link, twin radius	TRACK F/R	58/57in - 1473/1447mm
CUBIC CAPACITY	2995cc		rods, outboard coil spring/damper, anti-roll bar	WEIGHT	1140lb - 517kg
CARBURATION	Lucas fuel injection	BRAKES F/R	Outboard 11.66in ventilated discs	PRINCIPAL DRIVERS	de Adamich
POWER OUTPUT	425bhp	WHEELS DIAMETER x WIDTH F/R	15x10/15x15in	IDENTIFYING COLOURS	Papaya

1969 M8B
CAN-AM

The competition in Can-Am during 1968 had been formidable, but the M8A had prevailed in stunning fashion and Bruce and his team were not about to rest on their laurels.

1969 saw this exciting class of unlimited sportscar racing peak, with 11 races and a $1 million purse. It was also to be a stunning triumph for McLaren, a perfect season in which it won all 11 races, scored an incredible eight 1-2 finishes, and at Michigan a unique Can-Am 1-2-3 as Dan Gurney joined Bruce and Denny. This was a period that saw McLaren under Bruce's management attain a peak of planning, preparation and performance.

The seminal M8B was a common sense evolution by Coppuck. The chassis was lightened and modified, with the aluminium 7.1-litre Chevrolet engine now producing 680bhp and once again acting as a structural member. The key change was the deletion of an unstressed chassis section behind the front wheels to create a cutaway area which appeared to be done to help brake cooling but actually avoided damage to the tub, when the car ran over kerbs or grounded heavily. Elsewhere the 75-gallon fuel system was revised, and the suspension geometry was worked over to help maximise the amount of travel available.

Bruce, Denny and Teddy Mayer all believed the M8B was quite simply the best racing car the factory had ever produced. It had a clean, functional shape, was neat and efficient, and a joy to drive. Denny in particular revelled in the way he could throw the big machine into corners and steer it on the throttle.

More power, and wider front and rear tracks to cater for wider tyres were typical of the improvements which accompanied refinements to the car's basic aerodynamics. The most obvious visual change on the M8B was the adoption of the high, strut-mounted aerofoil that had already made the Chaparrals iconic. These devices were mounted on the rear suspension uprights and thus generated their high downforce loadings directly through the rear wheel hubs. Over the winter of 1968 the concept had famously been tested by the team on one of its Minivans on the roads around Colnbrook, although how it affected the handling of a little roadcar is best left to the imagination!

The problem with the M8B, if there was such a thing, was that others argued that its total dominance was actually scaring off rivals, and certainly other factory teams had promised cars and full support for the 1969 series but then cried off, apparently unwilling to waste time and money failing to beat the ratings of the 'Bruce and Denny Show'. But in hindsight, so many of their rivals' efforts seemed half-hearted. McLaren, at that period of its existence, was a totally professional racing team that had its act finely honed. It had, in Bruce's words, learned how to go motor racing properly, and it showed.

Dan Gurney believed that the high-winged machine was: "*Light years ahead of the rest of the cars running in Can-Am.*" Indeed, when the Chevrolet in his M6B-based 'McLeagle' died in practice at Michigan – the first and only time the series visited that state – he literally jumped at the chance to drive Bruce's spare car. Not having qualified it (Jack Brabham did that) he had to start at the back of the grid, but in typical Gurney style he soon fought his way through the traffic until he was lying third behind Bruce and Denny's team cars and was the only other runner on the same lap. At the time he said: "*What a great car to drive!*" The result: that spectacular 1-2-3 for the M8B.

At the third round of the 1969 Can-Am season at Watkins Glen, Bruce (above) and Denny scored their third consecutive 1-2 finish of the season.

Having won the 1968 Can-Am Championship, in 1969 despite winning five races in the M8B Denny Hulme had to concede his crown to Bruce.

With Bruce winning the 1969 Canadian-American Challenge Series and Denny finishing second, both drivers scored twice as many points as their nearest challenger. The team had suffered only four non-finishes and the season's winnings totalled a staggering $305,000. This brought the Bruce McLaren Motor Racing Team's earnings in the Can-Am series to well over half a million, very welcome, US dollars.

Writing in that year's Autocourse annual, Pete Lyons explained McLaren's success thus: "*It is not Bruce's budget that makes him win, but the manner in which he goes about the whole job. He has a very practical conception of what machines he needs to win. He starts to build and test on time. He hires the best brains and keeps them happy. He organises bases, transport and supply lines in a paramilitary manner. He keeps close tabs on the life of each component and has a continuing programme of refinement that amounts to a restless search for perfection. He keeps himself liberally supplied with spares, even to a second driver and a third car. Perhaps most important of all, he never lets his men ease up. They are taught to think of themselves, at all times, as racers.*"

Lyons had captured the McLaren culture that remains to this day, while unwittingly outlining the blueprint for F1 teams of the future.

Over the course of the ensuing seasons, as had happened with the original M8A cars, the three team M8Bs were cannibalised in order to build cars for the new season and to keep the existing cars running. Eventually no complete example of the legendary M8B was known to exist so, a decade later, Chuck Haines and McLaren mechanic and fabricator Tom Frederick set about finding all the original parts to recreate a truly genuine replica. After 20 years of searching they managed to assemble all the components necessary to complete the car photographed here.

MODEL	McLaren M8B	TRANSMISSION	Hewland LG500 4-speed	TYRES F/R	Goodyear
TYPE/FORMULA	Can-Am	CHASSIS	Aluminium sheet monocoque with steel bulkheads	LENGTH	154in - 3911mm
YEAR OF PRODUCTION	1969	BODY	Monocoque sides, GRP body sections, aluminium wing	WIDTH	75in - 1905mm
DESIGNER	Gordon Coppuck/Jo Marquart	FRONT SUSPENSION	Single top link & radius arm, lower wishbone,	HEIGHT OF BODY	32in - 812mm
EXAMPLES BUILT	3		outboard coil spring/damper, anti-roll bar	WHEELBASE	94in - 2387mm
ENGINE	Chevrolet V8	REAR SUSPENSION	Reverse lower wishbone, single top link,	TRACK F/R	58/56in - 1473/1422mm
CUBIC CAPACITY	6997cc		twin radius rods, coil spring/damper, anti-roll bar	WEIGHT	1405lb - 637kg
CARBURATION	Lucas fuel injection	BRAKES F/R	Outboard 12in ventilated discs	PRINCIPAL DRIVERS	McLaren, Hulme, Gurney
POWER OUTPUT	680bhp	WHEELS DIAMETER x WIDTH F/R	15x11/15x16in	IDENTIFYING COLOURS	Papaya

1969 M9A
FORMULA 1

Clever, controversial, but destined to disappear rather than rewrite the rules of Formula 1, the McLaren M9A designed by Jo Marquart made its public debut at the British GP in 1969 with Derek Bell at the wheel.

There was nothing particularly new about four-wheel-drive (4WD) in F1. Tractor king Harry Ferguson and Le Mans winner Tony Rolt had first unveiled an all-wheel drive Formula 1 car called the Ferguson P99, driven in particular by Stirling Moss, as far back as 1961. BRM produced a similar sort of car in 1964. Towards the end of that decade, however, it was widely felt within the sport that all-wheel drive held the key to harnessing the considerable power of the latest generation of 3-litre engines, in particular the 405bhp Ford Cosworth DFV. Unfortunately, while such cars were still at the concept stage during 1968, the development of wings gathered so much pace that, ultimately, they would render 4WD an expensive blind alley.

Lotus, Matra, McLaren and Cosworth all produced such cars for the 1969 season. Lotus's 63 was an elegant wedge-shaped car that was a very serious effort on Colin Chapman's part to make the concept work. Matra's MS84 was slightly less so, since designer Derek Gardner opted for a spaceframe chassis for ease of manufacture, maintenance and modification of the experimental prototype. The slab-sided Cosworth was the work of Bruce's former designer Robin Herd, the man behind the M7A.

It was typical of Bruce that the M9A most closely rivalled the Lotus, for he did nothing by halves. While Gordon Coppuck worked on the M7A, B and C derivative cars in F1, Marquart looked after the M9A. Like the Lotus it was a monocoque design, but the McLaren differed in employing the engine as a fully stressed member. The DFV was turned back to front with the gearbox positioned ahead of it in the chassis, and the drive taken out to the left as in the Lotus, via a two-shaft McLaren-designed, Ferguson-style gearbox with five Hewland ratios. Inboard brakes were used, with hollow discs for more efficient cooling, in conjunction with conventional suspension that featured inboard coil spring/damper units. The rear wheels were marginally wider than the fronts and power was fed to them via differentials fitted with Hewland-ZF spin locks as Marquart sought to avoid the need for limited-slip units. The central differential had been designed with quick-change torque-split ratios; these could be changed in less than 15 minutes. It is also interesting to note that despite all the additional equipment, the finished car was said to weigh a little over 10lbs more than the conventional rear-wheel-drive M7A. This caused not inconsiderable dismay at Colnbrook at the time, but a 10lb weight penalty sounds pretty modest today.

Even before the car first ran in public, Bruce was having serious reservations about it. In his book McLAREN The Grand Prix, Can-Am and Indy Cars, Doug Nye outlines Teddy Mayer's recollections of a conversation that BRM's chief

designer Tony Rudd had with Bruce. *"When Tony heard we were building a four-wheel-drive car he said to Bruce: 'Have you tried fitting a hundredweight of cement in your car?' No, Bruce hadn't. 'Well, have you tried setting up your brakes so that they bind all the time?' No, Bruce hadn't. 'Well have you tried de-tuning your engines to run only 300 horsepower?' No, we hadn't tried that either. And Tony said: 'Well you might just as well, 'cos that's what it's like with four-wheel-drive."*

The press seemed optimistic and impressed with early test results, but by the time the team arrived at Silverstone for the British Grand Prix several key members were already uncomfortably aware that they had almost certainly been barking up the wrong technological tree. One that, at £70,000, had probably accounted for a sixth of the total 1969 budget, according to Mayer. As Bruce put it, piloting the M9A, *"was like trying to write your signature with somebody jogging your elbow."* Why bother, was the question he put to workshop staff after the car had undergone its first test at Goodwood. Certainly, designing and building such a novel and technically complex machine took the team's eye off several other, arguably more worthwhile exercises and progressing the project from first drawings to finished prototype took at least four months of very hard - and costly - work. It now seems incredible that McLaren was reportedly hoping to build half a dozen M9As. In reality only that prototype was ever completed.

In its original guise (as seen here) with nothing more aerodynamic than a pair of small front wings during early practice at Silverstone, Bell described the car as, *"A right royal handful. Its handling characteristics were completely different to a conventional car. I found that the only way to get it around a corner was to back off the throttle momentarily, give a great wrench on the steering wheel and then go hard on the power again."* Subsequently the team fitted a rear tea tray assembly from one of the M7s and Bell, taking part in only his third Grand Prix, qualified the recalcitrant machine 15th with a lap of 1m 26.1s. That compared with Jochen Rindt's pole time of 1m 20.8s and Denny's third fastest 1m 21.5s in the M7A. In contrast, John Miles lapped his better sorted Lotus 63 in 1m 25.1, Jo Bonnier the other 63 in 1m 28.2s, and Jean-Pierre Beltoise the Matra MS84 in a slightly unrepresentative 1m 31.2s. Bell ran 12th, ahead of the other 4WD cars, on the opening lap, but fell back quickly before retiring after sixlaps with a broken rear suspension carrier. It was the end of the road for the M9A.

Interest in 4WD evaporated soon after Bell's abortive run, and not just at McLaren. In theory it offered advantages that, in reality, failed to match those conferred instead by aerodynamic devices which added download to the tyres. But if the M9A was a flop, it yet again endorsed Bruce's belief in experimentation, and his commonsense ability to admit when something was wrong and cut his losses.

Top: With the DFV turned 180° in the chassis, the gearbox and torque split unit was situated in the space between the engine and the driver's seat back.

Above: This is how the new M9A first appeared in the paddock at Silverstone. Before practice was over it had gained a huge rear wing taken from the spare M7A.

Opposite page: In the M9A's only race, Derek Bell qualified 15th but lasted only six laps of the British Grand Prix at Silverstone in July, before the suspension failed.

MODEL	McLaren M9A	TRANSMISSION	McLaren 4-wheel drive 5-speed	TYRES F/R	Goodyear
TYPE/FORMULA	Formula 1	CHASSIS	Aluminium monocoque, steel bulkheads, tubular subframe	LENGTH	148in - 3759mm
YEAR OF PRODUCTION	1969	BODY	Monocoque sides, GRP nose & cockpit surround	WIDTH OF CHASSIS	36in - 914mm
DESIGNER	Jo Marquart	FRONT SUSPENSION	Upper wishbone/rocker arm, lower link & radius	HEIGHT OF ROLLBAR	37in - 940mm
EXAMPLES BUILT	1		arm, inboard coil spring/damper, anti-roll bar	WHEELBASE	95in - 2413mm
ENGINE	Ford Cosworth DFV	REAR SUSPENSION	Upper rocker arm, lower wishbone, twin radius	TRACK F/R	63/59in - 1600/1499mm
CUBIC CAPACITY	2993cc		rods, inboard coil spring/damper, anti-roll bar	WEIGHT	1160lb - 526kg
CARBURATION	Lucas fuel injection	BRAKES F/R	Outboard/Inboard Girling 12in ventilated discs	PRINCIPAL DRIVERS	Derek Bell
POWER OUTPUT	420bhp	WHEELS DIAMETER x WIDTH F/R	13x12/13x14in	IDENTIFYING COLOURS	Papaya

1969 McLAREN-TROJAN M10A FORMULA 5000 & FORMULA A

With the majority of the main test and evaluation work being carried out by Bruce himself, the handsome Chevrolet-powered McLaren-Trojan M10A was designed by Gordon Coppuck to be a production Formula A/Formula 5000 car for both the works team and for customers. 20 of them were built in 1969, along with an additional 21 M10B versions the following year for Formula 5000.

The M10A monocoque was based on the previous year's Formula 1 M7A but with full 'up-and-over' aluminium-alloy panelling bonded and riveted to the steel bulkheads to form a cigar tube rather than a bathtub. There were also pontoons that extended rearwards to support the 5-litre American V8 engines which, unlike the Ford Cosworth DFV, couldn't be used as fully stressed members.

Suspension was by the familiar single top link with a radius arm, lower wishbone, anti-roll bar and outboard coil spring/damper at the front, and single top link, reversed lower wishbone, twin radius arms and with the spring/damper unit at the rear. Wheels were McLaren cast magnesium 15 inch diameter items, 11 inch wide at the front and 16 at the rear.

Since its inaugural race in the US in 1967 Formula A had been a category with classes for 3.0, 1.6 and 1.1-litre racing engines, but in the absence of sufficient numbers of serious contenders, the governing authorities at the Sports Car Club

of America (SCCA) took the decision for 1968 to extend the formula, to include stock-block engines of up to 5-litres. Opening the floodgates for such production-based 302 cubic inch pushrod engines such as the Chevrolet and Ford V8s proved to be the major breakthrough for what came to be called Formula 5000 worldwide.

This change in rules caught the interest of several chassis manufacturers, and many of the sport's big names – including Eagle, Lola and McLaren – rushed to complete their own designs. The formula grew accordingly, with a similar class being announced in Britain for 1969, and South African, New Zealand and Australian national championships being launched.

The papaya orange M10A prototype in full 'high-wing' format was the star of the 1969 Racing Car Show in London and was to be run as a works-assisted entry under the banner of Church Farm Racing, in the Guards European Championship in the UK. It was driven by 28-year-old Peter Gethin who took the car to early wins at Oulton Park, Brands Hatch and Mallory Park. He so dominated the early going that the team ventured abroad to race successfully in America. While it was absent, former F1 driver Trevor Taylor also amassed four victories in new constructor John Surtees' eponymous TS5 chassis, and it was only after Gethin returned to defend his title chances that he succeeded narrowly in the final round at Brands, after both men were put off the road by a backmarker.

The M10A was one of the first monocoque Formula 5000 cars, and besides its performance its superior safety factors quickly obliged Lola to follow suit for 1970 as its new T190 superseded the spaceframe T140 and T142 models.

The M10A was derived from the previous season's M7A Formula 1 car. When it was launched in early 1969 the 'high wings' developed for Formula 1 were still legal, but not for long.

The McLaren also came at a competitive price. Supplied as standard with a Bartz-tuned Chevy V8, it cost £7,055 ex-works at its launch in 1969, or £4480 as a rolling chassis. Drivers quickly sensed the way things were moving and switched to McLarens as soon as they could for the forthcoming season.

Typical of these was Canadian Eppie Wietzes of Formula Racing. He made the decision during the off-season to switch from his Chevrolet powered Lola T142 to a McLaren M10B and never looked back. In 1970 he would go on to win five out of the seven rounds of the Gulf Canada F5000 Series and clinch the title.

MODEL	McLaren-Trojan M10A
TYPE/FORMULA	Formula 5000/Formula A
YEAR OF PRODUCTION	1969
DESIGNER	Gordon Coppuck
EXAMPLES BUILT	20
ENGINE	Chevrolet V8
CUBIC CAPACITY	5000cc
CARBURATION	Lucas fuel injection
POWER OUTPUT	500bhp

TRANSMISSION	Hewland LG600 5-speed
CHASSIS	360° aluminium monocoque, steel bulkheads
BODY	Monocoque sides, GRP nose & cockpit surround
FRONT SUSPENSION	Single top link & radius arm, lower wishbone, outboard coil spring/damper, anti-roll bar
REAR SUSPENSION	Reverse lower wishbone, top link, twin radius rods, outboard coil spring/damper, anti-roll bar
BRAKES F/R	Outboard Lockheed 12in ventilated discs
WHEELS DIAMETER x WIDTH F/R	15x11/15x16in

TYRES F/R	10.55x15/12.50x15
LENGTH	161in - 4089mm
WIDTH	75in - 1905mm
HEIGHT TO TOP OF SCREEN	26.5in - 673mm
WHEELBASE	97in - 2464mm
TRACK F/R	59.5/58.5in - 1511/1485mm
WEIGHT	1285lb - 583kg
PRINCIPAL DRIVERS	Gethin
IDENTIFYING COLOURS	n/a

With the designation M11 left out in order to avoid confusion with the 1966 M1B Trojan-built McLaren MkII, the M12 was the McLaren production sportscar for the 1969 season. Trojan made 15 examples to compete in Can-Am and Group 7 racing.

Naturally it was based on the phenomenally successful works McLaren team's M8-series cars, bringing together an M8A-style body and a chassis not dissimilar to that of the M6. The latter was a straightforward version of the simple but successful stressed-skin hull, the structure once more being formed from bonded and riveted magnesium and aluminium alloy panel box structures. Again, these were attached to a square-section tube frame. Power came from an aluminium-block 7-litre Chevrolet V8, the engine on which Can-Am continued to depend, which now developed a reliable 600bhp. A true M12 is easily identifiable by the fact that side sections of the chassis are curved under, like the M6's, rather than flat-sided as on the M8, and extend all the way to the front wheels, again like the M6, rather than tapering behind the front wheel arch.

The M12 was never going to topple the high-wing works-run M8Bs, but it was nevertheless to acquit itself adequately. In particular, 1966 Can-Am champion John Surtees made no bones about the fact that he far preferred the car Jim Hall purchased, while finishing off his radical, and ultimately hugely unsuccessful, Chaparral 2H with its exceptionally narrow track and reduced frontal area.

Surtees qualified fourth and finished third in the season opener at Mosport, then collided with Bruce while disputing second place at St Jovite. He fought with Chris Amon's Ferrari for third at Watkins Glen prior to retirement, then returned to the M12 for the Bridgehampton race after unhappy outings in the Chaparral, and ran strongly until another failure to finish. Surtees' F5000 driver, Andrea de Adamich, took over the M12 to finish fifth at Michigan Raceway after the Englishman fell ill.

Two other stand-out M12 combinations finished ahead of ninth-placed Surtees in the final reckoning: Canadian George Eaton and American Lothar Motschenbacher in fifth and seventh respectively. Eaton's best results were a second, a third and a fourth, Motschenbacher's two fourths.

At least two M12s went east, where Toyota planned to rebody and re-engine them to take on Nissan's all conquering machines in the Japanese Group 7 series. According to reports at the time, the company had an impressive 5-litre quad-cam V8 unit it wanted to race, though Toyota's car only ran with it once.

Several years later, one M12 resurfaced in Japan. Hiroshi Kazato's bright yellow machine spent 26 years in a shrine-like display in a local restaurant window after the young driver had been killed at Mount Fuji Raceway. The restaurant owner eventually sold the car to the Bruce McLaren Trust in New Zealand. After receiving minimal attention – the Trust believes it to be the most original Can-Am car in the world and wanted it to retain its patina – it fired up and took to the track at Whenuapai, more than 30 years after it had last turned a wheel in anger.

A one-off car designated M12C, with an older M6 style body and carburettors rather than the regular injection on the 7.2-litre Nicholson McLaren engine, was commissioned by UK hillclimb expert Phil Scragg. After crashing the car in his first event at Doune, he sold it to fellow competitor Tony Harrison who campaigned it for several years in the major British speed championships. The car was once loaned to Patsy Burt of M3 fame. She used it, equipped with fuel injection borrowed from the factory and streamlined bodywork, on another of her speed record breaking runs but the engine blew up in a big way.

Above: John Surtees drove Jim Hall's M12 in the first three races of the 1969 season. Here he passes Johnny Servoz-Gavin's Matra M650 during the round at Watkins Glen. Later in the season when the engine on his Chaparral expired in practice at Bridgehampton, he used the back-up M12 for one last race.

Top: Commissioned by British hillclimb driver Phil Scragg, chassis M12C-60-11 was built at the factory with an M6B-style body and regular carburation. It was then sold to Tony Harrison who campaigned it on the hills for many years.

M12-60-08 was sold to the Toyota Corporation in Japan and fitted with its 5-litre V8 engine. Seemingly, it raced only once, in a sportscar race at the Mt. Fuji circuit.

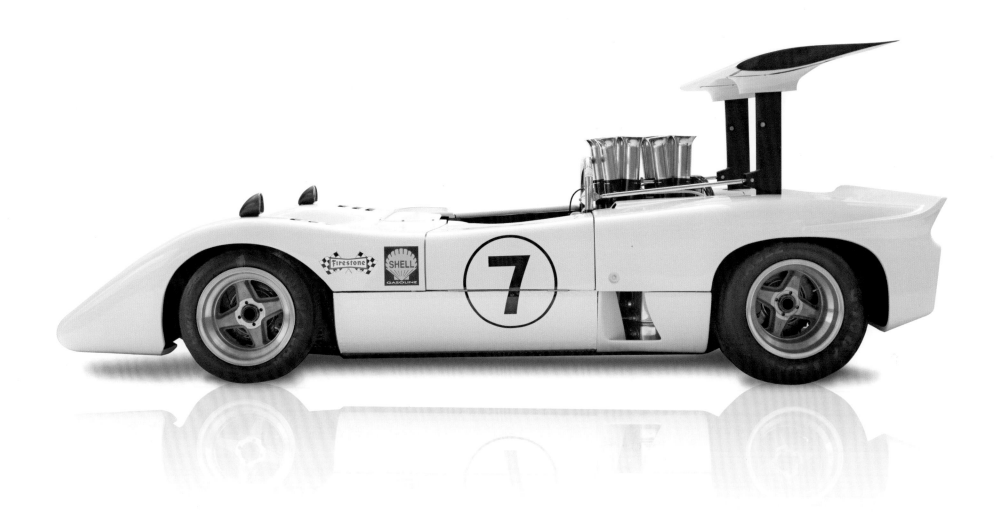

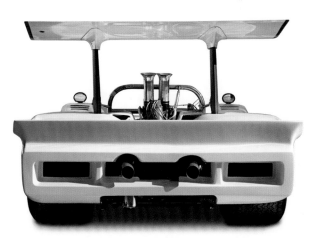

MODEL	McLaren-Trojan M12
TYPE/FORMULA	Can-Am/Group 7
YEAR OF PRODUCTION	1969
DESIGNER	Gordon Coppuck
EXAMPLES BUILT	15
ENGINE	Chevrolet V8
CUBIC CAPACITY	6997cc
CARBURATION	Lucas fuel injection
POWER OUTPUT	590-615bhp

TRANSMISSION	Hewland LG 5-speed
CHASSIS	Aluminium alloy sheet monocoque, steel bulkheads
BODY	Formed by monocoque sides with GRP top panels
FRONT SUSPENSION	Wide based unequal length double
	wishbones anti-roll bar, coil spring/damper
REAR SUSPENSION	Reverse lower wishbone, single top link,
	twin radius arms, coil spring/damper, anti-roll bar
BRAKES F/R	Outboard 12in Girling ventilated discs
WHEELS DIAMETER x WIDTH F/R	15x10/15x15in

TYRES F/R	Goodyear
LENGTH	155in - 3937mm
WIDTH	75in - 1905mm
HEIGHT AT WINDSCREEN	31in - 787mm
WHEELBASE	93.5in - 2375mm
TRACK F/R	57/55in - 1448/1397mm
WEIGHT	1300lb - 590kg
PRINCIPAL DRIVERS	Surtees, Motschenbacher
IDENTIFYING COLOURS	n/a

CHAPTER

02

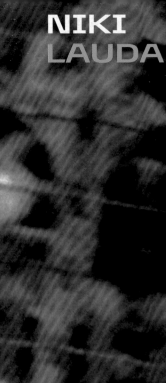

When I quit racing at the end of 1979 I did so completely, I didn't even watch the races on TV but concentrated 100 per cent on my airline. Ron Dennis would call me though, every three or four months, and we'd chat and he started to break my resolve. Finally, in 1981, I went to a Grand Prix again, as a TV commentator in Austria. There was a huge startline crash during a support race and for the first time I thought: 'This is good stuff,' and could feel the old spirit coming back.

A month after that I accepted an invitation from Ron to go to Monza. I saw John Watson's huge crash at the exit of the second Lesmo corner when he went off going flat in fourth and hit the guardrail backwards so hard that the car broke in two parts. The engine and the gearbox came apart from the carbon-fibre monocoque but the latter survived remarkably well – John Barnard had clearly built an incredible car – so when Ron rang on the Monday and offered me a test, I said yes.

I'd had another approach, from Frank Williams, but when I went to Donington and saw the McLaren set-up and how they worked as a team it was clear to me that I would only ever go there. Eventually I decided I would do just that. 1982 was a good year and I won two races with the Cosworth-engined MP4/1B. That said, 1983 was a disaster, because we had no chance against the turbo guys at Ferrari, Renault and BMW, unless they crashed or retired. Because of this I went to Ron and said why don't we introduce the turbo car this year, do a couple of races and then we are much better prepared for the following year?

John Barnard, ever the perfectionist, said no way and Ron went with him, so I called the president of Philip Morris, told him my worries and asked him to ask the team to run the turbo engine earlier. Ron thought I was crazy, but we got to run the car from Zandvoort onwards and it was the right decision as it prepared us well for the 1984 season.

Of the eight races I won with McLaren, the best was probably Monza that year. It was the toughest of races and gave me the impetus to go on and win the '84 Championship. As ever we had very little emotion in the team but always very high quality cars. Other teams are driven by emotions and as long as you perform they love you, but if you don't perform you get sacked like anybody else. But McLaren is the opposite, being a high quality, high-tech team, making the best racing cars ever built, and run with Ron's British coolness.

Niki Lauda
Drivers' World Champion 1984
McLaren MP4/2

One of the works M8Bs was retained as a development mule for the new M8D which appeared in 1970, leaving only two chassis available for purchase by non-works drivers eager to emulate Bruce and Denny's outstanding 1969 successes. It came as little surprise then, that the company announced the launch of a new M8B-based customer car for others, the McLaren-Trojan M8C. Given that the 1969 customer car had been the M12, the nomenclature was slightly confusing to those who didn't understand its origins.

The 15 examples of the M8C that were built differed in several details from the M8Bs, and in real terms were not based around it at all but more on the 1968 M8A. For example, instead of simply feeding the stresses directly through the slightly larger 7.4-litre Chevrolet V8 as the works cars did, the M8C used a supporting structure. As a consequence, however, customers could opt to fit the Ford V8 or other engines.

With the high wings which had sprouted on almost all of the front-running cars the previous year now significantly truncated by new regulations, the M8C sported a low wing on its tail. It was rather less prominent than its counterpart on the M8D. The side sections of the M8C chassis were very much the same as on the M8B, with the area behind the front wheel cut away in a long tapered section extending to a point below the front edge of the door.

The M8C made its first race appearance at the opening round of the 1970 Can-Am Championship held at Mosport Park in June. With ace privateer Lothar Motschenbacher and colourful Pole Oscar Kovaleski running the two ex-works M8Bs, it was left to Roger McCaig and John Cordts to debut the new customer car. With McCaig qualifying in fifth and Cordts back in 17th it wasn't exactly a dream start, but McCaig finished the race in a strong fifth place as the first of the non-works McLarens.

These two cars were the only M8Cs to run in that year's series. McCaig finished a creditable 10th, albeit with another pair of fifth places being the best results he could muster. For the final two races of the year Cordts passed his M8C over to Motschenbacher who had started the season campaigning his M8B before switching to an M12 after damaging the former. At the season finale at Riverside, 'Low Tar' too managed to bring the car home fifth and the points from the race lifted him to an excellent second place in the Can-Am standings for 1970. But on 65 points, he had less than half the score of championship winner Denny Hulme's total of 132.

Throughout 1971 four M8Cs raced in Can-Am, all of which had by now sprouted the large low rear wing that was also fitted to the 1971 customer car from Trojan, the M8E. Cordts, George Drolsom, Charlie Kemp and Bill Wonder were their drivers, though by the end of the season Cordts, who in 12th overall was the best placed M8C pilot in the series, had switched allegiance to Lola's T163.

A few M8Cs stayed in Europe. The Interserie sportscar championship was founded in 1970 as a European version of the Can-Am series and during the early seasons many original Can-Am cars – from McLaren, Lola, Porsche, March and BRM – raced against Group 5 and 6 cars from the World Championship of Makes.

One car was bought by British privateer team Ecurie Evergreen for F3 and saloon racing star Chris Craft to drive and was modified to run with 3-litre Cosworth DFV power. It

Left: With a rather interesting triple layer rear spoiler, Tom Dutton dives down the Corkscrew at Laguna Seca in George Drolsom's M8C Chevrolet. He retired from this, the 8th round of the 1972 Can-Am series, with gearbox problems on lap 18.

Above: The M8C of Chris Craft and Trevor Taylor arrives for the 1970 Brands Hatch 1000km. Craft retired with ignition problems on lap 25, before Taylor even got to drive. Bruce McLaren was on the entry list as a third driver but chose not to drive.

proved very quick in several UK sportscar races, and at the British round of the Interserie championship at Croft in July Craft put chassis M8C-70-07 on pole position and set the fastest lap before retiring from the lead after a spin. At the Swedish Grand Prix (for sportscars) in August, Craft and co-driver Alain de Cadenet scored a superb win ahead of a strong field including several Porsche 917s and Lola T70s.

Ironically, McLaren's only other strong performance in the series that year came from Vic Elford, who took a 7-litre M6B/12 to victory in the Solituderennen at Hockenheim.

Another M8C was adapted to accept a Toyota engine, although according to Bill Meace, a manager at Trojan, this proved to be an "exercise which unfortunately did not work out." The engine started to misfire badly, and rather than tinker with the internal mechanisms of a unit that was on loan the crew decided to return it to its maker and the project was terminated abruptly.

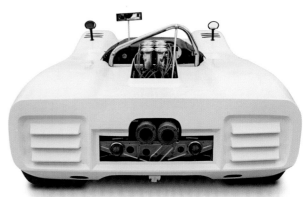

MODEL	McLaren-Trojan M8C		TRANSMISSION	Hewland LG500 4-speed		TYRES F/R	Goodyear
TYPE/FORMULA	Can-Am		CHASSIS	Aluminium sheet monocoque with steel bulkheads		LENGTH	153in - 3886mm
YEAR OF PRODUCTION	1970		BODY	Monocoque sides with 4 GRP body sections		WIDTH	74in - 1880mm
DESIGNER	Gordon Coppuck/Jo Marquart		FRONT SUSPENSION	Single top link & radius arm, lower wishbone,		HEIGHT	30in - 762mm
EXAMPLES BUILT	15			outboard coil spring/damper, anti-roll bar		WHEELBASE	94in - 2387mm
ENGINE	Chevrolet/Ford V8		REAR SUSPENSION	Reverse lower wishbone, single top link,		TRACK F/R	58/55in - 1473/1397mm
CUBIC CAPACITY	7000-7500cc			twin radius rods, coil spring/damper, anti-roll bar		WEIGHT	1425lb - 646kg
CARBURATION	Lucas fuel injection		BRAKES F/R	Outboard 11.9in ventilated discs		PRINCIPAL DRIVERS	McCaig, Cordts, Craft, De Cadenet
POWER OUTPUT	650-700bhp		WHEELS DIAMETER x WIDTH F/R	15x11/15x16in		IDENTIFYING COLOURS	n/a

1970 McLAREN-TROJAN M10B FORMULA 5000 & FORMULA A

The M10B cars built for the 1970 season differed from the M10A in several respects. Revising the engine bay and lowering the engine by almost two inches necessitated revisions to the rear suspension, and the stronger DG300 Hewland gearbox replaced the previous LG600. The steering geometry was also slightly revised, as was the shape of the nose. Overall, the M10B was also slightly lighter than the M10A.

Many drivers had complained that the M10A could be a bit of a handful and you needed arms of steel to turn the car into a corner. The solution was to move the kingpin inclination closer to the centre of the contact patch of the tyre and changing length radius arms. This, matched to a deeper inset front rim, moved the kingpin closer to the centre of the contact patch. Thus the new car was sharper, lighter and altogether better.

Of all the M10A/B drivers, Peter Gethin's record was probably the most outstanding. The new 5-litre cars were as powerful as their Formula 1 contemporaries, if not quite so agile, so he had ample opportunity to demonstrate that he could handle the extra power. His domination of the 1970 UK series, with eight victories, further prompted McLaren to give him the chance to drive in F1, and his successor in the Sid Taylor Racing car that year, Reine Wisell, simply took up where he left off. Both Wisell and New Zealander Howden Ganley also got their Formula 1 breaks on the strength of their F5000 performances in a McLaren.

In their day, the M10A and M10B McLarens were the class of the field in Formula 5000. They made champions of

Gethin, former M1C racer John Cannon, David Hobbs, Eppie Weitzes and Graham McRae, and besides them provided championship race wins for a list of drivers that reads like a veritable "Who's Who" of single-seater racing, drivers such as, Neil Allen, Kevin Bartlett, Howden Ganley, Ron Grable, George Eaton, Derek Bell, Frank Matich, Sam Posey, Brian Redman, Mike Walker and Reine Wisell.

Left: This is Teddy Pilette in the 'Team VDS' M10B at Snetterton in August 1971. In the two-heat race he finished third overall behind Graham McRae in his heavily modified M10B and the Lola T192 of Mike Walker.

Above: Peter Gethin in the Sid Taylor M10B, chassis #400-06, at the Silverstone International Trophy F1/F5000 race in April 1970. Having finished seventh overall and first in the F5000 category in the first heat, he retired from the second.

It was the two 'works' drivers, Gethin in 300B-06 and Ganley in 300B-05 who would set a circuit record which was to stand for some fifteen years against far more modern machinery, their cigar shaped F5000 McLarens hustling round the Castle Coombe circuit in tandem to ultimately smash the hitherto unbroken one minute lap record, reducing it to an astonishing 56.6 seconds.

Herein lies an interesting 'M10' snippet. Bruce McLaren didn't want to be seen beating his customers in what was essentially a car built for retail sales, so to get around this problem McLaren entered Formula 5000 by backing Church Farm Racing in what was essentially a full 'works' M10A, strangely enough though, the cars had "McLaren Racing" on the sides of the cockpit, rather letting the cat out of the bag as they say!

The two McLaren F5000 models (M10A & M10B) were also a great favourite of club racers as well as sprint and hillclimb competitors throughout Europe. Driving an M10A Sir Nicholas Williamson won the RAC Hillclimb Championship in 1970, and in 1972 Bob Rose used an M10B to win the British Sprint Championship. Not to be out done, in both 1975 & '76 the Sprint title was won by Dave Harris also driving an M10B. It really was the perfect customer car.

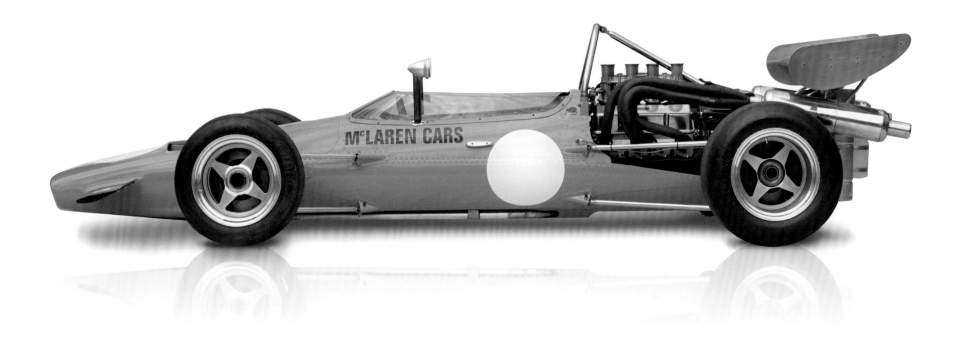

MODEL	McLaren-Trojan M10B	TRANSMISSION	Hewland DG300 5-speed	TYRES F/R	10.55x15/12.50x15
TYPE/FORMULA	Formula 5000/Formula A	CHASSIS	360° aluminium monocoque, steel bulkheads	LENGTH	157.5in - 4000mm
YEAR OF PRODUCTION	1970	BODY	Monocoque sides, GRP nose & cockpit surround	WIDTH	77in - 1956mm
DESIGNER	Gordon Coppuck	FRONT SUSPENSION	Single top link & radius arm, lower wishbone,	HEIGHT TO TOP OF SCREEN	26.5in - 673mm
EXAMPLES BUILT	21		outboard coil spring/damper, anti-roll bar	WHEELBASE	98in - 2489mm
ENGINE	Chevrolet V8	REAR SUSPENSION	Reverse lower wishbone, top link, twin radius	TRACK F/R	59/60.5in - 1499/1536mm
CUBIC CAPACITY	5000cc		rods, outboard coil spring/damper, anti-roll bar	WEIGHT	1251lb - 567kg
CARBURATION	Lucas fuel injection	BRAKES F/R	Outboard Lockheed 12in ventilated discs	PRINCIPAL DRIVERS	Gethin, Pilette
POWER OUTPUT	500bhp	WHEELS DIAMETER x WIDTH F/R	15x11/15x16in	IDENTIFYING COLOURS	n/a

1970 McLAREN M8D CAN-AM

The McLaren M8D is inevitably remembered as the car in which Bruce died, but it gave his team one of its best years in Can-Am. Rallying superbly after the tragedy, McLaren took nine wins from 10 rounds, and Denny Hulme his second title despite driving with his hands still bandaged after the fire in the M15 at Indianapolis.

The M8D inspired confidence. Peter Gethin, brought onboard after Bruce's death when a clash between the team's Gulf Oil sponsorship and Dan Gurney's Castrol associations eased the American out of the team, admitted that the first time he saw an M8D going past the pits with Denny driving: *"The ground literally shook, and I wondered what I had let myself in for."* After taking the wheel himself, he discovered: *"The car was fantastic... and of course by the end of the session you were asking for another 100bhp."*

The M8D differed visually from the M8B. With new rules banning the strut-mounted wings that had proliferated in 1969, the solution at McLaren comprised a pair of tail fins which acted as fences to channel airflow over a wide, low-mounted wing located eight inches above the rear bodywork. The distinctive appearance earned the car the nickname 'the Batmobile'. It was less efficient aerodynamically without the M8B's high wing, so to maintain performance the team sought even greater horsepower. A new deal with Reynolds Aluminium gave it access to that company's new silicon-aluminium Chevrolet blocks, 8-litre versions of which were said to be capable of producing 700bhp. In the interests of reliability, a slightly smaller 7.6-litre was chosen giving 670bhp.

Jo Marquart's new car was wider and longer than any previous Can-Am racer, with the additional girth being used to provide even greater fuel capacity. With both the V8 and the transmission now forming part of the rear chassis structure, the monocoque was constructed using aluminium sheets and a magnesium floor.

Bruce's death came during a test session on a Tuesday at Goodwood. New Zealand mechanic Cary Taylor warmed up the M8D, as Bruce lapped in an M14A that Gethin would race at Spa in place of the injured Denny. Bruce then switched to the M8D, popping in and out of the pits for adjustments to the rear wing to reduce oversteer. At 12.19 he left the pits for the last time. In a fast, left-hand kink leading on to the main straight, part of the tail section lifted at 170mph, causing the car to spin. It struck a marshals' protective embankment on the right-hand side of the track with enormous impact. Bruce was thrown from the wreckage and killed instantly.

The team was told not to report to work the following day, but Bruce's men were racers to the core, and not one of them was missing that Wednesday. The F1 cars were withdrawn from the following weekend's Belgian GP, but two M8Ds were on the grid when the Can-Am series kicked off with the Labatt's Blue Trophy race at Mosport on June 14th, because that's how racers react to crises.

Dan Gurney was drafted in to replace Bruce, and qualified on pole despite never having driven the car before. And he won. Denny, who had been devastated by Bruce's death, demonstrated his towering inner strength. His hands were still healing after Indianapolis, and every time he grasped a steering wheel, let alone used one to fight a 670bhp race car through a corner, the tender skin cracked, and the healing process had to start all over again. In Bruce's name he raced home third, after qualifying alongside Dan. It was one of many acts of genuine heroism from 'The Bear' that were so instrumental in helping the shattered team to regroup.

At St Jovite Dan led from start to finish, and Denny only quit when his engine overheated. He had a smaller 7.1-litre engine in his car at Watkins Glen, but led from start to finish. In his final race in the M8D, Gurney fell back to ninth with rising coolant temperatures. Like Denny, he had done what he set out to do, which was to support Bruce's team when it most needed it.

At Edmonton in late July, Peter Gethin made his debut, qualifying second behind Denny, and finishing second to his team-mate. Denny won at Mid-Ohio, where Gethin suffered engine problems.

At Elkhart Lake, Wisconsin, Gethin inherited victory after Denny had been disqualified for a push-start. Both were outqualified at Road Atlanta by Vic Elford in the Chaparral 2J 'sucker' car and damaged their cars in a chaotic race won by privateer Tony Dean's 3-litre Porsche 908. At Donnybrooke the team recovered its form with another Denny-led 1-2, and he won again at Laguna Seca. Once again Elford upstaged the M8Ds in qualifying at Riverside's finale, but Denny took an early lead and was never challenged. Gethin lost second in the Championship after his engine blew.

In the most trying circumstances, McLaren had pulled through. It had been shaken to the core, but it was a tribute to the philosophy with which Bruce had imbued every member, that they were able not just to carry on, but to keep winning.

The familiar 'stack' of injection trumpets on the works cars fed the Chevrolet V8 engine which was now enlarged to over 7.5- litres in capacity. Benefiting from something approaching 700bhp the 'works' cars completely dominated the 1970 Can-Am series.

MODEL	McLaren M8D
TYPE/FORMULA	Can-Am
YEAR OF PRODUCTION	1970
DESIGNER	Jo Marquart
EXAMPLES BUILT	4
ENGINE	Chevrolet V8
CUBIC CAPACITY	7100-7600cc
CARBURATION	Lucas fuel injection
POWER OUTPUT	680bhp

TRANSMISSION	Hewland LG500 4-speed
CHASSIS	Aluminium sheet monocoque with steel bulkheads
BODY	Monocoque sides, GRP body sections, integral wing
FRONT SUSPENSION	Single top link & radius arm, lower wishbone,
	outboard coil spring/damper, anti-roll bar
REAR SUSPENSION	Reverse lower wishbone, single top link,
	twin radius rods, coil spring/damper, anti-roll bar
BRAKES F/R	Outboard 12in ventilated discs
WHEELS DIAMETER x WIDTH F/R	15x11/15x16in

TYRES F/R	Goodyear
LENGTH	164in - 4166mm
WIDTH	76in - 1930mm
HEIGHT AT TAIL	45in - 1143mm
WHEELBASE	94in - 2387mm
TRACK F/R	62/58.5in - 1575/1486mm
WEIGHT	1398lb - 634kg
PRINCIPAL DRIVERS	Hulme, Gurney, Gethin
IDENTIFYING COLOURS	Papaya

Having already clinched the Championship, Denny Hulme easily won the Can-Am race at Riverside, California, in 1970. He finished the season with more than double the points of second place finisher Lothar Motschenbacher's M12.

By 1971 the works M8Ds had passed into the hands of privateer drivers. Here at Road Atlanta the M8D of Lothar Motschenbacher leads Bob Bondurant (M8E/D), Tony Adamowicz (M8B) and British driver Vic Elford (M8E).

Peter Gethin's last race in the works M8D was in the final race of the 1970 Can-Am series at Riverside in November. After suffering engine problems he retired on lap 21. Having won one race, Gethin finnished second in the series.

1970 M14A & M14D FORMULA 1

Superstition ruled out any model under the designation M13 so the new Formula 1 design for 1970 – with Bruce's personal race car the first chassis to be completed – became the M14A.

It was another full monocoque design, Bruce making a contribution to the evolutionary concept as Gordon Coppuck and Jo Marquart handled the detailing. It bore evidence of the lessons learned from the Formula 5000 M10A as well as the derivative M7C, using fully-stressed sections fore and aft of the cockpit. 18-gauge aluminium skinned the tub, bonded and riveted over a series of internal bulkheads formed from mild steel.

Whereas on the M7s the front suspension had incorporated rearward trailing links those on the new car ran forward, thereby negating the need for an additional bulkhead to provide anchorage points. This saved weight and left more room for fuel in the pontoons running down either side. Additionally, the M14A now enjoyed an improved degree of steering lock.

Further weight was saved by using tubular Can-Am style anti-roll bars and new front uprights. At the rear Coppuck and Marquart followed popular practice by mounting the 10.9-inch brake discs inboard to reduce unsprung weight. The coil spring/damper unit were mounted inboard as before, and with larger McLaren-cast 15-inch diameter wheels it was possible to clean the airflow by concealing larger front discs within the wheels, together with the twin-pot Lockheed calipers.

Forward of the scuttle, a simple detachable glass-fibre panel finished off the cigar tube section, while the M10B-style nose enclosed a larger but lighter radiator slung out front on a tubular frame. Power for the 1180lb car came from the trusty Ford Cosworth V8. McLaren owned four and ordered two more.

The team travelled to Kyalami in March for the M14A's debut in the South African GP. An ageing M7A went along as a spare car, as a third M14A would not be completed until later in the year. Bruce failed to finish after his engine expired on lap 40 when he was running fourth, but Denny came in second, eight seconds adrift of the victorious Jack Brabham in his BT33.

Bruce crashed on oil at Clearways in the Race of Champions, requiring a rebuild for M14-1 around a new monocoque, but Denny was third. Both cars sported 13-inch front wheels in Jarama for the Spanish GP, where Denny retired when his distributor's rotor arm shaft sheared but Bruce finished second behind Jackie Stewart's March 701. His final race appearance, his 101st Grand Prix start, came on May 10th at Monaco. The M14As had been fitted with stronger driveshafts, new uprights and the larger front wheels, but he damaged the front suspension badly enough to be forced into retirement on lap 19 after misjudging the chicane while trying to overhaul Jo Siffert. Denny kept the team respectable with fourth place ahead of the Swiss pilot who was also driving a March 701.

The M14 was the last Formula 1 car to be driven by Bruce. His final appearance in the 1970 Monaco Grand Prix was just 12 days short of four years since his first GP in a car bearing his own name at Monaco in May of 1966. In five seasons he competed in 34 GPs and scored a total of 60 World Championship points.

MODEL	McLaren M14A
TYPE/FORMULA	Formula 1
YEAR OF PRODUCTION	1970
DESIGNER	Gordon Coppuck/Jo Marquart
EXAMPLES BUILT	3 +1 (M14D)
ENGINE	Ford Cosworth DFV
CUBIC CAPACITY	2993cc
CARBURATION	Lucas fuel injection
POWER OUTPUT	430bhp

TRANSMISSION	Hewland DG300 5-speed
CHASSIS	18/16swg aluminium skins over mild steel bulkheads
BODY	Monocoque sides, GRP nose & cockpit surround
FRONT SUSPENSION	Single top link & radius arm, lower wishbone,
	outboard coil spring/damper, anti-roll bar
REAR SUSPENSION	Reverse lower wishbone, top link, twin radius
	rods, outboard coil spring/damper, anti-roll bar
BRAKES F/R	Outboard/inboard 10.9in discs
WHEELS DIAMETER x WIDTH F/R	15x11/15x16in

TYRES F/R	Goodyear
LENGTH	156in - 3962mm
WIDTH	27in - 686 mm
HEIGHT AT WING	36in - 914mm
WHEELBASE	95in - 2413mm
TRACK F/R	62.5/60in - 1585/1524mm
WEIGHT	1180lb - 535kg
PRINCIPAL DRIVERS	McLaren, Hulme, Gurney, Gethin, Oliver
IDENTIFYING COLOURS	Papaya

Peter Gethin was the sole representative of Bruce McLaren Motor Racing at the Silverstone International Trophy meeting in May 1971, when he drove M14A-2 in the two-heat event. After finishing sixth in the first race and fourth in the second, he was classified second overall, 1m 30s behind Graham Hill's last F1 win in his 'Lobster Claw' Brabham BT34.

The 1970 Spanish GP at Jarama would be Bruce's last Grand Prix finish. In a race of attrition, he finished an excellent second, albeit a full lap down on winner Jackie Stewart's March 701. The six points left him a posthumous 14th in the Drivers' World Championship at the end of a tumultuous year for F1.

McLaren withdrew from the Belgian GP at Spa early in June in the immediate aftermath of Bruce's death, and when it returned for the Dutch race later that month Dan Gurney had taken over Bruce's M14A-1 and Peter Gethin had replaced Denny, whose hands were still too raw after the Indianapolis fire, in M14A-2. The former's engine broke its timing gears after he had started from the back of the grid, while the latter crashed out on the 19th lap, necessitating a rebuild around a fresh tub.

Denny made a brave return at the French GP at Clermont-Ferrand to claim fourth place right behind Brabham in M14A-1, officially listed in the entry as M14D-1. He took that to third place in Britain after a very close battle with rookie, Clay Regazzoni's Ferrari which was only four-tenths of a second adrift at the flag. In Germany he was third again, in what was effectively a new car, although the chassis plate concealed this having been swapped over in order to ease the company's progress through international customs. He drove M14A-3 which bore the chassis plate from M14A-2. He went on to finish fourth at Monza, where in practice he had seen the tragedy in which Jochen Rindt was killed, and third in Mexico.

Gurney scored the final point of his illustrious F1 career with sixth place in France, before electing to retire from the category after suffering engine failure in Britain. Thereafter Gethin had a patchy season as Hulme's team-mate, with only sixth place in Canada to celebrate.

McLaren ran the M19 in 1971, but for a while an M14A reappeared alongside it as Gethin's race car. The South African, Spanish and Monaco GPs yielded little, though he was generally competitive in the ageing car. His best result came at Oulton Park's Spring Cup, where he was able to show his true mettle as he beat Jackie Stewart's Tyrrell, challenged eventual winner Pedro Rodriguez's BRM and set a new lap record before dropping back to finish second, just under five seconds adrift after inadvertently hitting the ignition switch on the 20th lap.

Jackie Oliver later raced this car as a third works entry in the British and Italian Grands Prix, without championship point-scoring success. Later the car was acquired by Tony Dean who converted it to Formula 5000 configuration with a Chevrolet V8, without notable success.

There was one other M14 built in 1970, the M14D, for Andrea de Adamich as part of the Autodelta agreement. It was similar to the M14A in all respects apart from modifications to the rear end to accept the Alfa Romeo V8. It first appeared in the Italian's hands at Zandvoort but yielded no upturn in the fortunes he had encountered with the M7D. He reverted to the latter briefly before resuming with the M14D at Hockenheim. At Österreichring, Monza and St Jovite he was competitive with Denny's Cosworth-powered M14 in qualifying, but his only notable finish was eighth place in the Italian Grand Prix and after non-starting in Watkins Glen he did not make the trip to Mexico City.

At Brands Hatch for the British Grand Prix in July, Denny Hulme once again finished third. This time Rindt (now in the new Lotus Type 72) was the winner, passing Jack Brabham halfway round the last lap when the Australian ran out of fuel.

The UK debut for the M14 was at the 1970 Brands Hatch 'Race of Champions' in March. Bruce crashed out on lap 21, while Denny finished third behind Stewart in Ken Tyrrell's March 701 and Rindt in the Gold Leaf Team Lotus Type 49.

1970 M15
INDYCAR

Bruce was pleased with certain aspects of the pannier-tanked M7B, which aimed to make the handling more consistent thanks to the weight distribution. This partly explains the genesis of the Gordon Coppuck-designed M15 built for Indianapolis, which was effectively a single-seat version of the outstanding M8.

The decision to tackle the lucrative 500-mile race was said to have been inspired by a radio broadcast detailing Denny Hulme's exploits there in Dan Gurney's Eagle in 1969, and team sponsor Goodyear's keenness to beat rival Firestone at the 'Brickyard'. Having conquered one series of American racing, Bruce characteristically decided: *"Let's have a go."*

The M15's monocoque terminated immediately behind the driver, and the 2.6-litre turbocharged four-cylinder Offenhauser engine was bolted to two plates on the rear bulkhead. Twin A-frames extended back to the bellhousing which joined it to the Hewland LG500 four-speed transaxle.

The rear suspension comprised reversed lower wishbones and twin radius arms, while up front there were single top links with radius arms, lower wishbones, anti-roll bars and outboard coil spring/damper units. The wheels were McLaren cast magnesium units with knock-off hubs. Goodyear safety fuel cells in the sills held 68 US gallons, helping to give the 1,380lb car the enhanced weight distribution Bruce sought, and its distinctive bulbous profile.

After the first test session at Goodwood in November 1969, Denny accompanied Bruce and Chris Amon to Indianapolis to help them familiarise themselves with the car, the circuit and the unique characteristics of turbo-lag in a 650bhp engine running at 9,000 rpm on Hillborn fuel injection. Hamstrung by a testing regime which allowed only one car out at a time, they nevertheless posted impressive results, Denny lapping the circuit at 168mph and Bruce 162mph. Chris, a driver in Jim Clark's class on his day, simply didn't like the concrete walls that lined the circuit. Eoin Young joked that they should paint some trees on them to make him feel at home.

Once again, with a new car and in a previously unknown motor racing environment, McLaren was beginning to look highly competitive. Pre-race modifications included systems to jack the weight across the car to cater for the high fuel load burning down or to alter the ride heights, adding more than 100lbs to Coppuck's original design weight, but it was still the lightest car in the field. Bruce admitted how much it meant to the company: *"Two months ago we were saying 'Right, remember now, it's just another race...' but there's never been a single race that we've got this excited about."*

On the first day of official practice in May 1970, the three McLarens really shook the establishment, and everybody remarked upon their high standard of construction. But tragedy lay around the corner.

First, came misfortune for Denny. A vibration in the 'Offy' engine caused the springs that were meant to hold the fuel filler caps closed, to flip them open at speed. Mechanic Alan McCall had been forced by scrutineers from the United States Auto Club (USAC) to change the original snap-down design to incorporate an extra spring so that they flipped open faster during pit stops. The caps opened as Denny was out on a fast run, and methanol was sucked from the tanks. At first he thought it was raining, as liquid sprayed the shallow windscreen, but when he braked for the next corner the weight transfer threw more fuel out of the now open left-hand tank. This was blown back by the slipstream on to the hot engine, particularly the turbocharger, and suddenly the car was on fire at 180mph. Methanol, which had been mandated at Indianapolis following the fiery 1964 accident which claimed the lives of Dave Macdonald and Eddie Sachs, burns with an invisible flame but when Denny felt the pain in his leather-clad hands he realised he was in serious trouble. All he wanted was out of the cockpit. He talked of watching the leather disappearing from his gloves and seeing the plastic screen melting before his eyes as, fearing an explosion, he braked harder. That sent more fuel to the fire. Finally, after his first attempt to bale out was thwarted when he forgot to undo his seatbelt, he leapt overboard at 70mph. Rescuers were more concerned about the car, and initially few noticed that the hapless driver's overalls were on fire as he rolled on the grass trying to quell the invisible flames. Denny sustained serious burns to his hands and would clearly be out of action for the race.

It was not Bruce's intention to race himself at Indianapolis, and with Denny out and Chris electing to give Indianapolis a miss, Peter Revson and USAC specialist Carl Williams were drafted into the cockpits at late notice, the team's plans now heavily compromised. Williams qualified 19th at 166.590mph and finished ninth, three laps down. Revson qualified 16th at 167.942mph but was classified 22nd after the magneto broke on the 88th lap.

Three days after the race, which was run on Memorial Day, May 30th, came the second hammer blow when Bruce died at Goodwood. Sadly, he would never know how successful McLaren would go on to become at Indianapolis.

The M15s were also raced in the 500 milers at Ontario and Pocono. At the former, Revson qualified strongly and was leading by his final pit stop but dropped to fifth after the coil needed changing. Gordon Johncock, another USAC star who had acquired one of the cars after Indianapolis, was fourth. He crashed that very same car at Indianapolis in 1971 after qualifying it 12th at 171.388mph. Other privateers raced M15s, with negligible success.

It is important not to underestimate the disruption caused to the M15 programme by Denny's burns at Indianapolis, then Bruce's death. It did a more than respectable job under traumatic circumstances.

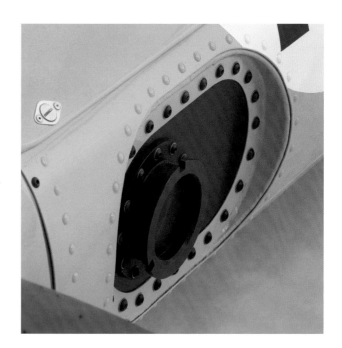

With fast fuel stops essential, quick release caps were fitted to both tanks allowing the air inside the each tank to escape and the 68 gallons of methanol fuel to enter faster. It was one of these caps that sprang open and triggered the fire in which Denny sustained the burns to his hands.

With fuel consumption of around 2mpg and the Indy 500 lasting 200 laps of the 2.5-mile circuit, cars were required to refuel several times. An Avery Hardoll 'spill-proof' aircraft style filler unit was fitted to the left side of the car.

After Hulme was injured and Amon just couldn't come to grips with an oval circuit, Peter Revson and Carl Williams were brought in as the team drivers for the 1970 Indy 500. Williams finished a solid ninth but Revson (above) retired after 87 laps.

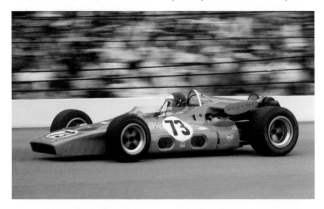

MODEL	McLaren M15
TYPE/FORMULA	Indianapolis/USAC
YEAR OF PRODUCTION	1970
PRINCIPAL DESIGNER	Gordon Coppuck
EXAMPLES BUILT	3
ENGINE TYPE	Offenhauser 4-cylinder turbo
CUBIC CAPACITY	2600cc
CARBURATION	Garrett turbocharger
POWER OUTPUT	650bhp

TRANSMISSION	Hewland LG500 4-speed
CHASSIS	Broad aluminium alloy sheet monocoque, steel bulkheads
BODY	Monocoque sides, GRP nose & cockpit, engine cover
FRONT SUSPENSION	Single top link & radius arm, lower wishbone, outboard coil spring/damper, anti-roll bar
REAR SUSPENSION	Reverse lower wishbone, top link, twin radius rods, outboard coil spring/damper, anti-roll bar
BRAKES F/R	Outboard 11.97in Lockheed ventilated discs
WHEELS DIAMETER x WIDTH F/R	15x10/15x14in

TYRES F/R	Goodyear
LENGTH	156in - 3962mm
WIDTH AT COCKPIT	45in - 102mm
HEIGHT	36in - 914mm
WHEELBASE	99in - 2515mm
TRACK F/R	57.75/58in - 1467/1473mm
WEIGHT	1490lb - 676kg
PRINCIPAL DRIVERS	Revson, Williams, (Hulme, Amon)
IDENTIFYING COLOURS	Papaya

1971 McLAREN-TROJAN M8E CAN-AM

Given McLaren's superb track record in sportscar racing and the high level of support it enjoyed from Chevrolet, Goodyear, Reynolds and Gulf, it was only natural that its continuing domination of the Can-Am series should bring in not just much-needed revenue but awards too.

Just before Bruce's death, Britain's Royal Automobile Club was preparing to announce the presentation to him of the prestigious Segrave Trophy. At the same time, loyal customers were clamouring for something similar to the all-conquering M8D. The result was a new McLaren-Trojan replica for the 1971 season. It received the type number M8E as the team cars' designation was M8F.

The M8D was a sizeable car – pictures taken at the time show the jockey-sized Peter Gethin almost disappearing from view in the cockpit – but though the M8E was based on it, it inherited dimensions from the more compact M8B. It had a four-inch narrower track and a low, strut-supported rear wing rather than the M8D's distinctive apparatus. The changes shaved a useful 22lb off the dry weight, making the total 1,425lb.

Construction was mostly of 16 and 20 gauge L72 aluminium alloy, using argon-welded steel bulkheads which were bonded and riveted into place. For the first time in a customer Can-Am McLaren the engine was employed as a stressed unit, although suspension pick-ups were taken from the welded steel bulkheads in order to impart maximum strength. Once again, a low centre of gravity was ensured by carrying 56 gallons of fuel in foam-filled rubber Marston cells located within the outer sections of the tub.

The customer cars also generally had larger powerplants than the outgoing M8D, typically a dry-sump aluminium-alloy 8-litre Chevrolet such as the unit shown here. With a stated output of 700bhp with this larger engine, the M8E's transmission was via the familiar Hewland LG500 gearbox with Trojan/BRD splined driveshafts and a triple-plate Borg & Beck clutch.

The M8E pictured here was originally delivered to Roy Woods Racing, to be driven by Vic Elford. It made its debut at Road Atlanta, where Elford qualified six places ahead of another M8E driven by Roger McCaig, before retiring after 35 laps with a broken clutch.

Both were back again two weeks later, however, by which time the field at Watkins Glen was crowded out with a variety of Group 4 and 6 sportscars from the previous day's six-hour endurance race. The M8Es qualified 14th and 21st, Elford eventually finishing a respectable eighth.

On August 22nd at Lexington, four M8Es took part, but none finished. Neither of the works cars finished either, suffering driveshaft failures. As Hulme's car spun in the pack, causing much confusion, McCaig shot through from 14th to fourth but eventually retired on lap 64 when his engine expired. He was classified 13th, well ahead of the other McLarens.

As the M8Fs dominated, the M8E's best day came at Elkhart Lake. Elford made a strong start from the third row of the grid and finished a well-deserved third behind Peter Revson's team car and Jo Siffert in the fast-improving Porsche 917.

Donnybrooke marked Elford's last drive in the car; he qualified on the third row and finished fourth behind the works cars of Revson and Hulme, and Greg Young's M8E/D.

By 1972 several of the customer cars in the M8 series had become outclassed in a Can-Am series increasingly being dominated by Porsche and began to find their way back to the UK for the Interserie Championship. Appearing alongside the few M8Cs which had been delivered directly to European customers as well as an M12 and the occasional M6B which had run in the series since 1970, the M8E (and later the M8F) was the stalwart of the larger-engine class until it was overcome by the turbocharged Porsche 917s of Willi Kauhsen and Helmuth Kelleners.

Top: In October 1972 Bill Cuddy finished 12th in the Cuddy Racing Inc. Chevrolet-powered M8E during a rather wet round of the Can-Am series at Laguna Seca. 1972 was the first year of Porsche domination and George Follmer's 917/10K won the championship with 130 points to Denny Hulme's 65.

Above: Teddy Pilette in the Team VDS M8E (chassis 70-08) finished eighth in the 70-lap Super Sports 200 Interserie Championship race at Silverstone in May 1972. The European series was also dominated by Porsche, with Leo Kinnunen in his 917/10 taking the title.

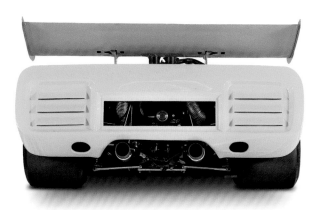

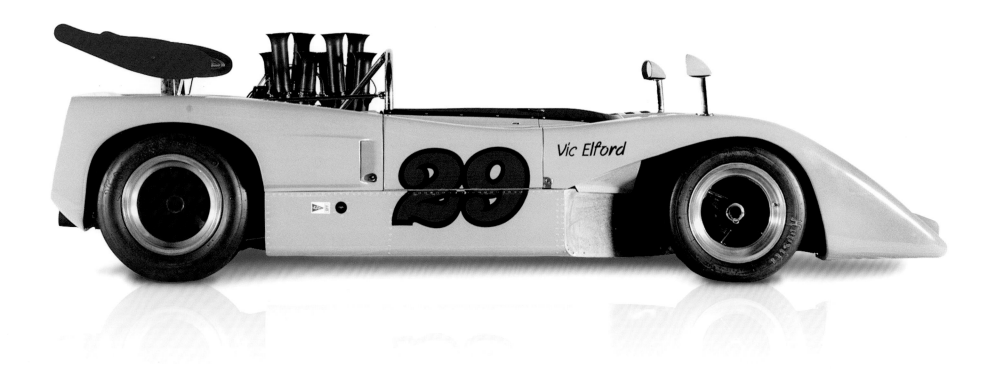

MODEL	McLaren-Trojan M8E
TYPE/FORMULA	Can-Am
YEAR OF PRODUCTION	1971
DESIGNER	Jo Marquart
EXAMPLES BUILT	15-18 (insufficient records)
ENGINE	Chevrolet/Ford V8
CUBIC CAPACITY	7000-8095cc
CARBURATION	Lucas fuel injection
POWER OUTPUT	650-700bhp

TRANSMISSION	Hewland LG500 4-speed
CHASSIS	Aluminium sheet monocoque with steel bulkheads
BODY	Monocoque sides, GRP body sections, aluminium wing
FRONT SUSPENSION	Single top link & radius arm, lower wishbone,
	outboard coil spring/damper, anti-roll bar
REAR SUSPENSION	Reverse lower wishbone, single top link,
	twin radius rods, coil spring/damper, anti-roll bar
BRAKES F/R	Outboard 11.9in ventilated discs
WHEELS DIAMETER x WIDTH F/R	15x11/15x16in

TYRES F/R	Goodyear
LENGTH	153in - 3886mm
WIDTH	74in - 1880mm
HEIGHT TO WINDSCREEN	30in - 762mm
WHEELBASE	94in - 2387mm
TRACK F/R	58/55in - 1473/1397mm
WEIGHT	1425lb - 647kg
PRINCIPAL DRIVERS	Elford, McCaig, Drolsom
IDENTIFYING COLOURS	n/a

1971 & 1972 M8F & McLAREN-TROJAN M8F/P CAN-AM

Somewhat belatedly, in 1971, Peter Revson became the first North American to win his 'home' Can-Am Championship. And though nobody knew it at the time, his success in the M8F would prove to be McLaren's last year of domination of the series. The baton would pass to Porsche and its turbocharged 917/10K, but not before M8s had chalked up 32 wins in 37 races, 19 of them in succession.

In a pattern which was becoming increasingly familiar, Gordon Coppuck created the strongest, longest, widest and heaviest Can-Am McLaren thus far. The chassis comprised another simple but effective monocoque with steel bulkheads, now employing Reynolds-sourced aluminium inner and outer skins of slightly heavier gauge than that used in previous M8s.

Two foam-filled rubber fuel cells on either side of the driver created a total capacity of 72 US gallons. Well-balanced as it undoubtedly already was, the additional size and ballast did much to improve the M8F's handling. The braking system was also improved, thanks to moving the rear discs and calipers inboard.

The track dimensions were reduced slightly to enable 17-inch rims to fit within the rear bodywork, but the uncompromisingly brutal body shape was otherwise very similar to the 'Batmobile' M8D, albeit with aerodynamic fences now running the full length of the body atop the wing line. These helped to channel airflow more efficiently over the top of the bodyshell to the low-mounted rear wing and, allied to a revised nose shape, helped the M8F to generate 1.5 tonnes of downforce.

By the first race of 1972, Peter Revson had been signed to partner Denny Hulme. In qualifying at Mosport in mid-June, it was clear that the M8F drivers' strongest competition all season was likely to come from 1969 World Champion Jackie Stewart in a bespoke Lola T260. The Scot took pole, but Denny soon put five seconds of clean air between himself and the rest of the field. The result was another one-two, with second an excellent result for new boy Revson.

At St Jovite a fortnight later pole was Denny's, with Revson starting third. Stewart's Lola was the filling in the McLaren sandwich, but in the race itself the Scot sprang a surprise by leading an unwell Denny and Revson home. Highly concerned, McLaren went to Road Atlanta to test prior to the next race, where Revson used a new lineless Reynolds

all-aluminium 7.9-litre Chevrolet V8. Stewart led again but retired, and Revson led Denny home in another one-two, even though the New Zealander was running out of brakes.

Stewart was on pole again at Watkins Glen on July 25th and led until the Lola sustained a puncture. Thereafter it was Revson all the way, using another new Reynolds-block engine this time enlarged to 8.4-litres. Denny was second. Stewart won at Mid-Ohio, where both McLarens suffered universal joint failures, while Denny led and looked set to head another M8F one-two at Elkhart Lake until a broken crankshaft forced him out, leaving Revson to take the honours. Revson led from start to finish at Donnybrooke, with Denny inheriting second place when Stewart's Lola retired.

Denny won at Edmonton and Revson at Laguna Seca, where he ignored a black flag at the start of his last lap for dropping oil. Riverside marked the last outing for the works M8-series cars. The championship was already wrapped up, so both drivers ran the sleeveless 8.3-litre engines. Denny smashed the course record to take pole by a full second from Revson, and won the race going away. Revson was happy to keep Stewart at bay, aware that sixth place would be sufficient to clinch him the title, and duly finished runner-up. He took the title with 142 points to Denny's 132, five wins to three. Lola had won twice, its first successes since John Surtees won at Vegas in 1967, but for McLaren the season had virtually been business as usual.

Above: At the third round of the 1972 European 'Interserie' Championship at Silverstone, the Helmut Felder-entered M8F/P was driven by Helmut Kelleners. After coming second in the first heat, he retired on the seventh lap of heat two with a broken cam follower.

Below: Peter Revson won four races to Hulme's three (and Stewart's two in the Lola) and took the 1971 Can-Am title with a second place at the final race at Riverside and a total of 142 points to Denny's 132.

MODEL	McLaren M8F
TYPE/FORMULA	Can-Am
YEAR OF PRODUCTION	1971
DESIGNER	Gordon Coppuck
EXAMPLES BUILT	3
ENGINE	Chevrolet V8
CUBIC CAPACITY	7900-8400cc
CARBURATION	Lucas fuel injection
POWER OUTPUT	700-720bhp

TRANSMISSION	Hewland LG600 5-speed
CHASSIS	Aluminium sheet monocoque, with steel bulkheads
BODY	Monocoque sides, GRP body sections, integral wing
FRONT SUSPENSION	Single top link & radius arm, lower wishbone,
	outboard coil spring/damper, anti-roll bar
REAR SUSPENSION	Reverse lower wishbone, single top link,
	twin radius rods, coil spring/damper, anti-roll bar
BRAKES F/R	Outboard 12in ventilated discs
WHEELS DIAMETER x WIDTH F/R	15x11/15x17in

TYRES F/R	Goodyear
LENGTH	167in - 4242mm
WIDTH	76in - 1930mm
HEIGHT	32in - 812mm
WHEELBASE	98in - 2489mm
TRACK F/R	60/58.75in - 1524/1492mm
WEIGHT	1520lb - 689kg
PRINCIPAL DRIVERS	Hulme, Revson, Gethin
IDENTIFYING COLOURS	Papaya

While the works team was developing the radically different M20 to run in the 1972 Can-Am, Trojan was putting the M8F into limited production — just 10 were built — as a customer car. Designated M8FP, these models were virtually identical to the 1971 team cars and as such were seemingly only ever referred to by the factory as M8Fs. With eight different drivers listed as driving M8Fs or M8FPs, the best result of the year and the only McLaren victory other than those taken by Denny in the works M20, came courtesy of Tyrrell Formula 1 star, François Cevert who pedalled Greg Young's M8F to a superb triumph at Donnybrooke in September, after the works cars failed, and the dominant turbo Porsches ran out of luck.

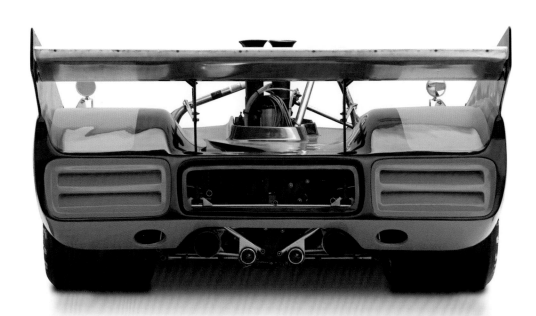

MODEL	McLaren-Trojan M8F/P	TRANSMISSION	Hewland LG600 5-speed	TYRES F/R	Goodyear
TYPE/FORMULA	Can-Am	CHASSIS	Aluminium sheet monocoque, with steel bulkheads	LENGTH	167in - 4242mm
YEAR OF PRODUCTION	1972	BODY	Monocoque sides, GRP body sections, integral wing	WIDTH	76in - 1930mm
DESIGNER	Gordon Coppuck	FRONT SUSPENSION	Single top link & radius arm, lower wishbone,	HEIGHT	32in - 812mm
EXAMPLES BUILT	10		outboard coil spring/damper, anti-roll bar	WHEELBASE	98in - 2489mm
ENGINE	Chevrolet V8	REAR SUSPENSION	Reverse lower wishbone, single top link,	TRACK F/R	60/58.75in - 1524/1492mm
CUBIC CAPACITY	8093cc		twin radius rods, coil spring/damper, anti-roll bar	WEIGHT	1520lb - 689kg
CARBURATION	Lucas fuel injection	BRAKES F/R	Outboard 12in ventilated discs	PRINCIPAL DRIVERS	McCaig, Cevert, Agor
POWER OUTPUT	710bhp	WHEELS DIAMETER x WIDTH F/R	15x11/15x17in	IDENTIFYING COLOURS	n/a

1971 M16
INDYCAR

The M15 performed more than adequately on its debut at Indianapolis in 1970 but having seen how effective Colin Chapman's wedge-shaped Lotus Type 72 was in the summer of that season, Gordon Coppuck was very taken with the idea of running a car of similar shape at the American oval.

He believed that McLaren had learned a lot about Indy from the M15, and while he wasn't convinced the 72 was the right shape for Grand Prix racing, he thought the basic concept would work well for an Indy car. He told Doug Nye in McLAREN The Grand Prix, Can-Am and Indy Cars: "For Indy we thought it must be a dead cinch. Your aerodynamic forces are very constant at Indy, with only about a 60mph difference in running speed at each corner; you're doing about 210mph on the straights and 150mph through the corners." Work on a new design started immediately after the 1970 race and the result, when the papaya orange cars were shown to the press at Colnbrook in January 1971, was quite sensational.

Without building a prototype the team had gone straight into production with a really striking car based on another L72 aluminium-skinned monocoque with steel bulkheads, but this time with a more wedge-shaped cross-section. Once again sponsorship came from Goodyear, Gulf and of course Reynolds Aluminium.

As in the M15, the Offenhauser turbo engine was mounted in a triangulated supporting frame. The 2.6-litre, overhead cam unit might have been one of the oldest powerplants then in production, tracing its origins to a Miller design of 1931, but with tweaks from Gary Knutson it was still good for around 700bhp while pulling up to 9000rpm. Allied to the familiar Hewland LG500 transaxle – McLaren favoured a three-speed unit over the usual Indy two-speed – it was to prove a formidable combination, with the additional ratio offering especially rapid acceleration out of the pits and after any yellow-light period.

With the radiators moved to the cars' hips, where they were enclosed by glass-fibre ducts, the Specialised Mouldings nosecone now contained little more than fire-extinguishing equipment, thereby creating a smooth and especially penetrative shape. To smooth the airflow still further the front suspension was moved inboard as the tub width was kept to a minimum. Coppuck incorporated a degree of rising rate in the suspension which offered greater resistance the greater the deflection, to help keep the car stable at high speeds.

There was space within the chassis for 75 US gallons of methanol-based fuel, via Goodyear cells on either side. This was crucial in a series where three fuel stops were mandatory per race and cars did well to achieve two miles per gallon.

In all its various guises the M16 concept would go down in motorsport history as one of the most successful cars in the long and illustrious history of the Indianapolis 500. Competing in 11 races and taking three victories, four seconds and two third places, it laid the foundations for an astonishingly fruitful adventure for what was still a small team.

The radical, Lotus-inspired wedge shape, while familiar in F1, caused astonishment at Indianapolis, where just as Coppuck had suspected, it proved ideal for the continuous high-speed running which characterised the racing. It generated significant aerodynamic downforce, though initially it proved quite challenging to balance this correctly over the front and rear ends. There was a lot of downforce at the front, and this had to be balanced by the large rear wing which operated in conjunction with a smooth engine cover, and by improving airflow over the whole car. Small canard fins either side of the nose helped with this trimming, while the turbocharger was sited as low as possible on a bespoke manifold to keep it out of the airstream.

In comparison with many other Indy cars of the time, which tended to metamorphose each year, the M16's engine installation was astonishingly tidy. Cleverly, Coppuck had also incorporated the rear wing into the bodywork, rightly suspecting that rivals would attempt to protest that wings were not allowed. The USAC scrutineers looked at the car, and said they were happy that its wings were bodywork and that it complied with the rules.

Within days of the 1,380lb racer being shown to the press, testing began in earnest with Denny Hulme and Peter Revson taking the controls at the new Ontario Motor Speedway in California. Subsequently M16-1 was taken over by Roger Penske, so that Mark Donohue could test further at Phoenix with engineer Don Cox. By March they had moved on to Indianapolis, where Donohue stunned rivals with a lap of 172mph. When official practice for the 500 started in May, he upped the Penske car's speed to 174.757mph against the previous best of 171.953 which dated back to 1968. Denny lapped in 172.944, and the old hands threw up their hands in horror. The following day Donohue hit 177.901mph, averaging 176.3 over four laps. And he wasn't finished. A week later he topped out at a staggering 180.900mph, while Revson lapped at 174 for second fastest time.

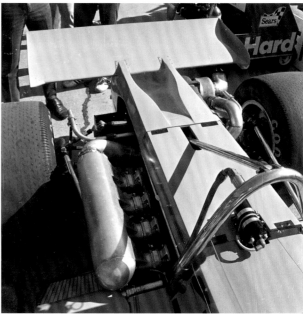

In early March 1971, prior to its first run at Indy, Denny Hulme tested the new M16 at Ontario Motor Speedway in California. He turned in some very fast lap times of well over 190mph.

This aerodynamic 'engine cover' which some felt was nothing more than a rear wing, caused a great deal of controversy at the '71 Indy 500. By '72 the authorities relented and allowed 'proper' wings.

Denny Hulme qualified fourth on the grid for the 1971 Indy 500 but retired from eighth position with engine problems on lap 138 of the race.

MODEL	McLaren M16	TRANSMISSION	Hewland LG500 3-speed	TYRES F/R	Goodyear
TYPE/FORMULA	Indianapolis/USAC	CHASSIS	Full aluminium monocoque, steel bulkheads	LENGTH	155in - 3937mm
YEAR OF PRODUCTION	1971	BODY	Monocoque sides, GRP nose & cockpit, engine cover	WIDTH AT RADIATORS	61in - 1550mm
DESIGNER	Gordon Coppuck	FRONT SUSPENSION	Welded cantilever rocker arm operating	HEIGHT OF ROLLHOOP	38in - 965mm
EXAMPLES BUILT	3		inboard coil spring/damper, lower wishbone	WHEELBASE	101in - 2565mm
ENGINE	Offenhauser 4-cylinder turbo	REAR SUSPENSION	Reverse lower wishbone, top link, twin	TRACK F/R	58/58in - 1473/1473mm
CUBIC CAPACITY	2600cc		radius rods, coil spring/damper, anti-roll bar	WEIGHT	1380lb - 626kg
CARBURATION	Hilborn injection, Garrett Airesearch turbocharger	BRAKES F/R	Drilled outboard 11.9in discs	PRINCIPAL DRIVERS	Hulme, Revson, Donohue
POWER OUTPUT	700+bhp	WHEELS DIAMETER x WIDTH F/R	15x10/15x14in	IDENTIFYING COLOURS	Papaya

1971 McLAREN-TROJAN M18 FORMULA 5000

The M17 designation was intended for a 3-litre sports prototype design which was abandoned and the next McLaren in line, the M18, was a new Formula 5000 car for the 1971 season.

Once again it was built by Trojan and power came from the usual 5-litre Chevrolet V8. As such it had much in common with the earlier M10A/M10B even though it used the five-speed DG300 in place of the LG600, but it also owed something to the M16 in an attempt to adopt a wedge shape and was substantially lighter than its class predecessors. As indicated by the Trojan suffix, it was always intended as a customer car although one owner, Irishman Sid Taylor, enjoyed some works support.

With most of the main test and evaluation work carried out by Bruce McLaren himself, the M10A was a successful machine that saw off the likes of Lola's T142 spaceframe contender and remained the class of the field against the monocoque offerings from that rival, Surtees and Leda. It followed that it would be a hard act to follow, and the Ralph Bellamy-designed M18 never really looked like the car to do it. Its performance was a disappointment both for the company and Trojan, although Brian Redman's talent at the wheel won the M18 early success in the UK until Surtees' TS8 and, later in the season, Lola's new T300, hit their stride. Altogether 10 cars were completed, eight with official chassis numbers and two more apparently built up from completed tubs at a later date. But many observers had the distinct impression that the older M10B was actually a quicker car than the £4,850 machine which replaced it.

Bellamy's penmanship ensured it was at least a handsome machine, its flatter nose redesigned with high-sited wings and a larger radiator, and the fuel tank had a central filler. With 45 gallons held in foam-filled Marston cells located in the side sections, the top fuel bag was eliminated, thereby lowering the centre of gravity. At the same time all the pipework for delivery and return of water was mounted externally to optimise cooling.

In a form which was by 1971 wholly familiar, the bonded and riveted monocoque weighing just 80lb was constructed from panels of 16-gauge aluminium formed around steel bulkheads. The front suspension used a lower wishbone with a top link and radius arm, whilst at the rear reversed lower wishbones were mated to top links and radius rods. Formula 1 Lockheed ventilated discs were standard, with actuation via twin master cylinders. The driven wheels were 15x16-inch magnesium alloys with similar 13x11-inch rims up front. All-up weight was 1,350lb.

McLaren made more than 50 Formula 5000 cars, but the M18's record fell a long way short of impressive. Chassis M18 500-1, Redman's Sid Taylor Racing car which was actually built by McLaren rather than Trojan, won one of its first three races, posted two seconds and another late season victory at Brands Hatch, to come fifth in the European Championship. It was then taken over by the McLaren team itself, but Reine Wisell crashed it out of the final race of the season, the Rothmans World Champion Victory Race at Brands Hatch. This chassis was then developed into the prototype M22 that was raced in the 1972 Tasman Series by David Hobbs.

The next car, the Trojan Team 500-02, was raced by Graham McRae in 1971 but crashed and described in Britain's Autosport magazine as destroyed. In any case, he preferred his heavily modified M10B. The whereabouts of 500-03, the so-called Eppie Wietzes car, are currently unknown, but the fourth car in the series was raced by Tim Schenken, Howden Ganley (who crashed it) and Jean-Pierre Jaussaud in Barry Newman's dark green livery. It raced into 1974, without distinction, and in at least one libre race.

Chassis 500-05 was another Team Trojan car, driven by Ulf Norinder before being sold to Speed International Racing which campaigned it throughout 1972 with David Prophet, Ray Allen and Gijs van Lennep. In 1973 it was sold to Shell Oil for use in static displays and popped up in HSCC events for several years before a bad crash at Oulton Park.

The history of 500-06 is far less clear, this 1971 car being rebuilt with a new tub after being destroyed by Al Lader in an end-of-season US crash. It joined the 1972 New Zealand Tasman series and then went on to the US, scoring a second place in its Edmonton debut but was crashed at Watkins Glen before being rebuilt yet again. Since then a car known as chassis 500-06A has appeared in California, perhaps having been built up from one of the damaged tubs, while another, 500-06B, surfaced in New Zealand and is thought to have been rebuilt from a new tub — originally supplied after Lader's wreck — for the 1974 Tasman series. The car still exists in this form and has been described as both a McLaren M18/22 and a McLaren M18C.

The existence of other M18 chassis has been suggested and the probable remains of 500-07 have also been traced, while parts thought to have come from 500-08 are believed to have been reused in the building of the rival Gardos F5000 machine.

Top: Round 11 of the 17-round European F5000 championship was the Esso Uniflo Trophy at Silverstone on August 14th 1971. Brian Redman in the pristine white Sid Taylor Castrol-GTX M18 qualified seventh but ran out of fuel on lap 22 of the 25 lap race.

Above: On the Saturday before the 1972 Brands Hatch Race of Champions there was a round of the European F5000 series. Teddy Pilette in the VDS Racing M18 finished fifth and qualified to take part in Sunday's RoC where he finished 11th overall and the second F5000 car home.

MODEL	McLaren-Trojan M18
TYPE/FORMULA	Formula 5000/Formula A
YEAR OF PRODUCTION	1971
DESIGNER	Ralph Bellamy
EXAMPLES BUILT	8
ENGINE	Chevrolet V8
CUBIC CAPACITY	5000cc
CARBURATION	Lucas fuel injection
POWER OUTPUT	530bhp

TRANSMISSION	Hewland DG300 5-speed
CHASSIS	Full aluminium monocoque, steel bulkheads
BODY	Formed by monocoque, GRP nose & radiator shroud
FRONT SUSPENSION	Single top link & radius arm, lower wishbone,
	outboard coil spring/damper, anti-roll bar
REAR SUSPENSION	Reverse lower wishbone, single top link,
	twin radius rods, coil spring/damper, anti-roll bar
BRAKES F/R	Outboard/inboard 10.5in discs
WHEELS DIAMETER x WIDTH F/R	13x11/15x16in

TYRES F/R	Goodyear
LENGTH	166.5in - 4229mm
WIDTH OVERALL	77in - 1956mm
HEIGHT TO WINDSCREEN	26.5in - 673mm
WHEELBASE	100in - 2540mm
TRACK F/R	59.5/59.75in - 1511/1517mm
WEIGHT	1350lb - 612kg
PRINCIPAL DRIVERS	Redman, McRae, Pilette
IDENTIFYING COLOURS	n/a

1972 M16B
INDYCAR

Immediately Donohue had seen McLaren's new M16, on a flying visit to the Colnbrook factory early in 1971 while he and Penske were shopping for a Can-Am car and were talking with Lola about a new Indy contender, he had said that he "knew they had a much better overall package than we were discussing with Lola. They had obviously learned a lot about wings in Formula 1 and were applying that knowledge to Indy.

The McLarens dominated official qualifying later that week, as Revson grabbed the pole at a towering 178.696mph, Donohue was right behind him on 177.087, their respective best laps in their mandatory four-lap qualifying averages being 179.354 and 178.60. Bobby Unser squeezed his Eagle into third place, but Denny was right behind him at 174.900mph to give the M16s three out of the top four grid slots for the race on May 29th. It was a quite remarkable performance, and as Donohue put it later: "The new McLarens obsoleted every other car on the track."

Following the traditional rolling start, Donohue led the way with Revson taking second place and Hulme spinning at Turn Three, though he later recovered to eighth place before a broken valve forced him out on lap 138. Donohue was also to experience problems and slowed with transmission difficulties, eventually dropping out after 66 laps. Revson, who had been suckered at the start by Donohue and Unser, had the last laugh, though the crew were disappointed that having lost confidence in his car's handling, he did not attack defending champion Al Unser Snr (Bobby's brother) in a Johnny Lightning Colt Ford in the closing stages as he headed for second place. He crossed the line 24s adrift.

One car finishing out of three was well short of what the team was aiming for, but its achievement was nevertheless considerable. Second place at an average speed of 183.378mph, and some record-breaking qualifying times, had enabled the distinctively designed McLarens to make their lasting mark on the home crowd at the Speedway. Pushing forward with a truly revolutionary design, the team hitherto best known to Americans for its Can-Am sportscars demonstrated in the clearest terms that it was one to watch out for in the future.

The Penske M16 had been written off at Indianapolis after its retirement when it was struck where it lay by the side of the track as Mike Mosley lost control of his Eagle on the exit of Turn Four. The chassis was rebuilt at Colnbrook, and in the inaugural Pocono 500 Donohue scored McLaren's first Indy racing victory. To prove it was no fluke, he backed it up by winning at Michigan. He could have won the California 500 at Ontario too, but for running out of fuel when unaccountably he missed pit signals.

Donohue, a highly respected and very well-liked figure on the US scene, was more than justified in his original view that by the time Penske had finished converting a Lola for Indy racing the result would be, in comparison with the McLaren, "cobbled together". His admiration for the totality of the M16 design, not to mention its storming performances in 1971, persuaded the factory of the wisdom of investing in further development of its existing car rather than designing a new one for 1972.

As Dan Gurney worked on a slippery new Eagle designed by Roman Slobodynskyj, the M16 morphed into the M16B. Together with deeper front and rear wings it gained revised steering geometry, a sleek new bullet-shaped fairing over the plenum chamber and 25 per cent larger radiators. The nose was shortened too, taking on a bluff shape rather than its pointed wedge, so that the rear wing could be moved even further back yet still stay within the stipulated 158-inch maximum car length.

Penske ordered two of the new cars immediately, one for Donohue and the other for Gary Bettenhausen, scion of one of Indy racing's most famous families. The works entered two cars at Indianapolis, for regular Peter Revson and private M15 owner Gordon Johncock, but it was for the Sunoco Penske team, rather than for McLaren itself, that the new M16B was to turn its most significant trick in the famed '500'.

The previous season the rest of the field had complained about what they saw as McLaren's unfair advantage; in particular there was a hue and cry about it having too much of the engine exposed and 'illegal' wings. Beaten rivals were quick to learn, however, and it was Bobby Unser in Gurney's new Eagle who took the top slot on the grid as speeds rocketed. The 1968 race winner averaged a staggering 195.940mph to take the pole for 1972 Indy 500. Revson got the closest to him, at 192.885mph in the fastest of the M16Bs. Donohue was third at 191.408.

In the race itself, however, both Unser and Revson retired early, with a broken distributor rotor and gearbox respectively. Then Gurney's second driver, Jerry Grant, made a pit stop on lap 188 to investigate a tyre vibration, handing the lead to Donohue. In the interests of reliability, Penske had insisted on his driver running less turbo boost, and the ploy paid off handsomely. Donohue had a clear run to the flag and didn't squander the opportunity. The M16B averaged 162.962mph, and while it wasn't a works car which achieved it, a car inspired by Bruce McLaren had won the Indy 500 for the first time.

Top: Prior to its departure for the 1972 Indy 500 Peter Revson and chief designer Gordon Coppuck pose with the sensational looking M16B. Having taken the pole in 1971, 33-year-old Revson was, to quote the Gulf-McLaren press release, "hoping to take it all" in that year's race.

Above: Team Penske bought a pair of M16Bs to run at the 1972 Indy 500 for their drivers Mark Donohue and Gary Bettenhausen. Donohue, seen here with Roger Penske, qualified third fastest and went on to take a first Indy '500' victory for McLaren.

MODEL	McLaren M16B
TYPE/FORMULA	Indianapolis/USAC
YEAR OF PRODUCTION	1972
DESIGNER	Gordon Coppuck
EXAMPLES BUILT	4
ENGINE	Offenhauser 4-cylinder turbo
CUBIC CAPACITY	2600cc
CARBURATION	Hilborn injection, Garrett Airesearch turbocharger
POWER OUTPUT	700-750bhp

TRANSMISSION	Hewland LG500 4-speed
CHASSIS	Full aluminium monocoque, steel bulkheads
BODY	Monocoque sides, GRP nose & cockpit, engine cover
FRONT SUSPENSION	Welded cantilever top arm operating
	inboard coil spring/damper, lower wishbone
REAR SUSPENSION	Reverse lower wishbone, top link, twin
	radius rods, coil spring/damper, anti-roll bar
BRAKES F/R	Drilled outboard 11.9in discs
WHEELS DIAMETER x WIDTH F/R	15x10/15x14in

TYRES F/R	Goodyear
LENGTH	158in - 4013mm
WIDTH	76in - 1930mm
HEIGHT	38in - 965mm
WHEELBASE	101in - 2565mm
TRACK F/R	58/58in - 1473/1473mm
WEIGHT	1380lb - 626kg
PRINCIPAL DRIVERS	Revson, Donohue, Johncock
IDENTIFYING COLOURS	Papaya/Blue

1971 M19A
FORMULA 1

The M19 was Australian Ralph Bellamy's 1971 Formula 1 contender, with which McLaren hoped to make amends for the rather disappointing M14 design. Wider and longer, the M19A's most distinctive feature was the way its belly swelled out in what Bellamy described as "a Coke-bottle shape, like a Matra MS80," referring to Jackie Stewart's 1969 World Championship-winning car.

Conceived by Jo Marquart around a longer wheelbase to accommodate the fuel as centrally as possible, the double curvature panelling was worked in 16-gauge NS4 aluminium by Don Beresford and Leo Wybrott.

Upon viewing the car Motor Sport magazine's technically minded writer, Denis Jenkinson, reported: *"As with all the McLaren racing cars the detail work is a joy to see, the standard of finish being very high indeed."*

As on the M14A the brakes were mounted outboard at the front and inboard at the rear, but the suspension differed radically as Bellamy opted for a degree of rising rate in which the resistance to movement increased as wheel deflection increased. This was achieved by using conventional, inboard-mounted linear springs activated by a novel linkage system which worked to compress both spring and damper to a greater or lesser extent as the wheels rose and fell over bumps.

The system was chosen not least because in the early 1970s F1 cars were sprung relatively softly, which meant running quite generous ride heights. When carrying a full fuel load cars were liable to bottom out on undulating circuits.

The Lotus 72 had to an extent demonstrated the previous year that rising rate suspension could be used to circumvent that problem with its complex torsion bar system; now McLaren believed it had discovered a simpler and less expensive alternative means.

The new system was more complicated to set up but Denny liked the car on the smooth surface of Kyalami and, having qualified only fifth for the season opener, was already fourth at the end of the opening lap. Then he overtook Jacky Ickx's Ferrari, Emerson Fittipaldi's Lotus and the leading Ferrari of Clay Regazzoni and soon pulled away. Then on the 76th of the 79 laps Denny began to feel the M19A squirming beneath him. Fearful of a puncture he dropped back to a sixth-place finish one lap down; later it transpired that the bolt securing the upper right radius arm in the rear suspension had sheared.

Thereafter Denny notched up fourths in Monaco and Canada and a fifth in Spain, and they would be his best results in a season that flattered only to deceive. McLaren had two M19As by the Dutch GP in June. Peter Gethin and Jackie Oliver both drove the second car, each taking a ninth, the former in France, the latter in Austria.

Left: Peter Gethin's M19A is prepared for the 1971 German Grand Prix at the Nürburgring. Of the 22 starters he could only qualify 20th and spun out of the 12-lap race on lap five. Team mate Hulme faired even worse, retiring on lap three with a fuel leak.

Above: On Monday 15th February 1971 the curvy Ralph Bellamy- designed M19 was shown to the press for the first time. Seen here inside the tidy-looking McLaren workshops at Colnbrook (it was raining), the pronounced 'Coke-bottle' shape of the M19 is clearly visible.

Ironically, the M19A's best performance was achieved by Grand Prix debutant Mark Donohue who drove a Penske-liveried version superbly to third place in the rain in Canada behind only Jackie Stewart and Ronnie Peterson. In his biography, The Unfair Advantage, Donohue described the result as a gift, thanks to the weather.

Problems in the M19A's inconsistent performance were put down to understeer induced by tyre vibration associated with the low-profile rubber that was becoming fashionable, continued difficulties setting up the rising rate suspension, and an imbalance in the aerodynamics. In the US GP at Watkins Glen late in the year, Denny ran his car with an experimental wide nose, without noticeable improvement in its performance.

In his first Formula 1 appearance, the 1971 Canadian Grand Prix at Mosport Park, Mark Donohue qualified Roger Penske's M19 eighth on the grid and ahead of Denny Hulme. He finished the rain-soaked race on the podium in third place. Hulme was fourth.

With Gordon Coppuck tied up working on the Indy cars, and Jo Marquart leaving to co-found junior formula race car manufacturer Huron, Bellamy had complete responsibility for the M19A, and he summarised the 1971 season thus: "The rising-rate suspension offered many clear theoretical advantages, but in practice it worked well enough at the front of the car and less well at the back. Trying to sort it out and find a set up that the driver felt happy with and could understand what was going on, proved rather tricky."

The answers were slow in coming even when Roger Penske agreed to put Donohue, a renowned car sorter, in an M19A for a prolonged test at Silverstone. He complained about the car oversteering, so more rear wing was added only for the car to oversteer even more. When the same thing happened again the team was even more confused until someone eventually suggested that the more downforce they were putting on the back of the car the more it tended to push the car into the stiffer part of the suspension's rate curve.

Eventually the radical rear suspension was ditched in favour of a non-rising rate M14A rear end. Bellamy thought the improvement was dramatic, but his podium position first time out in Canada notwithstanding, Donohue was forever frustrated that even he couldn't figure out the rising rate front suspension properly. He finally concluded that half the problem was that the rear wing rarely worked efficiently.

The big change as the M19A headed into the 1972 season was a change of colour scheme, a consequence of Yardley Cosmetics switching from BRM. The new white livery with the black, brown and gold Yardley 'Y' did however leave a small space for some papaya orange flashes on the sides.

MODEL	McLaren M19A
TYPE/FORMULA	Formula 1
YEAR OF PRODUCTION	1971/1972
DESIGNER	Ralph Bellamy
EXAMPLES BUILT	2
ENGINE	Ford Cosworth DFV
CUBIC CAPACITY	2993cc
CARBURATION	Lucas fuel injection
POWER OUTPUT	440bhp

TRANSMISSION	Hewland DG300 5-speed
CHASSIS	Full aluminium monocoque, steel bulkheads
BODY	Formed by monocoque, GRP nosecone
FRONT SUSPENSION	Double wishbone, with push rod and rocker operating inboard coil spring/damper, anti-roll bar
REAR SUSPENSION	Lower wishbone, top link, push rod acting on inboard coil spring/damper, twin radius rods, anti-roll bar
BRAKES F/R	Outboard/inboard 10.5in ventilated discs
WHEELS DIAMETER x WIDTH F/R	13x11/13 or 15x16in

TYRES F/R	Goodyear
LENGTH	160in - 4064mm
WIDTH OF CHASSIS AT COCKPIT	42in - 1066mm
HEIGHT OF REAR WING	34in - 864mm
WHEELBASE	100in - 2540mm
TRACK F/R	63/62in - 1600/1575mm
WEIGHT	1230lb - 558kg
PRINCIPAL DRIVERS	Hulme, Gethin, Oliver, Donohue, Hobbs, Redman
IDENTIFYING COLOURS	Papaya, Blue

1972 M19C
FORMULA 1

The other crucial change, initially made on the M19As but then carried over once the new M19Cs arrived later in the season, was the permanent adoption of conventional rear suspension.

That, and other subtle changes which led to better understanding of the rising rate front suspension, transformed the M19A. Peter Revson had done so well for McLaren in USAC and Can-Am in 1971 that he was promoted to the F1 team, returning to the category after initial outings in the mid-1960s as a privateer.

Back at Kyalami for the South African GP, Denny in M19A-2 was able to expunge his 1971 disappointment by winning as former motorcycle champion Mike Hailwood's Surtees retired. Revson brought M19A-1 home third to complete a highly satisfying weekend for the revitalised team. Later, the duo completed a McLaren 2-3 at the Österreichring, finishing just a second behind Emerson Fittipaldi in the all-conquering Lotus 72 that took the Brazilian to that season's title.

By then Denny was driving a revised car designated M19C-1 with Revvie taking over M19A-2 which had received some updated modifications itself when it had to be rebuilt around one of the simpler and lighter new monocoques after being crashed by Brian Redman, who stood in at Monaco and Clermont-Ferrand when Revson was racing in USAC events.

The M19C, which first appeared at the Race of Champions in March, took up where the revised M19A left off. Minor changes, such as the front bulkhead being fabricated rather than cast, together with lighter suspension wishbones, solid driveshafts of smaller diameter than the previous tubular components, and less complex mounts for the rear wing, all contributed to making the M19C lighter than its predecessor.

Denny scored points regularly: besides South Africa and Austria there were thirds in Belgium, Italy (which he inherited as Chris Amon's Matra lost its brakes and leader Jacky Ickx's Ferrari retired in the pits), Canada and America, plus a fifth in Britain. Revson also kept his end up; besides that third in South Africa he repeated the result in Britain and Austria, took second in Canada and fourth in Italy. Denny started from the front row five times, Revson once, and Denny set one fastest lap. The M19 had proved itself at last.

M19A-1 was rebuilt with larger fuel tanks for Redman to drive in the unique Rothmans 50,000 Formula Libre race at Brands Hatch, where he earned well for the team by finishing second behind Fittipaldi's Lotus.

Gordon Coppuck's new M23 was ready for 1973, but the M19Cs continued into the new season until sufficient M23s had been constructed. Modifications were limited to minor tweaks such as new F2 upright castings for the rear suspension, a new fabricated rear bulkhead, and a revised profile for the roll-over hoop. The rear suspension was also revised again, the better to accommodate the requirements of Goodyear's massive new 26-inch wide rear tyres.

The season kicked off this time in Argentina, where Denny avoided a big shunt when his throttle jammed open in qualifying. He finished a lapped fifth, Revson eighth. In the Brazilian Grand Prix at Interlagos he was lying in third place when his clutch began to malfunction, obliging him to drive the rest of the race in top gear. He got away with it, retaining his podium place in the wake of another Fittipaldi victory. Revson, fighting food poisoning, lasted only three laps before suffering gearbox failure.

The Rothmans 50,000 race at Brands Hatch in August 1972 was officially a Super Formula Libre race with everything from Group 6 sportscars to works Formula 1 cars taking part. Brian Redman drove the heavily revised M19A-1 chassis and was the only serious challenge to winner Emerson Fittipaldi in his JPS Lotus 72.

New sponsor for 1972, the Yardley cosmetics company, brought a change of colours and a new driver to the team. Peter Revson joined Denny Hulme and scored his first World Championship points in only his second race for the team at Kyalami. At the Belgian Grand Prix (left) he could only finish seventh.

Jody Scheckter took over Denny's car as a third works entry in his native South Africa, as the New Zealander got his hands on the new M23. The young South African started from the front row, took the lead when Denny sustained a puncture, but was overhauled by Jackie Stewart's victorious Tyrrell and was forced to retire with tyre problems and a broken engine. Revson fought his way home second, half a second ahead of an attacking Fittipaldi, and stayed there when a protest from McLaren that Stewart had passed Scheckter under a yellow flag was thrown out.

That was the end of the Grand Prix road for the M19, but an early car was acquired by club racer Brian Robinson, who had it fitted with a Chevrolet V8 for Formula 5000 racing. In 1973 his best results were a seventh, an eighth and a ninth, but 1974 yielded joint 12th overall in the European Formula 5000 Championship as he scored a fourth, a fifth, a seventh and two 10ths to add to second place in a race of attrition at Snetterton in October. In 1975, with the wide nose fitted, he finished ninth overall, netting a third, a fourth, two sixths, a seventh, an eighth and a ninth. There was also talk in the Press of upcoming Frenchman René Arnoux racing a Shell-backed M19A mid-season, but nothing came of it.

MODEL	McLaren M19C
TYPE/FORMULA	Formula 1
YEAR OF PRODUCTION	1972/1973
DESIGNER	Ralph Bellamy
EXAMPLES BUILT	2
ENGINE	Ford Cosworth DFV
CUBIC CAPACITY	2993cc
CARBURATION	Lucas fuel injection
POWER OUTPUT	450bhp

TRANSMISSION	Hewland DG400 5-speed
CHASSIS	Full aluminium monocoque, steel bulkheads
BODY	Formed by monocoque, GRP nosecone
FRONT SUSPENSION	Double wishbone, with push rod and rocker
	operating inboard coil spring/damper, anti-roll bar
REAR SUSPENSION	Lower wishbone, adjustable top link, twin radius
	rods, outboard coil spring/damper, anti-roll bar
BRAKES F/R	Outboard/inboard 10.5in ventilated discs
WHEELS DIAMETER x WIDTH F/R	13x11/13x16 or 17in

TYRES F/R	Goodyear
LENGTH	178in - 4521mm
WIDTH	84in - 2134mm
HEIGHT OF AIRBOX	45in - 1143mm
WHEELBASE	100in - 2540mm
TRACK F/R	63/63in - 1600/1600mm
WEIGHT	1257lb - 570kg
PRINCIPAL DRIVERS	Hulme, Revson, Scheckter
IDENTIFYING COLOURS	White/Papaya/Brown

1972 M20
CAN-AM

The M8 concept had finally reached its conclusion by the end of 1971, and the M20 became the staple for the 1972 Can-Am Championship. Underlining the intensity of the latest challenge, reigning World Champion Jackie Stewart joined Denny Hulme, to replace Peter Revson, who planned to concentrate solely on Formula 1.

In response to Porsche's monster turbocharged 917/10K, Gordon Coppuck planned a car quite different to the M8, with bigger brakes, the weight concentrated within the wheelbase, and the driver isolated from the radiators which were now located amidships.

McLaren had hoped to produce a turbo engine of its own using a Chevrolet block as the basis, but lack of development time ultimately obliged it to settle for another normally aspirated V8, Chevy's aluminium 8.1-litre. In addition to mounting this slightly forward, the new chassis also relocated the 79 US gallon fuel load in twin cells mounted in each of the side pontoons and linked them via an 18-gallon tank located behind and beneath the driver's seat across the full width of the structure.

The M20 also featured a wing across the front, working in conjunction with a strut-mounted rear wing slung between the usual M8D/M8F-style fins. Once again, the car also featured full-length fences atop the bodyshell to control airflow. It was hoped that the revised front end would fix a perennial understeer problem. The engine, still a stressed member, transaxle, suspension, brakes and wheels were all familiar. The chassis was constructed from 16 and 20-gauge L72 aluminium alloy with argon-welded steel bulkheads providing suspension pick-up points.

Only three M20s were built, but once pre-season testing began hopes for the new car were high. With happy

memories of 19 consecutive wins between 1968 and '70, McLaren was confident it could retain its mastery of Can-Am despite Porsche's burgeoning challenge.

In testing at Silverstone Denny and Jackie clocked up record-breaking lap times, but before the start of the Can-Am season Stewart was forced to stand down on doctors' orders after being diagnosed with a stomach ulcer. Revson was hastily called up. The other unsettling news was that Porsche's campaign would be run by Roger Penske, and that naturally meant that technically minded Mark Donohue would pilot the awesome 917/10K.

The first race of the season – the 50th in Can-Am history – was at Mosport in June where, in a foretaste of what was to come, Donohue's Porsche took pole. Revson was second on the grid and Denny third. Donohue lost the lead with induction issues and, despite jumping the start Revson was able to take the advantage from Denny, whose engine was sick. Then Revson's engine broke with two laps to go, handing the win to Denny. Revson was classified third. Already the alarm bells were beginning to ring in Colnbrook thanks to Porsche's competitive pace.

McLaren improved the brakes, tyres and aerodynamics in time for practice at Road Atlanta, where Revson blew an engine. Denny took the pole after running neck and neck with George Follmer in the Penske 917. Follmer had been drafted in to replace Donohue, who had been injured in an accident during a test the previous week which had written off his 917/10K. In a dramatic race, Follmer surged to victory first time out after Denny backflipped his M20 at over 180mph while giving chase. Revson had stopped at that very spot with an ignition problem, saw the whole incident, and helped to rescue Denny who was knocked out and briefly hospitalised but otherwise unhurt. The M20 was written off.

At Watkins Glen a fortnight later, tough old Denny was back at the wheel of the M20 prototype. Despite a lingering headache he qualified right behind Revson, who took the pole. In the race that order was quickly reversed as Denny raced to his 22nd Can-Am win and he and Revson secured McLaren's first 1-2 of the season. At Mid-Ohio, however, Denny finished only fourth after five tyre changes, and Peter retired. Follmer won. Road America saw Denny on pole and leading until ignition problems on the 12th lap; after Revson retired, Follmer won again.

At Donnybrooke both McLaren drivers struggled in practice as a recovered Donohue joined Follmer for an all Porsche the front row. None of them finished; François Cevert won in Greg Young's M8F after Denny's engine blew. Revson took up the cudgels until a valve dropped. Donohue blew a tyre, and Follmer ran out of fuel on the last lap while leading. Edmonton saw another second place for Denny and sixth for Revson, but Donohue won with Follmer third after dropping back with a puncture. Porsche was steadily pulling ahead, and when both McLarens retired in the Monterey GP at Laguna Seca, and Donohue let Follmer by into the lead close to the finish to win, the American veteran took the title.

At the Riverside finale 'The Bear's' final Can-Am race ended with another engine failure, leaving Revson to finish second behind Follmer. An era had ended, and with-it McLaren's domination of the Canadian American Challenge Cup series. With its place in the record books assured, the works team never returned.

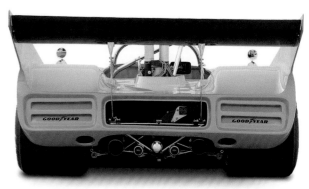

MODEL	McLaren M20
TYPE/FORMULA	Can-Am
YEAR OF PRODUCTION	1972
DESIGNER	Gordon Coppuck
EXAMPLES BUILT	3
ENGINE	Chevrolet V8
CUBIC CAPACITY	8095cc
CARBURATION	Lucas fuel injection
POWER OUTPUT	750bhp

TRANSMISSION	Hewland LG MkII 4-speed
CHASSIS	Aluminium sheet monocoque, with steel bulkheads
BODY	Monocoque sides, GRP body sections, integral wing
FRONT SUSPENSION	Single top link & radius arm, lower wishbone,
	outboard coil spring/damper, anti-roll bar
REAR SUSPENSION	Twin parallel lower links, single top link,
	twin radius rods, coil spring/damper, anti-roll bar
BRAKES F/R	Outboard/inboard 11.8in discs
WHEELS DIAMETER x WIDTH F/R	15x11/15x17in

TYRES F/R	Goodyear
LENGTH	178in - 4521mm
WIDTH	81in - 2057mm
HEIGHT AT TAIL	46in - 1168mm
WHEELBASE	100in - 2540mm
TRACK F/R	61.8/60in - 1570/1524mm
WEIGHT	1520lb - 689kg
PRINCIPAL DRIVERS	Hulme, Revson, Hobbs
IDENTIFYING COLOURS	Papaya/Blue

The key ingredient in McLaren's short-lived return to Formula 2, after an absence of four years, was the Impact-sponsored M21 that upcoming South African Jody Scheckter chauffeured to a classy victory over champion-elect Mike Hailwood at Crystal Palace. Another Ralph Bellamy design, and the best-looking car in its class at the time, the neat little machine boasted a low monocoque, distinctive large cockpit surround and a sharp nose with a pronounced and aggressive lower lip.

The M21 was designed to accept both the Broadspeed-developed 1.8-litre BDA engine or one of only four specially prepared 2-litre Cosworth BDGs. The simple monocoque used 16-gauge aluminium side panels, with 18-gauge material employed elsewhere. Lower wishbones were employed at both ends together with outboard spring/ damper units; the front suspension incorporated a single top link and rearward radius rods with the wishbone reversed. At the rear transverse links and twin radius rods were used. It was just about the biggest car in that year's F2 series, but in Scheckter's hands it proved highly effective.

After successful testing by team stalwarts Denny Hulme and Peter Gethin, the papaya orange car was first shown to the press with no visible sponsorship livery. Shortly afterwards the commercial building and property group, Impact BS Holdings Limited, came on board keen to raise its profile via motorsport after moving into vehicle rental and petrol retailing. World Champion-to-be Scheckter was entered in all the European F2 and John Player F2 Championship rounds. Hopes went unrealised for a second car to be built for Barry Newman or Howden Ganley to drive.

Scheckter made his debut with the M21 at Mallory Park on March 12th for the opening round of the European Championship, which was also the opener for the John

Player series. The car ran on Goodyear tyres and with the larger capacity Cosworth engine, the Broadspeed having blown a head gasket earlier in the week. Being a McLaren, reported Autosport four days later, the M21 "was of course immaculately turned out."

The results were an aggregate of two heats, and underrated Briton David Morgan's Brabham took the flag ahead of Niki Lauda and Carlos Reutemann. Scheckter was fourth, 42.2s behind Morgan after a suffering a misfire and trouble selecting the right gears. With the McLaren finishing ahead of the works cars of Mike Hailwood (Surtees) and Ronnie Peterson (March) in a 20-car field, Autosport suggested that it was "a very deserving fourth after a sensible first outing."

Scheckter non-started at Hockenheim, then ran with the Broadspeed engine at Pau for the fourth round of the European Championship. Despite finishing a good sixth in his heat, he was denied a place in the final following some 'creative' rule bending to allow Frenchman Jean-Pierre Beltoise to participate.

The Whitsun weekend in May provided the highlight of the year for the M21 and for McLaren as its cars scored wins in three major categories worldwide. Mark Donohue in Roger Penske's M16B triumphed in the Indianapolis 500; Denny won the Oulton Park Gold Cup in an M19A, and Jody won the Euro round at Crystal Palace after a performance that stunned the more experienced graded drivers and rival F2 teams. He beat Hailwood by two seconds after a gripping wheel-to-wheel battle.

A month later at Rouen, Scheckter was quickest in a wet practice session on the Friday. Then, after leading his heat comfortably until he was forced into the pits, he fought hard

Left: The European Formula 2 round at Crystal Palace in May of 1972 was the bright orange, M21's finest hour. South African driver Jody Scheckter won an exciting race from champion elect Mike Hailwood in his Matchbox-Surtees TS-15.

Above: After three years away from Formula 2 McLaren returned with the purposeful looking Ford BDA-engined M21. The Ralph Bellamy-designed M21 was modelled on his M19 design and was the biggest car on the F2 grid in 1972.

in the final to overhaul Hailwood, Emerson Fittipaldi and Reutemann. He was scorchingly fast, matching the pace of the leaders as he ran 10s behind, and eventually neither Reutemann, François Cevert nor Beltoise could resist his challenge. He was safe in third place and was just about to challenge for second, after Hailwood had spun, when his engine failed due to a crack in the block caused earlier in the day when it had overheated. He was classified 11th.

Generally, the luck ran against Scheckter and the Impact M21 that season, and they ended the year eighth overall in the European F2 standings. The result was not a genuine reflection of the combination's potential, and consideration was given to putting the car into limited production for 1973, but plans were eventually shelved.

The design lived on, however. After considering converting the M19A into a production Formula 5000 car, Trojan elected to take the simpler chassis from the M21 and the rear end from the M22 to create a contender for the 'big banger' single seater series which was initially codenamed M21X. Completed by a concave, full-width nose, the design eventually became the 1973 Trojan T101. It was not a pukka McLaren, but its antecedents were clear and it upheld McLaren honour in the formula by scoring five victories in the UK series that year.

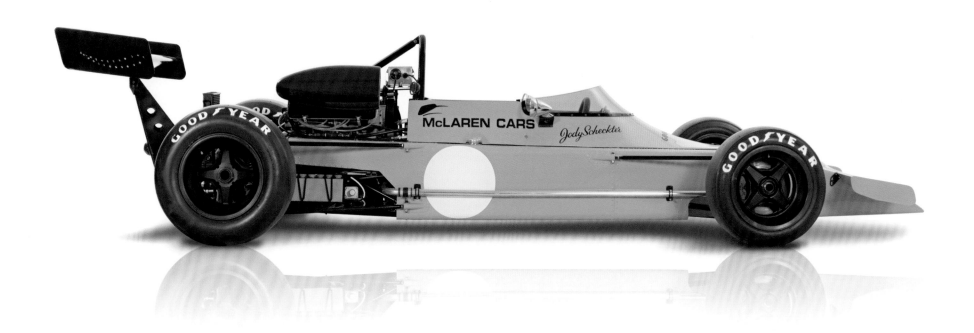

MODEL	McLaren M21	TRANSMISSION	Hewland FG400 5-speed	TYRES F/R	Goodyear
TYPE/FORMULA	Formula 2	CHASSIS	Full aluminium monocoque, steel bulkheads	LENGTH	160in - 4064mm
YEAR OF PRODUCTION	1972	BODY	Formed by monocoque, GRP nosecone	WIDTH	74in - 1880mm
DESIGNER	Ralph Bellamy	FRONT SUSPENSION	Single top link & radius arm, lower wishbone,	HEIGHT AT WING	36in - 914mm
EXAMPLES BUILT	1		outboard coil spring/damper, anti-roll bar	WHEELBASE	92in - 2337mm
ENGINE	Ford Cosworth BDA or BDF 4-cylinder	REAR SUSPENSION	Reverse lower wishbone, single top link,	TRACK F/R	58/60in - 1473/1524mm
CUBIC CAPACITY	1899/1998cc		twin radius rods, coil spring/damper, anti-roll bar	WEIGHT	1036lb - 470kg
CARBURATION	Lucas fuel injection	BRAKES F/R	Outboard ventilated/inboard solid discs	PRINCIPAL DRIVERS	Scheckter
POWER OUTPUT	250+bhp	WHEELS DIAMETER x WIDTH F/R	13x10/13x16in	IDENTIFYING COLOURS	Papaya

1972 McLAREN-TROJAN M22 FORMULA 5000

With McLaren devoting more of its time to the increasingly prestigious and more lucrative Formula 1, Indy and Can-Am championships, the Formula 5000 M22 became one of the least known of its single seaters.

The company's M10A and M10B models had been the class of Formula 5000 in 1969 and '70, in both the UK and America, and later in Australia and New Zealand. The replacement model, the stressed-engine M18, proved to be much less successful. It was hard to set up and its handling could be unpredictable, and even a driver of Brian Redman's talent could only muster two victories in the 1971 season. In a bid to improve the car another British F5000 star, David Hobbs, was brought into the fold in late 1971 to test a modified M18. Described as the M18/22, or sometimes even just M22, in contemporary reports it was intended to be the prototype for a totally new M22 which would race in 1972.

Hobbs and the car were sent to Pukekohe in New Zealand in January that year for the opening round of the Tasman Championship. Once a series for 2.5-litre Formula 1 cars, it had adopted Formula 5000 rules as well from 1970 onwards. Against the likes of former F1 driver Frank Gardner in a Lola T300, Mike Hailwood in a works Surtees TS8B and local hero Graham McRae in a Leda GM1, Hobbs took the M18/22 with its additional cooling courtesy of a pair of side-mounted radiators, to seventh on the grid. In the 101.5-mile race he reached third position by the 48th lap and eventually finished there, half a minute behind winner Gardner but a more respectable 4.1s shy of runner-up Hailwood. It was

nevertheless clear that the M18/22, which was still running with the M18's squared nose rather than the M21-inspired scooped version that would follow, had inherited rather too much from the M18.

The car failed to score in Levin, Wigram, Teretonga and Warwick Farm, but after another third at Sandown Park and fourth at Surfers' Paradise, Hobbs struck gold in Adelaide when he won the final round from Hailwood and Teddy Pilette's M10B.

The Autosport story from Sandown had reported: "*David Hobbs, who has not been having a happy time recently in the Kirk F White-entered M22, seems to have got it sorted out.*" and suggested that the car "*was much improved.*" In Adelaide Hobbs was second only to local star Frank Matich in his eponymous Matich A50, qualifying ahead of McRae, Hailwood and Pilette. He got away third, fell to fourth behind Hailwood, survived a spin, and then inherited victory when McRae's engine failed, Matich broke his differential, and Hailwood lost time with a rear tyre failure on the main straight on the 48th of the 70 laps. The result lifted him to joint fifth overall with M10B-mounted Kevin Bartlett on 20 points, compared to the 39 of champion McRae.

Back at Colnbrook the works was completing the first production version of the M22 for the European F5000 series. This to all intents and purposes resembled the M18/22, but now had the shovel-shaped nose with protruding lower lip. At some point Trojan would have been expecting to

In the July round of the European F5000 championship at Brands Hatch, Teddy Pilette drove the VDS Racing M22 for the first time. During the early part of the season he had been forced to rely on the team's older, heavily modified 18/22 chassis.

The M22 was the last car to be built under the McLaren-Trojan partnership and the car photographed here was the last of the three M22s built. McLaren was to concentrate its efforts on Formula 1 and Indianapolis, while Trojan went on to build its own cars.

productionise the new car for private customers, but by this time McLaren's interest had waned to such a degree that there was little point in continuing.

Pilette raced the M22 in Europe for Count Rudi van der Straaten's VDS Racing Team. Delivery of the car was delayed and he too had to resort to the old M18/22, but met with little success. He was the slowest to qualify for the Race of Champions at Brands Hatch in March, a full six seconds off Emerson Fittipaldi's pace and, in the race itself, finished three laps behind in 13th place overall but second in F5000 to Allan Rollinson's Lola T300.

The following month, at Silverstone for the International Trophy, he improved his overall finishing position by only two places and was fourth in F5000. The M22 was ready for the Oulton Park Gold Cup meeting in May where, after finishing fifth in the F5000 race and as Denny won in the M19A, Pilette finished ninth, and fifth F5000 home in the Gold Cup race. Elsewhere, in the Rothmans European F5000 series, he picked up two seconds, a fourth and a fifth in the M18/22, then a third, a fourth, a fifth, and an eighth in the M22 to finish fifth overall on 25 points to Surtees-mounted champion Gijs van Lennep's 65. It had been an up and down season that provided a muted postscript to McLaren's otherwise illustrious time in Formula 5000.

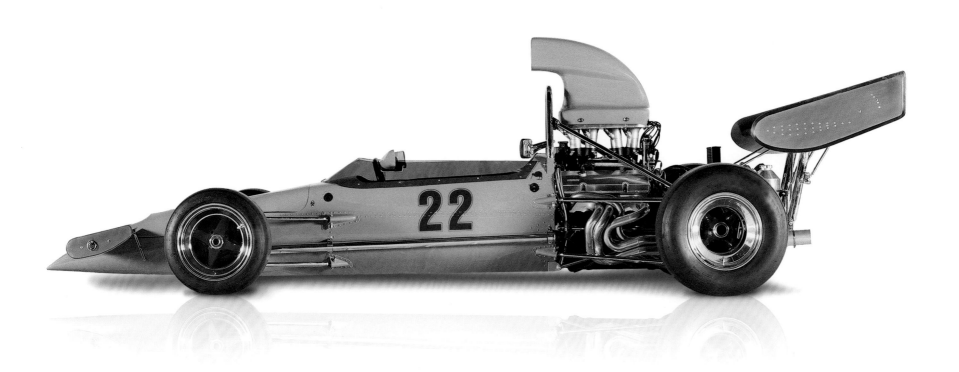

MODEL	McLaren-Trojan M22		TRANSMISSION	Hewland DG500 5-speed		TYRES F/R	Goodyear
TYPE/FORMULA	Formula 5000		CHASSIS	Full aluminium monocoque, steel bulkheads		LENGTH	176in - 4470mm
YEAR OF PRODUCTION	1972		BODY	Formed by monocoque, GRP nose & radiator shroud		WIDTH	77in - 1956mm
DESIGNER	Gordon Coppuck		FRONT SUSPENSION	Single top link & radius arm, lower wishbone,		HEIGHT OF AIRBOX	50in - 1270mm
EXAMPLES BUILT	3			outboard coil spring/damper, anti-roll bar		WHEELBASE	100in - 2540mm
ENGINE	Chevrolet V8		REAR SUSPENSION	Reverse lower wishbone, single top link,		TRACK F/R	59.5/59.75in - 1511/1517mm
CUBIC CAPACITY	4950cc			twin radius rods, coil spring/damper, anti-roll bar		WEIGHT	1450lb - 657kg
CARBURATION	Lucas fuel injection		BRAKES F/R	Outboard/inboard 10.5in discs		PRINCIPAL DRIVERS	Hobbs, Pilette
POWER OUTPUT	540bhp		WHEELS DIAMETER x WIDTH F/R	13x11/15x16in		IDENTIFYING COLOURS	n/a

1973 M23
FORMULA 1

The McLaren M23 was one of the most outstanding designs of its era and was designed by Gordon Coppuck for new regulations which, from the Spanish GP on April 29th, required fuel tanks to be protected by new deformable structures. He opted for a wedge shape and integral sidepods to achieve that. A modified form of the M19's complex rising-rate suspension was used at the front, and a much simpler interpretation at the rear.

It was immediately obvious that McLaren's new car was a very serious contender. Denny Hulme liked it straight away and in testing at Kyalami, prior to its debut in the South African GP, it easily chalked up faster times than the M19A. *"It oversteers and stays out there in a nice comfortable slide,"* he said.

He revelled in it as he secured his first-ever Grand Prix pole position. And he led from the start, as Jody Scheckter pushed his M19C into second place ahead of Emerson Fittipaldi's Lotus and Revson's M19C. Denny seemed capable of running away with the race, but there had been a fiery accident on the third lap and he picked up a puncture on debris and pitted for a replacement tyre on the fifth lap, then had to do the same thing again four laps later. As Jackie Stewart raced through to win from Revson, Denny recovered to fifth place after a strong run back from 19th place on lap 10.

It took a while to recapture the Kyalami form, however. Clutch trouble cost Denny his chances in the Brands Race of Champions and he was lucky to finish second only millimetres ahead of hungry debutant James Hunt, in a Surtees TS9B hired by Lord Hesketh. Revson was fourth in the International Trophy race at Silverstone. Back on the Grand Prix trail, the American was fourth and Denny sixth in Spain, but a front-row start for Denny in Belgium resulted in only seventh place after he slid off on oil. In Monaco they were fifth and sixth, Revson leading Denny home. And then came Sweden, and payback for Kyalami.

Denny qualified only sixth, behind Ronnie Peterson's Lotus, the Tyrrells of François Cevert and Jackie Stewart, Emerson Fittipaldi's Lotus and Carlos Reutemann's Brabham. Revson was seventh. Early on he was happy to follow Peterson, Fittipaldi, Cevert, Stewart and Reutemann, before picking off the Argentinian. Then he was baulked by Jackie Oliver in a Shadow, who threw dirt into the M23's throttle slides. He resigned himself to the almost inevitable pit stop, but suddenly the slides freed up. By now he had lost 15 seconds and was angry. Switching off his rev limiter, he charged. He caught Cevert on lap 61, then Fittipaldi and Stewart hit brake problems. Suddenly the M23 was second and hauling in Peterson, the local hero. Maybe Denny could have done it without the intervention of Fate, but with two laps to run the Lotus picked up a puncture, and the race was McLaren's. It was the M23's first triumph, and richly deserved.

Another victory was on the cards in the French GP at Paul Ricard, as Jody Scheckter had his first outing in an M23. He qualified on the front row between polesitter Stewart and Fittipaldi, and grabbed the early lead. Neither Peterson nor Fittipaldi could dislodge him, but the stalemate ended when Fittipaldi's attempt to overtake Scheckter backfired on the 42nd lap and they collided. Jody got going in second place as Emerson retired on the spot, but a lap later McLaren number eight was in the pits with damaged suspension. Denny was a delayed eighth.

Revson made it three M23s when he returned at Silverstone, and prior to qualifying on the front row with a time equal to Denny's he bet £100 on himself to win at 14 to 1. It was a prescient move.

Peterson led the opening lap from pole position, but Stewart leapt up from the second row and suckered him for the lead at Becketts. As they approached the finish line at the end of

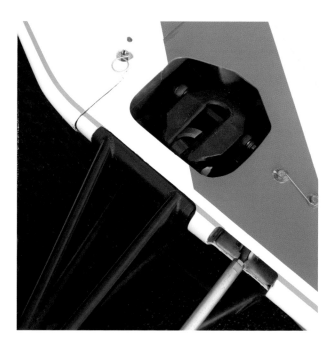

the lap, Reutemann was chasing them and then came two McLarens, side by side as Jody squeaked past Denny. But the South African's car slid ever wider until it was on the grass on the exit to Woodcote corner and then spun a complete 360 degrees before crunching head-on into the pit wall and bouncing back into the path of the rest of the field. Mayhem ensued. By the time the dust settled, and the race was red flagged, nine cars were out of the running. When the race was restarted, Peterson soon established a lead from Fittipaldi, Revson, Denny and James Hunt, now driving a March. Fittipaldi broke a driveshaft on the 37th lap, and Revson closed in on Peterson and passed him on the 39th before pulling away to score his maiden Grand Prix triumph. It was 'Champagne Peter's' greatest day. Denny just fended off Hunt for third.

Peter finished fourth in Holland as Denny's engine broke, then Ickx had a one-off ride deputising for USAC-occupied Revson in Germany to finish third. In Austria Revson lost his clutch on the first lap and, having had handling trouble at the Nürburgring, Denny now ran into problems with a plug lead while fighting the Lotuses for the lead. Monza yielded third for Revson as Denny had brake trouble. Then came Canada, where Revson was awarded a second victory after complications with deployment of the pace car for the first time in a Grand Prix threw lap charts into hopeless confusion. Denny was 13th as Scheckter blotted his copybook again by colliding with Cevert as they squabbled over fourth place. In the final race of the season, the USGP at Watkins Glen, Denny led Revson home in fourth place, as Jody retired with broken rear suspension.

Three victories, and the other good placings, left McLaren a strong third in the Constructors' World Championship, behind Lotus and Tyrrell.

Denny Hulme qualified a strong third on the grid for the Monaco Grand Prix but made a terrible start and slipped down to ninth place. A later spin dropped him down the order and he could only finish sixth, two laps down on winner Jackie Stewart.

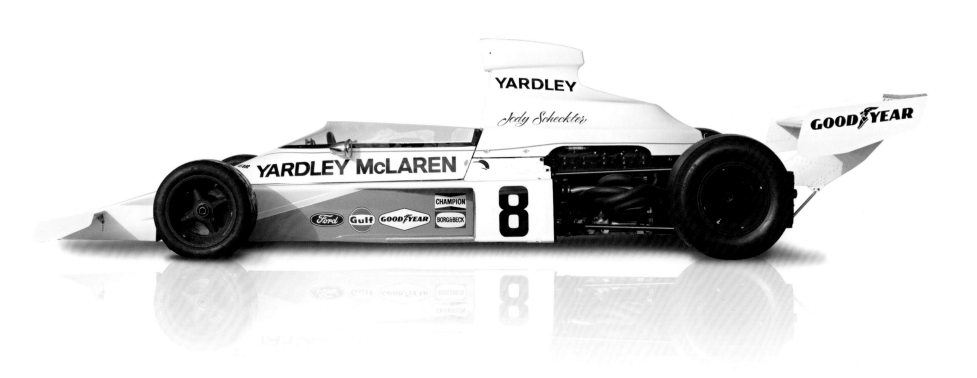

MODEL	McLaren M23	TRANSMISSION	Hewland DG400 5-speed	TYRES F/R	Goodyear
TYPE/FORMULA	Formula 1	CHASSIS	Deformable double skinned aluminium monocoque	LENGTH	170in - 4318mm
YEAR OF PRODUCTION	1973	BODY	Monocoque lower, GRP nose, cockpit & engine cover	WIDTH	80in - 2032mm
DESIGNER	Gordon Coppuck	FRONT SUSPENSION	Tubular upper rocker arm, operating inboard	HEIGHT OF AIRBOX	46in - 1169mm
EXAMPLES BUILT	4		coil spring/damper, lower wishbone, anti-roll bar	WHEELBASE	101in - 2565mm
ENGINE	Ford Cosworth DFV	REAR SUSPENSION	Adjustable top link, reverse lower wishbone,	TRACK F/R	65.5/62.5in - 1664/1587mm
CUBIC CAPACITY	2993cc		twin radius rods, coil spring/damper, anti-roll bar	WEIGHT	1270lb - 576kg
CARBURATION	Lucas fuel injection	BRAKES F/R	Outboard/inboard ventilated discs	PRINCIPAL DRIVERS	Hulme, Revson, Scheckter, Ickx
POWER OUTPUT	460bhp	WHEELS DIAMETER x WIDTH F/R	13x11/13x18in	IDENTIFYING COLOURS	White/Papaya/Brown

1973 M16C, M16C/D & M16E
INDYCAR

Throughout 1972 Indy racing speeds had soared. After qualifying at Indianapolis at 195.940mph, Bobby Unser had taken his Eagle round Michigan International Speedway at 199.889 and, after team-mate Jerry Grant did one lap at 201.414 at Ontario, Unser upped that the next day to 201.965s. The rulemakers at USAC, realising they had opened Pandora's Box when they relaxed wing regulations, attempted to reduce speeds for 1973.

McLaren built six new M16Cs, which sported a new full-length cowling to smooth airflow between the headrest and a new rear wing that was similar to that fitted to the Formula One M23. Airflow was further improved by adopting a more rounded cockpit surround, and the radiator ducts were also subtly reshaped.

Joining Peter Revson this time for the Indy 500 was the fleet but often unlucky Johnny Rutherford, 'Lone Star JR' from Texas. He quickly set the scene by qualifying on pole at 198.413mph and was the quickest driver/car combination of the whole weekend. Revson qualified 10th at 192.606, but for the works team that was to be as good as it got. Rutherford was soon black-flagged after a fuel leak, then lost boost pressure and ultimately finished ninth. The race was initially rained off, restarted two days later and then spiralled into a nightmare involving Swede Savage's ultimately fatal accident and the death of STP mechanic Armando Teran. Revson crashed after just three laps, in Turn Four. The best placed McLaren was the blue and white Lindsey Hopkins Buick-sponsored ex-works M16A of Roger McCluskey, which finished third. Later, McCluskey used the same car to win the Michigan 200.

Rutherford later won twice at Ontario and at Michigan, while Gary Bettenhausen won the Texas 200 in Penske's M16C. The fly in the works team's ointment was the withdrawal of Gulf Oil's sponsorship at the end of the season.

USAC sought to enhance safety for 1974, requiring smaller 40-gallon fuel tanks to be more safely accommodated within the centre section of the monocoque and on the left of the car, away from the more vulnerable right-hand side that was always nearer to the unforgiving wall. Overall length was also reduced in order to restrict wing size and an 80in/Hg pop-off valve was mandated on all turbo-engined cars to restrict boost. Cars would now be required to stop at least six times during 500-mile races.

McLaren's response was the new version of the trusty M16 designated M16C/D, which gained a much more pronounced M23-style cockpit cowling, had its nose truncated again, and was fitted with a new monocoque-pillar rear wing with a sharply curved-section aerofoil, also taken from its Formula 1 cousin. The engine cowl was also modified to stop short of the wing.

After missing the first weekend of qualifying and the chance to be at the front of the field, Rutherford could only qualify a lowly 25th. But his speed of 190.446mph was impressive and would have put him second on the grid. David Hobbs, in the second, Carling Black Label-sponsored, M16C/D qualified ninth at 184.833 mph.

Rutherford still had a chance. By lap 65 he was fighting for the lead with 191.632mph polesitter A. J. Foyt's Coyote. Then Foyt's scavenge pump broke on lap 143 and Rutherford was left leading Bobby Unser's Eagle by a margin of 22s. Reeling off the remaining laps without incident, he handed McLaren a second Indy victory, and the first for the works team.

The winner's purse was $245,032 from the total prize money pool of $1,015,686. To add to the euphoria, Hobbs brought his car home fifth. Once again Rutherford triumphed in the Ontario 100, as well as in the Milwaukee 150 and another 500-miler, at Pocono.

In 1975 the now five-year old design morphed again, the new M16E being the work of Coppuck's new assistant, John Barnard, as he himself was flat-out on the F1 side. Indy veteran Lloyd Ruby joined Rutherford in the team, but the car's longer wheelbase and new parallel lower-link rear suspension failed to stem the bad luck which seemed to dog the career of the man whom a biography described as *the greatest driver never to win the Indy 500*. Having qualified his white, red and blue Allied Polymer car sixth at 186.986mph, Ruby was out with a burned piston on lap seven. For the rest of the field a freak rain storm cut the race to just 174 laps, with Bobby Unser's Eagle taking the flag after a long battle with A.J. Foyt and a disappointed Rutherford who had to be content with another second place for McLaren after qualifying his white, green and orange Gatorade-sponsored car seventh at 185.998mph. The race was also notable for the horrific mid-race accident which destroyed Tom Sneva's Norton Spirit Penske M16C/D which he had qualified fourth at 190.094mph. Miraculously, he was unharmed.

The even years were good for McLaren at Indianapolis at this time, and JR won once again in 1976 in a slightly updated M16E sponsored by Hy-Gain, which he had planted on the pole at 188.957mph. That was not the fastest speed of qualifying, however. Mario Andretti in Penske's Cam 2 Motor Oil M16C/D achieved 189.404mph, albeit on the second weekend which thus obliged him to start 19th under Indy's rules. Rutherford struggled initially until the front wing angles were adjusted and the right-hand side tyres were changed. Then the M16E suddenly came to life and he established a comfortable lead by the time the race was flagged off because of rain after only 102 of the scheduled 200 laps. It was the shortest 500 on record, but that didn't bother JR who took McLaren's third, and final, victory in five years as the curtain came down on the M16's works career.

Johnny Rutherford at speed in the Boyd Jeffries McLaren-Offy M16C, August 1973. This shot was taken during the second heat run prior to the following week's 500-mile race at Ontario Motor Speedway in California.

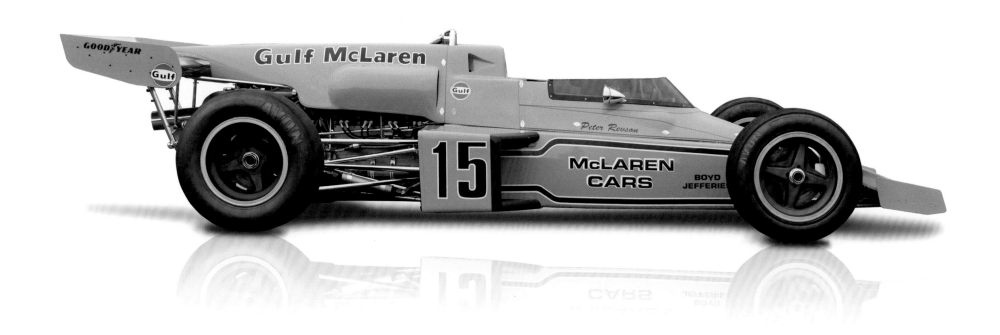

MODEL	McLaren M16C		TRANSMISSION	Hewland LG500 4-speed		TYRES F/R	Goodyear
TYPE/FORMULA	Indianapolis/USAC		CHASSIS	Full aluminium monocoque, steel bulkheads		LENGTH	162in - 4115mm
YEAR OF PRODUCTION	1973		BODY	Monocoque sides, GRP nose & cockpit, engine cover		WIDTH	76in - 1930mm
DESIGNER	Gordon Coppuck		FRONT SUSPENSION	Welded cantilever top arm operating		HEIGHT	39in - 991mm
EXAMPLES BUILT	6			inboard coil spring/damper, lower wishbone		WHEELBASE	101in - 2565mm
ENGINE	Offenhauser 4-cylinder turbo		REAR SUSPENSION	Reverse lower wishbone, top link, twin		TRACK F/R	58/58in - 1473/1473mm
CUBIC CAPACITY	2600cc			radius rods, coil spring/damper, anti-roll bar		WEIGHT	1380lb - 626kg
CARBURATION	Hilborn injection, Garrett Airesearch turbocharger		BRAKES F/R	Outboard 11.9in discs		PRINCIPAL DRIVERS	Rutherford, Revson
POWER OUTPUT	770bhp		WHEELS DIAMETER x WIDTH F/R	15x10/15x14in		IDENTIFYING COLOURS	Papaya

MODEL	McLaren M16C/D	TRANSMISSION	Hewland LG500 4-speed	TYRES F/R	Goodyear
NAME/FORMULA	Indianapolis/USAC	CHASSIS	Full aluminium monocoque, steel bulkheads	LENGTH	175in - 4445mm
YEAR OF PRODUCTION	1974	BODY	Monocoque sides, GRP nose & cockpit, engine cover	WIDTH	76in - 1930mm
DESIGNER	Gordon Coppuck	FRONT SUSPENSION	Welded cantilever top arm operating	HEIGHT	39in - 991mm
VOLUME	6 (included in M16C)		inboard coil spring/damper, lower wishbone	WHEELBASE	104in - 2642mm
ENGINE	Offenhauser 4-cylinder turbo	REAR SUSPENSION	Reverse lower wishbone, top link, twin	TRACK F/R	58/58in - 1473/1473mm
CUBIC CAPACITY	2600cc		radius rods, coil spring/damper, anti-roll bar	WEIGHT	1380lb - 626kg
CARBURATION	Hilborn injection, Garrett Airesearch turbocharger	BRAKES F/R	Outboard 11.9in discs	PRINCIPAL DRIVERS	Rutherford, Hobbs, Hiss
POWER OUTPUT	780bhp	WHEELS DIAMETER x WIDTH F/R	15x10/15x14in	IDENTIFYING COLOURS	Papaya

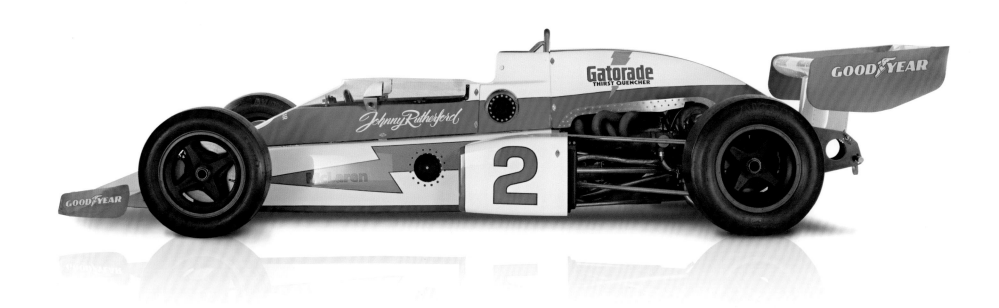

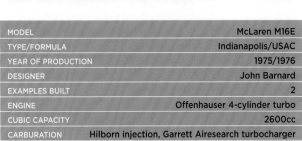

MODEL	McLaren M16E	TRANSMISSION	Hewland LG500 4-speed	TYRES F/R	Goodyear
TYPE/FORMULA	Indianapolis/USAC	CHASSIS	Full aluminium monocoque, steel bulkheads	LENGTH	177in - 4496mm
YEAR OF PRODUCTION	1975/1976	BODY	Monocoque sides, GRP nose & cockpit, engine cover	WIDTH	78in - 1981mm
DESIGNER	John Barnard	FRONT SUSPENSION	Welded cantilever top arm operating	HEIGHT	39in - 991mm
EXAMPLES BUILT	2		inboard coil spring/damper, lower wishbone	WHEELBASE	106in - 2692mm
ENGINE	Offenhauser 4-cylinder turbo	REAR SUSPENSION	Reverse lower wishbone, top link, twin	TRACK F/R	58/58in - 1473/1473mm
CUBIC CAPACITY	2600cc		radius rods, coil spring/damper, anti-roll bar	WEIGHT	1380lb - 626kg
CARBURATION	Hilborn injection, Garrett Airesearch turbocharger	BRAKES F/R	Outboard 11.9in discs	PRINCIPAL DRIVERS	Rutherford, Ruby
POWER OUTPUT	780bhp	WHEELS DIAMETER x WIDTH F/R	15x10/15x14in	IDENTIFYING COLOURS	White/Green

The M23 had plenty of development left in it for 1974, and the really significant change was the creation of the Texaco-Marlboro McLaren superteam, as 1972 World Champion Emerson Fittipaldi quit Lotus to join Denny in M23s that were now painted red and white. It was a major coup for McLaren that brought in the sponsorship dollars to stage a major title assault, but a high degree of juggling was needed to placate Yardley. In the end, agreement was reached to run a third works car in its livery. Teddy Mayer's initial plan was to run Peter Revson in it, but the American finally lost patience with the ongoing negotiations and left to join Shadow in a decision that would ultimately cost him his life when he was the victim of suspension failure during testing at Kyalami. In his place, Phil Kerr would run the M23 for Mike Hailwood.

Prolonged winter testing by the enthusiastic Fittipaldi at Paul Ricard led to changes to the car, such as a longer wheelbase and wider track, based on his considerable experience of the Lotus 72. Years later, historic racer Willie Green would call it *"easily the best"* of the many 1970s Formula 1 machines he had driven round Brands Hatch. Good aerodynamics, he contended, *"were one of its strong suits and the lack of buffeting in the cockpit at high speeds bears this out."*

Gordon Coppuck described the car a decade and a half on as, *"The best F1 car for three years. Yes, it was a good design, but it also benefited from a lot of good development. The chassis changed very little, but we did a great deal of suspension work to keep it competitive. The chassis was much stiffer than those of our rivals' cars, but it was pretty flexible by modern standards."*

Compared to the previous season the M23's weight distribution had been improved by fitting a new bellhousing spacer between the engine and gearbox, hence the three-inch longer wheelbase. With an additional two inches of track, traction was also improved out of slow corners, while the rear wing was brought forward by 10 inches in order to comply with a new set of regulations. During the season three different wheelbase variations were employed, together with a distinctive narrow 'winklepicker' nose which saw

service at Brands Hatch, Jarama and Monaco where its wider wings generated more front-end downforce.

Fittipaldi loved testing. According to Coppuck, *"He enjoyed this side of his job more than the races."* That was to prove a valuable factor as a tough season progressed. It began superbly for the new team, though it was Denny who won the opening race in Argentina after passing Reutemann's ailing Brabham with two laps to run. Emerson inadvertently delayed himself while in a position to challenge for the win by knocking off the ignition. He finished 10th. But the Brazilian did not have to wait long to make amends, as he won his home event from pole position, finishing 13s ahead of Regazzoni.

In a year characterised by the battle with a newly emergent Ferrari team and its drivers, Niki Lauda and Clay Regazzoni, and the threats from Reutemann, Tyrrell's Jody Scheckter and Lotus's Ronnie Peterson, all of whom enjoyed victories, Emerson won again in Belgium and Canada to head into the final race, at Watkins Glen, neck-and-neck with Regazzoni.

Denny Hulme gets airborne on his way to seventh on the grid for the German Grand Prix at the Nürburgring. He was involved in a first lap accident that stopped the race, took to the spare car for the restart but was then disqualified.

In the Yardley car, meanwhile, Hailwood had some strong races, most notably the Dutch GP where he matched Fittipaldi as he raced home fourth behind the Marlboro car to add to another fourth in Argentina and third in South Africa. But his F1 career ended when his M23 landed badly on a jump at the Nürburgring and crashed heavily, inflicting leg injuries. David Hobbs drove the car in Austria and Italy, before upcoming German Jochen Mass left Surtees to take over the car for the two final races.

The American shootout went Emerson's way as he brought the M23 home fourth to clinch his second world title, and the first-ever World Championship for the McLaren marque. That day was historic for two other reasons: it marked the end of McLaren's association with Yardley; and Denny's final Grand Prix appearance. His engine failed after four laps. Without 'The Bear's' mountainous courage in the aftermath of Bruce's death, there might not have been a McLaren team for Fittipaldi to drive for.

The M23's outstanding combination of performance, predictable and controllable handling, superb preparation and reliability had left an indelible mark in the record books.

Far left: In 1974 Emerson Fittipaldi won three races for his new team, Brazil, Belgium and Canada. Here at the Spanish GP the team experimented with a narrow 'winklepicker' nose.

Left: David Hobbs drove the Yardley car in two races in 1974. He qualified 17th for the Austrian GP (above) and finished seventh. After a ninth place at Monza he was replaced by Mass.

MODEL	McLaren M23	TRANSMISSION	Hewland DG400 5-speed	TYRES F/R	Goodyear
TYPE/FORMULA	Formula 1	CHASSIS	Deformable double skinned aluminium monocoque	LENGTH	165in - 4191mm
YEAR OF PRODUCTION	1974	BODY	Monocoque lower, GRP nose, cockpit & engine cover	WIDTH	80in - 2030mm
DESIGNER	Gordon Coppuck	FRONT SUSPENSION	Tubular upper rocker arm, operating inboard	HEIGHT OF AIRBOX	48in - 1219mm
EXAMPLES BUILT	4		coil spring/damper, lower wishbone, anti-roll bar	WHEELBASE	104.2in - 2647mm
ENGINE	Ford Cosworth DFV	REAR SUSPENSION	Adjustable top link, reverse lower wishbone,	TRACK F/R	64.2/66in - 1631/1676mm
CUBIC CAPACITY	2993cc		twin radius rods, coil spring/damper, anti-roll bar	WEIGHT	1270lb - 576kg
CARBURATION	Lucas fuel injection	BRAKES F/R	Outboard/inboard ventilated discs	PRINCIPAL DRIVERS	Fittipaldi, Hulme, Hailwood, Hobbs, Mass
POWER OUTPUT	460bhp	WHEELS DIAMETER x WIDTH F/R	13x11/13x18in	IDENTIFYING COLOURS	Red/White or White/Papaya/Brown

1974 M25
FORMULA 5000

The M25, detailed by John Barnard, was another car derived from the World Championship-winning, Gordon Coppuck-designed, M23. The sole car to be built was McLaren's last official entry into the Formula 5000 arena. With just two races to its credit in F5000, and a further nine as a Ford Cosworth DFV-powered F1 car, its only real claim to fame is that it was mistakenly thought by many to have been the last McLaren single seater to race from new in the company's trademark papaya orange.

Trojan had by this time moved on to build its own F5000 cars, so M25-1 was built in the Colnbrook factory around the customary Chevrolet V8 and uncharacteristically brought little that was new to the mix. It was tested by Howden Ganley and engine builder-cum-Formula Atlantic racer John Nicholson in 1973, and possibly later by Denny Hulme, but it was never a works racer and eventually the tub, in the words of motoring historian Doug Nye, "lay unloved for long months on a rooftop at Colnbrook."

In February 1974 the car was sold to Brazilian Carlos Avallone, who some believe may have commissioned it. He wanted to race in European F5000 as a precursor to making it to F1. However, no sooner had he taken possession than the M25 was impounded over a dispute concerning a proposed sportscar series in Brazil that Avallone had been involved with, and sat out the rest of the 1974 season under lock and key. In early 1975 it found its way into the hands of Yorkshire hillclimber David Hepworth, only for another legal battle to ensue. When the dispute was finally resolved early in 1976, Hepworth decided to take the car racing.

Carrying number one on its nose and painted in the Hepworth Racing Organisation colours of Alfa-Romeo Yellow Ochre, the Shell-backed car finally made its race debut in the ninth round of the 1976 Shellsport G8 Championship at Brands Hatch on August 30th. Driving what Autosport confusingly described as a *Brand new, three-year-old 5-litre McLaren M25,*" in the 35-lap race, Bob Evans came an excellent second behind David Purley's 3.4-litre Chevron B30. This result was extremely promising given that the team had done absolutely no testing and that a minor coming-together early in the race had bent the front left nose wing upwards at more than 30 degrees.

Two weeks later, at the Thruxton round of the series, the McKechnie Racing-run car again looked competitive before it retired with piston problems after just 19 laps. With no spare engine and very little money available, this sadly spelt the end of the season for the underfinanced team. Evans was later to comment that despite being so beautifully built, with its rising-rate suspension it was, "*The twitchiest car I've ever driven in seven years of racing.*"

Hepworth then advertised the car for sale stating that: "*I would love the car to go to an 'ace' since I still believe it could be a winner. It would mop up on both sides of the Atlantic.*" For a while there were rumours that American Can-Am star George Follmer was keen to buy the car so that he could race it in the high-profile US Formula 5000 series. Hepworth let it be known that McLaren would be consulted as to whom the car could be sold and suggested that Mike Hailwood might be a contender.

In the end it was acquired by Giuseppe Risi's Iberia-backed team for Spanish bank manager Emilio de Villota, a true gentleman racer who was later to have some reasonable success in the Aurora AFX F1. Acquiring the M25 following some experience in the 1977 BRSCC Group 8 series with the ex-F1 Lyncar, Risi replaced the Chevy V8 with a Cosworth DFV to give M25-1 a new life as a second-string back-up car to M23-6 that de Villota had attempted to qualify for several GPs in 1977. To bring the car up to then current Formula 1 regulations, most of the M25's original features, such as its early M23 style wings and nose, along with its unusually shaped airbox, were to disappear. Much of its 1973 style suspension was also reworked to later M23 specification, and to all intents and purpose the M25 was transformed into an M23, complete with a front roll-hoop which had become mandatory in F1 midway through 1976.

In 1978 de Villota attempted to qualify what the press rather confusingly referred to as M25/23-1, or even mistakenly as M23-7, for the Spanish Grand Prix, only to fail after spinning spectacularly at the exit of the corner leading to the main straight. As he sat at the side of the circuit waiting for help from marshals, he let his foot slip off the brake and the car rolled backwards on to the track, causing a collision with fellow McLaren driver James Hunt. Having damaged his M26 race car quite severely Hunt was forced to use his back-up car, something which didn't go down too well with the works Marlboro-McLaren team.

Away from the Grand Prix circuit, de Villota nevertheless enjoyed better results with the M25, and in the Aurora AFX Championship that same year finished in third place overall behind champion Tony Trimmer's Melchester Racing M23.

After de Villota and his Iberia team had moved on to running a Lotus 78, the M25 was sold to David McLaughlin before becoming part of the John Foulston collection. Now in the hands of collector and historic racer Abba Kogan, the one-of-a-kind M25 has been restored to something approaching its original F5000 specification, complete with Chevrolet engine and resplendent in the Hepworth Racing Organisation colour scheme in which it first raced.

Emilio de Villota (above) drove the heavily modified ex-F5000 M25, now virtually a Grand Prix spec M23 to second in the 1978 Oulton Park Gold Cup. He finished the race just half a second behind Tony Trimmer in M23/14, the last Formula 1 car supplied to an outside team, Chesterfield Racing, in 1977.

Although the one-off M25 has now been restored to its original Formula 5000 specification it does still retain the front cockpit roll-hoop (top) that had become mandatory in Formula 1 halfway through the 1976 season and had been fitted during the cars Aurora AFX period.

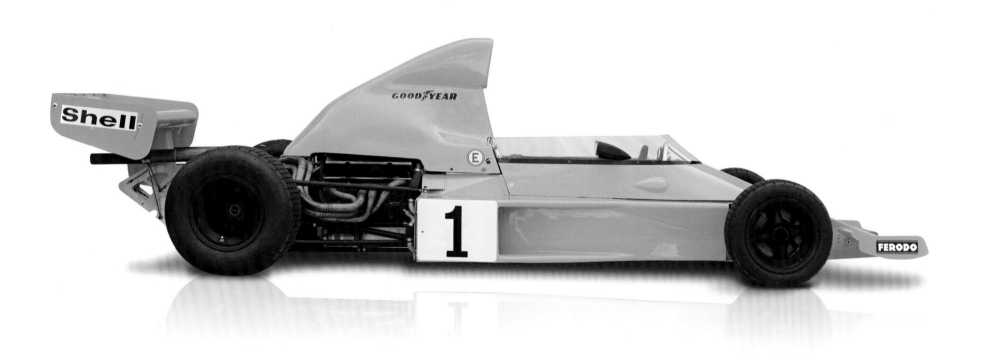

MODEL	McLaren M25	TRANSMISSION	Hewland DG500 5-speed	TYRES F/R	Goodyear
TYPE/FORMULA	Formula 5000	CHASSIS	Deformable double skinned aluminium monocoque	LENGTH	166in - 4216mm
YEAR OF PRODUCTION	1974	BODY	Monocoque lower, GRP nose, cockpit & engine cover	WIDTH	78in - 1981mm
DESIGNER	John Barnard	FRONT SUSPENSION	Upper rocker arm, operating inboard coil	HEIGHT OF AIRBOX	46in - 1168mm
EXAMPLES BUILT	1		spring/damper, lower wishbone, anti-roll bar	WHEELBASE	104.2in - 2647mm
ENGINE	Chevrolet V8	REAR SUSPENSION	Adjustable top link, parallel lower links,	TRACK F/R	64.2/66in - 1631/1676mm
CUBIC CAPACITY	5000cc		twin radius rods, coil spring/damper, anti-roll bar	WEIGHT	1420lb - 644kg
CARBURATION	Lucas fuel injection	BRAKES F/R	Outboard/inboard ventilated discs	PRINCIPAL DRIVERS	Bob Evans
POWER OUTPUT	500bhp	WHEELS DIAMETER x WIDTH F/R	13x11/13x16in	IDENTIFYING COLOURS	Yellow Ochre

Jochen Mass now joined new World Champion Emerson Fittipaldi in the two-car Marlboro team, as the M23 went into its third season largely unchanged. The most significant mechanical development, in the search for better front-end grip, was a new front suspension along Brabham lines for Fittipaldi to try. The original tubular links and rocker arms were replaced by a much sturdier and sweptback fabricated upper rocker with pull-rods actuating the coil spring and damper. After several iterations of the idea, the team finally settled on a non-rising rate set-up for the first time.

Gordon Coppuck still fondly recalls the Brazilian's *"fantastic testing mileages"*, which enabled the team to generate small but crucial changes from race to race as the season progressed. And McLaren needed all it could find as Niki Lauda and the new Ferrari 312T proved the dominant combination. Fittipaldi's input was invaluable, Coppuck making no bones about it being *"crucial in our development of the car"*.

There was also experimentation with the length of the wheelbase, and incorporation of a cockpit-adjustable front anti-roll bar. At the same time John Nicholson worked progressively to boost the Ford Cosworth DFV's 440bhp, adding some 20bhp during the season while also improving the torque curve. Attempts were also made to fit transparent skirts around the lower edge of the chassis to maintain an area of low pressure beneath the car to generate some ground effect. Coppuck had tried the idea the previous season without convincing himself that the skirts worked. This time around the experiment was not successful as the skirts ground away on the track surface as the suspension moved up and down. Some other aerodynamic innovations proved more worthwhile, with a variety of different bodywork styles being tested including revised nose profiles, kick-ups ahead of the rear wheels, and extended bodywork to accommodate the oil coolers. Many were adopted and also appeared on the car's eventual successor, the M26.

In Argentina Fittipaldi drove a brilliant tactical race. Sitting back initially while Carloses Reutemann and Pace in their Brabhams fought for the lead with Niki Lauda and James Hunt, he then began to force the pace as the Englishman found himself leading in the Hesketh Ford. Hunt spun under the pressure, leaving Emerson to claim his 12th Grand Prix victory by 5.9s. In Brazil, however, there was to be no repeat of his 1974 success. Pace won, with Emerson leading Mass home in a McLaren 2-3.

Scheckter won for Tyrrell in South Africa, where Fittipaldi failed to score thanks to a misfire and Mass finished sixth. In Spain Mass scored the only Grand Prix victory of his career in trying circumstances, only earning half points as the race was stopped before half distance following an horrific accident when Rolf Stommelen's leading Embassy Hill suffered rear wing failure and killed four spectators as it

vaulted a guardrail. This had already developed into an acrimonious weekend for Formula 1 as bitter feelings were aroused in practice by the poor state of safety measures around the track. Many team personnel were obliged to pick up spanners to tighten loose securing bolts on the Armco barriers. Fittipaldi, in particular, an active member of the Grand Prix Drivers' Association, was outraged. He qualified on the back row after deliberately doing the bare legal minimum of running, and then withdrew after the race warm-up lap in protest.

There were times in the year when several observers questioned the Brazilian's commitment. When victory was possible, he went for it. But when it did not appear to be he seemed content merely to pick up points. This prompted speculation that he was considering retirement, but his performance in appalling conditions at Silverstone demonstrated that he could still exhibit his inherent class when he chose to. The M23 had been updated with a new rear wing which sported a vee-shaped leading edge not dissimilar to Mario Andretti's Parnelli, but once again he only qualified on the fourth row of the grid and was content to sit back in the early stages before moving up to challenge Pace for the lead as it began to rain after 20 laps. Several drivers pitted for wet tyres, but Fittipaldi did not. Driving beautifully on a track that was as slippery as a skating rink, he moved back into the lead by the 43rd lap as conditions changed again, prompting further stops for those who had changed to wet tyres. Then came a downpour of almost Biblical proportions, prompting him to pit for wet tyres on the 56th lap. He did one more lap before bemused officials called a halt to the farce after 16 drivers had crashed as a consequence of the cloudburst, and was declared victorious.

Above: After the race was halted by a torrential downpour, Emerson Fittipaldi was declared winner of the 1975 British Grand Prix held at Silverstone. His M23 sported a forward vee-shaped rear wing, first seen on both the Parnelli Indy and Formula 1 cars.

Opposite: In April 1975 Jochen Mass driving M23/8 won the shortened Spanish Grand Prix. This would be the only GP win of his career. Emerson Fittipaldi in M23/9 refused to start the Spanish race over concerns about the safety of the poorly constructed guardrails.

It was not until Monza in September that the real Emerson Fittipaldi reappeared, driving a feisty race. As Lauda won to secure his first World Championship, Fittipaldi split the Ferraris to head Clay Regazzoni home. At Watkins Glen he was only narrowly beaten by Lauda for the pole. In the race he was right on the Austrian's tail until they came up to lap Regazzoni, who shamelessly blocked the red and white car. That let to scenes in the pits as Ferrari team manager Luca di Montezemolo scuffled with the Clerk of the Course who had shown the Swiss driver the black flag. By the time Fittipaldi found a way by, Lauda was long gone. Mass supported him by taking a strong third.

In the end, Lauda's Championship triumph was well deserved and Fittipaldi had to be content with second place, nearly 20 points behind. In the final reckoning, Brabham pipped McLaren by a single point for the runner-up slot behind the red cars. It had been a curate's egg of a season, good and bad in parts, and there was to be a final sting in the tail. Far from retiring, Fittipaldi suddenly announced his intention to leave the team in order to join his older brother Wilson's fledgling Copersucar outfit. Suddenly, McLaren was in dire need of a new number one driver for 1976.

MODEL	McLaren M23	TRANSMISSION	Hewland DG400 5-speed	TYRES F/R	Goodyear
TYPE/FORMULA	Formula 1	CHASSIS	Deformable double skinned aluminium monocoque	LENGTH	167in - 4242mm
YEAR OF PRODUCTION	1975	BODY	Monocoque lower, GRP nose, cockpit & engine cover	WIDTH	82in - 2083mm
DESIGNER	Gordon Coppuck	FRONT SUSPENSION	Upper rocker arm, operating inboard coil	HEIGHT OF AIRBOX	49in - 1245mm
EXAMPLES BUILT	2		spring/damper, lower wishbone, anti-roll bar	WHEELBASE	105.75in - 2686mm
ENGINE	Ford Cosworth DFV	REAR SUSPENSION	Adjustable top link, parallel lower links,	TRACK F/R	64.2/65in - 1631/1651mm
CUBIC CAPACITY	2993cc		twin radius rods, coil spring/damper, anti-roll bar	WEIGHT	1325lb - 601kg
CARBURATION	Lucas fuel injection	BRAKES F/R	Outboard/inboard ventilated discs	PRINCIPAL DRIVERS	Fittipaldi, Mass
POWER OUTPUT	465bhp	WHEELS DIAMETER x WIDTH F/R	13x10/13x18in	IDENTIFYING COLOURS	Red/White

After the shock of Emerson Fittipaldi's sudden decision to leave the team, the problem of selecting his replacement was quickly solved. The Brazilian's defection coincided with a plea for further funding from Lord Hesketh, who announced that without it he could not afford to keep his eponymous team running in the style to which the upcoming James Hunt had become accustomed for the past three years.

Teddy Mayer and John Hogan of Marlboro lost no time in snapping up the Englishman. They signed him within 36 hours of Fittipaldi informing them that he was heading to his brother's team, at what would subsequently look like an absolute bargain basement price for a World Champion.

Gordon Coppuck had a new M26 design in preparation, but the M23 was pressed into service now bearing a new dayglo shade of Marlboro red and McLaren's own six-speed development of the Hewland FGA transmission which Team Manager Alastair Caldwell had calculated would enable them to make better use of the trusty DFV's torque curve. With lighter body panels, lower wishbone rear suspension, an innovative compressed air start and, from the Spanish GP onwards, new low-line airboxes, regular driver Jochen Mass and his new partner would race cars that were also 30lb lighter.

The first race of 1976 was the Brazilian GP at Interlagos where Hunt made the best possible start to his time at McLaren by qualifying ahead of reigning World Champion Niki Lauda and his Ferrari. It was James's first-ever pole position for a Grand Prix. A confused, controversial, traumatic and ultimately magnificent year was about to kick off.

Both Lauda and team-mate Clay Regazzoni made much better getaways, but the second Ferrari subsequently slipped back with a puncture as Hunt pressured Lauda. But Niki went on to win as the M23 lapsed on to seven cylinders due to a dislodged fuel injection trumpet, which later jammed the throttle open and spun James into the fence.

Despite McLaren being forced to remove new underskirts after protests in South Africa, Hunt again took pole but, wary of burning his clutch, got away gently and ran fourth initially. Once he was able to stop worrying about a minor oil leak, he got the hammer down and began to chase after Lauda, who was 10s ahead. Then the Austrian's left rear tyre slowly began to deflate, setting up a gripping conclusion in which he held on by 1.3s to lead the McLaren across the line. Mass had a strong race too, finishing third.

At Brands Hatch in March James's early promise was realised when, for the second time in front of his home crowd in a non-championship race, he won the Race of Champions after overhauling the Surtees TS19 of early leader Alan Jones.

Using 35 per cent larger Can-Am style brakes at Long Beach for the US GP West, James qualified alongside Lauda on row two behind Regazzoni and the Tyrrell 007 of Patrick Depailler. James beat Depailler away and stayed ahead despite a momentary vapour lock, but then a coming together with the Frenchman put him hard into the wall on lap three to his intense chagrin. He worked out his frustration by standing by the side of the track for several laps, shaking his fist at his rival.

Back home at Silverstone for the non-championship International Trophy, he thrilled the crowd to win that race for the second time, starting from pole and setting the fastest lap as well.

By the Spanish GP at Jarama in May it was increasingly apparent that James was becoming the team's big winner even though, for all his poles and fastest laps, he was still one place lower in the rankings than Jochen. Then he scored his first win for McLaren after catching and passing Lauda, who was suffering bruised ribs after a tractor accident the previous week. But then the win was taken away from him in parc fermé when post-race scrutineering showed that the M23, around which a new dimensional regulation had been specifically formed since it was the largest F1 car, was 1.8cm, five-eighths of an inch, too wide across the rear wheels. McLaren tried everything it could think of to rectify the problem, but the organisers disqualified James.

In a season in which the politics were already fast becoming unsavoury, Mayer lodged an immediate appeal only to have it thrown out by the Spanish organisers. He then appealed to the FISA, but for the time being Lauda was the winner.

Niki won in Belgium and Monaco, where engine and transmission problems respectively stymied James and left McLaren with only Mass's fifth and sixth places as consolation. Jody Scheckter won in the six-wheeled Tyrrell in Sweden, where Lauda was third and James fifth. Then James put a run of three superb races together, winning in France and Britain, where he vanquished Lauda fair and square, and Germany where Niki crashed.

The same weekend he won in France Hunt learned that the FISA had given him back his Spanish victory, but then his British win was taken away on a technicality after his car was deemed to have been worked on, in contravention of the rules, having sustained damage after the original start had to be abandoned. That news was not imparted on a day when the British crowd let its anger be known when officials initially sought not to let their hero take part in the restart. Ironically, Clay Regazzoni was the culprit who had triggered the accident on the first attempt to start the race, after crashing into team-mate Lauda.

Far worse was the news at Nürburgring. James won, but Lauda lay at death's door after his Ferrari crashed heavily at

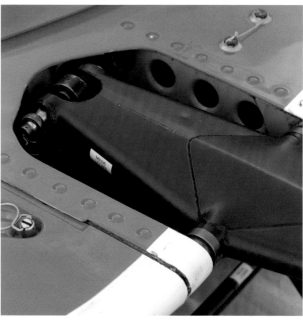

the Bergwerk corner following suspension failure and was engulfed in flames. He survived, having received the last rites, but his title challenge seemed precarious, especially as James went on another winning spree.

He had to be content with fourth in Austria after fighting with eventually victorious John Watson's Penske, then won in Holland, Canada and America. Between the European race and the north American rounds, however, there was yet more controversy when allegations about the McLaren's fuel octane, since disproved, saw Italian authorities place James and Jochen at the back of the grid. In his frustration, the former spun out early on. Lauda's come back at this race was truly heroic, finishing fourth to keep his title hopes alive.

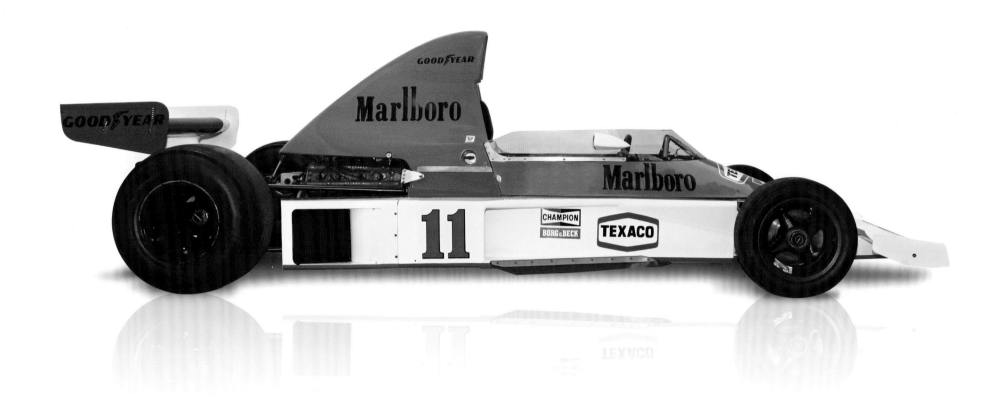

MODEL	McLaren M23	TRANSMISSION	Hewland FG400 6-speed	TYRES F/R	Goodyear
TYPE/FORMULA	Formula 1	CHASSIS	Deformable double skinned aluminium monocoque	LENGTH	165in - 4191mm
YEAR OF PRODUCTION	1976	BODY	Monocoque lower, GRP nose, cockpit & engine cover	WIDTH	82in - 2083mm
DESIGNER	Gordon Coppuck	FRONT SUSPENSION	Upper rocker arm, operating inboard coil	HEIGHT	36in - 914mm
EXAMPLES BUILT	4 modified (No new chassis for 1976)		spring/damper, lower wishbone, anti-roll bar	WHEELBASE	107in - 2718mm
ENGINE	Ford Cosworth DFV	REAR SUSPENSION	Adjustable top link, parallel lower links,	TRACK F/R	64.2/65in - 1631/1651mm
CUBIC CAPACITY	2993cc		twin radius rods, coil spring/damper, anti-roll bar	WEIGHT	1295lb - 587kg
CARBURATION	Lucas fuel injection	BRAKES F/R	Outboard/inboard ventilated discs	PRINCIPAL DRIVERS	Hunt, Mass, Villeneuve, Giacomelli
POWER OUTPUT	465bhp	WHEELS DIAMETER x WIDTH F/R	13x10/13x18in	IDENTIFYING COLOURS	Red/White

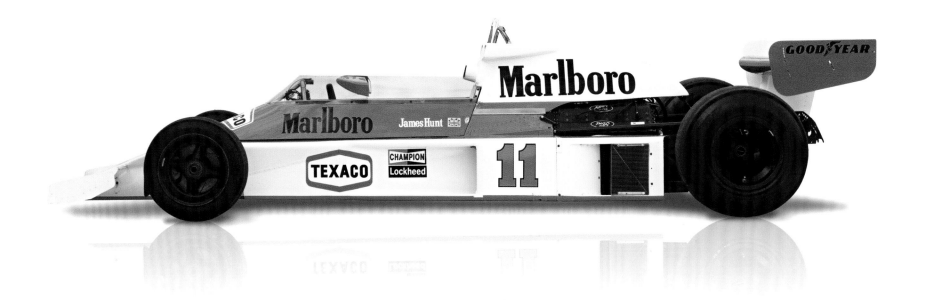

Most famously, the 1976 World Championship came to its showdown at a wet Mt. Fuji for the Japanese GP. It was run in appalling conditions that saw Lauda, his burned eyelids still improperly healed, withdrawing after two laps in which visibility was minimal. James, perhaps more desperate to win his first title than Lauda was for a second, led for 61 of the 73 laps, then had to make a dramatic pit stop to have a deflating wet weather tyre replaced as the conditions improved. He was lucky to make it, as the tyre blew just before the pit lane entry. He was able to duck in to have it replaced, but the stop dropped him to fifth and for a moment the title was Lauda's. James drove the remaining laps in a red mist as he recovered to the third place he needed to beat the Austrian by a single point. No Hollywood scriptwriter could have dreamed that one up.

The Hunt/Lauda battle completely overshadowed Mass's contribution that year, and surely the most frustrating day of his career came at the Nürburgring. Braving slicks on a track surface initially dampened by pre-race rain, he had disappeared into the distance when Lauda's crash brought

that part of the event to a halt. On the restart he had to be content with third place behind his team leader, and Jody Scheckter. Besides his third in South Africa, he took fourth in America, fifths in Long Beach, Monaco and Canada, and sixths in Brazil and Belgium.

The lighter and stiffer M26 was scheduled to appear in 1977, but initially McLaren played it safe and the mighty M23 soldiered on into its fifth season. James put M23-8 on pole position for the Argentine GP at Buenos Aires and easily led the first 32 laps before a suspension bolt sheared, sending him off the road and into the catchfencing. A couple of weeks later, at Interlagos in Brazil, he again led from pole but could only finish second to Reutemann's Ferrari. He led in South Africa too until a problematic front tyre slowed him enough for Lauda and Scheckter, now driving for Wolf, to overtake. Towards the end, Depailler also pushed his Tyrrell past the McLaren. Back home in the UK, James won the only non-championship race of the season, at Brands Hatch.

Later, while still awaiting his M26, Jochen led very briefly in

the wet in Belgium before spinning on lap 39 after he had switched to dry tyres, then scored a good second in the Swedish GP at Anderstorp before emergent Canadian Formula Atlantic racer Gilles Villeneuve made a stunning debut in an M23 at Silverstone. Qualifying ninth, ahead of Jochen's M26, the former skidoo racer was running a comfortable seventh when a faulty water temperature gauge tricked him into making a precautionary and unnecessary pit stop which dropped him to 11th. But for that he would have finished fourth in his first-ever Grand Prix.

Over its long working life, the iconic M23 was piloted in its heyday by some of the greatest names in Formula One: Denny Hulme, Peter Revson, Jody Scheckter, Jacky Ickx, Emerson Fittipaldi, Jochen Mass, James Hunt and Gilles Villeneuve. Even after it was past its best, it provided a ride for the emergent Nelson Piquet courtesy of BS Fabrications in 1978, and was also driven by the likes of Bruno Giacomelli, Brett Lunger and Emilio de Villota. More than any other car, even the M7A, it was the machine that truly put McLaren on the Formula 1 map.

Gilles Villeneuve's first Grand Prix was the 1977 British GP at Silverstone. Driving M23/8 he finished 11th, two laps down on James Hunt who took the first win for the M26.

After a long, hard-fought and controversial season, James Hunt clinched the 1976 Drivers' title with third place at the wet Japanese Grand Prix held at the Mt. Fuji circuit.

Despite making a brief debut at the Dutch GP in 1976, the M26 was still under development at the start of 1977, and although Ferrari, Lotus and Wolf were all strong, teething problems with the M26 obliged reigning World Champion James Hunt to continue relying on the older M23 for the first four rounds, and team-mate Jochen Mass for the first nine.

In testing at Kyalami M26-1 had been seriously damaged when a bolt came loose from a front brake caliper, throwing James off the track. By the time the season reached Jarama for the Spanish GP in May, however, chassis M26-2 was ready for its 'second' debut. James found its handling unbalanced and unpredictable, qualified only seventh and retired with a misfire on lap 10. He returned to the M23 for the next race, at Monaco, and it was not until Zolder for the Belgian GP in June that the M26 reappeared. The wings had been modified, and the oil cooler was now relocated in the nose. The car proved better balanced, but Mass, in the older M23 still outqualified Hunt. Choosing slicks for the race in the belief that the rainswept circuit would soon dry out, James was lapped as Mass led briefly. Hunt finished out of the points, in seventh.

At Dijon for the French GP James put the M26 on the front row alongside Mario Andretti's Lotus, and led the American away at the start until Ulsterman John Watson pushed his Brabham Alfa Romeo past both of them. As the McLaren's began to understeer Andretti overtook Hunt for second on lap 17 and took the win when the Brabham faltered on the final lap and stuttered home second. James was third.

The breakthrough came at Silverstone, where Mass had an M26 for the first time and Gilles Villeneuve joined the team in an M23. Hunt grabbed pole but failed to prevent Watson from thrusting the Brabham Alfa into the lead for the first 50 laps. Then further fuel delivery problems sent the red car into the pits, and James took the flag in front of the predictably partisan crowd. With Jochen finishing fourth it was a long overdue successful day.

Using the same car and engine at Hockenheim, James was running third before a broken exhaust pipe and a faulty fuel pump handed the position to Jochen, who soon lost it when his gearbox failed. The Austrian race was little better: Hunt led for 43 laps before his engine expired, but Mass took a point for sixth place.

Hopes were higher for Zandvoort, where Hunt had won the two previous races. From third on the grid he took an early lead from a challenging Andretti. Then they touched wheels on the exit to the Tarzan Hairpin on lap six as the American attempted to run round the outside. An angry Mario spun; James landed hard after momentarily becoming airborne and sustained damage to the M26's suspension and a water pipe. His day was over. Jochen, too, had a short run, getting turfed off by Alan Jones's Shadow at the start.

At Monza McLaren fielded its regular M26s and an M23 for Formula 2 star Bruno Giacomelli. James qualified on pole, Jochen ninth, and after brake problems accounted for the Englishman, the German took fourth place.

James was buoyant at Watkins Glen for the US GP East, despite spinning into a barrier on Friday. After taking his third pole position of the season, he found himself trailing German Hans Stuck's Brabham-Alfa in the early wet going. Inheriting the lead after Stuck went off after 14 laps, and with a comfortable lead over Andretti, he was nevertheless stalked by trouble. His engine was overheating, and as the field nursed their wet weather rubber on a rapidly drying track, he pressed on with a slowly deflating tyre. He pulled it off, winning his second GP of the season and his second consecutive one at the Glen, but it was a close call as Andretti was only two seconds behind at the finish.

Canada went less well, and was a tense weekend despite Hunt joking about Mosport being a great circuit to drive on, *"But not so nice to drive off."* He and poleman Andretti had all but lapped the field by lap 59 and were about to overhaul Mass, in third place, when Mario lost ground and leader James was accidentally taken out by his own team-mate. He hit the wall head-on, wrecking the M26's tub, and was briefly trapped in the car by his feet. Jochen recovered to finish third.

The final race of the year at Mount Fuji saw Andretti pip Hunt for pole position. Having damaged M26-2 at Mosport and been dissatisfied with M26-1, James was now driving Jochen's chassis M26-3, and as the flag dropped he leapt into the lead as Andretti hit Jacques Laffite's Ligier and was forced out. When Jochen moved up to second place on lap six it seemed that the M26 really had come good, but the total McLaren domination ended when his engine broke on the 28th of the 73 laps. For Hunt, however, it was to be an easy run home as he led every lap to take what would be his last-ever Grand Prix victory. It left him fifth in the World Championship, a long way adrift of Lauda. The success would also be McLaren's last for three and a half years.

Despite the performance of the ground effect Lotus 78 in 1977, McLaren went into 1978 feeling very optimistic, which was understandable given the performance of James and the M26 in the final two races of the previous season. As he replaced Jochen Mass, popular Frenchman Patrick Tambay could be excused for thinking he had gone to the right place at just the right time. History would prove otherwise.

At the Brazilian GP at the new Jacarapagua circuit in Rio, that optimism did not seem misplaced as James qualified M26-4 on the front row alongside poleman Peterson's Lotus Type 78. At the start he chased eventual winner Carlos Reutemann, in his Michelin-shod Ferrari, then Andretti once the American had overtaken him, but the pace destroyed a front tyre and he pitted for a replacement on the ninth lap.

Running three cars at the 1978 British GP at Brands Hatch made for hard work but, after Hunt (top seen in practice with 'high' front wing) crashed out on lap 7 the team was at least rewarded by finishes from the other two drivers. Tambay (middle) made it home sixth and in the points whilst Giacomelli (lower) was right behind him in seventh.

MODEL	McLaren M26	TRANSMISSION	McLaren/Hewland 6-speed	TYRES F/R	Goodyear
TYPE/FORMULA	Formula 1	CHASSIS	Double skinned aluminium & Nomex monocoque	LENGTH	172in - 4368mm
YEAR OF PRODUCTION	1976/1977	BODY	Monocoque lower, GRP nose, cockpit & engine cover	WIDTH	83in - 2108mm
DESIGNER	Gordon Coppuck	FRONT SUSPENSION	Upper rocker arm, operating inboard coil	HEIGHT	34.5in - 876mm
EXAMPLES BUILT	7		spring/damper, lower wishbone, anti-roll bar	WHEELBASE	108in - 2743mm
ENGINE	Ford Cosworth DFV	REAR SUSPENSION	Adjustable top link, parallel lower links,	TRACK F/R	65/66in - 1651/1675mm
CUBIC CAPACITY	2993cc		twin radius rods, coil spring/damper, anti-roll bar	WEIGHT	1300lb - 589kg
CARBURATION	Lucas fuel injection	BRAKES F/R	Outboard/inboard ventilated discs	PRINCIPAL DRIVERS	Hunt, Mass
POWER OUTPUT	465bhp	WHEELS DIAMETER x WIDTH F/R	13x10/13x18in	IDENTIFYING COLOURS	Red/White

Reigning World Champion
James Hunt had a tough season
in 1977. After having to use an
updated M23 in the first four
races of the year, the M26
finally made its debut in Spain.
Here in the Belgian Grand Prix,
the M26 finally finished a race,
but out of the points in seventh.

Trying to make up time, he tangled with Riccardo Patrese's new Arrows and was out after 26 laps. Kyalami went little better. After qualifying third James ran fourth until his engine quit on the fifth lap, and Patrick, who qualified alongside James on the second row, only managed an unclassified last place in M26-5 after clutch trouble cost him time at the start and he later slid off on oil.

In Long Beach the McLarens were out of luck again, James crashing on the fifth lap and Patrick finishing 12th. An uneasy feeling began to pervade the team. James qualified sixth at Monaco, Patrick 11th, but the former's anti-roll bar broke as the latter finished seventh, out of the points. Not only had the new Lotus 79 rewritten the design parameters, but the Brabham Alfa Romeos had plentiful horsepower and the Michelins on the Ferraris endowed them with a significant advantage on some circuits. McLaren was beginning to struggle.

Hunt and old rival Niki Lauda collided on the grid in Belgium, where they had started fifth and fourth respectively. Bruno Giacomelli was elevated to second-car status after a leg injury sustained in the Pau F2 race the previous Monday kept Tambay out of action. The Italian finished eighth. In Spain Hunt tried a high (but just legal) front wing to try to cure the M26's inherent understeer problem, but though he qualified fourth it was not used in the race. He struggled home sixth after a tyre stop, as the returned Tambay dumped his car in the gravel after spinning on lap 17.

The Swedish Grand Prix was all about Lauda's controversial victory in the Brabham 'fan car', which detracted from the M26's poor performance. Neither qualified well, and Hunt finished out of the points as Tambay dragged his machine home fourth. The cars were better suited to the smoothness of Paul Ricard, where James qualified fourth and Patrick sixth, as 'Jack O'Malley' put the third car 22nd in the line-up. In a halfway decent car James drove one of his stronger races to place third, Patrick ninth; Giacomelli's engine broke.

In a desperate attempt to revive its flagging fortunes, McLaren took no fewer than six M26s of varying specification and two M23s to Brands Hatch for the British GP. The most interesting was M26-4, whose chassis had been rebuilt to incorporate large sidepods which, curiously, did not contain the crucial shaped underwings that were the secret of the Lotus's ground effect. The entire rear end was also boxed in. Teddy described it as being: "*Thirty per cent of the way to being a Lotus, but only twenty per cent of the way towards our new car.*" Sometimes mistakenly referred to as the M26E, this designation has no entry in the drawing register at McLaren and thus is not registered as a McLaren type.

In the race James raced his regular M26-3, which he crashed in very unusual circumstances along the Bottom Straight early in the race. Patrick was sixth. Bruno inadvertently helped Carlos Reutemann to win by blocking Niki Lauda to

Left: In the 1978 United States Grand Prix at Watkins Glen and the following Canadian race in Montreal, both the works M26 cars appeared in the colours of Löwenbräu beer.

Above: Despite the support of the home crowd for the 1978 British GP at Brands Hatch, Hunt (top) seen here in his brief run on Friday in the 'M26E', could only qualify 14th. In the race he lasted just seven laps before spinning off in front of his fans at South Bank.

the point where the Argentinian was able to use superior momentum out of Clearways corner to overtake the Brabham driver; Giacomelli finished a chastened seventh only two seconds behind Tambay.

In Germany James sustained a punctured left front tyre and was disqualified for taking a short-cut to the pits; Patrick crashed after picking up a puncture of his own. Austria brought two more accidents, Holland ninth and 10th places and a retirement for Bruno.

It was crystal clear to Teddy Mayer and the McLaren management that the poor performance of their car was not inspiring their former World Champion driver, and tensions between the parties were high. Teddy was adamant that James was no longer "*really*" interested in driving and found him little help in trying to resolve the ongoing technical problems. Soon, it became clear that when Hunt's contract expired at the end of the season, it would not be renewed. Instead, Mayer turned to Ronnie Peterson, the prodigal son at Lotus. Lured by the promise of an all-new ground effect McLaren M28 for 1979, 'Superswede' signed for the Marlboro-backed team and the news was announced shortly

before the Italian Grand Prix at Monza. A week later, Ronnie was dead, and Teddy admitted that, after the euphoria of signing the highly popular racer, his death was an even bigger blow than Bruce's. In the tragic circumstances, Patrick's fifth place went unnoticed.

After Monza Mayer tried to keep James, but his new contract with Walter Wolf was binding and in the end the little American opted for the fast but underrated and sensitive John Watson, who in Austria and Holland in 1976, and France and Britain in 1977, had shown himself capable of challenging James even when the latter had the fire of victory in his heart. Against this sad backdrop McLaren's 1978 season petered out with lowly placings at Watkins Glen after tyre troubles, and more disillusionment in Canada.

While the works team switched to the M28 in 1979, and American privateer Brett Lunger did not drive his M26 (chassis six) beyond 1978, an M26 was resurrected for Patrick Tambay to race in Brazil in 1979 before his M28 was ready to use in Argentina. A car that had won three races, it nevertheless flattered to deceive as it was left floundering by the development of ground effect.

1977 & 1978 M24 & M24B
INDYCAR

Long since out of Can-Am and Formula 5000, McLaren's presence in the US during the mid- to late-1970s was nevertheless still significant, with the works continuing to make good showings at the Indianapolis 500.

While many privateers continued running ex-works or ex-Penske M16s of varying vintages into the 1980s, by 1976 it was clear that as far as frontline racing was concerned the M16E had come to the end of its competitive life. But the factory was ready with its replacement for 1977, in the shape of the new M24.

Five years earlier the back end of an M19, complete with the Ford Cosworth DFV, had been grafted onto an M16 Indy car front end as Gordon Coppuck sought solutions to the F1 design for 1973. He was pleased with the outcome, much of which was to find expression in the double World Championship-winning M23.

In 1976 Cosworth had unveiled its new Indy engine, a 2.65-litre turbocharged version of the famed DFV known as the DFX. Now, as the four-cylinder Offenhauser was finally coming to the end of the road it was time for that 1972 experiment to come full circle and Coppuck leapt at the chance to create an Indy version of the M23. The basic M23 chassis design was metamorphosed with a heavier gauge aluminium skin and heftier bulkheads to comply with USAC safety regulations, and fitted with M16E-style suspension. The result, while very obviously an oval racer, could not conceal its F1 ancestry.

The works team, now sponsored by First National Citibank Travellers' Checks, ran a car for Johnny Rutherford in 1977, while Penske Racing took one for Mario Andretti to race with Cam 2 Motor Oil backing. In such capable hands they made their mark immediately. In the first four races of the season Rutherford took a pole for the works, led two races and won one. Andretti became the first to lap Indianapolis over 200mph in his M24, running 200.311mph when practice began. In official qualifying that honour fell to Tom Sneva, driving Penske's second car under Norton Spirit sponsorship as he lapped the two-and-a-half-mile oval at 200.401mph.

Sneva eventually took the pole at 198.884mph. Rutherford qualified third fastest behind Sneva but under Indy rules he was obliged to start 17th. It wasn't his year at the Brickyard, however, as he retired after 12 laps with gearbox failure. Sneva, though, brought his M24 home second.

1978 marked McLaren's ninth year at Indianapolis, and Rutherford's sixth as the team's number one driver. The new M24B was slightly lighter and had the oil cooler repositioned horizontally to the left of the transmission. A third win for JR soon began to look unlikely as engine trouble twice forced the M24B into the pits. On a day when Al Unser Snr won for Lola and JR was classified an unhappy 13th, the highest-placed McLaren was the quaintly named Sugaripe Prune M24 driven to fifth by Wally Dallenbach.

The 1979 season was riven with controversy as CART was founded in direct competition to USAC. The latter retained control of the prestigious Indy 500, and added to the controversy by reducing turbo boost from 80 to 50 inches of manifold pressure for qualifying and to 70 for racing. The plan was not just to reduce speeds, but also to give stock block engines a fresh lease of life. McLaren's development for the race embraced heavy revision of the M24B's monocoque, albeit not of sufficient magnitude to warrant a new type number, and an attractive slimmer nose profile similar to the M26's but without that car's oil cooler.

Rutherford found himself on the third row, eighth fastest at 188.137mph and in the works team's final outing at the Brickyard, JR lost 30 laps in the pits with gearbox problems and was classified 18th. Veteran Roger McCluskey was left to salvage McLaren's honour, with 13th place in Warner Hodgdon's National Engineering M24. By the end of the season Rutherford was still fourth in the new USAC/CART series, albeit courtesy of results such as thirds at Phoenix and Michigan and a fourth at Ontario. McLaren's real star that year was Sneva, who wrung great speed out of Jerry O'Connell's Sugaripe Prune M24; he was second at Atlanta and Michigan, and third at Trenton.

The writing was on the wall, however, written largely by the

The 1977 Indy 500 saw the appearance of another car derived from the M23 Formula 1 car, the Cosworth DFX-engined M24. Mario Andretti in the CAM2/Penske-entered car (top) finished sixth.

speed of the ground effect Chaparral 2K designed by former McLaren man John Barnard, who had further chapters yet to write in the marque's story. By the end of a tough season, Team McLaren faced 1980 with no sponsorship and a car that was no longer a match for Penske's own chassis, let alone the Chaparral, and growing trouble on the Formula 1 front. The only option was withdrawal.

That did not quite mark the end of the McLaren story in Indy racing, however, as Rutherford moved over to drive the Chaparral. For much of 1980 Sneva thrilled spectators with his now three-year-old Jerry O'Connell-owned M24. Second at Ontario for the opening race of the season, he was forced to start at the back of the grid for the Indy 500 after cutting a tyre on his brand new Phoenix ground effect racer and crashing it in practice heavily enough to warrant a switch to a back-up chassis. The only alternative was 'Ole Hound', as O'Connell's faithful M24 was nicknamed. In a superb drive he climbed from 33rd place to the lead by lap 72 until, ironically, Rutherford's Chaparral caught and passed him on lap 148.

Other private McLarens would continue to race in the USAC/CART National Championship until 1981. In that year's controversial 500, Australian former Formula 1 driver Vern Schuppan dragged his Theodore Racing M24B from 18th starting slot to a superb third behind disputed winner Bobby Unser and an angry Mario Andretti.

MODEL	McLaren M24	TRANSMISSION	Hewland LG500 4-speed	TYRES F/R	Goodyear
TYPE/FORMULA	Indianapolis/USAC	CHASSIS	Deformable double skinned aluminium monocoque	LENGTH	178in - 4521mm
YEAR OF PRODUCTION	1977	BODY	Monocoque lower, GRP nose, cockpit & engine cover	WIDTH	78.5in - 1994mm
DESIGNER	Gordon Coppuck	FRONT SUSPENSION	Upper rocker arm, operating inboard coil	HEIGHT AT WING	36in - 914mm
EXAMPLES BUILT	6 (+3 M24B)		spring/damper, lower wishbone, anti-roll bar	WHEELBASE	107in - 2718mm
ENGINE	Ford Cosworth DFX	REAR SUSPENSION	Adjustable top link, parallel lower links,	TRACK F/R	66.5/62.5in - 1689/1587mm
CUBIC CAPACITY	2650cc		twin radius rods, coil spring/damper, anti-roll bar	WEIGHT	1521lb - 690kg
CARBURATION	Hilborn injection, Garrett Airesearch turbocharger	BRAKES F/R	Outboard/inboard ventilated discs	PRINCIPAL DRIVERS	Rutherford, Sneva, Andretti
POWER OUTPUT	820bhp	WHEELS DIAMETER x WIDTH F/R	15x10/15x14in	IDENTIFYING COLOURS	White/Red/Blue

The M27 was intended to be a non-ground effects car but circumstance rendered it obsolete even before it had been built. Thus, the design team moved on to the M28 in time for the 1979 season as Patrick Tambay was joined by John Watson, the replacement for James Hunt.

Gordon Coppuck quickly set to work on a second replacement for the M26, a ground effect machine dubbed the M28. Not surprisingly, it was the World Championship-winning Lotus Type 79 that most influenced his thinking. By harnessing airflow beneath the chassis to generate downforce, and going one better than he had with the revolutionary Lotus 78 in 1977, the fertile Colin Chapman had caught the opposition unawares.

In order to increase the downforce figures that McLaren calculated for the 79, the new DFV-powered M28 took its chassis and bodywork dimensions to the limit prescribed by the governing body. Accordingly the most obvious feature of the aluminium Nomex honeycomb monocoque was the two vast sidepods. Each accommodated not only a Marston radiator and an oil cooler but also a fuel cell (with a third one placed behind the driver to give a total capacity of 40 gallons) and the shaped underwings which were intended to optimise the undercar airflow.

To facilitate the latter the Koni-damped suspension was moved inboard, out of the airstream. At the front this meant top rocker arms, lower wishbones and inboard coil spring/ dampers, at the rear lower and upper wishbones together with lower rocker arms and inboard spring/ dampers. With a wheelbase of 113-inch wheelbase, a 70-inch front track and 64-inch rear track, the 1,378lb car looked somewhat slab-sided and bulky.

The prototype was running by the end of 1978 and with time for plenty of testing ahead of the Argentine opener, so by that race numerous detail changes had already been made which included a repositioned rear anti-roll bar and minor modifications to the bodywork.

The team was confident it had ironed out earlier problems with the bonding of various magnesium castings to the monocoque's honeycomb sections, but it soon became apparent that there were still technical issues to be ironed out even though some were effectively masked by some excellent Goodyear tyres. As Jacques Laffite dominated the race for Ligier, chased by Lotus's Carlos Reutemann, John Watson brought his M28 from sixth on the grid to what seemed a promising third place. He struggled in Brazil, however, finishing eighth.

By Kyalami the M28s had undergone further modifications following experiments with and without nose fins, and with a double-deck rear aerofoil and a low-mounted one. Unfortunately, Tambay's new M28-3 refused to run correctly and he was forced back into M28-1. He finished 10th, three

laps down on the winning Ferraris, as Watson wrestled with M28-2 before retiring on lap 63 with ignition trouble.

When the series reached Spain, the cars had morphed again with reduced front and rear tracks, a shorter wheelbase and heavily revised aerodynamics. But both were still well off the pace, running three seconds slower than Laffite's pole winning Ligier. "Little better than the old design" was Autosport's post-race judgement on cars that were never in contention.

Such a large machine was no better suited to Monaco either, and by the time the McLaren team reached the Principality they had another new version ready, this one christened M28C. Though built up from the monocoque of M28-3 the changes were now more substantial - hence the C suffix. Again, the inspiration had come from Lotus, this time Chapman's Type 80 'wingless wonder'. The M28C now had a longer, slimmer nose and the front suspension pick-ups were moved inboard with the suspension components themselves reprofiled to present a tidier appearance. The theoretical aerodynamic advantage allowed the air a clearer route through to the radiator intakes and beneath the sidepods.

Watson took this car, with Tambay taking over the B-variant which had been developed using M28-2 as a base. Wattie at least finished fourth out of six survivors, still on the lead lap, but Tambay didn't even qualify. In France Patrick was 10th, Wattie 11th. The unloved M28's final appearance was in Tambay's hands in the British GP, where he finished seventh. Watson by then was driving its replacement, the hastily conceived M29.

Teddy Mayer did not spare anyone in his criticism of the M28, which was overweight, slow on the straights, aerodynamically weak and had poor grip despite the plan-form size of its ground effect areas. It was, he said trenchantly, "Ghastly, a

Throughout 1979 the M28 appeared in several different guises. Early in the season the car ran with a low sidepod set-up. At Long Beach where both works cars once again ran in Lowenbräu livery, Tambay (top) retired on lap one.

At the Race of Champions Watson (middle) was out by lap 17. By the time of the British Grand Prix both cars had high side fences to help direct air over the rear wing. Tambay (bottom) was seventh.

disaster, quite diabolical." Querying Coppuck's track record, Mayer continued: "We ignored all the crucial design precepts that a car should be as light, agile and as compact as possible." In creating a car designed to get as much air underneath it as possible, McLaren had gone too far in the wrong direction.

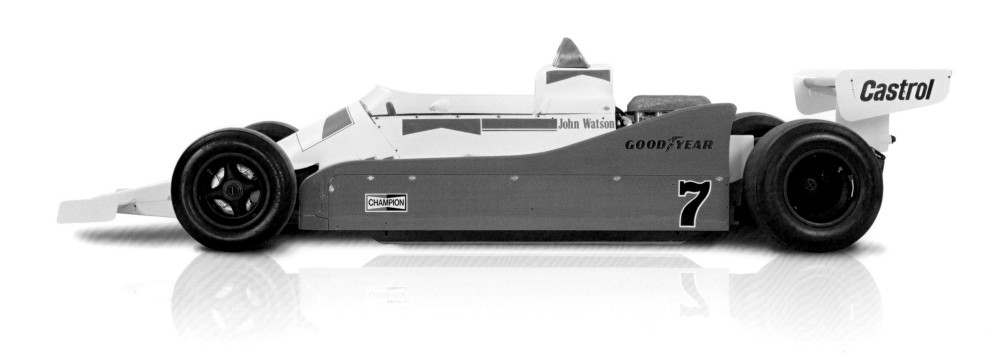

MODEL	McLaren M28	TRANSMISSION	McLaren/Hewland 6-speed	TYRES F/R	Goodyear
TYPE/FORMULA	Formula 1	CHASSIS	Double skinned aluminium & Nomex monocoque	LENGTH	174in - 4420mm
YEAR OF PRODUCTION	1979	BODY	GRP nose, side pods, cockpit & engine cover	WIDTH	84in - 2134mm
DESIGNER	Gordon Coppuck	FRONT SUSPENSION	Upper rocker arm, operating inboard coil	HEIGHT OF ROLLBAR	40in - 1016mm
EXAMPLES BUILT	3		spring/damper, lower wishbone, anti-roll bar	WHEELBASE	113in - 2870mm
ENGINE	Ford Cosworth DFV	REAR SUSPENSION	Upper wishbone/rocker arm operating inboard	TRACK F/R	70/64in - 1778/1626mm
CUBIC CAPACITY	2993cc		coil spring/damper, lower wishbone & link	WEIGHT	1378lb - 625kg
CARBURATION	Lucas fuel injection	BRAKES F/R	Outboard/inboard ventilated discs	PRINCIPAL DRIVERS	Watson, Tambay
POWER OUTPUT	470bhp	WHEELS DIAMETER x WIDTH F/R	13x11/13x18in	IDENTIFYING COLOURS	Red/White

Though they proved extremely resistant to all attempts to alleviate them, the McLaren M28's numerous shortcomings had not taken long to identify. Nor did it take long for the team to complete and commission its replacement once Teddy Mayer had stepped in at the start of May demanding that a brand-new car be ready in time for the British Grand Prix in July 1979.

By Gordon Coppuck's own admission more of a Williams FW07 copy than a replica of the Lotus 79, the M29 was accordingly much more compact than its unloved predecessor. With some elements of Ligier thinking in its design and make-up, the car's cockpit was now situated well forward within the wheelbase, and the new monocoque was constructed in a more conventional manner using sheet aluminium in place of the M28's radical honeycomb.

Still powered by the evergreen Ford Cosworth DFV mated to a Hewland gearbox, and with a new Williams FW07-style secret heat exchanger hidden away within the left-hand sidepod, the car also incorporated a single fuel cell in place of the three which featured on the older car. The wheelbase was slightly shorter and the track narrower, and the M29 weighed in 58lb lighter than the M28. It was duly ready in time for the Silverstone race, as per Mayer's order, but once again the team took along M28-3C as a spare car just in case. Tambay was still using M28-2. He qualified that car 18th, while Watson was a promising seventh in the new car. He got caught out at the start and dropped down to 16th, fought back, but then had to pit to replace a tyre. Thereafter he fought back again, slicing past Scheckter's understeering Ferrari to claim fourth in front of his 100,000-strong home crowd. Nobody could have known it at the time, but it was to be the best performance of the M29's life.

By just missing out on a podium place, Wattie was able to demonstrate that his own spirit and drive had not been damaged by the disappointments with the M28. But no matter what the team did to the M29 after Silverstone, it became increasingly clear that it was not the answer to the inherent problems. Experiments continued with undercar aerodynamics and the rear suspension, but to little avail. Watson could only pick up minor placings. By the end of the season it was abundantly clear that Tambay's confidence had not survived the difficult couple of years he had spent with the team. He headed off to pastures new, and his place alongside Watson for 1980 was taken by fellow countryman Alain Prost, who had starred in Formula 3 that season.

The diminutive Frenchman had been introduced to Mayer by Marlboro's Paddy McNally and participated in a test at Paul Ricard that November. Wattie had lapped a modified M29C, with outboard rear suspension, 2.7s faster than the standard car, to everyone's delight. When Prost went faster than Wattie in 10 laps, Teddy went running to his car for a contract. The little Frenchman immediately became a McLaren team member.

His early promise was quickly borne out in 1980 with the lighter, M29C. 'The Professor,' as he quickly became known, finished sixth on his Grand Prix debut in Argentina and followed that with fifth in Brazil, outpacing the experienced Watson to establish himself as the team's number one.

Things went awry at Kyalami during the South African GP meeting. A suspension failure pitched Prost's M29C off the road in practice and left him with a broken wrist. That forced him to miss the race and the following Long Beach event. There, clutch problems prevented promising British F2 driver Stephen South from qualifying. Watson recovered form sufficiently to cross the line in fourth place, but that was something of a false dawn.

Eventually, after crashing in Spain and then again at Watkins Glen, having taken sixths in Britain and Holland, the injured Prost decided to quit to join Renault. Against this backdrop, pressure continued to mount for a merger between McLaren and Ron Dennis's Project Four Racing team.

The previous year, 1979, Dennis and Marlboro had suggested such a thing to Teddy Mayer, who rebuffed the idea. Having been angered not to get the credit he felt was his due for designing Jim Hall's revolutionary Indianapolis Chaparral 2K, John Barnard had turned down a previous offer from Mayer to head McLaren's design department fearing his input might be diluted by the presence of his former boss, Gordon Coppuck. Mayer refused to consider sacking Coppuck, so the situation reached stalemate. Barnard instead joined forces with Ron Dennis and began designing a revolutionary Formula 1 car for Project Four. Now John Hogan of Marlboro was again pressing Mayer to reconsider a merger between the two parties. In the end it came down to a simple ultimatum: take the Project Four deal or face the loss of Marlboro's funding. Mayer knew how tough it was to find a major corporate sponsor at short notice and conceded. The merger went ahead in September, with Dennis and Mayer as joint-Managing Directors of a new entity called McLaren International. Towards the end of 1980 work began on the

Top: The M29's first race appearance was at the 1979 British GP at Silverstone. It proved much faster than the M28 and John Watson qualified the car seventh, finishing the race an encouraging eighth.

Above: The 1980 Monaco Grand Prix was a dismal weekend for the McLaren team. Watson failed to qualify and Prost (here) who at least made the race, was out by the first corner.

construction of Barnard's all-new car, the carbon fibre MP4 which would, the following year, turn F1 design on its head and play a significant role in restoring the team's fortunes.

In the meantime, the M29 soldiered on into 1981, with more detail changes, including a switch from Goodyear to Michelin tyres. Watson picked up two points for fifth place in the South African GP, which was promptly declared not to be of Championship status by the governing body, and the M29Fs were outclassed at Long Beach and Brazil, the MP4 could not come soon enough.

MODEL	McLaren M29		TRANSMISSION	McLaren/Hewland 6-speed		TYRES F/R	Goodyear
TYPE/FORMULA	Formula 1		CHASSIS	Double skinned aluminium & Nomex monocoque		LENGTH	173in - 4394mm
YEAR OF PRODUCTION	1979/1981		BODY	GRP nose, side pods, cockpit & engine cover		WIDTH	81in - 2057mm
DESIGNER	Gordon Coppuck		FRONT SUSPENSION	Upper rocker arm, operating inboard coil		HEIGHT	40in - 1016mm
EXAMPLES BUILT	3 (+2M29C)			spring/damper, lower wishbone, anti-roll bar		WHEELBASE	106in - 2692mm
ENGINE	Ford Cosworth DFV		REAR SUSPENSION	Upper wishbone/rocker arm operating inboard		TRACK F/R	68/62in - 1727/1575mm
CUBIC CAPACITY	2993cc			coil spring/damper, lower wishbone & link		WEIGHT	1295lb - 587kg
CARBURATION	Lucas fuel injection		BRAKES F/R	Outboard/inboard ventilated discs		PRINCIPAL DRIVERS	Watson, Tambay
POWER OUTPUT	470bhp		WHEELS DIAMETER x WIDTH F/R	13x11/13x18in		IDENTIFYING COLOURS	Red/White

SAIMA

2

Pros
BOS

TAG turbo

Marlb

CHAPTER

03

ALAIN
PROST

Before I started racing, McLaren was obviously one of the top names you heard about. With Bruce himself, the Formula One cars, the Can-Am cars, the Indy cars, and of course the orange livery - which I have very strong memories of as a boy - it was already so strong from a marketing point of view.

Even so, in 1979 I turned down the chance to take part in my first Grand Prix and drive for the team at Watkins Glen. It was almost my only opportunity at that time – I had started talks with Ligier, and with Bernie Ecclestone at Brabham – but when Marlboro's Paddy McNally contacted me and asked if I would drive, I knew it was too soon. I said that I would prefer to do some testing on a track I knew. He agreed, and in January of 1980 I went to Paul Ricard with McLaren. Without that opportunity I wouldn't be writing this now.

After that I was very happy to be at McLaren, with a good team-mate in John Watson, good relations with Teddy Mayer and the guys, and everyone made me very welcome. That first year I had many accidents, some were bad ones, but otherwise it was a very good year for me.

In 1981 I moved to Renault, at a time when the new technology was improving but the turbos were unreliable. I always remained on good terms with Ron Dennis and after three seasons at Renault I was really happy to go back to McLaren. Even though I am French I prefer to work with English people, the ambience at McLaren was more the way I like it and I felt comfortable. Everyone goes in the same direction at McLaren, it is well organised and has key people who are experienced. It's so much easier when you are professional and serious – much better!

In fact, looking back, of my four World Championships, the one with McLaren in 1986 was the toughest and the one I am most proud of. By then McLaren was my family. We had a difficult time in my last year with the team, fighting with Ayrton, but today, you know, I don't care too much about that. It's a shame how it worked out and why I left in 1990, because 'my team' really was McLaren.

After I stopped racing, I worked with McLaren again and was involved on the technical side alongside Ron. It was a really good time for me but in 1997 I left again but only to try and build my own team in France, you must realise. If I have one regret it is that I would have preferred to stay at McLaren, to have an involvement and to continue working with the team. To be part of the great team that it continues to be.

Alain Prost
Drivers' World Champion 1985, '86 & '89
McLaren MP4/2B, MP4/2C & MP4/5

The M30 was Gordon Coppuck's last design for McLaren, and the last Formula 1 contender to be raced by the team prior to the arrival in September 1980 of Ron Dennis and new Technical Director John Barnard. It was also the machine that contributed to Alain Prost leaving the team, following successful overtures from Renault.

It was introduced mid-season at Zandvoort, and despite having a two-inch shorter wheelbase and inch-wider track both front and rear, it weighed the same as the M29C, 1,320lbs. The running gear such as engine, transmission, suspension, brakes, wheels, steering assembly and instruments, was largely a carry-over from the M29C but crucially the honeycomb aluminium chassis was 50 per cent stiffer and the aerodynamics were improved. This was after Teddy Mayer himself had taken an M29 to the Motor Industry Research Association's (MIRA) wind tunnel. A major effort went into improving downforce with the M30 in the hope of restoring McLaren's competitiveness, but the results were patchy.

Though Alain Prost thought the car was an improvement over the M29, he was overshadowed in Holland as Watson put the spare M29C on the fifth row despite a heavy crash in practice with his intended race car. The Frenchman qualified the M30 in 18th, half-a-second slower, after complaining of oversteer. While Watson raced strongly and was running seventh when his engine broke, Prost also chased hard and brought his new car home a reasonably encouraging sixth on its debut. That would, however, be its sole World Championship point.

Two weeks later the M30 was back in action as the Italian GP switched briefly from Monza to Imola. Again, Watson in the M29C was faster as Prost struggled on to the back row of the grid after problems with his brakes and clutch and the handling. After a smooth drive he brought it home seventh, just outside the points.

In Canada later that September Watson was again quicker in qualifying in the old car, and Alain retired after 41 laps. John Barnard's arrival as Technical Director generated more development on the car in the form of a revised engine cover and floor and revisions to the suspension, but on the opening lap Prost clashed with Arrows driver Riccardo Patrese, and subsequently suffered suspension failure. The story was no happier in the US GP East at Watkins Glen, where the M30 was still almost a second slower than the M29C before Prost had a nasty accident when the car went straight on in a fourth-gear left-hander in practice. Another suspension failure was suspected. The Frenchman was still feeling giddy on race morning and having tried out the spare M29C wisely opted not to start.

At the time it was widely reported that the only M30 ever built had been destroyed in the incident, but in all honesty that was more because the team felt it would be better to stick with a revised version of the M29 for the start of the 1981 season. Thus the car, which had enjoyed a very limited topline racing career that encompassed just 172 competition laps and barely more than 485 miles, was left back in the stores in Colnbrook, slightly damaged and accompanied by a complete spare monocoque.

With hindsight it is easy to argue that using the M29 as a starting point, a car which was itself a stop-gap, meant the basic design of the M30 was always going to be compromised. But it came at a time when McLaren was struggling for its very survival as a competitive racing team and every avenue had to be explored. Subsequently the car was restored by Tony Dunne using the spare tub and raced in the UK by Irishman Alo Lawler. He won two non-F1 championships with it in 1984 and '85. Then it was sold to a collector in the USA before passing into the hands of a well know vintage racer who currently campaigns the one-off in US historic events.

Top: The M30 made its first press appearance (top) at a mid-year Silverstone test day. At the Canadian Grand Prix in Montreal (above) Prost ran as high as fourth in the race before suffering suspension failure and spinning out on lap 42.

Above: The squared-off front roll-hoop of the M30 is clearly visible in this high angle shot taken in the pit lane at the Italian Grand Prix. Alain Prost started last on the 24-car grid and made it to the finish just out of the points in seventh.

MODEL	McLaren M30
TYPE/FORMULA	Formula 1
YEAR OF PRODUCTION	1980
DESIGNER	Gordon Coppuck
EXAMPLES BUILT	1
ENGINE	Ford Cosworth DFV
CUBIC CAPACITY	2993cc
CARBURATION	Lucas fuel injection
POWER OUTPUT	470bhp

TRANSMISSION	McLaren/Hewland 5-speed
CHASSIS	Double skinned aluminium & Nomex monocoque
BODY	GRP nose, side pods, cockpit & engine cover
FRONT SUSPENSION	Upper rocker arm, operating inboard coil
	spring/damper, lower wishbone, anti-roll bar
REAR SUSPENSION	Upper wishbone/rocker arm operating inboard
	coil spring/damper, lower wishbone & link
BRAKES F/R	Outboard/inboard ventilated discs
WHEELS DIAMETER x WIDTH F/R	13or15x11/13x16or18in

TYRES F/R	Goodyear
LENGTH	169in - 4293mm
WIDTH	82in - 2082mm
HEIGHT	38in - 965mm
WHEELBASE	104in - 2642mm
TRACK F/R	69/63in - 1752/1600mm
WEIGHT	1320lb - 598kg
PRINCIPAL DRIVERS	Prost
IDENTIFYING COLOURS	Red/White

1981 MP4/1
FORMULA 1

"It was a big step into the unknown..... like flying Concorde when you've only ever flown a Boeing 707". If anything, John Watson's famous description of his first drive in John Barnard's completely new McLaren MP4/1 vastly undersold the concept. In reality what is arguably still the most significant car in McLaren's long history had more to do with space travel than commercial airline flying, even such a swift and elegant one such as Concorde.

The MP4/1 brought a change to McLaren's established nomenclature, standing for McLaren Project Four, and bore the distinction of being the first carbon composite Formula 1 design. The material had been used for small components since Graham Hill's eponymous Embassy-backed cars had used it for their rear wing supports in 1975, but not until the MP4/1 made its bow on March 5th 1981 had it been used for the entire chassis. Together with Lotus chief Colin Chapman whose controversial Lotus 88 would also use the material, Barnard had come to appreciate not just the lightness of carbon fibre but also its tremendous strength, and his new car would set a trend every bit as influential as Chapman's introduction of the monocoque chassis two decades earlier. It laid the groundwork for material innovation that has become such a hallmark of the McLaren Group's activities with cars such as the three-seater F1, the world's first fully composite road car, and the later Mercedes-Benz SLR McLaren as the world's first series production carbon composite car.

Born out of a singular vision, the MP4/1 remains as much as anything a testament to Barnard's character, drive and imagination. He had cut his teeth with Lola, and then McLaren in the early 1970s, before moving to Parnelli and Chaparral in the United States, yet it was his relative inexperience in F1 that paradoxically freed him to think outside the box. The focus in F1 at that time, he said, was very much on ground effects. *"The objective was to optimise it, and that meant using the biggest underwing I could get, which entailed a very small section chassis. I wanted to get my chassis down to not too much bigger than the driver's bum."* To Barnard, the only way to reduce the chassis section while retaining the necessary torsional stiffness was to use an entirely new material rather than just a different gauge of aluminium.

Sometimes controversial but never anything less than a highly gifted and always adventurous designer, he had been thinking about this particular problem long before the merger between Marlboro McLaren and Project Four Racing. He had also been hearing good things about carbon fibre composites: given the correct application it was clearly light, stiff, and extremely strong – perfect, in theory, for Formula 1.

Very few people knew much about it, however. A contact at British Aerospace provided some clues at a time when the material was being used for engine cowls for the Rolls-Royce RB211 turbofan engine. At the same time, however, its mysterious properties were called into question, Barnard

remembers, when someone easily snapped a piece of it in half (actually, a unidirectional piece which he bent the wrong way). Perhaps it was not, after all, the ideal material with which to build an entire Formula 1 car.

Others too, Barnard confirmed years later, *"thought we were mad,"* and even the man he describes as his design hero, Colin Chapman who was busy working on his technically brilliant but ultimately doomed Type 88 with its complex composite-mix 'twin chassis', went on record to say that a pure-carbon car of the sort McLaren was planning simply would not be safe enough.

Typically, Ron Dennis showed a far more positive approach, or as Barnard characterised it, *"He was very gung-ho. It was a very simple deal between us. He said, 'You tell me what you want to do technically, and I'll get the money.' That's how it went, and it worked, too!"*

Around this time a contact from Barnard's IndyCar days with Parnelli and Chaparral pointed him towards the Utah-based Hercules Corporation which had 'Skunk-Works' research and development section, and finally he was in business. Expressly conceived to think the unthinkable and play around with crazy ideas and odd one-offs, Hercules was the obvious place to start building his dream.

Barnard jumped on a flight to Salt Lake City with a quarter scale model of his proposed design in the cabin alongside him, and soon after the staff at Hercules set to work the MP4/1 began to take shape. As they lacked the technology and know-how to create curved pieces, the first monocoque was assembled using five major components, each one with flat faces. It had only a single major aluminium component, the internal front suspension bulkhead, compared to a conventional F1 car of the time which boasted around 50. Perhaps it looked a little rough and wrinkled in places, but it turned out even stronger than Barnard felt necessary, so for the next chassis plies were pulled out of the skin to make it lighter still.

Unfortunately, the new car wasn't ready for the start of the 1981 season, so John Watson and his new team-mate Andrea de Cesaris found themselves campaigning the outdated M29C. But it was well worth the wait.

In its first two races the sole MP4/1 qualified eleventh and seventh, making it to the line for its first race finish in San Marino in tenth. Watson qualified the MP4/1 a promising fifth on its debut at Zolder in the Belgian GP and ran a comfortable fourth until the late stages when gearbox problems dropped him back to seventh by the flag. He qualified tenth at Monaco and was heading for fourth place when the engine broke. Then came the start of what Wattie would later refer to as his 'Ted Rodgers' sweep, referring to the comedian's popular Three Two One game show. From fourth on the grid he finished third in Spain; in France a

front-row starting position translated into a superb race drive and second place just over two seconds behind first-time winner Alain Prost. Suddenly, McLaren was back. And then came the 1981 Marlboro British Grand Prix at Silverstone.

Watson and de Cesaris qualified fifth and sixth respectively as the turbocharged Renaults headed the grid. Watson's performance that day, July 18th, would be a vindication of so many things: Marlboro's faith in the team; Ron Dennis's faith in his inspired designer; and of course, John Barnard's faith in novel materials and a whole new way of doing things. It also represented a stunning return to form for the team Bruce McLaren had founded.

Alain Prost led initially for Renault, with team-mate René Arnoux riding shotgun. Watson was seventh at the end of the first lap, then was delayed further as he dropped to tenth by the fourth avoiding an accident in the Woodcote chicane at the end of lap three involving de Cesaris, Alan Jones and Gilles Villeneuve. But then he got his head down and charged. Nelson Piquet crashed his Brabham heavily; then Prost's car burned a valve. Suddenly, the McLaren was up to second place, albeit 25s adrift of Arnoux. And there it stayed for 30 laps. But on lap 50 the Renault's engine note changed; as Arnoux slowed, Watson went quicker and quicker and began scything down the gap, cheered on by an expectant crowd of his fellow countrymen. On lap 61 he swooped into the lead, and seven laps later was flagged off the winner of the British GP. It was McLaren's first Grand Prix victory since Fuji, four years earlier. And the first for a carbon fibre composite car.

Later, came the big shunt at Monza where Watson's MP4/1 was cut in half after he went off the road in the two fast Lesmo corners. But even as the engine and gearbox were

The official name for the new car, MP4 was understood to stand for 'Marlboro Project 4'. It wasn't until 1982 and the MP4/1B was announced that the original car became known as the MP4/1.

As this was only testing for the 1981 British Grand Prix at Silverstone it meant that the MP4/1 was able to run in its full Marlboro livery.

By the time of the race the following weekend the cars carried what was officially called 'Strobe' livery. John Watson scored a memorable victory.

MODEL	McLaren MP4/1
TYPE/FORMULA	Formula 1
YEAR OF PRODUCTION	1981
DESIGNER	John Barnard
EXAMPLES BUILT	4
ENGINE	Ford Cosworth DFV
CUBIC CAPACITY	2993cc
CARBURATION	Lucas fuel injection
POWER OUTPUT	470bhp

TRANSMISSION	McLaren/Hewland 5-speed
CHASSIS	Moulded carbon fibre/honeycomb monocoque
BODY	Carbon fibre composite panels
FRONT SUSPENSION	Upper rocker arm, operating inboard
	coil spring/damper, lower wishbone
REAR SUSPENSION	Upper wishbone/rocker arm operating
	inboard coil spring/damper, lower wishbone
BRAKES F/R	Outboard McLaren/Lockheed twin caliper
WHEELS DIAMETER x WIDTH F/R	13x11/13x16in

TYRES F/R	Michelin
LENGTH	170in - 4318mm
WIDTH	81in - 2057mm
HEIGHT	40in - 1016mm
WHEELBASE	104in - 2640mm
TRACK F/R	68/66in - 1730/1676mm
WEIGHT	1290lb - 585kg
PRINCIPAL DRIVERS	Watson, de Cesaris
IDENTIFYING COLOURS	Red/White

torn off, the monocoque structure remained intact. Wattie had walked away from a 140mph crash, and while the car did not look very pretty afterwards it had not, as so many sceptics had expected, exploded into a cloud of black dust.

When it had first been shown to the media, Tyler Alexander held aloft the 70lb monocoque, which boasted a quite amazing torsional stiffness of 15,000lb per degree, well over twice what could reasonably have been expected of an aluminium chassis at that time. Now, after the remarkable demonstration of the inherent strength of its chassis in the Monza accident, the team was approached by Britain's Civil Aviation Authority. Still wrestling with the problem of how it could certify composite components as safe for aircraft construction, its technical officers wanted to share the data arising from the Lesmo crash. Later still, having of course borrowed much of this new technology from the aerospace industry, McLaren found itself a supplier to that very industry, even gaining a commendation from NASA itself.

It was a win-win situation. The McLaren MP4/1 not only radically improved McLaren's chances but genuinely reinvigorated the sport as well. No less significantly, as rival teams looked at ways of building carbon composite cars of their own, the construction methods introduced by Barnard's MP4/1 made possibly the largest single contribution to driver safety of any innovation in the sport's history. By feeding loads along the axis of the strands in the material, carbon composite cars were able to boast a much higher stiffness-to-weight ratio, making them not just lighter and faster but safer too.

For all its success, the MP4/1 was not the finished article, and with its tendency to porpoise there was certainly room for further aerodynamic development. Nor was it ever a particularly easy car to drive. The nickname earned by de Cesaris — 'de Crasheris' — gives some indication as to how well his season went, and also explains in part why after finishing with only a single point he was replaced by Niki Lauda for 1982.

Watson quickly discovered that there were some downsides to the new material, notably that it had no 'give'. "If you banged your elbow in the cockpit, it really hurt." He had also been concerned about its crashworthiness and admitted that initially at least it had been hard to keep faith with Barnard's belief in it. The Monza accident finally convinced him, and others.

It changed many perceptions, inside and outside the sport. The McLaren MP4/1 had always been interesting because it had become a winner, but now the true advantages of its ground-breaking technology had been demonstrated worldwide. Potential applications for the new material were being identified almost weekly, and videos of Watson's crash were soon being used in the US to convince the military of the material's value as cladding for attack helicopters in need of underbody protection against fire from below. For this, and for the major leap forward that F1 safety took, the remarkable McLaren MP4/1 deserves all the credit it can get.

1982 MP4/1B
FORMULA 1

After the seismic changes which had been necessary to enable the progression from M30 to MP4/1, the further evolution in 1982 to 'B' specification required what seemed like only relatively modest changes. Barnard attempted to make the innovative chassis even stiffer and to pare off a little more weight. Stiffer suspension was also offered together with a switch to Michelin tyres, and carbon brake discs made an appearance on the cars during the year.

Behind the scenes, however, the activity in and around McLaren International to make all this happen had been considerable. Mechanically the car was still quite conventional, still using rocker-arm suspension and relying on the trusty Ford Cosworth DFV, but Ron Dennis was already looking to the future and work at Porsche was well underway on a new turbocharged V6, the funding for which was coming from the Paris-based, Saudi-financed, Techniques D'Avant Garde (TAG). TAG boss Mansour Ojjeh became a very close friend of Ron and would go on to become a major shareholder in the McLaren Group.

The team's own moving-ground wind tunnel was meanwhile installed in the National Maritime Institute facility at Feltham in Middlesex, to simulate the most realistic environment possible in which to study the dynamic interface between a car body and the road surface. Further real-time aerodynamic work was carried out at Paul Ricard in southern France, and at Michelin's Ladoux test facility.

The switch to Michelin tyres was to be one of the most significant changes. Crossply tyres such as Goodyear's grew at speed because of the centrifugal force, thus compensating for the way in which aerodynamic downforce also increased at speed. By contrast, John Watson observed, the Michelins seemed to squash down under high centrifugal loading at high speed, thereby affecting the behaviour of the aerodynamic skirts beneath the chassis and occasionally even causing the car to bottom out over bumps. This required even more fine tuning in the chassis set-up to allow for this 'squidging' effect and for the car to settle under aerodynamic loading out on the circuit. As a consequence, much time was spent adjusting spacers and bump rubbers to avoid taking up too much of the critical skirt travel.

Fortunately, Michelin was keen to help the newly successful McLaren team, building bespoke 15-inch front tyres which showed better reactions than either of the conventional 13s. With all this help from Michelin, McLaren soon discovered that the mechanical traction levels were so good that it could afford to run narrower rear tyres than its turbocharged rivals. As a result, the MP4/1B benefited from another small but measurable aerodynamic gain via reduced drag, especially compared to the fast-improving Renaults.

Throughout the season the team experimented with various set-ups, varying both the track and wheelbase of the cars by as much as four inches in the latter case before settling on a two-inch extension. The carbon discs were similarly fitted for two races, in California and Brazil, although McLaren later admitted that in this case it simply didn't fully understand the technology it was acquiring from the aviation industry.

On the one hand carbon discs brought a valuable saving in weight, as Brabham's Gordon Murray had discovered nearly six years previously. They also held out the promise of a better coefficient of friction than conventional steel discs because they could run at very high temperatures, but unfortunately in 1982 it could take half a year to make a set and in a sport as fast-moving as F1 that just wasn't practical. Similarly, their extremely high operating temperature was fine when a car was running but posed all sorts of problems if it should pit, or if it was running in the wet.

The season started well, with Niki Lauda and Watson both in the points for the first race at Kyalami, in fourth and sixth places respectively. At Long Beach, however, the tables were turned. Following an early spin during testing, and despite losing pole to – of all people – de Cesaris who was now with Alfa Romeo, Lauda won the race and Watson came sixth after a variety of mechanical problems.

After just three races with McLaren, Lauda and the team were second in the World Championships behind Renault, with Watson lying third. Boycotting the San Marino race, as many leading British teams did, McLaren returned for the Belgian race which was overshadowed by the death of

The 1982 season saw the return of Niki Lauda to the Grand Prix scene. At the British Grand Prix, held at Brands Hatch, he scored his second victory of the season in MP4/1-6.

Ferrari's great star Gilles Villeneuve. Watson set fastest lap and eventually took his first victory in the MP4/1B, putting him just a point behind Prost's Renault, but Lauda was disqualified from third place when a post-race check revealed his car was 1.8kg under weight. McLaren had miscalculated the weight loss through tyre and brake wear. Wattie's car was legal, by a kilo.

Another superb win in the inaugural street race in Detroit round put Watson and McLaren ahead in their respective World Championships, the Ulsterman having called in for harder Michelins during a brief stop before charging back to victory. Watson lost his points lead after finishing third behind the Brabhams in Canada, whilst Lauda posted a fourth in Holland and won well at Brands Hatch before a wrist injury forced him to miss the German race. By this time the turbocharged Ferraris and Renaults were dominating, and although Lauda went on to pick up points in Austria and at Dijon for the Swiss Grand Prix, it wasn't enough. At Monza, Watson scored his first points in three months and went to the finale in Las Vegas still in contention for the title. But second place there to Michele Alboreto's Tyrrell was too little too late. Losing out respectively to Keke Rosberg and Ferrari, McLaren had to content itself with runner-up slots in both the Drivers' and Constructors' World Championships.

MODEL	McLaren MP4/1B		TRANSMISSION	McLaren/Hewland 5-speed		TYRES F/R	Michelin
TYPE/FORMULA	Formula 1		CHASSIS	Moulded carbon fibre/honeycomb monocoque		LENGTH	175in - 4445mm
YEAR OF PRODUCTION	1982		BODY	Carbon fibre composite panels, sliding skirts		WIDTH	81in - 2057mm
DESIGNER	John Barnard		FRONT SUSPENSION	Upper rocker arm, operating inboard		HEIGHT	40in - 1016mm
EXAMPLES BUILT	5 (3 converted from MP4/1)			coil spring/damper, lower wishbone		WHEELBASE	105.6in - 2682mm
ENGINE	Ford Cosworth DFV		REAR SUSPENSION	Upper wishbone/rocker arm operating		TRACK F/R	71.5/66in - 1816/1676mm
CUBIC CAPACITY	2993cc			inboard coil spring/damper, lower wishbone		WEIGHT	1290lb - 585kg
CARBURATION	Lucas fuel injection		BRAKES F/R	Outboard McLaren/Lockheed twin caliper		PRINCIPAL DRIVERS	Watson, Lauda
POWER OUTPUT	480bhp		WHEELS DIAMETER x WIDTH F/R	13x11/13x16in		IDENTIFYING COLOURS	Red/White

1983 MP4/1C, MP4/1D & MP4/1E FORMULA 1

With personnel changes, new regulations and a new engine on the horizon, this was to be a season of momentous changes at McLaren, and following negotiations with Ron Dennis and John Barnard those great stalwarts from Bruce's days, Teddy Mayer and Tyler Alexander bowed out of the company.

The new season also brought new rules which outlawed ground-effect tunnel sections and required all cars to run flat-bottom chassis. While some management of the airflow beneath the car was still permitted, the intention was dramatically to reduce any associated benefits and thus to reduce downforce.

Some degree of ground effect could be restored by using an upswept diffuser at the rear and by smoothing the airflow around the rear wheels, but the overall effect of the rule changes was to disadvantage the less-powerful non-turbo cars quite significantly since they could no longer use their superior downforce to offset the greater horsepower of the turbocars. This remained the case even when Cosworth responded with a new short-stroke DFY version of its long-established V8, and with the 1499cc TAG Turbo V6 engine not yet up and running, this was to be a major cause for concern at McLaren International.

Any performance loss resulting from the abandonment of ground effect would have to be made up elsewhere, the most obvious answer being to compensate for the loss of undercar downforce by running larger front and rear wings. Unfortunately, any gains would come at the expense of increased drag, which would again inevitably affect the less powerful V8-engined cars rather more than it would the turbocharged Renaults, Ferraris and Brabhams.

This left McLaren, in particular, in a dilemma. Clearly in the V8 camp at the start, the team needed to modify its cars in line with the new aerodynamics regulations. But the engineers and aerodynamicists fully expected mid-season to be joining the turbo brigade with their own new engine. As John Barnard put it, "*It might be counter-productive to go all the way with a new Cosworth car for what might be less than a full season.*"

Meanwhile other teams, including Brabham, Ferrari, Ligier, Tyrrell and Renault, quickly moved to slim down their designs in an attempt to take advantage of the changes. For Barnard, however, it was to be more a case of continuing along his chosen path so that by the time the 1983 season started the new MP4/1C, but for its flat underside and the absence of skirts, looked not unlike its predecessor. There were modest low-level aerodynamic trays immediately ahead of the rear wheels, a waisted platform behind the side radiator mountings and a slight coke-bottle effect, but the family resemblance was certainly unmistakable.

The arrangement of the Cosworth engine, rear suspension and transmission was exactly as before, but in order to accommodate the turbo engine when it came with its additional pipework, extra radiators, twin KKK turbochargers and intercoolers, no attempt was made to slim down the rear end too much. Barnard was convinced that he could compensate for this, believing: "*We still have one of the best lift/drag ratios amongst current cars.*"

Once again, the car needed care when it came to setting it up, as there was sensitivity to ride height and suspension-rate changes. And the design of the front and rear wings was to be even more critical than before, now that they were providing 80 per cent of the total downforce.

Things started well, with Lauda third in Brazil, then Watson heading him home for an historic and totally unexpected back-to-front 1-2 in Long Beach after they struggled to get temperature into their qualifying tyres and started near the back of the grid. Watson was third in Detroit with fastest lap, third again in Holland, fifth in Germany and sixth in Canada, while Lauda added sixths in Britain and Austria. The nadir came at Monaco when the drivers struggled again to get sufficient temperature into Michelin's qualifying tyres and failed to qualify even though the French company had responded to McLaren's entreaties for improved rubber by sending new tyres to the Principality which arrived in time for practice and enabled them to shave an astonishing 1.8s off their dry lap times.

When the tyres worked, the MP4/1C could lead its Cosworth-brethren, but that was no longer sufficient to challenge the turbos. That made it doubly fortunate that by July, after a shakedown at Weissach, the new TAG Turbo TTE-P01 V6 engine was installed in what was officially termed the MP4/1D for some serious testing at Silverstone ahead of the Dutch GP in August.

Perhaps irked that Lauda got the sole new car for that event, Watson drove outstandingly to take a podium finish and to upstage the debut of the new MP4/1E, which clearly still needed substantial sorting. With an estimated 700bhp at 11,700rpm Niki found that his new TAG-powered car was very fast in a straight line, but still lacked grip.

Subsequent races saw both drivers run the new cars, but they were still under development and did not show significant performance improvements relative to their opposition and were not reliable. But this development phase would be crucial in ironing out the faults ahead of 1984, when things would be very different.

MODEL	McLaren MP4/1C	TRANSMISSION	McLaren/Hewland 5-speed	TYRES F/R	Michelin
TYPE/FORMULA	Formula 1	CHASSIS	Moulded carbon fibre/honeycomb monocoque	LENGTH	167in - 4242mm
YEAR OF PRODUCTION	1983	BODY	Carbon fibre composite panels	WIDTH	84in - 2133mm
DESIGNER	John Barnard	FRONT SUSPENSION	Double wishbone, push-rod operating	HEIGHT	40in - 1016mm
EXAMPLES BUILT	1 (+3 converted from MP4/1B)		inboard coil spring/damper	WHEELBASE	105.8in - 2687mm
ENGINE	Ford Cosworth DFV/DFY	REAR SUSPENSION	Upper wishbone/rocker arm operating	TRACK F/R	71.5/66in - 1816/1676mm
CUBIC CAPACITY	2993cc		inboard coil spring/damper, lower wishbone	WEIGHT	1191lb - 540kg
CARBURATION	Lucas fuel injection	BRAKES F/R	Outboard McLaren/AP Racing twin caliper	PRINCIPAL DRIVERS	Watson, Lauda
POWER OUTPUT	480-510bhp	WHEELS DIAMETER x WIDTH F/R	13x11/13x16in	IDENTIFYING COLOURS	Red/White

1984 MP4/2
FORMULA 1

Having spent three seasons preparing to win on a regular basis, notwithstanding the six triumphs since 1981, McLaren at last had everything in place to sweep the board. It may have been slightly late joining the turbo generation, but the preparation for it had been typically thorough and from now on the team was ready to stamp an indelible mark on the 1980s.

By the start of 1984 everything that had been learned from the interim MP4/1E had been incorporated into the design of the new MP4/2, which John Barnard believed was far more integrated. The team had a much better understanding of the 80-degree one million Deutschmark TAG V6 and it was now producing an extra 50bhp compared to the previous season. Everything was neatly packaged, in one of the first truly homogenous F1 designs of the era, and after strenuous testing the MP4/2 was ready to catapult the team into the front rank.

The new car shared much in common with the outgoing MP4/1E, but the monocoque was redesigned to accommodate the shorter engine and the larger, 220-litre fuel cell that it required. The curve of the sidepods changed too, as the turbochargers were positioned as far forward as possible so that the pods could curve in at the rear to maximise the coke bottle and enclose the engine and gearbox in the most aerodynamically efficient way.

Remarkably, McLaren would dominate the season using just three cars: MP4/2-1 for Niki Lauda, MP4/2-2 for Alain Prost, and a T-car numbered MP4/3. Lauda, indeed, used just that one car throughout the entire 16-race season, the odd knock never severe enough to compromise the strength of the Hercules-built CFC monocoque.

Prost's return was a major coup, giving the team a tremendously strong driving partnership. The Frenchman was now a seasoned Grand Prix winner, and he had a point to prove after being fired by Renault when the French manufacturer's World Championship challenge collapsed in the South African denouement the previous year.

It quickly became apparent that in the MP4/2 Prost and Lauda had the tool to dominate the 1984 season from start to finish. With two World Championships under his belt, Lauda as the incumbent star insisted that he would do the majority of the testing and development of the car. However, as the season progressed there was no escaping the fact that the younger Prost was the faster driver. This was particularly so in qualifying, but over the course of the season 'The Professor' was also to win seven races to Lauda's five.

If the car had any weakness it was in the areas of braking and the gearbox. The team was still relying on a transmission unit designed for the less powerful Cosworth era. As for the brakes, it was still experimenting with CFC components whose performance under stress remained a major limiting factor. Different forms and shapes of cooling ducts were developed and tested, but as the season progressed all that really emerged was that on circuits demanding frequent heavy braking the time between one application and the next was insufficient to allow for cooling.

On the plus side, the performance of the new engine completely vindicated Ron Dennis's decision to commission Porsche. BMW had also been considered, but the need for bracing struts for its turbocharged four-cylinder engine was incompatible with Barnard's intended rear-end design and he was similarly unhappy with the compromises which would have been required by the adoption of Renault's own V6. With the TAG engine he could dictate from the outset where key components were located, thus harmonising the installation in a manner not seen since Colin Chapman first worked with Cosworth to install the DFV in the Lotus 49.

McLaren's wind tunnel expertise was also key. Barnard told Motor Sport readers in 2005: "*I think we were well ahead of the other teams in terms of... the way we could anchor and move [our scale models]. So we had faith in our aero numbers. The combination of rear wing, winglets and diffuser worked tremendously on the MP4/2.*" By generating plenty of rear-end grip in this way, the car inspired great confidence in both drivers.

"*We knew from that first test that we had a strong car,*" Barnard said, but he admitted that he was frustrated with the new rule changes, calling the period of this highly successful car's gestation, "*One of my most annoying times in F1*". In particular he felt that the switch to flat-bottomed cars effectively robbed the team of up to 50 per cent of the engine's potential, nullifying much of the advantage it should have brought at a time when no other team had gone quite so far as to have a whole new engine built to suit the regulations then in force.

Even compromised in this way, however, the MP4/2 was to give McLaren those 12 wins from the 16 races, lead Lauda to his third Drivers' World Championship, and massacre the opposition in winning the Constructors' Cup by an incredible 86 points. True, a loose front wheel cost Prost the win at Dijon, Porsche still had some work to do on its engine, and the brake-cooling issue still needed to be resolved, while one can only imagine Prost's frustration at winning more races but losing out to Lauda by half a point. But in every other regard the MP4/2 provided McLaren with a near-perfect season, and everyone else on the grid with a warning shot that no-one could ignore.

During 1983 a development TAG engine was squeezed into a Porsche 911 Turbo roadcar and run on the test track in Germany. By the start of the 1984 season the engine was producing around 750bhp.

The previous season's engine development program paid dividends and meant that the 1984 season started off well. Alain Prost's first race back at McLaren resulted in a fine win in the Brazilian GP.

Two weeks later at Monza Lauda qualified fourth but benefited from the misfortune of others and took an easy win, his fifth of the season.

MODEL	McLaren MP4/2
TYPE/FORMULA	Formula 1
YEAR OF PRODUCTION	1984
DESIGNER	John Barnard
EXAMPLES BUILT	5
ENGINE	TAG Turbo TTE PO1 V6
CUBIC CAPACITY	1496cc
INDUCTION	Twin KKK turbochargers
POWER OUTPUT	750bhp

TRANSMISSION	McLaren/Hewland 5-speed
CHASSIS	Moulded carbon fibre/honeycomb monocoque
BODY	Carbon fibre single piece cockpit/engine cover & nose
FRONT SUSPENSION	Double wishbone, push-rod operating
	inboard coil spring/damper
REAR SUSPENSION	Upper wishbone/rocker arm operating
	inboard coil spring/damper, lower wishbone
BRAKES F/R	Outboard SEP carbon discs/McLaren twin caliper
WHEELS DIAMETER x WIDTH F/R	13x11/13x16in

TYRES F/R	Michelin
LENGTH	171in - 4343mm
WIDTH	84in - 2133mm
HEIGHT	39in - 991mm
WHEELBASE	109in - 2768mm
TRACK F/R	71.5/66in - 1816/1676mm
WEIGHT	1191lb - 540kg
PRINCIPAL DRIVERS	Prost, Lauda
IDENTIFYING COLOURS	Red/White

Yet another McLaren driver crowned World Champion, and another Constructors' Championship win for the team itself, can leave the misleading impression that life at Woking in 1985 went on pretty much as it had the previous season – but that was far from the case.

McLaren was certainly still the team everyone had to watch, and the MP4/2B the car to catch. But while development work had continued apace with John Barnard and his colleagues beavering away to keep Alain Prost and Niki Lauda ahead of the pack, and KKK had devised a completely new pair of 'mirror image' blowers for the TAG V6, Michelin had withdrawn and obliged the team to revert to Goodyear. Later, a wrist injury forced Lauda to miss the European Grand Prix, so John Watson returned in a stand-in role, and the Austrian's wretched final year in F1 ended with only 14 points. Prost, however, romped home with a title-winning 73 and five GP victories to Lauda's one.

The MP4/2B went from strength to strength, somewhat to the surprise of the opposition who had dared to hope that their own developments over the winter would have rendered the defending team slightly less competitive. The leading teams which were already using Goodyears certainly hoped so, having convinced themselves that after the less consistent performance of Goodyear's new radials during much of the previous season, Michelin's withdrawal would put McLaren on a more equal footing with them. Some observers also felt that the latest round of regulation changes – outlawing rear wing extensions in a bid to reduce downforce – would affect McLaren disproportionately.

Instead, Barnard's new turbocharger arrangement helped to keep the McLaren TAG firmly in play. He devised a typically innovative enhancement to alleviate problems experienced during the previous season. At that time the inlet for the KKK turbos was ahead of the rear wheel, in a high-pressure area which left the delicate impeller blades vulnerable to grit and debris. To resolve this, he asked KKK to make right and left-handed turbos which could then be positioned closer to the engine, front-to-back, so that the inlet could be relocated behind the intercooler.

Externally, the new car looked at first glance much like its predecessor, most of the changes being detail ones beneath the skin, such as subtle aerodynamic detailing, and new suspension which incorporated pushrods for the first time, together with inboard auxiliary rockers and upper wishbones.

Any optimism in rival camps received something of a boost at the first race of the season in Brazil when it quickly became apparent that Ferrari, Williams and Lotus were usually going to qualify ahead of the MP4/2Bs. This was largely thanks to the more powerful engines supplied to those teams solely for qualifying, whilst the TAG-powered cars, unable to run at such high boost pressures, chose to rely on a better race package to (hopefully) win the day.

That confidence was borne out in Rio, the McLarens fronting the field during the warm-up and Prost dicing fiercely with Michele Alboreto's Ferrari before romping home in first place as an electrical failure took out Lauda. The Austrian was similarly unlucky at the next round in Portugal, his V6 refusing to function effectively above 10,000rpm, while Prost who had been lying second behind Ayrton Senna's Lotus Renault crashed out after aquaplaning on the straight.

Imola for the San Marino GP looked more promising, the MP4/2Bs playing their trump card in the shape of a trip computer set up to show how much fuel remained onboard.

This was a crucially important weapon at a time of restricted fuel loads, and 'The Professor' used his to establish that he would run dry if he tried to keep pace, initially, with Senna. He sat back whilst both Senna and the Ferrari of Stefan Johansson ran out of fuel. It was a cunning, race-winning manoeuvre - until the scrutineers found his MP4/2B to be two kilogrammes underweight and disallowed the win. One of McLaren's key strengths had rebounded badly, costing nine points.

With his rigorously applied and highly professional driving skills more than making up for the turbo problems he was suffering for much of the race, Prost won at Monaco for the second year in succession. Canada and Detroit were markedly less successful, brake cooling proving a major headache thanks to the stop-start nature of the latter race, but despite problems with the CFC discs McLaren stuck with them, and when the circus returned to Paul Ricard the cars' inherently superior aerodynamics provided some ammunition against the more powerful Williams-Hondas. Lauda led Prost until he was removed by mechanical failure (possibly linked to running with too much boost) and Prost eventually finished third.

In Austria Lauda confirmed he was going to retire at the end of the season and failed to win in front of his home crowd, a turbo shaft fracturing on lap 40 after some magnificent driving. At Zandvoort he was finer still, beating Prost into second place although the latter was looking secure as the first-ever French World Champion. Lauda then missed the Belgian race due to a wrist injury and failed to finish in both South Africa and Australia, winding up a disappointed 10th overall after a season of bitter ill-fortune. Prost though took the World Championship easily, and McLaren picked up another Constructors' trophy with a resounding 90 points.

The Monaco Grand Prix in May gave Alain Prost his second win of the 1985 season. He took the lead from Senna on lap 12 and fought off a strong challenge from Alboreto's Ferrari to win by five seconds.

MODEL	McLaren MP4/2B	TRANSMISSION	McLaren 5-speed	TYRES F/R	Goodyear
TYPE/FORMULA	Formula 1	CHASSIS	Moulded carbon fibre/honeycomb monocoque	LENGTH	172in - 4369mm
YEAR OF PRODUCTION	1985	BODY	Carbon fibre single piece cockpit/engine cover & nose	WIDTH	83in - 2108mm
DESIGNER	John Barnard	FRONT SUSPENSION	Double wishbone, push-rod operating	HEIGHT	39in - 991mm
EXAMPLES BUILT	5		inboard coil spring/damper	WHEELBASE	109in - 2768mm
ENGINE	TAG Turbo TTE PO1 V6	REAR SUSPENSION	Upper wishbone/rocker arm operating	TRACK F/R	71.5/66in - 1816/1676mm
CUBIC CAPACITY	1496cc		inboard coil spring/damper, lower wishbone	WEIGHT	1191lb - 540kg
INDUCTION	Twin KKK turbochargers	BRAKES F/R	Outboard SEP carbon discs/McLaren twin caliper	PRINCIPAL DRIVERS	Prost, Lauda
POWER OUTPUT	750bhp	WHEELS DIAMETER x WIDTH F/R	13x12/13x16.5in	IDENTIFYING COLOURS	Red/White

1986 MP4/2C
FORMULA 1

Finland's fast and aggressive ex-World Champion Keke Rosberg moved into Lauda's seat for 1986, but his and Alain Prost's new MP4/2Cs yet again looked pretty much like the previous year's cars.

Once again, however, the changes were under the skin. One of the most important was a smaller fuel tank, as new regulations limited cars to a maximum capacity of 195 litres instead of 220. This was to be John Barnard's last season with the team but until the end he continued to refine his pioneering design, instigating a new six-speed gearbox and a revised version of Bosch's superb Motronic engine management system. The car's overall dimensions remained unchanged, but maximum power was up to something approaching 800bhp at 12,000rpm.

Together with the arrival of Rosberg — allegedly 'the fastest man in Formula 1' — McLaren fans had plenty to look forward to. Many were keen to see whether Prost could buck the opinion of former champion Jackie Stewart, who long ago had mentioned how hard it was for both driver and team to remain hungry enough to win when they had already tasted success. Others wondered whether the flying Finn would manage to unseat Prost to become the de facto number one.

The answers to both questions took very little time to surface: a definite yes to the first — Prost was still ravenous — and an equally forthright no to the second, not least because of Barnard's refusal to change his car to reduce the understeer and better suit it to Rosberg's driving style.

As Barnard had designed it, the MP4/2C could not have been more perfect for Prost. It suited his smooth and scrupulously considered driving style. Rosberg was inherently just as quick, but his speed came from his press-on style, and that just did not work with the MP4/2.

Imola provided all the evidence anyone needed of the value of the new car, Prost romping home brilliantly despite a computer glitch which denied him an accurate reading of his fuel status. He crossed the line to the accompaniment of tyre and crowd noise only, having run out of fuel. Rosberg was less fortunate, however, and looked a tad foolish when he too ran dry two laps from the end. He later protested, "*I'm not a fool. I can read a fuel gauge!*" The same glitch was to blame.

Monaco was much better, however. Prost's third victory on the famous street circuit — he won by 25s — was supported by a fantastic drive from Rosberg who fought his way up to second using some thrilling overtaking manoeuvres to charge through the traffic from his ninth place start position.

And for Prost, at least, Belgium was eventful since a first-lap collision meant that instead of winning, which he certainly deserved, he came away with only a single Championship point. Canada was more fruitful, the Williams-Hondas of Mansell and Piquet taking first and third, with Prost and Rosberg managing to sandwich the Brazilian to take second and fourth. Detroit yielded a third place too, despite Prost's well-advertised dislike of the course and a shunt in practice.

France provided a repeat of the Canadian race, which meant points at least, but things went badly at Brands Hatch with Prost actually being lapped but taking third and Rosberg out with another gearbox failure. Hopes now rested on the German event, which in a sense was a semi-home fixture thanks to the immense contribution made by Porsche and Bosch, the latter even then busy making further revisions to the Motronic engine management set-up. Rosberg now had the set-up he had wanted and, having announced earlier in

After an absence of five years the Spanish GP returned to the calendar. The team scored its first points of the year with Prost third and Rosberg fourth.

Having challenged for the lead of the German Grand Prix both McLarens ran out of fuel on the penultimate lap. Rosberg was classified fifth and Prost sixth.

the week his decision to retire at the end of the season, he took his first pole of the season. He had a fine battle with Nelson Piquet, harrying the Williams-Honda driver, before running out of fuel just a lap from the end. Prost too ran dry, and made his feelings clear by pushing his car towards the line even though he knew this was technically not allowed.

In Hungary both drivers qualified well for the inaugural event but then attempted to pit at the same time, with Rosberg being forced to go back out with a deflating tyre while the crew wrestled with an electrical fault in the T-car which Prost had been forced to use. Both eventually retired but in Austria things looked more promising with Rosberg charging hard against the apparently unstoppable Benetton-BMWs before having to pull out with a dead engine when second place looked secure. Once again Prost's experience shone through, however, and despite suffering similar problems he nursed his car along to a somewhat lucky victory.

In Italy he was less fortunate, his engine blowing up, whilst Rosberg took fourth for his last-ever GP points. Prost managed second, and in high-altitude Mexico he repeated that result, despite losing a cylinder. He then headed to Adelaide for the final showdown where a fantastic win — after Nigel Mansell blew a tyre and Piquet was called in for a precautionary stop — brought him a second consecutive Drivers' World Championship. McLaren finished second to Williams in the Constructors' title.

MODEL	McLaren MP4/2C		TRANSMISSION	McLaren 6-speed		TYRES F/R	Goodyear
TYPE/FORMULA	Formula 1		CHASSIS	Moulded carbon fibre/honeycomb monocoque		LENGTH	173in - 4394mm
YEAR OF PRODUCTION	1986		BODY	Carbon fibre single piece cockpit/engine cover & nose		WIDTH	83in - 2108mm
DESIGNER	John Barnard		FRONT SUSPENSION	Double wishbone, push-rod operating		HEIGHT	39in - 991mm
EXAMPLES BUILT	5			inboard coil spring/damper		WHEELBASE	110in - 2794mm
ENGINE	TAG Turbo TTE PO1 V6		REAR SUSPENSION	Upper wishbone/rocker arm operating		TRACK F/R	71.5/66in - 1816/1676mm
CUBIC CAPACITY	1496cc			inboard coil spring/damper, lower wishbone		WEIGHT	1191lb - 540kg
INDUCTION	Twin KKK turbochargers		BRAKES F/R	Outboard SEP carbon discs/McLaren twin caliper		PRINCIPAL DRIVERS	Prost, Rosberg
POWER OUTPUT	750bhp		WHEELS DIAMETER x WIDTH F/R	13x11.5/13x16.25in		IDENTIFYING COLOURS	Red/White

With John Barnard gone, Steve Nichols, who had worked alongside Barnard since 1981, stepped in as McLaren's Formula 1 Project Leader. Stefan Johansson came on board to partner Alain Prost. The Swede had won the 1980 British Formula 3 Championship, driving a Project Four Racing Ralt.

Nichols laid the groundwork for a new design, hence the revised nomenclature. It was similar in concept to the MP4/2, but with a different monocoque. It was narrower at the back in order to improve airflow around the rear wheels and over the wing, and also had a different profile around the cockpit.

Otherwise there were, as Nichols was the first to admit, "*A lot of good things about the existing MP4/2*," so with time short and most of the team responsible for the Barnard car still in place, it was agreed to establish just how much could be done in the time available, and how much of that actually needed to be done.

The push-rod suspension was left alone, since it was thought at the time that it would take considerable work on it to make even the most marginal gains. The previous car had performed very well in terms of its basic handling and being kind to its tyres. McLaren's own six-speed gearbox remained unchanged too, along with the basic rear wing design.

There was scope, however, to pare weight from the chassis, since this had only partly been modified when the smaller fuel cells had been introduced for 1986. Work in the wind tunnel also pointed towards some further development of the aerodynamics, and the introduction of new sidepods with side-exiting radiator outlets instead of top ones to optimise some changes to the cooling system. The new tub still made use of the same processes and materials as before, but now had new bodywork and a lower engine cover which gave the car a noticeably sleeker appearance.

There was much work to do in the engine, the once-envied TAG-Porsche V6 now beginning at last to show its age. Throughout the winter Porsche worked hard on the engine

management systems. In a bid to raise power, to 850bhp at 12,000rpm, and to improve overall economy and throttle response, Porsche increased the compression ratio three times, but the law of diminishing returns made its presence felt and a misfire would sometimes set in. The engine's boost was also now controlled to accommodate a new requirement for pop-off valves to prevent boost pressure rising higher than 4.0bar.

While the V6 was still capable of turning in outstanding performances – most obviously Prost and Johansson's first and second at Spa – the increase in power came at a cost of increased weight, which upset the balance of the engine slightly. This led to some problems with vibration, which together with the misfires was accompanied by a number of alternator drive-belt breakages.

In Brazil, after very little testing, Prost expressed himself mostly pleased with the car, especially its increased downforce, although his race engineer still had some work to do to cut the level of understeer. The engineer was Gordon

At Hockenheim, Johansson equalled his best-ever GP result with second place behind Piquet's Williams. It was a close call, though. Halfway round the last lap, a front tyre deflated and he crossed the line with a wheel hanging off.

Murray, who had joined from Brabham, and he was soon aided by the arrival of Neil Oatley from Haas-Lola, further strengthening the new McLaren line-up.

The season got off to a good start, with Prost winning in Rio and Johansson two places behind. At Imola, where both cars had a mixture problem, Prost retired on lap 15 with an alternator failure, and Johansson came fourth after losing a wing endplate. At Spa things flipped back the other way again, with Prost winning to equal Jackie Stewart's historic tally of 27 Grand Prix wins and Johansson the runner-up.

In Monaco, vibrations, computer glitches and belt breakages forced both drivers out and in the French round Johansson once again suffered belt failure although Prost at least managed third behind Nigel Mansell and Nelson Piquet's Williams-Hondas, even with his engine misfiring badly.

At Silverstone rumours began to surface that representatives of Honda had been spotted in Woking, and Prost confirmed he was remaining with the team for the next season. In Germany, Johansson came second despite losing a tyre, but Prost quit four laps from the end with yet another broken belt. The Frenchman won in Portugal, but overall the year belonged to Piquet and Williams.

Away from the circuit there was more to celebrate. At Monza it was confirmed that Honda would join McLaren at the end of 1987, and that Ayrton Senna would come onboard to partner 'The Professor'. For the first time since 1983 a McLaren driver had not won the World Championship, but the team came second in the Constructors' Cup with a respectable 76 points.

MODEL	McLaren MP4/3	TRANSMISSION	McLaren 6-speed	TYRES F/R	Goodyear
TYPE/FORMULA	Formula 1	CHASSIS	Moulded carbon fibre/honeycomb monocoque	LENGTH	172in - 4369mm
YEAR OF PRODUCTION	1987	BODY	Carbon fibre single piece cockpit/engine cover & nose	WIDTH	84in - 2134mm
DESIGNER	Steve Nichols	FRONT SUSPENSION	Double wishbone, push-rod operating	HEIGHT	38in - 965mm
EXAMPLES BUILT	6		inboard coil spring/damper	WHEELBASE	109in - 2768mm
ENGINE	TAG Turbo TTE PO1 V6	REAR SUSPENSION	Upper wishbone/rocker arm operating	TRACK F/R	71.5/66in - 1816/1676mm
CUBIC CAPACITY	1496cc		inboard coil spring/damper, lower wishbone	WEIGHT	1191lb - 540kg
INDUCTION	Twin KKK turbochargers	BRAKES F/R	Outboard SEP carbon discs/McLaren twin caliper	PRINCIPAL DRIVERS	Prost, Johansson
POWER OUTPUT	850bhp	WHEELS DIAMETER x WIDTH F/R	13x11.5/13x16.25in	IDENTIFYING COLOURS	Red/White

1987 MP4/3B
FORMULA 1 TEST CAR

Dimensionally the same as the MP4/3, and with identical suspension, the MP4/3B was created by taking Steve Nichols's 1987 car and converting it to run Honda's new RA 108E V6 engine in place of the TAG built Porsche V6.

For much of 1987 Honda had been the dominant engine supplier, and once fitted with its new V6 the McLaren MP4/3B ran as an engine test-bed during the 1987/88 off-season. With Alain Prost and then Ayrton Senna behind the wheel it fulfilled this crucial role right up until the first race of the new season, with some additional development work being carried out on the car at Honda's own circuit, Suzuka, in Japan.

Although it used a standard moulded carbon fibre/honeycomb composite-type MP4/3 chassis, the 3B was equipped with a special new casing for the McLaren six-speed gearbox and oil tank in order to accommodate the Honda engine. Oil and water-cooling arrangements remained as before, however, with special air-intercoolers installed, again to suit the Japanese engine.

The latter also called for a new engine cover and this had a slightly revised profile, although in every other respect the two cars built to this specification retained most of the existing MP4/3 bodywork and to most observers would have looked much the same. Underneath, however, the big change, the new engine, was to prove truly decisive for the team – as the astonishing results with the soon-to-be-revealed MP4/4 would show.

Nothing lasts forever and much of McLaren's problems during the 1987 season were down to its choice of engines. While the continuing development of the once famously clean-sheet TAG Porsche design – for a good while (and understandably) much coveted by McLaren's rivals – had achieved a few miracles in its time, by this point it had all but reached it's the end of its development road.

The team at Porsche had worked long and hard to wring additional power from the unit, increasing its compression ratio in order to raise it to 850bhp at 12,000rpm whilst managing to improve both its throttle response and fuel consumption. In this form Prost claimed he was happy with the car, but there was no escaping its shortcomings, in particular the extra weight which came with the power hike and the loss of overall balance which resulted from this, and the lack of horsepower compared to rivals such as Honda, Ferrari and Renault.

Before long, vibrations, regular misfires and a number of alternator drive-belt breakages were sending a clear message that the package needed more than a simple overhaul. For McLaren, Honda's defection from the Williams camp (they stayed with Lotus for the 1988 season) could scarcely have come at a better time.

Designed for the new 1988 regulations which reduced fuel capacity to only 150 litres and introduced a new mandatory 2.8-bar turbo boost limit, the RA108E V6 underlined that Honda was in fighting form, determined to end the turbo era

Over the winter of 1987/88 Ayrton Senna and Alain Prost took the hot seat and tested the Honda engined MP4/3B extensively. The cockpit was devoid of most of the electronics and adjustment controls used during races.

To most observers the MP4/3B looked identical to the regular MP4/3. Minor changes to the engine cover hid the major difference - the installation of the Honda RA108E V6 engine and a special gearbox/oil tank casing designed to suit the Honda engine.

on a high. As a result, the V6, whilst in a sense 'transitional' and 'interim' was to more than compensate for the changes which – with a total ban on turbo engines clearly imminent – would otherwise have heavily favoured McLaren's normally aspirated rivals.

As well as allowing for the new lower boost pressure, the engine's designers had brilliantly conceived a unit that could be located as low as possible in the chassis. That in turn enabled the drivers of what was to become the outstanding MP4/4 to lie even closer to the horizontal; Steve Nichols, Gordon Murray and Bob Bell were thus able to produce a car with an even shallower body profile than before as well as a much reduced frontal area.

Given what was to come, and despite the fact that it never raced itself, the MP4/3B was a significant machine in McLaren's history.

MODEL	McLaren MP4/3B	TRANSMISSION	McLaren 6-speed	TYRES F/R	Goodyear
TYPE/FORMULA	Formula 1 Test Car	CHASSIS	Moulded carbon fibre/honeycomb monocoque	LENGTH	173in - 4394mm
YEAR OF PRODUCTION	1987	BODY	Carbon fibre single piece cockpit/engine cover & nose	WIDTH	84.25in - 2140mm
DESIGNER	Steve Nichols	FRONT SUSPENSION	Double wishbone, push-rod operating	HEIGHT	37in - 940mm
EXAMPLES BUILT	2 converted from MP4/3		inboard coil spring/damper	WHEELBASE	109in - 2768mm
ENGINE	Honda RA108E Turbo V6	REAR SUSPENSION	Upper wishbone/rocker arm operating	TRACK F/R	71.5/66in - 1816/1676mm
CUBIC CAPACITY	1496cc		inboard coil spring/damper, lower wishbone	WEIGHT	1191lb - 540kg
INDUCTION	Twin IHI turbochargers	BRAKES F/R	Outboard SEP carbon discs/McLaren twin caliper	PRINCIPAL DRIVERS	Prost, Senna
POWER OUTPUT	850bhp	WHEELS DIAMETER x WIDTH F/R	13x12/13x16.5in	IDENTIFYING COLOURS	Red/White

1988 MP4/4 FORMULA 1

Having completed just a handful of laps in the new 1988 MP4/4, Alain Prost reportedly told Team Principal Ron Dennis that he knew the car would win the World Championship. Indeed, not long after that, Neil Trundle, McLaren's chief mechanic at the time and Dennis's former partner in Rondel Racing, admitted that many people in the team, *"Already felt we could even win all the races."*

The high level of optimism at McLaren, following the arrival of its new Honda V6 engine and of Ayrton Senna as Prost's partner, was not diluted by rule changes for the 1988 season. These brought in a further reduction in fuel capacity to 150 litres and a mandatory 2.8-bar turbo boost limit, the benefit of both in theory going to McLaren's normally aspirated rivals in a move clearly made ahead of the imminent ban on turbo technology which would come into effect for 1989.

So swingeing was the fuel capacity rule that many expected 1988 to be a transitional year for the turbo teams rather than a winning one. But for McLaren at least it was to be nothing of the sort.

The new MP4/4 won 15 out of 16 races, losing only Monza which many felt was a self-inflicted defeat after Senna tripped over back marker Jean-Louis Schlesser's Williams-Judd in the first chicane. The Brazilian started on pole no fewer than 13 times and won eight races to take the World Championship despite having been disqualified in the opener in Brazil. At the same time, winning a scarcely less remarkable seven rounds, Prost found himself just three points adrift of the top slot leaving McLaren's nearest rival, third placed Gerhard Berger, literally miles behind. By the end of the season McLaren had scored a phenomenal 199 points in the Constructors' Cup, almost three times the tally of runner-up Ferrari.

The car which enabled them to achieve all this, a design which Trundle still insists is, *"The perfect package, still the lowest and sleekest-looking car on display at the team HQ,"* was not only a highly effective development of the 1981 carbon composite concept but also one which was correct in its tiniest details. With light overall weight, outstanding downforce, highly efficient brakes and suspension, and a fabulous V6 in the form of Honda's RA168-E, Trundle is one of many who has no doubts that it was McLaren's best-ever car.

In the hands of two of the world's best drivers, the McLaren Honda MP4/4 was quickly to prove itself unbeatable. Honda's new engine was mounted so low in the chassis that it required a new six-speed, three-shaft gearbox, devised by David North in the UK and Pete Weisman in the US. With a shallower body profile, the drivers were also made to lie more prone – something which suited Senna's driving style but to which Prost objected until wind tunnel results rendered his arguments untenable.

Lowering everything in this way enabled Murray and aerodynamicist Bob Bell to reduce the car's frontal area by ten per cent, which in turn helped improve the lift-to-drag ratio by six per cent because a simpler rear wing could be kept further away from the upper deck of the car. The wheelbase was four centimetres longer, and the car's longer nose housed a mandatory deformable structure.

Only when it came to the distance from the ground did Murray resist the temptation to go lower still, choosing instead *"To build with lots of wheel travel, sacrificing a little downforce by not running the car too close to the ground. That made it more comfortable and easier to set up."*

Crucially his skill and famous attention to detail and determination to get it right were matched point-for-point by Ron Dennis, who told him: *"You have carte blanche – anything you don't like, change. Anything you want, you can have. I want to win World Championships."* According to Murray, *"He stuck to that absolutely, and that was key in the MP4/4's success."*

This singular commitment brought new facilities to McLaren just when it needed them most. These included the team's first autoclave, but also new meeting rooms, new procedures to be rigorously applied, better record-keeping and above all much more detailed analysis of every performance, component and race (won or lost) to establish precisely what happened, when and why. Detail, detail, discipline and more detail – the hallmark of modern McLaren.

Alain Prost on the way to his 31st Grand Prix victory in Mexico 1988. His third win of the season meant he led the title race and would do so until the 11th round at Spa in August.

In the dry qualifying session for the Belgian Grand Prix at Spa, Ayrton put MP4/4-5 on pole position for the ninth time that season. The wet race gave him his seventh win of 1988.

The results were quick in coming and speak for themselves. Reliability problems dropped off almost completely – Senna had gear linkage problems in Rio, and something similar at Imola and again at Ricard – and as the record books show the MP4/4 achieved such dominance over the course of a season that any minor failings are now more or less forgotten. Finishing the season with a points total just two shy of the combined total of every other team on the grid, it simply towered over its opposition even though it was the lowest car out there.

MODEL	McLaren MP4/4	TRANSMISSION	McLaren 6-speed	TYRES F/R	Goodyear
TYPE/FORMULA	Formula 1	CHASSIS	Moulded carbon fibre/honeycomb monocoque	LENGTH	173in - 4394mm
YEAR OF PRODUCTION	1988	BODY	Carbon fibre single piece cockpit/engine cover & nose	WIDTH	84in - 2134mm
DESIGNER	Steve Nichols/Gordon Murray	FRONT SUSPENSION	Double wishbone, push-rod/roller track system	HEIGHT	37in - 940mm
EXAMPLES BUILT	6		operating inboard coil spring/damper	WHEELBASE	113.2in - 2875mm
ENGINE	Honda RA168E Turbo V6	REAR SUSPENSION	Upper wishbone/rocker arm operating	TRACK F/R	71.8/65.8in - 1824/1670mm
CUBIC CAPACITY	1494cc		inboard coil spring/damper, lower wishbone	WEIGHT	1191lb - 540kg
INDUCTION	Twin IHI turbochargers	BRAKES F/R	Outboard SEP carbon discs/McLaren twin caliper	PRINCIPAL DRIVERS	Prost, Senna
POWER OUTPUT	900bhp	WHEELS DIAMETER x WIDTH F/R	13x11.75/13x16.25in	IDENTIFYING COLOURS	Red/White

While meeting the challenge of revised turbocharger regulations for the 1988 season with its V6, and with a new, much larger normally aspirated engine formula set for introduction the following year, winning once was clearly not going to be enough for Honda during its time with McLaren. Back home in Japan the company quickly established a second project team quite independent from the current V6 engineers, to concentrate on the creation of a new 3.5-litre 'atmospheric' V10 for 1989.

On the track the close cooperation between the two organisations was to bring forth an immediate and outstanding harvest: In a thrilling season the MP4/4 rapidly established itself as the most successful single car in Formula 1 history with an unprecedented 199 points from a single season and no fewer than 15 wins and 10 superb one-two finishes. But in Honda's own workshops the progress was arguably just as impressive, with an all-new-for-1989 V10 motor quickly taking shape in the form of the 3.5-litre RA109A. Interestingly, only Renault and Honda opted for the 10-cylinder format initially, accepting it as the perfect compromise between outright power and torque, and external dimensions and ease of installation. Several key rivals, notably Ferrari who initially preferred a V12, were in due course obliged to follow suit and move to a V10.

To test the new engine the team at first considered using what had become known as the MP4/3C, a testbed created from a substantially revised MP4/3 chassis and running gear. This, however, was quickly abandoned in favour of MP4/4B shown here – as the name suggests a version of the 1988 race car – the change of vehicle choice being made in order to keep the project more up

to date. Neil Oatley's MP4/4B thus became the principal development mule for the earliest iterations of the ground-breaking new Honda V10.

Once again, the car used a carbon fibre composite monocoque chassis based on that of the turbo powered machines, but this was now fitted with a substantially larger fuel tank as allowed by the new regulations, as well as a completely new installation for the engine. A special gearbox casing was also designed to mate with the engine while the cooling system was heavily revised to suit a unit running more cylinders and of course one with no intercoolers.

Although from every angle the car looked familiar with its carbon fibre one-piece cockpit, engine cover and nose section assembly, it needed a change in the form of its overhead air intake which replaced the side intakes previously seen on the turbocar. It also gained revised bodywork to the rear of the sidepods, this was to accommodate the new engine installation. The wheelbase remained almost the same, however, at 114-inches, and the McLaren six-speed transmission, the McLaren SEP brakes, and the front and rear suspension were all direct carryovers.

Thus equipped, the MP4-4B first ran on European tracks in the mid-summer of 1988, and in the early part of 1989 it was flown to Suzuka where development continued under the Japanese. Over this period two further MP4/4B chassis were built. These would be driven and comprehensively evaluated not just by the Alain Prost/Ayrton Senna 'dream team' but ahead of their individual input by Britain's Jonathan Palmer who was at that time McLaren's test driver.

The move from small-capacity turbo engine to larger-capacity, normally aspirated unit was a major shift both for McLaren and Honda. The transition from V6 to innovative V10 was also an exciting development for the sport. For these reasons alone, and even leaving aside McLaren's status as the title defenders, the MP4/4B found itself with quite a task on its hands and is thus an extremely important car in the team's long and illustrious history even if it remains relatively unknown. The work done with it enabled Honda to give the team an emphatic power advantage over its rivals.

From the middle of 1988 many thousands of miles were covered by the three contracted McLaren drivers, Senna, Prost and official test driver Jonathan Palmer. The V10 engine required a bespoke cooling system and the bodywork from sidepods rearward was revised to suit the engine installation.

The MP4/4B was built to help the team test and develop the new 3.5-litre Honda V10 engine. After being used extensively over the winter of 1988/89, as with the MP4/3B one of the two cars built was shipped to Honda in Japan for continued engine development.

MODEL	McLaren MP4/4B	TRANSMISSION	McLaren 6-speed	TYRES F/R	Goodyear
TYPE/FORMULA	Formula 1 Test Car	CHASSIS	Moulded carbon fibre/honeycomb monocoque	LENGTH	174in - 4420mm
YEAR OF PRODUCTION	1988	BODY	Carbon fibre single piece cockpit/engine cover & nose	WIDTH	83.5in - 2120mm
DESIGNER	Steve Nichols	FRONT SUSPENSION	Double wishbone, push-rod/roller track system	HEIGHT	37in - 940mm
EXAMPLES BUILT	3		operating inboard coil spring/damper	WHEELBASE	114in - 2895mm
ENGINE	Honda RA109E V10	REAR SUSPENSION	Upper wishbone/rocker arm operating	TRACK F/R	71.8/65.8in - 1824/1670mm
CUBIC CAPACITY	3490cc		inboard coil spring/damper, lower wishbone	WEIGHT	1085lb - 492kg
ELECTRONICS	Honda PGM injection/ignition	BRAKES F/R	Outboard SEP carbon discs/McLaren twin caliper	PRINCIPAL DRIVERS	Prost, Senna, Palmer
POWER OUTPUT	645bhp	WHEELS DIAMETER x WIDTH F/R	13x11.75/13x16.25in	IDENTIFYING COLOURS	Red/White

1989 MP4/5
FORMULA 1

1989 meant all change for McLaren as the 3.5-litre normally aspirated Formula 1 came into force. The change had been flagged clearly many months in advance, and McLaren and Honda had been working on a car and engine package even as the MP4/4 was dominating the 1988 season. Even at Woking, however, few would have predicted that the first season of the non-turbo era would match the incredible results of the previous year, with McLaren walking away with further Drivers' and Constructors' World Championships.

Under Neil Oatley's guidance, the design team had created an all-new monocoque, new double wishbone suspension with pullrods up front and pushrods at the rear, and expected almost 700bhp from the 72-degree Honda RA109E V10. This drove through a longitudinal version of the David North/Pete Weismann three-shaft, six-speed gearbox, with a transverse unit arriving in mid-season. Honda's Osamu Goto made available eight new engines for the start of the year, though there was a slight delay to allow for a switch from belt- to gear-drive for the camshaft operation.

In the interests of aerodynamic flexibility Oatley's team stuck with the established practice of having a separate upper body, and though the monocoque looked similar to its forebears it incorporated a number of modifications as a result of a comprehensive review of the car's aerodynamic performance.

McLaren soon began to dominate the season, albeit not quite to the degree it had the previous year as the MP4/5 was not devoid of problems. There were some lubrication issues, which had reared their head during testing, and also some questions over the balance of the handling once Oatley's team had shaved off even more weight to meet the 505kg limit.

Even as the storm clouds were gathering over the relationship between Alain Prost and Ayrton Senna, it was clear that McLaren was once again the team to beat. Senna's collision in the first corner at Rio didn't alter the fact; neither did the clutch trouble which prevented Prost making an important pit stop, nor indeed complaints from both drivers about their respective throttle responses.

Much of this was resolved during some frenetic testing and development on the run-up to the San Marino GP. Upon arrival at Imola Prost promptly broke Nelson Piquet's three-year old lap record, while Senna won the race at an average speed of 125.479mph, making him more than three per cent faster than the previous year.

So far, so good – at least until Monaco where Prost publicly denounced Senna as a "Man of no honour". At Imola, he alleged, the latter had breached a no-passing agreement for which he, Senna, had apologised only belatedly and somewhat reluctantly. Thereafter the two spoke to each other only rarely, preferring to communicate with the other via Oatley, Steve Nichols or Jo Ramirez. The fact that they still won 10 races between them, enabling McLaren again to clinch the World Championship, speaks volumes for both the fundamental structure of the Honda-McLaren team and the quality of the MP4/5.

The new gearbox was still not ready for Monaco but new Brembo brakes were and these helped remove some more weight from the car. Once again Senna won, despite losing

After Senna retired on the first lap with gearbox problems, polesitter Alain Prost won the French Grand Prix for the fourth time in his career.

Senna was desperate to win his home Grand Prix but a lengthy pitstop to replace the nose of his car on the first lap meant he could only finish 11th, two laps down.

second gear, before more trouble flared up in Mexico where apparent disparities in the amount of fuel consumed by the two cars led Prost to question how fairly the team was dealing with the two drivers. It is more likely Senna simply drove further at high revs and that Prost's relatively lighter right foot (which had been such a benefit during the turbo era) worked slightly against him.

When the new transverse gearbox finally had its debut at Silverstone, a series of misfires and engine and gearbox failures followed. None of this prevented McLaren qualifying first and second, but in the race itself Senna ended up in a gravel trap. Indeed, despite all his complaints, it was to be Prost's season.

At Monza he announced that he was leaving again, this time for Ferrari. Senna, meanwhile, having won three races out of four, found his luck starting to unravel. Prost won in Italy, clinching for McLaren the Constructors' World Championship for the second year in a row and with four races still to be run, and by the season's end his 76-point total handed him yet another World Drivers' Championship. But not before the season had been sullied by the infamous coming-together of the two McLaren drivers in the Suzuka chicane, as they battled for the Japanese GP.

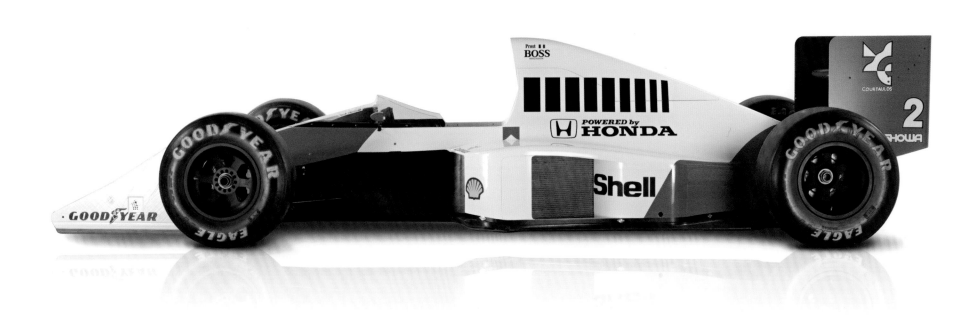

MODEL	McLaren MP4/5		TRANSMISSION	McLaren 6-speed/transverse 6-speed		TYRES F/R	Goodyear
TYPE/FORMULA	Formula 1		CHASSIS	High modulus carbon fibre/honeycomb monocoque		LENGTH	177in - 4496mm
YEAR OF PRODUCTION	1989		BODY	Carbon fibre single piece cockpit/engine cover & nose		WIDTH	84in - 2134 mm
DESIGNER	Neil Oatley		FRONT SUSPENSION	Double wishbone, pull-rod operating		HEIGHT	39in - 991mm
EXAMPLES BUILT	8			inboard coil spring/damper		WHEELBASE	114in - 2895mm
ENGINE	Honda RA109E V10		REAR SUSPENSION	Double wishbone, push-rod operating		TRACK F/R	71.8/65.75in - 1824/1669mm
CUBIC CAPACITY	3490cc			inboard coil spring/damper		WEIGHT	1102lb - 500kg
ELECTRONICS	Honda PGM injection/ignition		BRAKES F/R	Outboard SEP carbon discs/McLaren twin caliper		PRINCIPAL DRIVERS	Prost, Senna
POWER OUTPUT	685bhp		WHEELS DIAMETER x WIDTH F/R	13x11.75/13x16.25in		IDENTIFYING COLOURS	Red/White

With Senna's car carrying the World Champion's number 1 on the nose of his car, Alain Prost carried number 2 and only won four races to Senna's season high six. However he took his third Drivers' title by a 16-point margin over the Brazilian.

The introduction of new engine regulations meant that the team relied on the Honda V10 engine. In testing Honda was quoting 600bhp, by the start of the 1989 season it was up to 650bhp and by the end of the year it had reached 685bhp.

The most significant changes over the previous year's car were Neil Oatley's aerodynamic improvements which met the requirements of the RA109E V10 engine and its need for much greater cooling than the previous years V6 Turbo.

At the next race, the San Marino Grand Prix at Imola, the team scored yet another 1-2 finish. On this occasion it was Senna ahead of Prost, both of them over a lap ahead of third-placed Nannini.

CHAPTER
04

MIKA
HÄKKINEN

When I was with Lotus in 1991-92 McLaren was for me the Number One superteam: a really interesting outfit which always looked good, got fantastic results, and had a very high profile.

People think I took a gamble when I signed for McLaren because it already had two drivers signed up, but I didn't. Gambling is gambling and you never know if you are going to win, so I don't do it. However, I knew that I was good, I was the best, I was the fastest and Ron Dennis had to give me a try. I was very, very, confident and I took the risk that if Ayrton came back to race in 1994 maybe I wouldn't have a race seat and would only be testing.

I had quite a few offers from other teams that year, but McLaren was the Number One for me, Ron had promised me a race that year and so I wasn't concerned. He has always been the person who makes the decisions, so I knew I could rely on him.

My first Grand Prix drive came in Portugal in 1993 and I was confident. Of course, Ayrton was my team-mate and being next to a great champion and seeing how hard I had to work to be on the same level was a real eye-opener. At that time we had the same Ford HB engine as Lotus had used, one which had never had any problems but was just not powerful enough. Everything else at McLaren was unbelievably fantastic though – gearbox, brakes, the materials it was using – so when Mercedes-Benz joined we had a really interesting time. They said we come here and we have to win and that kind of attitude gave me a lot more confidence.

Obviously, it took some time to get it right – I had my first win only after seven years in Formula 1 – but it was worth the wait. Sometimes you look at the other side of the fence and think the grass is greener but, really, I had a great team behind me and to be honest I always thought we can do it, we can win, and I can win the World Championship. I saw the development work that was going on in 1995, '96, and '97 and after that last year and I knew that we were going to do it. At McLaren everyone was so motivated, with so much energy. We had a good programme, good mechanics, good designers, and in 1998 a fantastic car, the ultimate machine in every respect, and I knew that it would happen.

Mika Häkkinen
Drivers' World Champion 1998 & '99
McLaren MP4-13 & MP4-14

With World Champion Alain Prost and Steve Nichols departing for Ferrari, thus cementing the Italian team's 1990 status as McLaren's strongest challenger, and Gordon Murray turning his attention to the McLaren F1 roadcar project, Neil Oatley and his design colleagues opted to refine the MP4/5 for Ayrton Senna and his incoming new team-mate Gerhard Berger rather than create an entirely new car.

The latter would probably have wished otherwise since he was too tall to fit into the car comfortably when he first tested it. It was otherwise clearly a winner, however, and while it was true that McLaren's principal challengers, Ferrari and Williams, were catching up, the opinion at Woking was that the existing car was a good basis on which to continue.

Honda produced a new derivative of its V10, the RA100E engine. The car's monocoque was broadly similar, however, but used a new high-modulus material from Hercules Corporation which promised even greater impact resistance. A new, slightly larger fuel cell was also installed, whilst the suspension geometry was altered at the front and the transverse gearbox substantially revised.

While the car still looked broadly similar, some evolutionary rather than radical revisions were also made to its aerodynamic profile with particular reference to the sidepods and radiator ducting. It also gained a new windscreen design and a distinctive multi-arched diffuser. That diffuser was superseded by mid-season, by which time Berger's seating position problems had finally been resolved by making his driving position slightly more upright than Senna's.

It was to be a busy time at McLaren. While one crew was designing and building MP4/5B race cars, work was starting in parallel on a MP4/5C test car to accommodate a new V12 Honda engine intended for the following season. The fact that the very first 'B' car then sustained some serious

damage in Senna's hands didn't help matters, although the incident during pre-season shakedown trials at Silverstone provided some useful evidence to support the driver's assertion that the new chassis was rather more responsive than the MP4/5.

The season itself got off to a good start, however, with Senna quickly negating Berger's pole in the Phoenix opener and blasting his way to victory after a brief battle with the forceful Jean Alesi's Tyrrell. Thereafter he took pole position 10 times, but it was nevertheless obvious from the moment the new cars were completed that the team faced a greater challenge than it had in 1989. Not just from Prost at Ferrari (where he was partnered by Nigel Mansell), but also from Williams where Thierry Boutsen and Riccardo Patrese were making their presence felt with Renault V10 power in the FW13B.

None of this seemed to worry Senna, who led every race of the season except Hungary, where he was forced to chase Boutsen's Williams all the way to the finish, and Suzuka, where he cynically took out former team-mate Prost's Ferrari to claim a controversial second World Championship.

Over the course of the season the car improved significantly – helped in no small part by a new underbody which made it both easier to control and more comfortable to drive – with the factory burning the midnight oil to test and perfect all sorts of new aerodynamic components. The responsibility for this, and in particular for Senna's car, now fell to American Gordon Kimball, as Oatley moved on to design the V12-engined MP4/6 for 1991.

Honda too continued the development of its engine package, so that Senna's V10 was at times producing around 710bhp thanks to increased rev limits and new, lower density fuel which he used in qualifying. At Hockenheim Osamu Goto and his team unboxed a slightly lighter Version 4 power unit, with

Version 5 coming along in time for Spa-Francorchamps and producing even better top-end results.

In the final analysis there is simply no arguing with any car which takes pole 12 times in a season. Nor with a car which handed its team yet another Drivers' World Championship and another Constructors' World Championship to sit alongside it. It was only for the second time in history that the latter had been won by the same team three times in succession, so the 1990 season says a lot about the quality of the McLaren operation. And given that the car the team relied on was evolutionary rather than an entirely new design, it says even more about the commitment both it and its engine supplier were willing to make in the face of greater challenges from increasingly strong competition.

Even though Gerhard Berger had started from pole position and Senna (above) was only fifth on the grid, Ayrton still managed to win the 1990 United States Grand Prix in Phoenix, Arizona.

MODEL	McLaren MP4/5B	TRANSMISSION	McLaren transverse 6-speed	TYRES F/R	Goodyear
TYPE/FORMULA	Formula 1	CHASSIS	High modulus carbon fibre/honeycomb monocoque	LENGTH	176in - 4470mm
YEAR OF PRODUCTION	1990	BODY	Carbon fibre single piece cockpit/engine cover & nose	WIDTH	84in - 2133mm
DESIGNER	Neil Oatley	FRONT SUSPENSION	Double wishbone, pull-rod operating	HEIGHT	38in - 965mm
EXAMPLES BUILT	7		inboard coil spring/damper	WHEELBASE	114in - 2895mm
ENGINE	Honda RA100E V10	REAR SUSPENSION	Double wishbone, push-rod operating	TRACK F/R	71.8/65.75in - 1824/1669mm
CUBIC CAPACITY	3490cc		inboard coil spring/damper	WEIGHT	1102lb - 500kg
ELECTRONICS	Honda PGM injection/ignition	BRAKES F/R	Outboard Brembo/Carbone Industrie	PRINCIPAL DRIVERS	Senna, Berger
POWER OUTPUT	690bhp	WHEELS DIAMETER x WIDTH F/R	13x11.75/13x16.25in	IDENTIFYING COLOURS	Red/White

1990 MP4/5C
FORMULA 1 TEST CAR

A derivation of the 1990 MP4/5B race car, and once again designed by Neil Oatley, the MP4/5C on which design work had started in May of that year, was conceived as a mobile test bed for the first of a new generation of engines, Honda's RA121E V12.

It first ran in the late summer of 1990 alongside the familiar V10, having been built using essentially the same chassis as before but with revised engine mounts and all-new, elongated bodywork to accommodate the motor's extra length. The overall length of the car didn't actually increase a great deal, however, thanks to clever work shortening the length of the gearbox internals and thus the overall dimensions of the casing. As was by now established McLaren practise with test vehicles, its working life continued through the winter until MP4/6 was ready. After this, one of the two chassis built was taken to Japan for additional development running by Honda, putting in many miles at Suzuka.

At its first shakedown test at Silverstone, the MP4/5C was driven by both Ayrton Senna and Gerhard Berger, as well as by two of the team's test drivers, Italian Emanuele Pirro and Scotsman Allan McNish, both of whom were later to make their names in sportscar racing. While the regular drivers were carrying out development work on the MP4/5B (including a Tyrrell-inspired 'high nose' variant) Jonathan Palmer also tested the MP4/5C for McLaren in a session at Monza in August 1990. He drove the car again at Chobham in southern England in October, at the same time trying out a 'semi-automatic' MP4/5B variant.

Later to join the team, David Coulthard also drove the development car fitted with the Honda V12 as part of his prize for winning the 1989 McLaren Autosport BRDC Young Driver of the Year Award. His first taste of Formula 1 power came in the hybrid MP4/5C on Silverstone's South Circuit on a cold, damp day in late November. Interviewed at the end of it, he said: "*It was nice to come here and see a McLaren with Coulthard on the side, and hopefully in a few years my name will be there again.*"

Finally, in one last test of the V12 MP4/5C combination before the new car for 1991 was ready to be unveiled, Berger took part in the week-long session for all the teams at Estoril in mid-December. With one of the two chassis now hidden away in Japan, and the team not wanting to let the other teams get too good a view of the new V12, McLaren kept the car pretty much under wraps for the whole week. Despite this, Berger finished fifth fastest and less than one second off the pace of Prost's Ferrari.

There was debate whether the extra two cylinders of the V12 were really needed, and some parties in McLaren favoured further development of the V10. In particular, they would have liked it to lose weight. But Honda politics dictated a V12, and the V10s were eventually supplied to Tyrrell for 1991. The pro-V10 parties pointed out that, while it might be more powerful, the V12 was heavier and thirstier, which negated much of that advantage.

The 60-degree RA121E V12 gained not just additional cylinders but also a much larger piston area and, potentially, an even higher rev limit as well. In testing in the MP4/5C it showed itself to be thirstier than the V10, partly as a consequence of its greater weight. There were also greater losses from internal friction to deal with, but nevertheless the expectation was that with an output rumoured to be in the region of 720bhp any downsides would be compensated for. At the Monza test, however, there wasn't

much to choose in terms of lap times between it and the V10-engined car as the benefits of the more powerful engine were offset by its additional weight.

Since it was not only heavier but longer, the new engine also necessitated a slightly stretched wheelbase, the final dimensions being some 3 inches longer than the V10-engined MP4/5B at 117 inches. At the same time substantial alterations were made to the cooling system radiators; special oil heat-exchangers were fitted to suit the new engine installation, and a new gearbox/oil tank casing assembly was introduced.

The suspension remained unchanged from the revised arrangement employed in the test car, however, but the monocoque was constructed using a new, even higher-modulus material from Hercules Aerospace in Utah. In the constant battle between overall strength, the weight of the complete monocoque, and torsional stiffness, this new formula for the grade of the carbon-fibre mix had been selected for its improved resistance to high-speed impact.

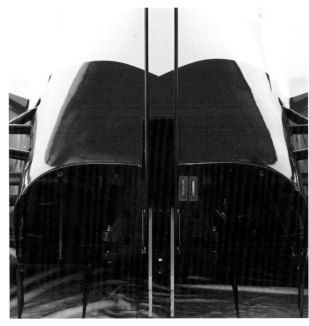

MODEL	McLaren MP4/5C
TYPE/FORMULA	Formula 1 Test Car
YEAR OF PRODUCTION	1990
DESIGNER	Neil Oatley
EXAMPLES BUILT	2
ENGINE	Honda RA121E V12
CUBIC CAPACITY	3493cc
ELECTRONICS	Honda PGM injection/ignition
POWER OUTPUT	700bhp

TRANSMISSION	McLaren transverse 6-speed
CHASSIS	High modulus carbon fibre/honeycomb monocoque
BODY	Carbon fibre single piece cockpit/engine cover & nose
FRONT SUSPENSION	Double wishbone, pull-rod operating
	inboard coil spring/damper
REAR SUSPENSION	Double wishbone, push-rod operating
	inboard coil spring/damper
BRAKES F/R	Outboard Brembo/Carbone Industrie
WHEELS DIAMETER x WIDTH F/R	13x11.75/13x16.3in

TYRES F/R	Goodyear
LENGTH	180in - 4572mm
WIDTH	83.5in - 2120mm
HEIGHT	39in - 990mm
WHEELBASE	117in - 2972mm
TRACK F/R	71.8/65.75in - 1824/1669mm
WEIGHT	1110lb - 503kg
PRINCIPAL DRIVERS	Senna, Berger, McNish, Pirro, Palmer
IDENTIFYING COLOURS	Red/White

While the V10 Honda RA100E had succeeded in holding off Renault's V10 and Ferrari's V12, the thinking within Honda was that it couldn't do for so much longer. For 1991, therefore, Ayrton Senna and Gerhard Berger found themselves seated ahead of yet another new engine, the RA121E Honda V12.

This was Honda's third engine configuration in just four seasons and was an entirely new 60-degree unit with a greater piston area than the outgoing engine and a potentially higher rev limit. It was longer, heavier and thirstier than the V10, but it was hoped that an output reputed to be 720bhp would compensate for that. However, the engine installed in the MP4/5C test mule failed to convince Senna. Concerned that it simply wouldn't be sufficient to defeat Renault's new, improved V10, he was quick to tell the Japanese what he thought of it in his usual candid terms.

Though naturally concerned to hear this, the Japanese stuck to their guns, Akimasa Yasuoka arguing that, "*Honda traditionally detunes its engines for the first race of the season; we tend to go for reliability rather than power.*" In retrospect, it was perhaps right to do so for McLaren's season got off to the best possible start with no fewer than four wins in a row, the increased engine weight partly offset by the latest development of McLaren's six-speed gearbox.

The car itself, whilst looking similar to MP4/5B, was quite different in terms of its aerodynamic profile as designer Neil Oatley and his team had received some valuable input from Henri Durand who had joined from Ferrari in mid-1990.

Numerous changes had also to be made to the chassis, not least in order to accommodate the longer engine and the enlarged fuel cell needed to satisfy its greater thirst. Even with four centimetres added to its length the new tub was much stiffer in terms of torsional rigidity and consisted of even fewer basic components than before. There were changes to the suspension too, an aspect of the car which had altered dramatically since the year before, with pushrod-activated coil-spring/dampers now mounted on top of the chassis ahead of the cockpit instead of being installed vertically either side of the footwell.

The changes called for some exterior alterations, so that the new suspension arrangement resulted in a slightly higher border round the cockpit while, with the larger water radiators now specified, the sidepods were also longer and taller. As the season progressed the aerodynamics were tweaked further, in part to offset the negative effects of increased weight and drag from the greater fuel load and revised cooling arrangements.

The increased fuel consumption posed challenges of its own, despite plenty of development on the engine management system, Senna twice ran out of fuel (at Silverstone and Hockenheim) but the Brazilian and his MP4/6 nevertheless

remained unbeaten up to and including Monaco, giving McLaren a comfortable lead in the Constructors' Cup. In Montreal two things quickly became apparent. The first was that the Honda's extra power was simply insufficient to offset its greater weight relative to the V10s, particularly when its internal frictional losses continued to rise. The other was that the Williams FW14s, particularly Mansell's, were really getting into their stride.

Undeterred, Honda continued developing its V12. The Spec 1, which had triumphed at Phoenix, Interlagos and in the Principality, eventually gave way to a Spec 2 variant which was actually introduced ahead of Monaco, at Imola, and offered better mid-range punch thanks to its new induction system. The friction problems were also addressed with a Spec 3 version at Silverstone. New linked rocker arms were also employed in a bid to reduce roll, and a cockpit-adjustable ride-height mechanism was also added.

The fuel metering issues that made themselves so painfully felt during the British and German rounds were largely to do with Shell's experimentation with different fuel densities and viscosities. At Paul Ricard, another inaccurate readout forced Senna to drive conservatively, although following this Honda's research and development effort accelerated dramatically so that by the time he arrived in Hungary he had a car which could be safely revved to 14,800rpm, albeit only for short bursts.

In Budapest McLaren regained its form in the nick of time. With a lighter-than-ever chassis, and yet another heavily reworked engine with lighter cylinder heads, camshafts and connecting rods, Senna pulled something out of the bag and pushed the Williams duo back to second and third places. Despite suffering a gearbox failure, he managed it again at Spa for the Belgian Grand Prix, where he nursed his failing car home and saw his lead over Williams grow enormously

While Ayrton Senna easily won the 1991 Monaco Grand Prix, Gerhard Berger was involved in a first-lap incident, pitted to repair the damage and was out by lap 10.

following another retirement by Mansell. McLaren's rival was quickly restored to good fortune, however, commanding the field in both the Portuguese and Spanish races, the last of which saw Senna struggling on the wrong tyres.

At Suzuka the order flipped again, the correct tyres and yet more successful engine development leaving Senna in an unassailable position on 96 points. He returned to Brazil with a resounding third title, while Berger finished fourth with 43 points, having been handed victory by Senna in Suzuka. McLaren again took the Constructors' World Championship.

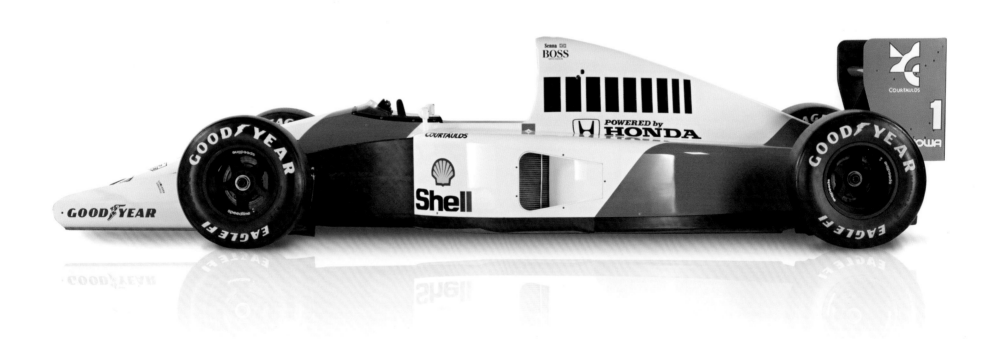

MODEL	McLaren MP4/6		TRANSMISSION	McLaren transverse 6-speed		TYRES F/R	Goodyear
TYPE/FORMULA	Formula 1		CHASSIS	High modulus carbon fibre/honeycomb monocoque		LENGTH	177in - 4496mm
YEAR OF PRODUCTION	1991		BODY	Carbon fibre single piece cockpit/engine cover & nose		WIDTH	83.5in - 2120mm
DESIGNER	Neil Oatley		FRONT SUSPENSION	Double wishbone, push-rod operating		HEIGHT	38in - 965mm
EXAMPLES BUILT	11			longitudinal inboard coil spring/damper		WHEELBASE	117in - 2972mm
ENGINE	Honda RA121E V12		REAR SUSPENSION	Double wishbone, push-rod operating		TRACK F/R	71.8/65.75in - 1824/1669mm
CUBIC CAPACITY	3493cc			vertical inboard coil spring/damper		WEIGHT	1113lb - 505kg
ELECTRONICS	Honda PGM injection/ignition		BRAKES F/R	Outboard Brembo/Carbone Industrie		PRINCIPAL DRIVERS	Senna, Berger
POWER OUTPUT	720bhp		WHEELS DIAMETER x WIDTH F/R	13x12/13x16.3in		IDENTIFYING COLOURS	Red/White

1992 MP4/7 FORMULA 1

In 1991 Ayrton Senna had been quick to accuse Honda of falling behind in its engine development. The following year there was no doubt that it had, and with the Williams team threatening to raise expectations yet again with its new, computer-controlled 'active' suspension FW14B, and with its drivers Nigel Mansell and Riccardo Patrese still in the ascendancy, it was soon apparent that the Woking team was in the now unfamiliar position of playing catch-up.

The previous year Honda had spent many hundreds of man-hours developing and improving the RA121E in order to stay ahead of Renault. One of the unfortunate consequences of this was that work on its replacement – the MP4/7's new 75° V10 RA122E/B – was substantially delayed. As a result, it hadn't even been bench-tested until December and when it did finally make it into a chassis it was clear that, like its predecessor, it was thirsty. Despite an estimated 740bhp this would prove a major handicap as rival V10s increased in sophistication. At the same time, rumours continued that Honda would withdraw at the end of the season.

Given the delays, and because the MP4/6 had in the end delivered the results needed the previous year, the decision was taken to stick with that car for the opening three races of the new season. The feeling was that the extra time could be spent in the wind tunnel, further refining the aerodynamics of the MP4/7; also perhaps that while the new engine wasn't quite up to scratch it was at least going to be paired with a chassis which was technically one of the best on the grid.

However, Ron Dennis soon reversed that decision, claiming to have had, "*A gut feeling that we would have to aim for a race debut in Brazil a month earlier*". A gut feeling, that is, which followed McLaren's observation of the Williams team in action. In testing it had become clear that with its increasingly fast and reliable Renault engine, and active suspension, the FW14B was a highly dangerous rival. As Dennis said: "*Williams clearly had a reliable package from the outset, so in order to stand a chance of winning the World Championship we just had to get the new car up and running as fast as possible.*"

Doing it this way, however, cut the remaining development time by as much as a third, something which inevitably piled on the pressure. No doubt, particularly as the new car was to represent a completely new concept for McLaren. The MP4/7's CFC monocoque was to be constructed within a 'female' mould rather than around a 'male' one, which had been the practice at McLaren since the company first pioneered composite materials with the ground-breaking MP4/1 more than ten years earlier.

As well as overturning a decade's experience with carbon composites, the car introduced another new, transverse six-speed semi-automatic gearbox that not only featured McLaren's own electro-hydraulic activation (devised in partnership with TAG) but also so-called fly-by-wire controls. Taken almost for granted these days, this aerospace practise replaced a conventional throttle cable with a system of electronic sensors. By monitoring and responding directly to a driver's pedal inputs, fly-by-wire was able to control engine speeds automatically, thereby removing the need for the driver to take his foot off the throttle whilst shifting up or down.

Despite the many and varied pressures on the team, three cars were readied in time for Interlagos, although the precaution was taken of freighting out three MP4/6s just in case. Once racing got underway, however, it was clear that there was still work to do. Senna complained of unpredictable handling going into fast corners. It was also felt that the new engine, despite sporting pneumatic valve actuation to facilitate higher revs, actually offered little if anything more than the old one had. At the same time it was to take until Monaco to sort out a flexing underbody section and for Honda to produce the power which had been promised. Unfortunately, by that time Williams had run away with four wins to McLaren's zero, so the pressure was intense.

Fortunately, Senna's commitment was still absolutely 100 per cent, and likewise McLaren's own when it came to ensuring that pre-race preparation was as good as it could be. Thus, its star driver was able to win in Monaco, Hungary and Italy. Berger, who was to leave at the end of his third season with McLaren and return to Ferrari, took wins in Canada and in Australia, in what was to be his final drive for the team. Together with Senna's second placing in Germany this was sufficient to leave McLaren in the runner-up position in the Constructors' World Championship with 99 points. Senna finished fourth overall in the Drivers' on 50, one ahead of Berger.

For a lesser team, that would have been a good year; for McLaren, however, after such an historically long run of spectacular victories, it was a bitter disappointment.

In December 1992, new team driver Michael Andretti tested the Honda-powered McLaren

MP4/7 at Paul Ricard. It was the last time a McLaren would officially run with Honda power.

MODEL	McLaren MP4/7	TRANSMISSION	McLaren semi-auto transverse 6-speed	TYRES F/R	Goodyear
TYPE/FORMULA	Formula 1	CHASSIS	High modulus carbon fibre/honeycomb monocoque	LENGTH	177in - 4496mm
YEAR OF PRODUCTION	1992	BODY	Carbon fibre single piece cockpit/engine cover & nose	WIDTH	83.5in - 2120mm
DESIGNER	Neil Oatley	FRONT SUSPENSION	Double wishbone, push-rod operating	HEIGHT	39in - 990mm
EXAMPLES BUILT	10		longitudinal inboard coil spring/damper	WHEELBASE	117in - 2972mm
ENGINE	Honda RA122E/B V12	REAR SUSPENSION	Double wishbone, push-rod operating	TRACK F/R	71.8/65.75in - 1824/1669mm
CUBIC CAPACITY	3493cc		longitudinal inboard coil spring/damper	WEIGHT	1115lb - 506kg
ELECTRONICS	Honda PGM injection/ignition	BRAKES F/R	Outboard Brembo/Carbone Industrie	PRINCIPAL DRIVERS	Senna, Berger
POWER OUTPUT	740bhp	WHEELS DIAMETER x WIDTH F/R	13x12/13x16.3in	IDENTIFYING COLOURS	Red/White

1993 MP4/8 FORMULA 1

With Honda leaving F1, McLaren did not announce its new engine supplier until November 1992, and when the name was eventually revealed it was Ford. The return to Cosworth power, for the first time since 1983, it was disclosed, would be via a team-financed development of Ford's HB powerplant.

This was a light and economical 3.5-litre V8 and by no means a bad engine, but there was no escaping the fact that, whereas McLaren had previously been able to call upon bespoke power units from the likes of TAG Porsche and Honda, its new hi-tech MP4/8 would have to rely on a proprietary unit. One, moreover, which would be one specification behind that used by Benetton in its B193 because Ford already had a supply contract with them.

Ron Dennis had tried very hard to secure a deal with Renault, and even considered buying Ligier in order to obtain its Renault engines. McLaren would naturally have wanted to use Shell fuel and lubricants, and ultimately this proved a stumbling block with Renault's sponsor, Elf. There was thus no alternative but to invest an estimated £6 million in developing the HB.

Design work on the new MP4/8 thus started without a clear idea of which engine would be used, although McLaren's computer-aided design capabilities would at least enable the design team to make up for lost time.

Featuring a battery of advanced new technologies, the car was the company's most sophisticated design yet with new electronic engine management software, chassis control, data acquisition and telemetry systems. Designed and manufactured by McLaren Group subsidiary TAG Electronic Systems exclusively for McLaren, these systems were accompanied by a new, lightweight electronic control panel in the cockpit. Fitted into a new, improved chassis, the fuel-efficient Ford HB engine gave McLaren cause to be optimistic. It was hoped that whatever the car lacked in outright horsepower it would make up for with even better preparation and engineering, clever race strategies, superb chassis and electronics from TAG. The new car was also to feature an even more advanced active suspension set-up and traction control.

And Ayrton Senna would drive it. Or would he? At times that seemed uncertain. For a while he appeared to be running on a race-by-race basis as he and Dennis negotiated over his financial demands with sponsors. Nevertheless, the season yielded five wins at a time when Williams Renault was the dominant force, compared to a singleton success for Benetton with the latest-spec engine. McLaren's tally in 1993 was all the more remarkable because, while Senna returned after a winter spent relaxing at home in Brazil, various rule changes meant that when Michael Andretti joined the team from the US, he was effectively denied adequate time to familiarise himself with the circuits. As a consequence, having

shown good speed when previously testing in the MP4/7 he failed to make his mark with the MP4/8 because of the lack of 'seat time' and was eventually replaced by one of the sport's coming-men, fresh from Lotus, Mika Häkkinen.

Senna really liked the MP4/8, particularly after testing at Silverstone where he ran his quickest laps there almost first time out. He proved his value to the team in the very first race at Kyalami by coming a close second to Prost's Williams despite suffering an active suspension problem. He quickly followed that with wins at home in Interlagos and in one of the greatest Grand Prix drives of all time in the wet at Donington Park. Andretti, meanwhile, crashed in all three events.

Despite a strong drive in France and a podium spot with third place at Monza, the American, the son of 1978 World Champion Mario Andretti, was unable to recapture the magic he showed in IndyCar racing and after the Italian race Häkkinen stepped up from test driver to team driver.

Senna, meanwhile, continued to impress, taking a record sixth win at Monaco despite a massive shunt at Ste Devote corner during practice. Nobody who watched him in action doubted the Brazilian's commitment, even though the MP4/8 let him down in Imola, Montreal, Estoril and the Hungaroring. Worst of all was at Silverstone, when the team used Ford's new Series VIII engine for the first time, only for yet another fuel-reading glitch to leave him stranded on the very last lap for the third year in a row. Nevertheless, his season ended on an upswing.

In one of the most sensational opening laps in history Senna started the rain-soaked European GP at Donington Park fourth on the grid, dropped to fifth and then passed four cars to lead at the end of the lap. He lapped everyone up to second place and won the race by over 30 seconds.

This squashed hedgehog appeared on the side of the MP4/8 was the McLaren team's response to the Sega hedgehog stickers that were put on the Williams cars to signify each Grand Prix victory by the Grove based team. McLaren added a sticker every time it beat Williams on track.

At Suzuka, and then again at Adelaide, Senna succeeded in pulling off superb victories. The Australian success, it transpired, would be his last and at the time enabled McLaren to declare itself the most successful Grand Prix team of all time.

Senna trailed that year's champion, Alain Prost, by 23 points, but had humbled him on more than one occasion, most notably at Donington, in what was seen to be a less powerful car. Long before Adelaide, where emotions in the team ran high, he had announced that he would be leaving McLaren after six seasons and three World Championships, to join Williams. The team, meanwhile, went towards an uncertain future testing a Lamborghini V12-engined MP4/8B before inking a supply deal with Peugeot for the coming season.

By the Portuguese Grand Prix Mika Häkkinen had replaced Andretti. In his first GP for McLaren, Mika qualified an incredible third, ahead of Senna and ran in the top 4 until he crashed out on lap 33.

MODEL	McLaren MP4/8
TYPE/FORMULA	Formula 1
YEAR OF PRODUCTION	1993
DESIGNER	Neil Oatley
EXAMPLES BUILT	8
ENGINE	Ford Cosworth HBE V8
CUBIC CAPACITY	3494cc
ELECTRONICS	TAG 2.12F ignition/injection
POWER OUTPUT	640bhp

TRANSMISSION	McLaren semi-auto transverse 6-speed
CHASSIS	High modulus carbon fibre/honeycomb monocoque
BODY	Carbon fibre single piece cockpit/engine cover & nose
FRONT SUSPENSION	Double wishbone, push-rod operating
	longitudinal inboard coil spring/damper
REAR SUSPENSION	Double wishbone, push-rod operating
	longitudinal inboard coil spring/damper
BRAKES F/R	Outboard Brembo/KH/Carbone Industrie
WHEELS DIAMETER x WIDTH F/R	13x11.5/13x13.8in

TYRES F/R	Goodyear
LENGTH	174in - 4420mm
WIDTH	78.8in - 2000mm
HEIGHT	39in - 990mm
WHEELBASE	114.25in - 2902mm
TRACK F/R	64/63.25in - 1626/1607mm
WEIGHT	1113lb - 505kg
PRINCIPAL DRIVERS	Senna, Andretti, Häkkinen
IDENTIFYING COLOURS	Red/White

1993 MP4/8B
FORMULA 1 TEST CAR

Another test mule that was developed for a potential engine partner, the McLaren MP4/8B was adapted from the Ford HB V8-engined MP4/8 in order to assess the Chrysler-Lamborghini V12 in the autumn of 1993.

Once again, the new engine, an 80º unit codenamed 3512, required both the wheelbase and bodywork of the original car to be stretched, the former by an additional 3.75 inches. The significantly longer engine also called for new mountings on the back of the monocoque and the front of the gearbox to be modified to mate with it. The latter was the standard transverse six-speeder with semi-automatic actuation, and the suspension was similarly unchanged from the regular season MP4/8 donor car with longitudinally mounted inboard spring/damper units operated by pushrods front and rear. Other changes included new McLaren Calsonic water and oil-cooling systems and a revised fuel cell. One familiar area was the Chrysler Lamborghini engine's TAG 2.12F injection system.

A top secret initial shakedown test of the car in this form was undertaken on the short South Circuit at far end of the Silverstone complex, on September 20th, after which the team travelled to South Wales for a couple more days of undercover testing at Pembrey, once again with Senna behind the wheel.

Immediately after the Portuguese Grand Prix the MP4/8B was shipped to the Estoril circuit in early October for a full week of F1 testing with all the other teams who had stayed on after the race. The car now had a modified engine with a power curve that had been revised at Senna's suggestion, and once again he drove. Mika Häkkinen also had a run. However, although Senna was very quick and set a best lap time of 1m 13.232s compared to Alain Prost's quickest time of the week for Ferrari of 1m 13.000s, and was reportedly 1.4s faster round Silverstone than he had been in the Ford HB-engined MP4/8, the MP4/8B project stalled.

The reason had everything to do with politics rather than with engineering. It was clear that the Ford deal offered little for the future, and there was disappointment that a proposed Ford V12 had been shelved. The Chrysler Lamborghini deal seemed promising, especially as Chrysler appeared keen to make a significant investment in it. But according to Technical Director Neil Oatley: *"We were only supplied with two Lamborghini engines for the initial development work, and since these came from its pool of engines that were also going to the Larrousse team, we really felt that Peugeot would be much more committed to working with us to develop a potential race-winning engine. To be honest, the Lamborghini engine was quite old technology, having been used by Lotus as far back*

The bodywork was revised to suit the longer wheelbase. Bespoke water and oil cooling systems as well as a modified fuel cell were designed to suit engine. All the suspension, however, was standard MP4/8A specification.

as 1990, and we really couldn't see much of a future in working with them."

Chrysler had a completely different interpretation of the discussions and believed a deal had been agreed and was livid when it fell apart as Ron Dennis inked supply terms instead with Peugeot. Lamborghini aspired to continue supplying the Larrousse team into 1994, but when the McLaren deal faltered, Chrysler withdrew from the sport and sold Lamborghini. Its brief sojourn as an F1 engine supplier was over.

The McLaren MP4/8B remains one of the sport's great what-might-have-been cars, and its story differs according to the teller. Fate, or perhaps Peugeot, intervened, and in the end only one chassis was ever built and tested. The car was never liveried in the familiar red and white Marlboro scheme, and remains in the McLaren collection in its virgin state. Its plain white bodywork carries nothing more than Goodyear logos on the front wing endplates and, complete with its V12 'Chrysler' engine, it provides an interesting insight into how a modern F1 car looks without the myriad sponsorship decals the world has become so used to since the late 1960s.

The MP4-8B was a special version of the 1993 race car built to accept the V12 Chrysler Lamborghini engine in place of the Ford V8 that the team used in 1993. With the engine mounting architecture modified to suit the longer motor the wheelbase was increased by 3.75 inches.

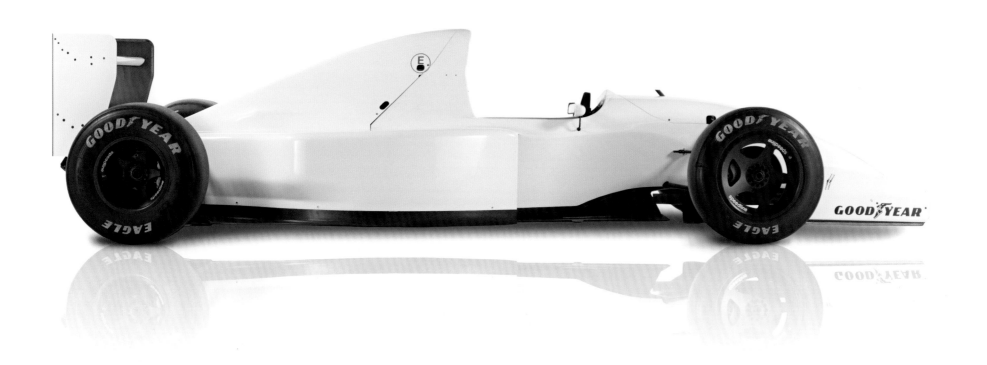

MODEL	McLaren MP4/8B	TRANSMISSION	McLaren semi-auto transverse 6-speed	TYRES F/R	Goodyear
TYPE/FORMULA	Formula 1 Test Car	CHASSIS	High modulus carbon fibre/honeycomb monocoque	LENGTH	177in - 4496mm
YEAR OF PRODUCTION	1993	BODY	Carbon fibre single piece cockpit/engine cover & nose	WIDTH	78.8in - 2000mm
DESIGNER	Neil Oatley	FRONT SUSPENSION	Double wishbone, push-rod operating	HEIGHT	39in - 990mm
EXAMPLES BUILT	1 (converted from MP4/8)		longitudinal inboard coil spring/damper	WHEELBASE	118in - 2997mm
ENGINE	Chrysler Lamborghini V12	REAR SUSPENSION	Double wishbone, push-rod operating	TRACK F/R	66/63in - 1676/1600mm
CUBIC CAPACITY	3498cc		longitudinal inboard coil spring/damper	WEIGHT	1113lb - 505kg
ELECTRONICS	TAG 2.12F ignition/injection	BRAKES F/R	Outboard Brembo/KH/Carbone Industrie	PRINCIPAL DRIVERS	Senna, Häkkinen
POWER OUTPUT	670bhp	WHEELS DIAMETER x WIDTH F/R	13x11.5/13x13.8in	IDENTIFYING COLOURS	White

1993 McLAREN F1 ROADCAR

On March 31st, 1998, at Germany's Ehra-Lessien Proving Ground, the McLaren F1 comprehensively beat the world speed record for production cars. Sportscar racer Andy Wallace drove a standard five-year-old factory car known as 'XP5' to an official, independently verified speed of 240.1mph on the 21-kilometre track. However, the story of the McLaren F1 had actually begun almost a decade before it went into the record books as the 'Fastest Production Car' in the world.

To trace its origins, one must travel back to the 1988 Italian Grand Prix, a race now chiefly remembered as the only one all season which the McLaren MP4/4s of Ayrton Senna and Alain Prost failed to win.

Hours later, while waiting for a flight out of Linate, Ron Dennis and Gordon Murray were discussing the possibility of the company designing and building a no-holds-barred McLaren roadcar. At the time it seemed everyone was racing towards a street legal 200mph: Jaguar unveiled its XJ220; Yamaha wheeled out its quite extraordinary tandem-seat OX99-11; Bugatti surfaced again, this time in Italy, and then there was a legion of strangely named newcomers, such as the 16-cylinder Cizeta-Moroder and the MCA Centenaire.

The McLaren, however, was to outdo them all, not just in terms of its outright speed and highly polished performance, but also in the numbers produced, the time spent in production, the design concept, the quality of the engineering and above all its sheer élan. It was, as Motor Sport reminded its readers some months before that record-breaking run at Ehra-Lessien: "A car created using the best brains and the greatest technological resources."

The simple truth, said the magazine, is that compared to every one of its rivals the McLaren F1, "Is an immeasurably greater car... great not because of the undoubted extravagance of its design but because of its sheer sense." Even more than this, the editor noted, "It is not simply the fastest mid-engined supercar ever built, but the most practical."

Murray was later to insist that its phenomenal speed was not the point of the car, "just a consequence of the other things it does". Even so, with such a blisteringly high top end, and with Autocar demonstrating in the F1's first full road test that it was quicker to 150mph than an ordinary sportscar was to 60, it was inevitable that the car would be noted first and foremost for its performance. After that came the price, a jaw-dropping £634,500 in the UK. The gold-lined engine bay and remote diagnostics also served occasionally to blind observers to the car's many other genuinely outstanding qualities.

Its trademark three-abreast seating layout, for example, was Murray's idea. Initially, Dennis had favoured an even more focused single-seater, but the South African had been thinking about his mid-seat supercar for many years, even doodling ideas for it as early as 1969. Murray also admitted to a number of supercar influences such as the Lamborghini Miura, and show cars such as the Bertone Caribou, as well as one of his all-time favourites, the Lotus Elan. "I like small cars and light cars," he told journalist Mick Walsh a decade after the car's launch. "I like everything that Colin Chapman liked. [The Elan] was incredibly well packaged, and packaging is everything."

Perhaps, surprisingly, given that work on the F1 didn't finally get underway for another two decades, the car was drawn entirely by hand, with no computer-aided design whatsoever. Responsibility for the exterior and interior fell to the highly regarded ex-Lotus stylist Peter Stevens who worked from the inside out, waiting until the seating buck was made before starting, "As I didn't want to create a style we'd fall in love with that would dictate the design."

It was, by any reckoning, a tight-lipped design team, and in the highly competitive world of supercars, where secrets are commonplace, details of this new road-going McLaren remained one of the very best of the best-kept secrets. For three years or more everyone with an interest knew something was going on; before getting the call, Stevens recalls seeing a piece in Autosport prompting him to assume the team was already sewn up, but

Even the grip shape of the specially made Nardi F1 steering wheel involved many hours of research, design and development. A minimal Formula 1 style dash panel created in carbon composite carried specially made analogue instrumentation.

The intricately crafted right-hand manual gearchange was situated in the carbon chassis rail that runs alongside the driver. This panel also housed the ignition switch, starter button and air conditioning controls, as well as the electric window switch and right-hand mirror control.

absolutely nobody outside the factory knew quite what to expect. The company would presumably be seeking to capitalise on its formidable Grand Prix record, but hopes were high that McLaren wouldn't simply try to cash in on its stellar name with 'just another' supercar.

At the car's launch party in Monte Carlo in May 1993, Murray was at pains to underline that it hadn't done this. "It's not just a case of going one step beyond," he said, speaking prior to the Grand Prix, "this is an entirely new starting point for supercars." It certainly was. Not because it was very fast, although it had a higher top speed than the Formula 1 cars, but, rather, because from stem to stern the 1138kg car showcased numerous new and exciting technical innovations.

Besides having the highest power-to-weight ratio of any previous production car, it was to be the first in the world to feature a complete carbon fibre composite monocoque and active aerodynamics to maintain a constant centre of pressure under hard braking. Taut-looking, tight and functional, it was also by supercar

MODEL	McLaren F1	TRANSMISSION	Transverse 6-speed, limited slip differential	TYRES F/R	Goodyear F1, Michelin SX-MXX3
TYPE/FORMULA	Roadcar	CHASSIS	Carbon fibre reinforced composite monocoque	LENGTH	169in - 4292mm
YEAR OF PRODUCTION	1993-1998	BODY	Carbon fibre composite panels	WIDTH	71.6in - 1820mm
DESIGNER	Gordon Murray/Peter Stevens	FRONT SUSPENSION	Double wishbones, Ground Plane Shear centre	HEIGHT	44.8in - 1140mm
EXAMPLES BUILT	64		sub-frame light alloy damper/co-axial coil spring, anti-roll bar	WHEELBASE	107in - 2718mm
ENGINE	BMW V12	REAR SUSPENSION	Double wishbones, Inclined Axis Shear mounting,	TRACK F/R	61.7/58in - 1568/1472mm
CUBIC CAPACITY	6064cc		light alloy damper/co-axial coil spring, toe-in/toe-out control links	WEIGHT	2502lb - 1140kg
INDUCTION	TAG 3.12 ignition/injection	BRAKES F/R	Outboard 13/12in ventilated discs	PRINCIPAL DRIVERS	n/a
POWER OUTPUT	627bhp	WHEELS DIAMETER x WIDTH F/R	17x9/17x11.5in	IDENTIFYING COLOURS	n/a

standards commendably light and small, and rather subtle in appearance. Murray's ground-breaking layout, with the seats staggered to give the centrally located driver elbow room, luggage in the flanks and fuel tank behind the driver, sounds and even looks quite simple, but has been recognised for what it is: a design of true genius.

Stevens later claimed that the car more or less designed itself around Murray's idea, and that only the details took time, but when one is seeking perfection it is precisely those small details which make the difference. There were no big wings or fins, nor ugly pop-up headlamps; the handbrake handle was wood to prevent it getting too hot; the accelerator pedal titanium.

In the deliberate absence of a radio, the 10-disc CD player was conceived by the Formula 1 team's sponsor Kenwood to be the smallest and lightest ever, while all essential cooling and ventilation ducts were neatly hidden or cleverly incorporated into the F1's singular but quietly dramatic shape. Customer cars were even fitted with modem sockets, each one neatly concealed behind caps bearing the F1 logo, so that the factory could download the engine diagnostics from a car anywhere in the world.

Similarly, the BMW Motorsport engine was unsurpassingly state-of-the-art. With 6.1 litres, 48 valves, a quartet of catalytic converters and developing 627 horsepower at 7,000rpm and 443lb of torque, it was almost as powerful as the famed Can-Am McLarens of yore but infinitely more driveable, and continued to redefine the supercar. With a dozen individual coils providing direct ignition, chain-driven camshafts and constantly variable inlet valve timing, it proved to be superbly tractable, enabling a driver to rocket from 30mph to 225mph+ in the highest of its six gears.

It was little surprise that it wasn't just the press that was queuing up to praise the car: the experts loved it too. Le Mans winner Derek Bell admired its reserved appearance, particularly the fact, "*That it isn't covered in spoilers or other add-ons and there's nothing on it that shouldn't be there. It isn't a case of style for style's sake, which is refreshing.*" Bell also found the car outstanding to drive, "*something with straight honest power – no turbos or anything, it really is astounding. There's no hesitation on take-off, just instant and seemingly never-ending acceleration and the sound of the BMW V12 behind you is incredible.*" The brakes too were singled out for comment, the F1's Brembo four-pot monobloc calipers making their presence felt on huge ventilated discs.

Many of those who drove the car in the early days also commented on how usable it was, and how easy to drive compared to many of its more conventional, more hardcore rivals. While ferociously fast at the limit, and capable of delivering pulverising levels of power when asked to, around town the car still showed itself to be amazingly docile.

Inevitably it was hailed as a classic from the moment the covers came off in Monaco, something which more than justified another part of Murray's original brief, namely that "*If one of these cars were to be discovered in a barn in 60 years time it could be restored.*" Among other things that meant no irreplaceable injection plastic mouldings, hence a decision to fabricate the instrument panel (as it happens, Murray's favourite feature) with stainless steel dials, hand-painted with etched numbers, and with each needle individually machined. In a project with no compromise, nothing was left unconsidered or to chance.

The F1 remains even now a unique and truly remarkable machine. Stationary or moving it looks as good today as it did at its launch, its iconic style having never even begun to date. Prices now exceed the original cost of the car, which, if one can be forgiven for the vulgarity of mentioning the money, is perhaps the definitive measure of a car's worth in the connected worlds of driving passion and automotive art. Most importantly, though, the McLaren F1 has not been surpassed, not in its combination of performance, practicality and breadth of ability, and certainly not when one calibrates the absolute clarity of its conception and the overwhelming intelligence of its design and execution.

At the heart of the McLaren F1 is the made-to-order, 6.1-litre
48-valve BMW V12 engine. With an output in excess of 600bhp
it produces one of the highest specific outputs for a large capacity
naturally aspirated unit in production sportscar history.

1994 MP4/9
FORMULA 1

The arrival of aggressive entrepreneur Bob Eaton at Lamborghini's US parent Chrysler might have made an Italian engine deal with McLaren look more likely: years earlier, when head of General Motors Europe, he had pushed hard to create an Opel F1 engine. In the end, though, Ron Dennis went with Peugeot, tying up the supply deal with remarkable speed given that the French company had only recently started work on its own 72° V10 F1 powerplant with the help of ex-Renault engineer Jean-Pierre Boudy.

Dennis was under no illusions that McLaren and Peugeot faced a very difficult task. *"It will,"* he said, *"take time to equal or surpass the level of Renault performance, but I have a very positive view of the season. Aided by the superior performance we anticipate from Peugeot I am quite certain [the MP4/9] will be competitive and will win races in 1994."*

The car was, nevertheless, insufficient to tempt Alain Prost out of retirement, although he did test it; so, the team recruited Briton Martin Brundle to drive alongside Mika Häkkinen. Peugeot-connected Frenchmen Philippe Alliot and Yannick Dalmas handling the testing. The former did get a McLaren race drive that year, standing in for Häkkinen in Hungary when the latter was given a one-race suspension following an incident in Germany.

When the new McLaren-Peugeot was unveiled at Woking on January 20th 1994, it was clear that it had much in common with the Ford-engined MP4/8 although there were numerous subtle aerodynamic changes to the floor and sidepods to take account of the new five-valve Peugeot A4 engine. In truth, the final configuration was not readily determined, and not just because Peugeot switched to the four-valve A6 before the season started. Significantly, as neither engine had actually been run by the time Neil Oatley's MP4/9 was coming off the drawing board, much of the data the McLaren team used to design the cooling system had to be derived from its previous experience, and from Peugeot's with its 905 Le Mans sportscar.

Other modifications included a clutch activated by steering column paddle controls, the resulting two-pedal car being very much to Häkkinen's liking since it meant he could left-foot brake very late into corners without compromising the car's aerodynamic balance as one would during the momentary delay between coming off the throttle and applying the brakes in a conventional car.

At this time the McLaren six-speed gearbox also had a fully automatic downchange facility, although this was later outlawed by a regulation change. Power steering made its debut on the car too and proved useful on some of the tighter circuits. McLaren's partner company TAG Electronics worked closely with Peugeot to refine its sophisticated onboard ignition/injection/data acquisition system. Providing a literally continuous flow of engine, chassis and performance data, this sort of telemetry was revolutionising the sport by

giving race engineers in the pits continuous access to a mass of real-time data.

Peugeot Sport, under the management of former F1 racer and turbo pioneer Jean-Pierre Jabouille, was to show steady progress with its engineering, adding an extra 20bhp for the Imola race, and finding another 500rpm and thus another 15bhp by the time the Version 2 engine was ready for the French GP. Achieving this with revised camshafts, it then developed a somewhat confusingly named 'Version 2 Mark 2' with an additional 15bhp in time for Hungary, and a 'Version 2 Mark 3' for Jerez which gave the drivers another 10bhp.

Throughout this period changes were made to the car's cooling, particularly when at Barcelona the FIA changed the aerodynamic rules in the aftermath of the deaths of Roland Ratzenberger and Ayrton Senna at Imola. This helped a good deal as shorter diffusers produced less back pressure and significantly lowered the engine's operating temperatures. Much of the testing of the all-new engine had taken place in cooler weather and Peugeot's V10 had not really performed as everyone had hoped it would when it came to operating at higher temperatures.

Brundle in particular experienced many mechanical difficulties during the season, but the introduction of a new underbody profile and rear wing in mid-summer helped to improve the cars' handling in slow corners. Even so, no one expected 1994 to be a vintage year for McLaren, and in this they were not to be disappointed. Brundle found his strength to be in race lap times rather than qualifying, and his best result of the year was second at Monaco. Häkkinen proved quick in both qualifying and the races themselves, and certainly hit the spot with the boss. Dennis firmly believed in the Finn and declared: *"He has what it takes to become a World Champion."*

New team leader Mika Häkkinen had a string of podium finishes in 1994. His best result of the season was a second in the Belgian Grand Prix (top) at Spa. Two weeks later he was third (above) in the Italian Grand Prix at Monza.

Senna's departure had clearly weakened the team, and at times it seemed that little progress had been made in a transitional year. With two races still to be run it came as little surprise when an announcement was made that the two parties had decided to dissolve their partnership. Dennis had agreed a deal with Daimler that would create perhaps the most outstanding racing partnership of the modern era.

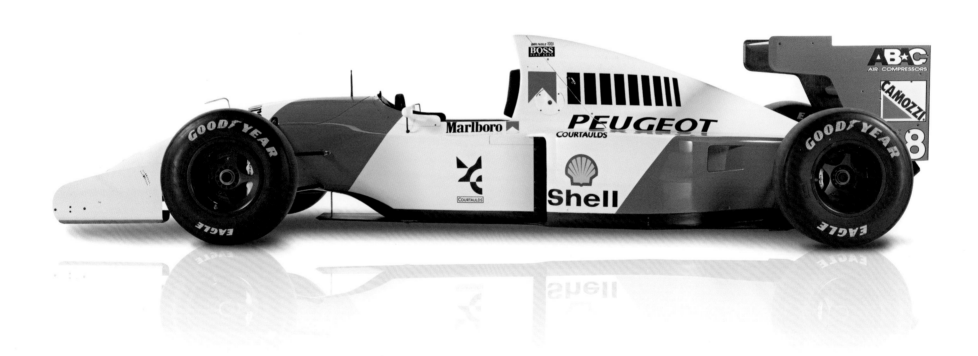

MODEL	McLaren MP4/9	TRANSMISSION	McLaren semi-auto transverse 6-speed	TYRES F/R	Goodyear
TYPE/FORMULA	Formula 1	CHASSIS	High modulus carbon fibre/honeycomb monocoque	LENGTH	177in - 4496mm
YEAR OF PRODUCTION	1994	BODY	Carbon fibre single piece cockpit/engine cover & nose	WIDTH	77.5in - 1970mm
DESIGNER	Neil Oatley	FRONT SUSPENSION	Double wishbone, push-rod operating	HEIGHT	39in - 990mm
EXAMPLES BUILT	8		longitudinal inboard coil spring/damper	WHEELBASE	117in - 2972mm
ENGINE	Peugeot A4 F1, A6 F1 V10	REAR SUSPENSION	Double wishbone, push-rod operating	TRACK F/R	66.6/63in - 1692/1600mm
CUBIC CAPACITY	3498cc		longitudinal inboard coil spring/damper	WEIGHT	1113lb - 505kg
ELECTRONICS	TAG 2.12F ignition/injection	BRAKES F/R	Outboard Brembo/KH/Carbone Industrie	PRINCIPAL DRIVERS	Häkkinen, Brundle, Alliot
POWER OUTPUT	740bhp	WHEELS DIAMETER x WIDTH F/R	13x11.75/13x13.7in	IDENTIFYING COLOURS	Red/White

1995 McLAREN F1 GTR
RACECAR

It was perhaps inevitable, given not just McLaren's whole raison d'etre but also Gordon Murray's professional background and expertise, that the F1 would eventually take to the race track, even though Ron Dennis had specifically denied such a possibility when the car was launched. Murray had no such plans either. He merely dreamed of building what was quickly and widely to become recognised as the 20th century's most exotic roadcar and at the conclusion of a three-year design-and-build process he had achieved exactly that.

Before long, however, customers were asking for a racing version, and as the 1995 GT season drew nearer the number of requests began to climb. Leading them was racing driver Ray Bellm who, together with fellow F1 owner and German banker Dr Thomas Bscher, approached McLaren with an idea to race the cars in the BPR Karcher Global Endurance GT series. Initially McLaren was not taken with the idea, so Bellm went direct to Dennis, an old friend.

Thereafter an agreement was reached initially to develop a three-car customer racing programme, the third car being assigned to Lindsay Owen-Jones. The factory was not slow to respond; it couldn't afford to be with just a few months left before the start of the season.

The racing version of the F1 that went to Le Mans in June, the GTR, was only slightly modified from the standard roadgoing model. The regulations pegged its power below 600bhp, so the racecar was actually slightly less powerful. The GTRs also had to be fitted with steel rollcages, the steering rack ratios were quicker, and the rubber bushing in the suspension was removed. Development of downforce was limited to a single day in the wind tunnel under Murray's direction, whilst the OZ Racing wheels concealed even larger discs and calipers. Bellm loved the car. "*As a result of the changes it didn't load up in the same way [as the standard car] and you could really zip it around,*" he revealed.

The fact that the F1 GTR entered by Tokyo Ueno Clinic Team went on to win the famed endurance classic at the first attempt underlined the integrity of the original design. There was also a simple moral correctness to such a car being victorious at Le Mans: the F1 GTR was essentially a roadcar which is, after all, what Le Mans had originally been all about. Seven GTRs started, four others finishing third, fourth, fifth and thirteenth.

By any standards the 1995 race was an epic. The weather was appalling – it rained for 16 of the 24 hours – but the McLarens rose to the challenge, despite never having been raced before in the wet. A couple fell victim to that, one of them Bscher's Team Competition car that crashed out during the night. It had led earlier on, as had the other casualty, the Gulf-sponsored GTR driven by Owen-Jones and Pierre-Henri Raphanel. Bellm recalled his worst moment: "*When the car got away from me through the Porsche curves and I slammed into the wall I thought, 'Oh Lord, this is it.'*" Instead he got back to the pits where repairs cost the team eight laps, enabling him to finish less than 30 minutes behind the winner. Once the car was fixed, he and co-drivers Maurizio Sandro Sala and Mark Blundell were able to make

up an incredible 31 places to finish fourth. Bellm expressed "*massive respect*" for the way eventual winner J.J. Lehto drove relentlessly all night through the weather. Even in the rain, in the Tokyo Ueno Clinic Team GTR he shared with Yannick Dalmas and Masanori Sekiya, the Finn was posting lap times up to 20 seconds faster than his rivals. After passing the lead car, the Harrods-liveried McLaren driven by Andy Wallace, Derek Bell and son Justin, Lehto was soon uncatchable and before long yet another McLaren-built machine had entered the racing record books.

Nor was it just that the La Sarthe classic that year was such a great race; it also represented several highly significant motorsport firsts. McLaren had won Le Mans at its first attempt. The F1 GTR had won the event in its first year of production, and not even Ferrari had managed that. As if that wasn't sufficient, the model also went on to win the 1995 Global GT Championship.

The greatest supercar of its generation had been transformed into probably the most successful British sports racing car of modern times.

MODEL	McLaren F1 GTR	TRANSMISSION	Aluminium case transverse 6-speed, lsd	TYRES F/R	Michelin
TYPE/FORMULA	Racecar	CHASSIS	Carbon fibre reinforced composite monocoque	LENGTH	169in - 4292mm
YEAR OF PRODUCTION	1995	BODY	Carbon fibre composite panels	WIDTH	71.6in - 1820mm
DESIGNER	Gordon Murray/Peter Stevens	FRONT SUSPENSION	Double wishbones, light alloy damper/	HEIGHT	44.8in - 1140mm
EXAMPLES BUILT	9		co-axial coil spring, anti-roll bar	WHEELBASE	107in - 2718mm
ENGINE	BMW V12	REAR SUSPENSION	Double wishbones, light alloy	TRACK F/R	61.3/58.6in - 1558/1488mm
CUBIC CAPACITY	6064cc		damper/co-axial coil spring	WEIGHT	2315lb - 1050kg
INDUCTION	TAG 3.12 ignition/injection	BRAKES F/R	Outboard 15/14in ventilated carbon discs	PRINCIPAL DRIVERS	n/a
POWER OUTPUT	600bhp	WHEELS DIAMETER x WIDTH F/R	18x10.85/18x13in	IDENTIFYING COLOURS	n/a

1995 marked another year of dramatic change at McLaren. Together with the introduction of the distinctive new MP4/10, the company was dealing with new drivers, a new engine supplier, in Mercedes-Benz, a key new technology sponsor in the Mobil Oil Corporation, a number of radical new ideas and more new regulations introduced by the sport's governing body.

The latter were an essential part of the FIA's safety drive and a desire to limit lap speeds following the tragic deaths the previous year of Roland Ratzenberger and Ayrton Senna at Imola. The package of measures included a return to the 3-litre formula which had held sway from 1966 until 1985. Only four-stroke engines were allowed, with no more than 12 cylinders, which effectively limited power to around 700bhp.

There were also strict limitations affecting other technologies, such as four-wheel drive and four-wheel steering, anti-lock brakes and electronic traction control mechanisms. Semi-automatic gearboxes were allowed, however, with a maximum of seven forward speeds. There were, inevitably, also restrictions on aerodynamics.

New regulations always kickstart engineers' creativity, so when McLaren unveiled its new car in the appropriate surroundings of London's Science Museum it was immediately obvious that it was quite unlike anything the company had produced before. The most striking features of its unconventional design were a new high nose located well above the full-width front wing and a small 50cm wide winglet mounted directly over the engine cover. Conceived to develop even greater downforce, the latter relied on a loophole which McLaren had discovered in the rule book which permitted a car's body at this particular point to extend up to 25cm either side of the centre-line.

The high nose was designed to enhance airflow around the front of the car, enhancing the wing's efficiency and the effectiveness of the barge boards. Separating the nose from the front wing in this way also meant it could form a deformable structure that did not need to be freshly crash-tested each time a change was made to the wing itself.

Beneath the car too the aerodynamics had received special attention, as a new requirement for a longitudinal step in the underbody obliged teams to look at more ways to control the airflow from front to back.

Just as it had with Honda, McLaren worked very closely in a fully integrated programme with its new engine partner, Mercedes-Benz, which in turn was partnered with the small British company, Ilmor Engineering. The new Mercedes-Benz FO 110D V10 was smaller than the outgoing Peugeot unit, and indeed some of the V8s, which greatly facilitated efficient packaging.

Mercedes-Benz and Ilmor conceived a completely new approach to engine architecture, in order to take advantage of the opportunities being offered by the new 50mm underbody step. It was clear that this arrangement would compromise the packaging of the engine, reducing the amount of space alongside it for ancillary equipment such as oil, water and hydraulic pumps. Ilmor proposed widening the vee angle to 75 degrees so that the hydraulic pump could lie between the two banks of cylinders and created a new exhaust manifold which was essentially a tight spiral that left room beneath for the water and oil pumps.

Meanwhile, at McLaren, Neil Oatley really wanted to use a new longitudinal transmission, but lacking the time contented himself with another transverse six-speeder, a semi-automatic with a hand clutch mounted on the steering wheel paddles and bespoke electronic controls from TAG.

At this point pressure from sponsors brought in Nigel Mansell, at 41 clearly looking for a highly competitive car to mark his return to the sport, while Mika Häkkinen stayed with the team for the second full season of his initial three-year contract. Unfortunately, both drivers found the car too tight for comfort; indeed, a completely new monocoque had to be built for the bulkier Mansell, requiring him to miss the first two races as Mark Blundell stood in while a wider version of the MP4/10B was created specifically for the 1992 World Champion.

The 1995 season saw the start of McLaren's relationship with Mercedes-Benz. The 3-litre Ilmor-built Mercedes-Benz FO 110D V10 engine was a smaller overall package than the previous year's engine and the MP4/10 chassis was smaller than ever.

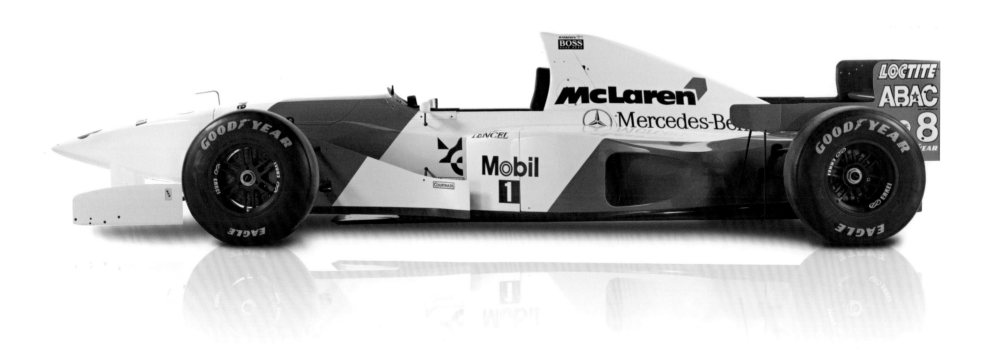

Both Häkkinen and Blundell started well in Brazil and Argentina against strong opposition from Williams-Renault drivers Damon Hill and David Coulthard, and Benetton-Renault's Michael Schumacher. Nevertheless, it was clear that the McLaren had a problem with front-end grip, and in Buenos Aires Häkkinen spun off with a puncture and Blundell succumbed to an oil leak from a cracked gearbox.

Thereafter, with Mansell back for the third race, in Imola, it became apparent that there were other problems too. Mansell complained about understeer in Barcelona, and although he qualified within half a second of his Finnish colleague, he was well off the pace by the time he slid off the road just before Schumacher threatened to lap him, and parked the car in the McLaren garage. By Monaco, he had quit for good, leaving his seat permanently to Blundell.

The younger Englishman was good for team morale, but the MP4/10B was still troubled. Things improved at Silverstone thanks to a new version of the Mercedes-Benz engine which had improved power, mid-range torque and driveability, and with this under his right foot Häkkinen set the fastest time during the race morning warm-up; at Hockenheim both rivers were running in the top six before their engines failed.

Much the same happened in Hungary, after which Mercedes-Benz worked hard to prepare fresh engines as McLaren went to work on its gearboxes and suspension readying the cars

In his first race for McLaren in Brazil, new recruit Mark Blundell scored a World Championship point for sixth place.

On lap 33 Mika Häkkinen retired from a strong third position in the German Grand Prix at Hockenheim with engine failure.

for a renewed assault at Spa. Unfortunately, Häkkinen spun there, but Blundell finished fifth before the team took second and fourth places at Monza following double retirements at Ferrari and Williams, and the early exit of Schumacher's Benetton.

The final iteration of the design, the MP4/10C, fared little better at Estoril, thanks to a series of minor problems with a new rear suspension arrangement, and at a very damp Nürburgring because of a decision to run slicks. Thereafter

Häkkinen missed the Pacific GP following an appendix operation, but returned to finish a good second behind Schumacher at Suzuka. Unfortunately, Blundell crashed heavily there in the 130R corner during practice, but raced bravely to seventh place. Then in Adelaide came Häkkinen's narrow escape from death after a heavy crash in practice, caused by a puncture. He survived thanks to a trackside tracheotomy, and with renewed heart McLaren laid its plans for a stronger challenge in 1996.

Mika Häkkinen had a strong qualifying session for the second race of the season in Argentina and put his MP4/10 fifth on the grid. He retired on the first lap of the race when a heavy collision with Eddie Irvine's Jordan knocked off his left front wheel.

MODEL	McLaren-Mercedes MP4/10	TRANSMISSION	McLaren semi-auto transverse 6-speed	TYRES F/R	Goodyear	
TYPE/FORMULA	Formula 1	CHASSIS	High modulus carbon fibre/honeycomb monocoque	LENGTH	182in - 4625mm	
YEAR OF PRODUCTION	1995	BODY	Carbon fibre single piece cockpit/engine cover & nose	WIDTH	78in - 1980mm	
DESIGNER	Neil Oatley	FRONT SUSPENSION	Double wishbone, push-rod & bellcrank	HEIGHT	39in - 990mm	
EXAMPLES BUILT	5 + (6 MP4/10B)		operating longitudinal inboard coil spring/damper	WHEELBASE	115in - 2925mm	
ENGINE	Mercedes-Benz FO 110D V10	REAR SUSPENSION	Double wishbone, push-rod & bellcrank	TRACK F/R	66.5/63.2in - 1690/1605mm	
CUBIC CAPACITY	2997cc		operating longitudinal inboard coil spring/damper	WEIGHT	1312lb - 595kg	
ELECTRONICS	TAG 2.12F ignition/injection	BRAKES F/R	Outboard 11in AP Racing/Carbone Industrie	PRINCIPAL DRIVERS	Häkkinen, Blundell, Mansell, Magnussen	
POWER OUTPUT	680bhp	WHEELS DIAMETER x WIDTH F/R	13x11.7/13x13.75in	IDENTIFYING COLOURS	Red/White	

1996 McLAREN F1 LM
ROADCAR

The F1 GTR had secured its place in motorsport history by achieving a resounding victory on its Le Mans debut in what is still widely regarded as the world's greatest motor race. A week later the winning car was in action, still bearing the stains of its high-speed travel in France, at Lord March's Goodwood Festival of Speed. McLaren Cars took the decision to mark the historic occasion with a limited edition commemorative model appropriately called the McLaren F1 LM.

'Limited Edition' really did mean precisely that, and despite the likely demand after the cars' stupendous performance at La Sarthe, just five production F1 LMs were made. There was one to commemorate each of the five McLaren finishers in the 1995 Grand Prix d'Endurance des 24 Heures du Mans, to give the race its full title. What's more, and in a warm and fitting salute to the company's late founder, three of the five were to be painted in McLaren papaya orange, the same, striking shade that had of course been used on many of Bruce McLaren's early Formula 1 and Can-Am race cars.

At the official launch of the car, Ron Dennis told the assembled press: "*It had been one of Bruce McLaren's dreams to produce the ultimate roadgoing sportscar. McLaren had achieved this initially with the standard production F1 model. Now in respect for Bruce's memory we finished the LMs – which really do provide a genuine racecar experience on the road – in the papaya orange colour which the team cars wore in Bruce's day. Our aim is always to produce excellence by design – the F1 LM simply underlines this commitment.*"

The concept of the F1 LM was to make as few changes as possible to a GTR racecar to enable its use on the public road. It was to run the most powerful engine of any F1 or F1-based derivative, roadcar or track star. All five were fitted with identical 1995 GTR-spec S 70/2 GTR LM engines and thanks to the absence of air restrictors – required on the track by FIA race regulations – this gave the LM a power output of 680bhp at 7,800rpm, and 703Nm of torque at just 4,500rpm. With a kerb weight of just 1,062kg the F1 LMs were also some 70kg lighter than the standard road-going cars, so they also boast the fastest in-gear acceleration of all the F1s; for example, 60 to 100mph in third gear took just three seconds, zero to 60mph could be reached in a fraction under three seconds and zero to 100mph inside a staggering seven seconds.

The car's racing heritage was much in evidence elsewhere too, for example, inside the cockpit where the driver was equipped with a carbon-fibre race seat while both passenger seats were moulded into the monocoque. The interior trim was kept to a minimum too, although all carbon materials in the cabin were painstakingly finished with several coats of high-gloss lacquer.

Outside, in addition to a full ground-effect underbody with diffuser, the cars featured special Le Mans front bodywork, 18in OZ magnesium alloy wheels – slightly wider than the standard car's nine and 11in rims at 10.85 and 13in respectively – and a distinctive carbon-fibre rear wing with a 'GTR-24 Heures du Mans Winners 1995' logo etched into the surface. Together with the bright orange finish and a discreet 'XP1 LM' logo on the sills, just ahead of the rear wheels, the completed cars were certainly unmistakable. As the rarest, most exclusive and most sought-after version of the McLaren F1 concept, they are almost certainly also the most valuable.

In the summer of 1999 at RAF Alconbury in Cambridgeshire, with McLaren's Ehra-Lessien driver Andy Wallace once more behind the wheel, the F1 LM set a new record for acceleration and braking. Travelling from zero to 100mph and back to zero in just 11.5seconds, the entire manoeuvre was completed in just 828ft of runway. Quite an achievement for a car which, as Gordon Murray himself was frequently at pains to point out, was never designed to break records.

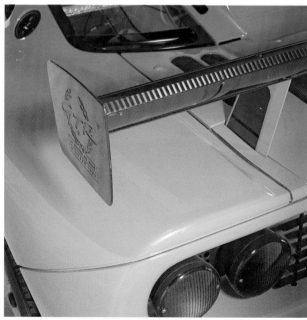

The distinctive carbon-fibre rear wing on the F1 LM carried a "GTR-24 Heures du Mans Winners 1995" logo, paying homage to the five cars that finished the 1995 Le Mans 24 hour race.

MODEL	McLaren F1 LM	TRANSMISSION	Transverse 6-speed racing unit, lsd	TYRES F/R	Michelin SX-MXX3
TYPE/FORMULA	Roadcar	CHASSIS	Carbon fibre reinforced composite monocoque	LENGTH	171.8in - 4365mm
YEAR OF PRODUCTION	1996	BODY	Carbon fibre composite panels	WIDTH	71.6in - 1820mm
DESIGNER	Gordon Murray	FRONT SUSPENSION	Double wishbones, light alloy damper/	HEIGHT	44.1in - 1120mm
EXAMPLES BUILT	5		co-axial coil spring, anti-roll bar	WHEELBASE	107in - 2718mm
ENGINE	BMW V12	REAR SUSPENSION	Double wishbones, light alloy	TRACK F/R	61.8/57.6in - 1570/1464mm
CUBIC CAPACITY	6064cc		damper/co-axial coil spring	WEIGHT	2341lb - 1062kg
INDUCTION	TAG 3.12 ignition/injection	BRAKES F/R	Outboard 13/12in ventilated carbon discs	PRINCIPAL DRIVERS	n/a
POWER OUTPUT	680bhp	WHEELS DIAMETER x WIDTH F/R	18x10.85/18x13in	IDENTIFYING COLOURS	n/a

1996 MP4/11A, MP4/11B & MP4/11C FORMULA 1

After a year of reorganisation and change 1996 was to be a year of consolidation rather than victory, with McLaren substantially reworking its chassis and Mercedes-Benz doing likewise with the V10 engine. David Coulthard joined from the dominant Williams Renault team and, even with Mika Häkkinen clearly back on form after his Adelaide accident, it was a sobering thought that the third anniversary of McLaren's last win was imminent.

The work undertaken on the new car was considerable, the new MP4/11 sharing no more than 7.5 per cent of components with the MP4/10C and featuring a new Phase 3 Mercedes-Benz engine in which every single component had been renewed bar the oil pumps. This was part of Mercedes-Benz's stated aim to raise its power output by five per cent, with the compact 120kg unit now able to run up to 16,500rpm and offering much improved low-speed torque.

The engine completed its bench testing just seven days before the new car was up and running, but Häkkinen liked it immediately and despite slight concerns about the handling balance promptly posted his fastest-ever lap in testing at Estoril in 1m 19.65s.

Once more the car was produced under Neil Oatley's direction, with considerable input from Steve Nichols who had returned to the fold after a spell with Ferrari. He was involved closely with the design and function of the suspension geometry and configuration, and introduced carbon flexures in place of ball joints on the front suspension to reduce friction and to increase the car's overall stiffness.

While Henri Durand took care of the aerodynamics, Oatley concentrated more on the installation of the engine and transmission. The latter comprised the all-new McLaren-designed longitudinal six-speeder that he had wanted for the MP4/10. This featured semi-automatic changing courtesy of TAG Electronics, the same McLaren Group subsidiary having devised a more fully integrated engine and chassis control data acquisition package.

Initially neither driver was convinced by the MP4/11's handling, both Häkkinen and Coulthard expressing dissatisfaction with its behaviour on turn-in. With some input from quadruple World Champion Alain Prost, who had returned to work with McLaren as a technical consultant and development driver, work was soon underway to rectify this and improvements were made in time for the European GP at the Nürburgring, where Coulthard finished third.

Further refinements were introduced for the San Marino Grand Prix at Imola, and later still came some revisions to the front wing mounting points to correct a degree of flexing at the point where the wing attached to its hangers. The team also produced a special short-wheelbase car MP4/11B which made its debut in Monaco before being adopted as the new standard by Magny-Cours, as Mercedes-Benz continued work on the engine to improve its responsiveness.

For Belgium the car gained yet another refinement, this time a new front suspension. Rather more aerodynamic than before, this had been designed in line with another new interpretation of the technical regulations which had allowed Tyrrell to campaign streamlined wishbones.

The best result all year, however, was to be Coulthard's second place at Monaco, where Häkkinen wrote off MP4/11-5 after losing control during an acclimatisation run in teeming rain; prior to this he had been two seconds faster than the rest of the field.

Fortunately, the Finn bounced back and was soon overhauling his team-mate with no fewer than four third places in the British, Belgian, Italian and Japanese races. Coulthard had never really got to grips with the car and admitted fighting "*to keep the rear end under control*".

As Coulthard discovered, the McLaren-Mercedes combination worked superbly on high-speed circuits such as Monza and Spa where less downforce was needed. Indeed, in Belgium he looked like he might win, before a spin on new tyres. Similarly, at Monza the car had enabled a hard-driving Häkkinen to climb from 17th to third place after an unscheduled pit stop had left him way down the field.

Elsewhere, though, it performed less well, particularly on bumpy or uneven circuits where McLaren paid a price for placing what Ron Dennis called "*significant emphasis on reducing the car's pitch sensitivity.*" It succeeded on that point, but as a consequence the team "*experienced problems in the optimisation of the car at circuits which demand performance in a broad range of corners*". The upshot of all this was fourth place in the Constructors' World Championship, with 49 points.

For the upcoming 1997 season the F1 Technical Regulations were to be changed to considerably narrow the overall width of the car. As a development exercise for this, the team converted a pair of 1996 race cars to run with rather crude, metal, narrow track suspension, this car being known as the MP4/11C. During the autumn/winter of 1996 the car was tested by both Häkkinen and Coulthard.

A little bit of history came to an end as the season closed, and Marlboro's sponsorship contract expired. Its relationship with McLaren spanned 23 years, at the time the longest such alliance in any sport.

The small high rear wing, designed to fit into a loophole in the regulations, and which had first appeared on top of the engine cover in the early races of the 1995 season, made a reappearance on the MP4/11A.

By the Monaco Grand Prix in May the team was using the revised spec MP4/11B. While David Coulthard was on the podium in second place, Mika Häkkinen (above) could only manage sixth.

MODEL	McLaren-Mercedes MP4/11A		TRANSMISSION	McLaren semi-auto longitudinal 6-speed		TYRES F/R	Goodyear
TYPE/FORMULA	Formula 1		CHASSIS	High modulus carbon fibre/honeycomb monocoque		LENGTH	179in - 4547mm
YEAR OF PRODUCTION	1996		BODY	Carbon fibre single piece cockpit/engine cover & nose		WIDTH	78.8in - 2000mm
DESIGNER	Neil Oatley		FRONT SUSPENSION	Double wishbone, push-rod & bellcrank		HEIGHT	39in - 990mm
EXAMPLES BUILT	6			operating longitudinal inboard coil spring/damper		WHEELBASE	120in - 3050mm
ENGINE	Mercedes-Benz FO 110E V10		REAR SUSPENSION	Double wishbone, push-rod & bellcrank		TRACK F/R	66.7/63.5in - 1694/1612mm
CUBIC CAPACITY	2997cc			operating longitudinal inboard coil spring/damper		WEIGHT	1320lb - 600kg
ELECTRONICS	TAG2000 ignition/injection		BRAKES F/R	Outboard 11in AP Racing/Carbone Industrie		PRINCIPAL DRIVERS	Häkkinen, Coulthard
POWER OUTPUT	700bhp		WHEELS DIAMETER x WIDTH F/R	13x12/13x13.75in		IDENTIFYING COLOURS	Red/White

Although it looked similar, the MP4/11 shared very little in the way of componentry with its predecessor. The new Phase 3 Mercedes-Benz FO 110E engine was a clean sheet approach.

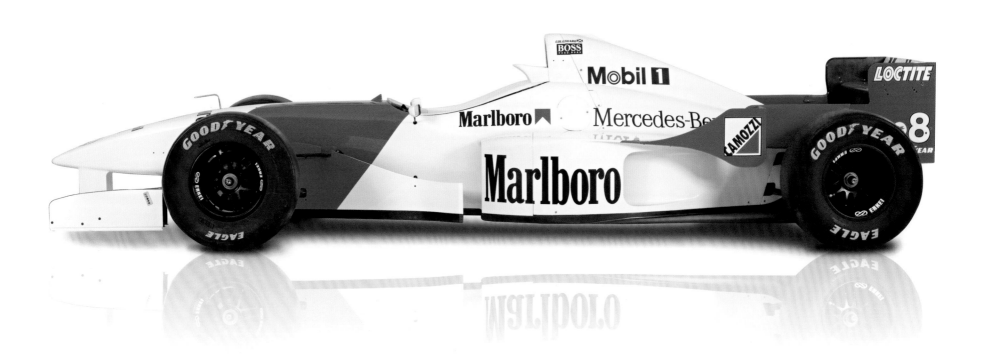

MODEL	McLaren-Mercedes MP4/11C	TRANSMISSION	McLaren semi-auto longitudinal 6-speed	TYRES F/R	Goodyear
TYPE/FORMULA	Formula 1 Test Car	CHASSIS	High modulus carbon fibre/honeycomb monocoque	LENGTH	179in - 4547mm
YEAR OF PRODUCTION	1996	BODY	Carbon fibre single piece cockpit/engine cover & nose	WIDTH	76in - 1930mm
DESIGNER	Neil Oatley	FRONT SUSPENSION	Double wishbone, push-rod & bellcrank	HEIGHT	39in - 990mm
EXAMPLES BUILT	2 (from MP4/11A)		operating longitudinal inboard coil spring/damper	WHEELBASE	120in - 3050mm
ENGINE	Mercedes-Benz FO 110E V10	REAR SUSPENSION	Double wishbone, push-rod & bellcrank	TRACK F/R	64/60in - 1625/1524mm
CUBIC CAPACITY	2997cc		operating longitudinal inboard coil spring/damper	WEIGHT	1320lb - 600kg
ELECTRONICS	TAG2000 ignition/injection	BRAKES F/R	Outboard 11in AP Racing/Carbone Industrie	PRINCIPAL DRIVERS	Häkkinen, Coulthard
POWER OUTPUT	700bhp	WHEELS DIAMETER x WIDTH F/R	13x12/13x13.75in	IDENTIFYING COLOURS	Red/White

1996 McLAREN F1 GTR RACECAR

In 1995 the factory had built just nine F1 GTRs, a figure it adhered to for the following season with two of the older cars (03R and 06R) being updated as the concept continued to develop to stay abreast of various new GT regulations. The car's first season in racing was in every sense going to be a hard one to beat. At the highest international level, the genuine if undeniably exotic roadcar had succeeded in overhauling several purpose-built sportsracers.

McLaren nevertheless stepped up to the challenge, with a car which while clearly a very close relation of the previous GTR, was now slightly lower and had significantly improved aerodynamics which endowed it with superior levels of downforce. The cars nevertheless kept very close to the original Peter Stevens profile while shedding more weight, reaching 1012kg for the new 1000kg limit BPR GT Series regulations.

Ground clearance was reduced slightly, by 15 mm at the front. A more aggressive chin spoiler served to accentuate this nose-down attitude as well as increasing the length overall by 80mm. The modest aerodynamic revisions incorporated a smaller cooling duct cut into the front compartment lid while some of the body panels were modified slightly to make them more easily removable for pit work and other repairs.

The trusty 600bhp Type S70/3 GTR V12 remained largely unchanged but sat lower in the car and was now mated to an uprated gearbox housed in a new magnesium casing.

During 1996 the McLaren F1 GTRs notched up nine international BPR GT victories together with another five race wins in the prestigious All Japan Grand Touring Car Championship.

In the Far East Team Lark had purchased a brace of GTRs, planning to campaign them in the GT500 class of the All Japan GT Championship. The cars debuted at Suzuka and scored another memorable McLaren 1-2 with Naoki Hattori and Ralf Schumacher at the wheel. Shortly afterwards, at Fuji, David Brabham and John Nielsen took another win.

At Sugo the Lark team badly damaged its own chassis but was able to borrow another from GTC Competition for the final round. Eventually, with four outright wins to its credit, Team Lark went on to capture the GT500 Championship well ahead of the Toyota and Nissan works teams.

In Europe McLaren once again started the season well, with the GTC Competition team car chalking up the model's first BPR Championship win in the hands of Ray Bellm and James Weaver. McLarens won the first three races, and GTC Competition successfully took the Championship.

Le Mans was clearly the big one, its history and heritage more than making up for it not being an official part of any single race series. McLaren was naturally keen to defend its title, but the competition from the Le Mans Prototypes (LMP) class was far stiffer than it had been the previous year with Porsche's factory team very much in the ascendant. As a result, and despite fielding another seven F1 GTRs, McLaren was unable to repeat its win. However, the now legendary reliability meant that six of the seven GTRs finished the race, in fourth, fifth, sixth, eighth, ninth and 11th places.

After delivery was taken days before the first race of 1996 at Paul Ricard (top), there was simply no time to paint the Lindsay Owen-Jones/Raphanel F1 GTR.

By the next race at Monza both the Gulf cars were in the familiar blue & orange acolours. James Weaver (above) shared the car with Ray Bellm at every race that season.

MODEL	McLaren F1 GTR
TYPE/FORMULA	Racecar
YEAR OF PRODUCTION	1996
DESIGNER	Gordon Murray
EXAMPLES BUILT	9
ENGINE	BMW V12
CUBIC CAPACITY	6064cc
INDUCTION	TAG 3.12 ignition/injection
POWER OUTPUT	600bhp

TRANSMISSION	Magnesium case transverse 6-speed, lsd
CHASSIS	Carbon fibre reinforced composite monocoque
BODY	Carbon fibre composite panels
FRONT SUSPENSION	Double wishbones, light alloy damper/
	co-axial coil spring, anti-roll bar
REAR SUSPENSION	Double wishbones, light alloy
	damper/co-axial coil spring
BRAKES F/R	Outboard 15/14in ventilated carbon discs
WHEELS DIAMETER x WIDTH F/R	18x10.85/18x13in

TYRES F/R	Michelin
LENGTH	172in - 4367mm
WIDTH	74.8in - 1900mm
HEIGHT	42.9in - 1090mm
WHEELBASE	107in - 2718mm
TRACK F/R	61.3/58.6in - 1558/1488mm
WEIGHT	2231lb - 1012kg
PRINCIPAL DRIVERS	n/a
IDENTIFYING COLOURS	n/a

A new era began for McLaren-Mercedes as the West tobacco brand came onboard as title sponsor in 1997, to replace Marlboro, and the other highly significant development later in the year was the arrival as Technical Director of Adrian Newey who joined from Williams-Renault at the start of August. A rather more subtle change was seen in the method of numbering the cars; whereas the generic nomenclature had previously been separated from the model number by a slash, now it was separated by a hyphen.

West's new race livery was initially kept under wraps, so that when the new MP4-12 made its debut at McLaren's Albert Drive factory in Woking on January 14th it was inished in McLaren's old trademark papaya orange, a neat touch. The new team colours of silver and black with red and white highlights were only shown later, at an official launch at London's Alexandra Palace complete with an all-star cast and live stage performances by '90s pop phenomenons the Spice Girls and Jamiroquai.

The fact that the first car was not completed until six o'clock on the morning of its launch – and was flown to Jerez for testing barely four hours after the event – gives some indication how comprehensively new this McLaren really was. It incorporated a number of technical innovations now required by new F1 regulations – including a rear crumple zone and collapsible steering column, reduced winglet area and suspension components of restricted depth-to-width ratio – and after every single component had been put under the microscope, 90 per cent of them were new or redesigned.

The MP4-12 was the result of many hours of research in the wind tunnel at the National Physical Laboratory in Teddington, Ron Dennis happily admitting to "*quantifiable gains*" here, although he was in little doubt that his rivals too would have made big advances in this area. But he felt that trying to evaluate such things was a waste of time: "*We just have to concentrate on developing the best car that we can.*"

This McLaren did, together with Mercedes-Benz which produced the FO 110E version of its V10 using an all-new, sand-cast aluminium alloy block whose design was determined by a range of different performance and installation parameters. Marginally heavier than before at 124kg, about the same as Ferrari's V10, it featured a new, lighter inlet system and a measurable hike in power. Significantly, though slightly wider than the old engine it was also 17mm lower, thereby reducing the car's centre of gravity. This in turn, with the reduced winglet area and rear crumple zone, required substantial aerodynamic work to be carried out on the rear end.

The car's preparation was immaculate, with Dennis declaring: "*Every component on the new car is better, and it is the sum of the total that will give us the performance we hope for. We have to play catch-up with Renault but we are closer than ever. If effort wins in motor racing, then we're going to win.*"

In pre-season testing his optimism seemed justified, and especially so when Coulthard won the first race of the season, in Australia, with Häkkinen finishing third. Though this was undoubtedly made slightly easier by the retirement of both Williams FW19s, the young Scot drove a cool race despite being under mounting pressure from Michael Schumacher's Ferrari. It was a fabulous result for the new West McLaren Mercedes team first time out.

Coulthard also won a superb race at Monza even though he was again concerned by the car's rear-end stability during much of the season. For his part Häkkinen, once again, seemed better able to adapt his driving style and was finally rewarded with a win at Jerez, his first in Formula 1, after Schumacher had controversially collided with the new World Champion, Jacques Villeneuve.

Elsewhere, McLaren's trademark resourcefulness demonstrated itself when it came to refuelling and pit strategies so that, at Buenos Aires, for example, where the car's harder compound tyres were not best suited, a one-stop strategy enabled Häkkinen to move from 17th to fifth place by the flag. Similar manoeuvring was on target to take the Finn to second place at Silverstone, where Coulthard was dogged by brake trouble, until his engine failed six laps from the end.

With a new F-spec version of the Mercedes-Benz engine, the cars were by this time enjoying a field-leading 740bhp at 16,000rpm, but even this proved insufficient to push McLaren's tally of wins for the season beyond three.

One of Adrian Newey's first moves when he joined as Technical Director in August was to introduce a revised front wing for the Austrian race to give the car improved front-end grip, as work continued on efforts to enhance its driveability with developments such as a sophisticated secondary braking system which (once ruled legal by the FIA) was mimicked in testing by some rival teams.

In the final race of the 1997 Formula 1 season, the European Grand Prix at Jerez, Mika Häkkinen took his maiden Grand Prix win and led David Coulthard home for a superb McLaren 1-2.

The Ilmor-produced Mercedes-Benz FO 110E engine was wider and lower than the previous year's unit. Although it weighed slightly more, its lower centre of gravity and increased power helped the MP4-12 to three wins in 1997.

The results of these improvements were not overwhelming, but they were at least now making themselves felt even if nothing in 1997 could quite eclipse the latest Williams Renault. What mattered was that McLaren was once again establishing itself as a Grand Prix winner. With resources already being poured into the following year's effort, as the team directed much of its testing effort towards detailed preparation for the new era of narrow-track, grooved-tyre F1 cars, McLaren was very clearly back on track to become the pacesetter.

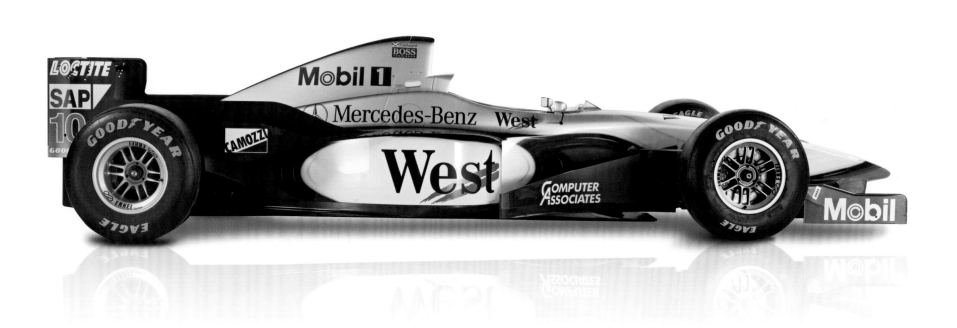

MODEL	McLaren-Mercedes MP4-12
TYPE/FORMULA	Formula 1
YEAR OF PRODUCTION	1997
DESIGNER	Neil Oatley
EXAMPLES BUILT	7
ENGINE	Mercedes-Benz FO 110E, FO 110F V10
CUBIC CAPACITY	2997cc
ELECTRONICS	TAG2000 ignition/injection
POWER OUTPUT	720, 740bhp

TRANSMISSION	McLaren semi-auto longitudinal 6-speed
CHASSIS	McLaren moulded carbon fibre/honeycomb composite
BODY	Carbon fibre single piece cockpit/engine cover & nose
FRONT SUSPENSION	Double wishbone, push-rod operating
	longitudinal inboard coil spring/damper
REAR SUSPENSION	Double wishbone, push-rod operating
	longitudinal inboard coil spring/damper
BRAKES F/R	Outboard AP Racing/Hitco/Carbone Industrie
WHEELS DIAMETER x WIDTH F/R	13x11.75/13x13.7in

TYRES F/R	Goodyear
LENGTH	179in - 4546mm
WIDTH	78.8in - 2000mm
HEIGHT	38in - 965mm
WHEELBASE	118.7in - 3015mm
TRACK F/R	66.6/63.5in -1692/1612mm
WEIGHT	1320lb - 600kg
PRINCIPAL DRIVERS	Häkkinen, Coulthard
IDENTIFYING COLOURS	Silver/Anthracite/Black/Rocket Red

1997 McLAREN F1 GT ROADCAR

After the sensationally quick F1 LM, McLaren had to build what was to be the final iteration of the F1 roadcar project. An even rarer car, this F1 GT was intended to be a genuine one-off roadcar, built solely to fulfil the new FIA homologation rules for the 1997 GTR racecar.

Given the go-ahead to develop the project in October of 1996, Gordon Murray and the team at McLaren had just three months before the deadline of January 1st 1997 which had been set for manufacturers to present their cars. Long hours in Woking resulted in the deadline being met, completion and road homologation of the GT road car within the allocated timeframe enabling the 1997 F1 GTR cars to compete in the first race.

Ironically, with several manufacturers not in a position to meet the deadline themselves, the regulation demanding homologation – a process which required a similar road-going version to be made and be available to paying customers prior to the start of the season – was suddenly postponed and set to take effect on the last day of the year instead. This effectively allowed rival manufacturers the luxury of building a no-holds-barred racecar and then turning that same chassis into a roadcar at the end of the year. It is interesting to wonder if McLaren would have built the same 97 GTR car if this regulation had been applied earlier.

However, for McLaren the F1 GT roadcar, which became popularly known as the 'Longtail', turned into another success story. The original intention was only to build one, but two further cars were soon built to order, each of them for existing F1 customers. These two very special clients had seen the prototype in production at Unit 12 Woking

Business Park and immediately placed an order. With typical attention to detail, these two customer cars acquired their own GT-specific parts and were handbuilt to the clients' requirements, being shipped to their new homes before the end of 1997.

It was the homologation of the GTR's bodyshape, the longer front and rear overhangs, the distinctive air intake and the large rear spoiler, which was to make the GT so striking. It also featured a much higher interior specification than even the F1 roadcar. The new interior design hinted at the classic era of Gran Turismo cars, and was hand-crafted in Connolly hide and Alcantara. Additional soundproofing and slightly higher gearing ensured relaxing and effortless high-speed cruising, which must surely be the raison d'etre for any GT car. In an official (and rare) McLaren Cars brochure for the F1 GT it was referred to as 'The Ultimate Grand Touring Car', a car with 'GT luxury with McLaren performance' and using 'an engine of total authority delivering instant performance, at any speed, in any gear.'

With the now-extended rear portions of the car cut with additional ventwork, NACA ducts set into the wings and its kick-up rear aerofoil, the car looked even more brutal than before. There was, nonetheless, no doubting the F1 GT's presence and entirely serious purpose.

The heavily revised bodywork of the F1 GT featured additional ventwork on top of the front wings, NACA ducts and a kick-up rear aerofoil.

All three F1 GTs were constructed around unmodified production monocoques and powered by the 627bhp version of the by-now familiar handbuilt McLaren-BMW S70/2 6.1-litre V12. Each was fitted with distinctive and GT-specific 18in diameter wheels, 10.85in wide at the front and 13 at the rear, which combined with the additional downforce meant the car carried special suspension settings. With nothing more than a simple GT badge on the rear left of the car to proclaim its identity, the modified bodywork of the F1 GT endowed the car with near-LM levels of downforce but less drag, thus making this F1 a fascinating vehicle in its own right.

'F1 GT, The Final Development' the brochure stated, and indeed it was. Thus, ended what was for now, anyway, the final chapter in the history of one of the world's greatest-ever cars.

1997 McLAREN F1 GTR RACECAR

According to Gordon Murray the change in emphasis in sportscar racing, and perhaps even more pointedly the people at Porsche, *"Forced us to build a racing car."* With more purpose-built machines taking to the track, and Le Mans once again in several manufacturers' sights as a most valuable tool when it came to boosting their overall image and marketing efforts, it was clear that McLaren would again have to raise its game.

The answer came in the form of the F1 GTR 97. The 1997 car was, according to a member of its development team, *"The only car in the championship built to the regulations. McLaren did it right; the car was based on a real roadcar."* Most obviously a descendent of the two previous racecars, it still retained the basic production monocoque, but was a much larger car with longer front bodywork and a radical 'longtail' design, generating considerably more downforce but with less drag. To meet the regulations, McLaren built the F1 GT roadcar to homologate this body shape (See F1 GT on previous pages for the full story). Including the development car, 10 examples of the F1 GTR 97 were built.

Despite its larger size it was a much lighter car, weighing in at just 915kg, an incredible achievement. Perhaps the most significant change, however, was mechanical. Whereas the earlier GTRs had retained the stock Paul Rosche production BMW engine, the capacity in the GTR 97 was dropped to 5990cc. Now designated the Type S70/3 GTR, and still producing 600bhp, the reduction was achieved by reducing the stroke by 1.1mm (from 87 to 85.9mm) although the bore stayed unchanged at 86mm. The result was significantly torque characteristics. At the same time a new sequential six-speed transmission was employed, along with new 20-spoke wheels and a host of detail improvements – no area of the car was left untouched from 1996.

With the BPR Championship having morphed into the FIA GT Championship, scratch-built racing cars were becoming the norm at the front of the grid. This meant the new GTR was preparing to duel with a variety of more obviously purpose-built machines, such as the powerful Mercedes-Benz CLK-GTR. For many this rule change threatened to ruin an otherwise appealing series, but it was good to see a number of McLaren privateers in 1995 and '96 specification cars keeping the spirit of the regulations alive. The major McLaren teams for 1997 were the BMW Motorsport-backed Schnitzer Motorsport and Team Davidoff.

At the start of the FIA Championship there was no denying the pace of the new Mercedes although it suffered mechanically during the first race of the season, dropping out before quarter distance. More significantly, however, by finishing 1-2-3-4, the new GTR 97 in the hands of the Schnitzer team demonstrated that McLaren had successfully closed in on Porsche's previous performance advantage and that it was back with a vengeance.

Mercedes fought back convincingly however, and in the next round at Silverstone Bernd Schneider and Alex Wurz finished less than a second behind the winning GTR of Peter Kox and Roberto Ravaglia. With J.J. Lehto and Steve Soper at the wheel, McLaren won again at Helsinki before Mercedes bounced back with its first win of the season, a resounding 1-2 on home ground at the Nürburgring. With a brief interlude to allow McLaren to slip in a win of its own in the Spa-Francorchamps 4 Hours, Mercedes followed up with three more 1-2 results.

Before another two end-of-season victories for Mercedes, a win at Mugello for Lehto and Soper gave the pair a total of four victories for the year and left the Schnitzer team, with a total of five race wins, second overall in the Championship, with Team Davidoff third. There is no doubt that the F1 GTRs' last season in frontline GT racing was hugely impressive.

The F1 GTR for 1997 featured the revisions that had been homologated following the construction of the F1 GT roadcar and was, according to Gordon Murray, *"the only car built to comply with the championship regulations"*

At the non-championship Le Mans race, the 'longtail' GTRs finished in honourable second and third places overall, the Gulf/Davidoff car in the hands of Jean-Marc Gounon, Pierre-Henri Raphanel and Anders Olofsson, also winning its class.

Perhaps the best footnote to describe the philosophy of the 1997 GTR is to remember that, in 1998, Steve O'Rourke took his unmodified 1997 car back to Le Mans as a privateer and finished fourth overall against the might of the works teams.

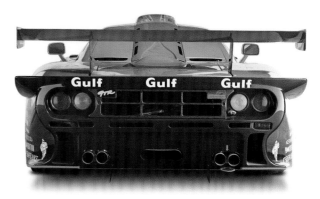

MODEL	McLaren F1 GTR 'Longtail'	TRANSMISSION	Magnesium case transverse 6-speed	TYRES F/R	Michelin
TYPE/FORMULA	Racecar	CHASSIS	Carbon fibre reinforced composite monocoque	LENGTH	194.2in - 4933mm
YEAR OF PRODUCTION	1997	BODY	Carbon fibre composite panels	WIDTH	75.6in - 1920mm
DESIGNER	Gordon Murray	FRONT SUSPENSION	Double wishbones, light alloy damper/	HEIGHT	47.2in - 1200mm
EXAMPLES BUILT	10		co-axial coil spring, anti-roll bar	WHEELBASE	107.2in - 2723mm
ENGINE	BMW V12	REAR SUSPENSION	Double wishbones, light alloy	TRACK F/R	63.7/62.3in - 1617/1582mm
CUBIC CAPACITY	5990cc		damper/co-axial coil spring	WEIGHT	2017lb - 915kg
INDUCTION	TAG 3.12 ignition/injection	BRAKES F/R	Outboard 15/14in ventilated carbon discs	PRINCIPAL DRIVERS	n/a
POWER OUTPUT	600bhp	WHEELS DIAMETER x WIDTH F/R	18x10.85/18x13in	IDENTIFYING COLOURS	n/a

1998 MP4-98T
TWO-SEATER FORMULA 1 CAR

Conceived with McLaren's characteristic flair, and engineered and executed with its trademark attention to quality and fine detail, the two-seater MP4-98T was a superb attempt to acquaint lucky individuals with the thrill and sensation of an F1 car. The design philosophy behind this unique machine served in 1998 to underline the innovation and technical excellence with which the McLaren Group has come to be most closely associated.

In 1989 the newly formed McLaren Cars had introduced its ground-breaking one-plus-two seating configuration with its world record-shattering McLaren F1 roadcar which positioned the driver in the centreline. Now, with the similarly novel MP4-98T tandem-seater, came a one-plus-one configuration.

Designed as a promotional vehicle, the world's first two-seater Formula 1 car was created to provide a unique opportunity for individuals associated with the team: namely a high-speed circuit drive with the chance for a passenger to experience the power, acceleration, braking, cornering and exhilaration of a modern race car.

No less significantly, however, the new car was also engineered from the outset to incorporate a full set of fully compliant frontal, side impact and driver/passenger head protection panels built to 1997 FIA safety regulations. To this end an extensive analysis was carried out in order to assess the likely load factors and to include these in the fundamental criteria of the design and build process. As a result, rather than merely stretching a conventional F1 monocoque by inserting additional panels, an entirely new shape was created featuring integral sidepod structures together with enhanced torsional rigidity and additional driver and passenger protection. As such it was also to prove an ideal advertisement for McLaren's speciality of providing truly unique design and engineering solutions.

Powered by a 3-litre Mercedes-Benz V10 similar to that fitted to the team's race cars, and driving through the same six-speed semi-automatic gearbox, the car made its debut in Australia at the beginning of the 1998 season, appropriately liveried in the authentic West McLaren Mercedes team colours that were all too familiar to those fortunate enough to secure a ride.

From McLaren Cars Technical Director Gordon Murray's perspective, however, it was important that the finished machine did not simply follow the line of Grand Prix cars, "*All looking the same*". Rather, and as he had with the F1, Murray took the opportunity to design something completely new from scratch, observing that, "*It was a really interesting project, with just the kind of packaging issues I like.*"

The car definitely retained the McLaren-Mercedes family look, something which was always one of the project's core aims. To a great degree this was helped by the fact that it was only 150mm longer than the previous season's racecar. This had been achieved by reducing the car's fuel capacity by two-thirds and placing the passenger where ordinarily a 120-litre fuel cell would have been. The reduced range was hardly a problem, since the immense forces inherent in Formula 1 cars would almost certainly leave the average passenger feeling somewhat queasy after just three laps – an out lap, one flier and the in lap.

At the same time various packaging considerations required the passenger seat to be located well above the base of the monocoque, something which obviously raised the car's centre of gravity above the ideal for a genuine F1 racer but which on the plus side afforded the passenger much greater visibility during the ride.

Ironically at 6ft 4in Murray himself was too tall to experience the car himself, something he dismissed on the grounds that he makes a lousy passenger. But others can confirm that the experience was totally authentic, aided by the fact that the second seat was located right on the 98T's centre of gravity. Murray went on the record to say that he thought the car wouldn't be, "*Far off the lap times a 1998 Grand Prix car would do at the start of the race, with a full fuel load.*" An extraordinary achievement.

This was borne out by Martin Brundle's experience, the ex-Formula 1 driver – promptly nicknamed 'Parker' by the staff at the UK monthly magazine F1 Racing – having been appointed to the post of official 185mph McLaren team chauffeur. "*The car,*" he said, "*is little different from an F1 car in terms of feel. It's quick, very quick. We did a 1m 36s lap at Silverstone. Compare that with this year's pole position time, and you'll see what I mean. It's not slow.*"

At a West McLaren Mercedes promotion in Hamburg, in September 2000 David Coulthard gave rides to celebrity guests around the part cobbled streets of Hamburg.

The MP4-98T wasn't just a modified Formula 1 car. It featured a new chassis with integrated sidepods and increased torsional rigidity. The passenger sat higher in the chassis than the driver and this protective headrest was placed between passenger and pilot to help the former cope with the huge g-forces.

MODEL	McLaren F1 GT
TYPE/FORMULA	Roadcar
YEAR OF PRODUCTION	1997
DESIGNER	Gordon Murray
EXAMPLES BUILT	3
ENGINE	BMW V12
CUBIC CAPACITY	6064cc
INDUCTION	TAG 3.12 ignition/injection
POWER OUTPUT	627bhp

TRANSMISSION	Transverse 6-speed, lsd
CHASSIS	Carbon fibre reinforced composite monocoque
BODY	Carbon fibre composite panels
FRONT SUSPENSION	Double wishbones, Ground Plane Shear centre
	sub-frame light alloy damper/co-axial coil spring, anti-roll bar
REAR SUSPENSION	Double wishbones, Inclined Axis Shear mounting,
	light alloy damper/co-axial coil spring, toe-in/toe-out control links
BRAKES F/R	Outboard 13/12in ventilated discs
WHEELS DIAMETER x WIDTH F/R	18x10.85/18x13in

TYRES F/R	Michelin
LENGTH	194in - 4928mm
WIDTH	76.4in - 1940mm
HEIGHT	47.2in - 1200mm
WHEELBASE	107in - 2718mm
TRACK F/R	63.8/62.3in - 1620/1582mm
WEIGHT	2469lb - 1120kg
PRINCIPAL DRIVERS	n/a
IDENTIFYING COLOURS	n/a

MODEL	McLaren-Mercedes MP4-98T
TYPE/FORMULA	Two-seater Formula 1
YEAR OF PRODUCTION	1998
DESIGNER	Barry Lett/Gordon Murray
EXAMPLES BUILT	1
ENGINE	Mercedes-Benz FO 110G V10
CUBIC CAPACITY	2997cc
ELECTRONICS	TAG2000 ignition/injection
POWER OUTPUT	700bhp

TRANSMISSION	McLaren semi-auto longitudinal 6-speed
CHASSIS	McLaren moulded carbon fibre/honeycomb composite
BODY	Carbon fibre single piece cockpit/engine cover & nose
FRONT SUSPENSION	Double wishbone, push-rod operating
	longitudinal inboard coil spring/damper
REAR SUSPENSION	Double wishbone, push-rod operating
	longitudinal inboard coil spring/damper
BRAKES F/R	Outboard AP Racing/Hitco/Carbone Industrie
WHEELS DIAMETER x WIDTH F/R	13x11.75/13x13.7in

TYRES F/R	Bridgestone
LENGTH	185.5in - 4712mm
WIDTH	78.8in - 2000 mm
HEIGHT	43.5in - 1105mm
WHEELBASE	122.6in - 3115mm
TRACK F/R	64/63in - 1625/1600mm
WEIGHT	1322lb - 600kg
PRINCIPAL DRIVERS	Brundle, Häkkinen, Coulthard, Turner, Lauda
IDENTIFYING COLOURS	Silver/Anthracite/Black/Rocket Red

1998 MP4-13
FORMULA 1

The creation of McLaren's unique two-seater did nothing to compromise the development of the 1998 team cars, and when these appeared it was evident that Adrian Newey had been working flat-out since joining the team from Williams in August the previous year.

Contractual restrictions meant he could not play an active role before that date, but clearly, he still had plenty of time to consider the impact of the new regulations and to find the most beneficial way to comply with them. As Mercedes-Benz poured their expertise into the development of the new FO 110G V10, Newey and his team spent an incredible 12,000 man-hours finding new ways to recover the downforce which would otherwise have been sacrificed to the new rules.

This, together with a switch to Bridgestone tyres and a very real rekindling of team spirit once Mika Häkkinen discovered for himself the joys of winning at the highest level, quickly put McLaren back into a dominant position on the grid. From a base of three race wins in 1997, the team went on to win yet another Drivers' and Constructors' World Championship double, and its first with Mercedes-Benz and West.

Neil Oatley nevertheless recalled: "*We didn't really expect to be so competitive, at least until the car went to Barcelona, and literally the first run we did was quicker than anyone else had managed all week, so that gave us an inkling that we had a reasonably competitive car.*"

Oatley also wondered whether, "*because from a novelty point of view the MP4-13 was probably fairly uninteresting, maybe that was why it was so good.*" The design process, he said, was relatively late in starting – "*it was a fairly hurried car in that respect*" – but Newey brought a strong influence to bear on the monocoque shape and its aerodynamics. These were two factors which inevitably drove the whole programme, while other team members battled with the demands of the new narrower track/grooved tyre regime.

The finished car was a neat and tidy package, relatively small and compact, and perhaps because there were no completely radical new features on it everything tended to work well from the very start. Still in place was the previous season's low-level nose design, but the front suspension was quite different with inboard vertical dampers and torsion bars in place of the previous car's horizontally mounted coil spring/damper units. The switch to Bridgestone cost the team some valuable time when it came to finalising the suspension geometry, but it proved worthwhile.

From the first race the team was, as Oatley observed, "*head and shoulders above everyone else*" with both Häkkinen and David Coulthard running "*like clockwork as well as being very quick.*" At Melbourne both drivers lapped the field, Coulthard leaving the way clear for Häkkinen to win the race.

Controversy followed in Brazil, with Ferrari querying the legality of McLaren's asymmetric braking system. Despite the FIA giving the okay during the winter, the stewards agreed with Ferrari. In the interest of the sport McLaren decided to withdraw the system rather than muddy the water in what it felt would be a Championship-winning year. This was a typically shrewd move, and even without the system the drivers managed another McLaren 1-2 leaving Ferrari's Michael Schumacher almost a lap behind.

At Buenos Aires, Schumacher fought back to win as Coulthard finished sixth. DC beat Häkkinen to win at Imola, and dominated again at Montreal until the throttle mechanism malfunctioned. "*Embarrassing,*" Ron Dennis called it, but the Finn soon reasserted his dominance after this and was never any lower than third on the grid, eventually posting nine poles, three second places and four thirds on the startline.

As the results show, Coulthard's throttle disaster was a rare failure, as was Häkkinen's retirement at Imola. Generally, the cars performed exceptionally well although DC experienced a couple of bottom-end failures at Monza and Monaco while Häkkinen's handling went awry in Budapest when the front anti-roll bar worked loose, costing the team a race win.

The team took full advantage of the downtime between races to test and refine the car, and towards the end of the season Häkkinen was able to find that little bit extra. Despite winning six races with just two still up for grabs, he was tied neck-and-neck with Schumacher. At the Nürburgring, however, he left nothing to chance, storming ahead to a

The 1998 German Grand Prix at Hockenheim was a perfect weekend for the team. From first and second on the grid, Häkkinen led Coulthard (top) all the way to the chequered flag, to score a memorable 1-2. David Coulthard (above) splashes round Monza during wet practice for the Italian GP.

victory which left the German trailing by a significant, but hardly decisive, four points. As a result, there was still everything to fight for at the last race in Japan. It was nail-biting stuff, a real down-to-the-wire situation.

Fortunately, the Mika magic held true. "*He drove an exceptional race at Suzuka.*" Oatley said. "*He was very quick all weekend, didn't make a single mistake, and the car was strong.*" By the end of the afternoon Häkkinen had delivered a great victory, and with exactly 100 points handed McLaren its first World Championship since Ayrton Senna's heyday. With one win of his own and six second places Coulthard came third with 56 points, sufficient to give West McLaren Mercedes and the MP4-13 the Constructors' title as well.

"*I don't know how to start explaining my feelings,*" Häkkinen said. "*It was easier than some of the races have been this year. I have been in much more difficult situations than at this Grand Prix, but obviously I was aware this morning of the pressure that was falling on me. It was disturbing my performance a little bit, but then I seemed to calm down quite a lot. But there is always one problem when you are leading easily – and it happened to me with about 10 laps to go – which is the tendency for your mind to start thinking about other things. I almost started whistling inside the car...*"

MODEL	McLaren-Mercedes MP4-13	TRANSMISSION	McLaren semi-auto longitudinal 6-speed	TYRES F/R	Bridgestone
TYPE/FORMULA	Formula 1	CHASSIS	McLaren moulded carbon fibre/honeycomb composite	LENGTH	179in - 4547mm
YEAR OF PRODUCTION	1998	BODY	Carbon fibre single piece cockpit/engine cover & nose	WIDTH	70.9in - 1800mm
DESIGNER	Neil Oatley/Adrian Newey	FRONT SUSPENSION	Unequal length wishbone, push-rod & bell	HEIGHT	40in - 1016 mm
EXAMPLES BUILT	7		crank operating inboard torsion bar/damper	WHEELBASE	120.5in -3060 mm
ENGINE	Mercedes-Benz FO 110G V10	REAR SUSPENSION	Unequal length wishbone, push-rod & bell	TRACK F/R	55.5/55in - 1410/1397mm
CUBIC CAPACITY	2997cc		crank operating inboard torsion bar/damper	WEIGHT	1322lb - 600kg
INDUCTION	TAG2000 ignition/injection	BRAKES F/R	Outboard AP Racing/Hitco carbon fibre	PRINCIPAL DRIVERS	Häkkinen, Coulthard
POWER OUTPUT	760bhp	WHEELS DIAMETER x WIDTH F/R	13x12/13x13.7in	IDENTIFYING COLOURS	Silver/Anthracite/Black/Rocket Red

According to Neil Oatley, the success of the MP4-13 allowed West McLaren Mercedes "*to push the design of the MP4-14 more than we would have been comfortable with the previous year. We had more time with the next car and could afford to be a little more adventurous in some of its mechanical aspects.*"

None of this prevented yet another season's racing being run down to the wire, but what was evident from the word go was that McLaren's new car was one of its most ambitious designs ever. With a lighter, lower V10 from Mercedes-Benz, it also showcased a host of new innovations brought in by Adrian Newey.

Accordingly, at its launch Dennis explicitly rejected the word evolutionary, describing it instead as a new car which "*represents the biggest single step we felt we could take for 1999 with perhaps the smallest-ever percentage of carry-over components from last year's car.*"

The new FO 100H now developed around 785bhp at 16,700rpm, and Newey battled to make the most of this by recovering as much grip as possible which would otherwise have been lost to a mandated, footprint-reducing fourth groove in the front tyres. The car now sported a new mid-height nose with a pair of high-sided bargeboards mounted either side of the cockpit. To the rear, but ahead of the driven wheels, large deflector panels made the car instantly recognisable.

Newey also reordered the packaging to a great degree, something he would clearly have done a year earlier had the timeframe allowed. He relocated the oil tank and hydraulic system and fitted a new, shorter gearbox, and the reduced weight of the new car allowed for some more creative ballasting with various ancillaries stowed within the walls of the monocoque. New torsion-bar rear suspension was added to the mix, while the front remained fundamentally been on MP4-13.

The increased complexity and lower weight did not at first inspire complete confidence on the part of David Coulthard and Mika Häkkinen, when compared to the previous year's Championship winner. At the limit it was able to perform quite brilliantly, but as Managing Director Martin Whitmarsh observed, "*In terms of riding the bumps, stability on the straight and sheer chuckability, it gave away something to the MP4-13.*"

The reality was that, more or less as a natural consequence of its more complex design, the MP4-14 just took longer to get right so that for much of the year it was very much a case of one step forward, one step back. No one foresaw the reduction in rear grip which was to affect the latest Bridgestones early on. Similarly, no one expected the year to start quite as badly as it did, with both cars stopping

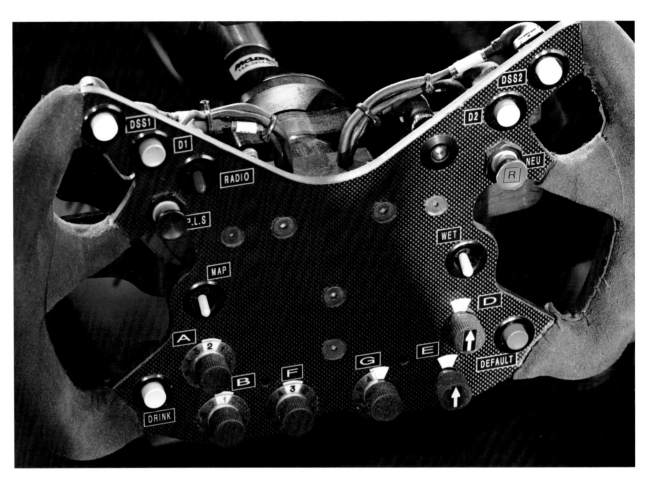

in the Australian opener. Later Häkkinen drove superbly to win in Brazil, where Coulthard was forced to retire with gearbox problems.

Thereafter Imola provided a glimmer of hope: Coulthard should have won, and might have but for difficulties with heavy traffic, and at Monaco Häkkinen finished third but was clearly unhappy with his car which was later stripped down and checked component-by-component. After that another reversal saw him win in Spain – actually it was a McLaren 1-2 – and again in Canada, before yet another change in fortunes left him qualifying in only 14th place at Magny-Cours. While Coulthard exited the French GP with electrical problems, the Finn was eventually able to recover and pull off second place. At Silverstone David Coulthard took a hugely popular win in front of his home crowd. Mika was forced to withdraw after shedding a wheel.

In Austria the two McLarens finished in the points immediately behind Eddie Irvine's Ferrari, but then at Hockenheim the Ulsterman was able to triumph again. In Hungary the old form reasserted itself, however, producing another McLaren 1-2 – the lead position Häkkinen's again – only for another reverse at Spa when the two cars touched wheels, leaving the Finn behind the Scot.

At Monza, the Nürburgring and Malaysia neither driver fared well so that by the time the circus reached Suzuka for the

Japanese and final round, Häkkinen's two-point lead over Irvine, and McLaren's eight-point advantage over Ferrari, had turned instead to four-point deficits. Once again it was to be a truly nail-biting finish to the season, but Häkkinen duly delivered, driving a superb race to beat Schumacher and Irvine and clinch his second Drivers' World Championship. Another strong performance by Ferrari denied McLaren another double, however, as the 1999 Constructors' World Championship went to Maranello by four points.

"*This has been a very difficult year,*" the elated Mika said after becoming, at that time, only the seventh driver in F1 history to win back-to-back titles. "*To have won the Championship in the last Grand Prix is nerve-wracking. It's an experience which I can't recommend to anyone!*"

Seven wins out of 16 was good, but not good enough. West McLaren Mercedes was still the team to beat but while Mercedes-Benz had demonstrated outstanding levels of mechanical reliability, the car never quite measured up to it. The team had won through in the end, but despite a relentless programme of development which continued right through the series – as late as Suzuka Newey was still introducing refinements – there was no escaping the conclusion that the MP4-14 could have won the Championship by the end of the summer.

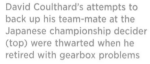

David Coulthard's attempts to back up his team-mate at the Japanese championship decider (top) were thwarted when he retired with gearbox problems on lap 39. Häkkinen didn't need his help though, and for the second year running took the title with a dominant victory in the last race of the season.

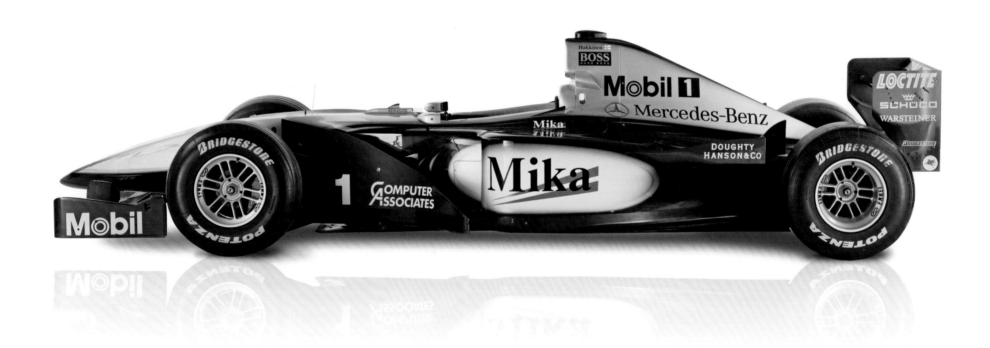

MODEL	McLaren-Mercedes MP4-14	TRANSMISSION	McLaren semi-auto longitudinal 7-speed	TYRES F/R	Bridgestone
TYPE/FORMULA	Formula 1	CHASSIS	McLaren moulded carbon fibre/honeycomb composite	LENGTH	179in - 4547mm
YEAR OF PRODUCTION	1999	BODY	Carbon fibre single piece cockpit/engine cover & nose	WIDTH	70.9in - 1800mm
DESIGNER	Neil Oatley/Adrian Newey	FRONT SUSPENSION	Unequal length wishbone, push-rod & bell	HEIGHT	40in - 1016mm
EXAMPLES BUILT	8		crank operating inboard torsion bar/damper	WHEELBASE	119in - 3023mm
ENGINE	Mercedes-Benz FO 110H V10	REAR SUSPENSION	Unequal length wishbone, push-rod & bell	TRACK F/R	55/56in - 1397/1422mm
CUBIC CAPACITY	2997cc		crank operating inboard torsion bar/damper	WEIGHT	1322lb - 600kg
ELECTRONICS	TAG2000 ignition/injection	BRAKES F/R	Outboard AP Racing/Hitco carbon fibre	PRINCIPAL DRIVERS	Häkkinen, Coulthard
POWER OUTPUT	785bhp	WHEELS DIAMETER x WIDTH F/R	13x12/13x13.7in	IDENTIFYING COLOURS	Silver/Anthracite/Black/Rocket Red

CHAPTER

05

LEWIS HAMILTON

I feel proud to have become part of the fabric of McLaren's long and tremendously successful history. Although I arrived at Melbourne in March 2007 as a Grand Prix rookie, in many ways I was already an old hand. I had known the Vodafone McLaren Mercedes team, and felt the benefit of its friendliness and professionalism for so long that I hardly felt like a new boy at all.

Everyone knows the reason: when I was just 10 years old, having won a karting award at the prestigious black-tie dinner hosted annually by Autosport magazine in London, I took a deep breath and marched right up to Ron Dennis on the night itself.

"One day I'm going to drive for McLaren," I told him – and within fewer than a dozen years it had happened.

I worked hard, very hard, to get there, but it has all been worth the effort. I was extremely fortunate to have McLaren and Mercedes-Benz supporting during those early days and therefore feel a lot of gratitude: gratitude to Ron, of course, for the opportunity, belief and support, but also to Norbert Haug of Mercedes-Benz and to Martin Whitmarsh at McLaren, and to many more people than I have space to name here. Most of all, though, I'm grateful to my dad, Anthony, who has sacrificed so much over so many years to push me to achieve my ambitions.

In my debut year, 2007, I finished second in the Drivers' World Championship. My car, the Vodafone McLaren Mercedes MP4-22, was a fantastic machine, and the unsung heroes behind me – the mechanics and engineers and everyone who works at Woking, Stuttgart and Brixworth – were just that: unsung heroes. As a team we got very close to taking the ultimate honours, but just missed out.

For 2008, we went one better, winning the Drivers' World Championship in the most dramatic way possible; on the last corner of the last lap of the last race! It was a great personal honour, of course, but I was also proud to have contributed to the team's illustrious championship-winning heritage and to have joined the select list of McLaren world champions.

I've been asked to write about McLaren's history since the dawn of the new millennium, and that's a great honour when you consider I've only been a part of the team for a relatively short era of the team's long history.

The decade kicked off with those two McLaren stalwarts, Mika Hakkinen and David Coulthard, in the cockpits. In 2000 Mika was in contention for what would have been a historic third straight Drivers' World Championship – he'd triumphed for McLaren-Mercedes in both 1998 and 1999 – but in the end he was edged out by Michael Schumacher and Ferrari.

When Mika retired, he was replaced at McLaren-Mercedes by Kimi Raikkonen – who would later become one of my fiercest rivals for World Championship glory. As a youngster watching Grands Prix in the early 'Noughties' on TV at home, I always rooted for Kimi – and I continued to respect him while we were racing wheel to wheel. He was a worthy World Champion in 2007, but you shouldn't forget that he and McLaren-Mercedes nearly took the honours in 2003 and 2005, too.

And through it all, leading and inspiring the team in equal measure, was Ron: the man who has done more than any other individual to make McLaren what it is today. It took great courage and vision, after so many years at the helm, to step aside from Vodafone McLaren Mercedes in 2009 and embark on the even bigger project of expanding the McLaren Group's wide-ranging business interests. Under the leadership of Martin Whitmarsh we continued to fight from the front, and it was my pleasure in 2010 to be joined by another World Champion, Jenson Button.

It has been, and remains, a privilege to be a McLaren driver; and I know that the team that Bruce McLaren created more than 40 years ago, and which Ron and Martin guided and nurtured so brilliantly, will continue to be a tribute to them for many years to come.

Lewis Hamilton
2008 FIA Formula 1 World Champion
Vodafone McLaren Mercedes MP4-23

2000 MP4-15 FORMULA 1

McLaren entered the new Millennium with the same engine partner, Mercedes-Benz, the same title sponsor, West, and for the fifth season in a row the same two drivers, Mika Häkkinen and David Coulthard. That made the pairing of the Finn and the Scot the longest-ever in the sport's history, and McLaren also became the first team ever to have three Grand Prix winners on board, as former Ligier and Prost racer Olivier Panis took over the duties as test driver.

His role was to be a key one. The new MP4-15 was more an evolution than a new car, but with continual changes to the aerodynamics and a new power-steering set-up coming on stream during the season, testing and development were to move even higher up the list of priorities. Coulthard was quick to acknowledge Panis's important place in the team, referring to the great benefit it was having, "*Somebody fulfilling this role whose judgement we could absolutely depend on and who was quick enough not to raise any doubts about the data he was inputting.*"

Adrian Newey's third car for McLaren incorporated a number of refinements which had been developed during the off-season during consultations with the FIA. Because of this Martin Whitmarsh maintained that, while some rivals might attempt to complain to the governing body, he had no worries about their legality even though some, such as the distinctive exhaust set-up with its central exit, and the hot-air radiator outlet 'chimneys' atop the sidepods, were novel.

Talk at the launch was not restricted to the car's technical aspects, however. Prior to the event, Daimler took the opportunity to confirm that it was exercising its right to buy 40 per cent of the TAG McLaren Group. At the same time Whitmarsh reflected on the considerable challenges facing the hitherto unfortunate Coulthard during the coming year.

"*He is,*" he remarked, "*intelligent enough to realise that we considered other drivers for this season.*"

The team had no intention of repeating the poor start it had made in 1999, but this proved unavoidable. After taking the top two qualifying positions in Australia both cars retired when their new FO 110J Mercedes-Benz V10s suffered valve seal problems. Two weeks later Häkkinen's engine blew up again at Interlagos while he was leading, and having finished second on the road Coulthard was then disqualified for a wing-height infringement. But on the positive side the new cars were very fast and better at responding to changes and more comfortable on the limit than the MP4-14 had been.

At Imola, Häkkinen held the lead for a long time, though once again Michael Schumacher's pace enabled him to win for Ferrari. It wasn't until Silverstone, courtesy of Coulthard, that the team had a victory to celebrate. Häkkinen made it a great day by finishing second, though he wasn't happy with his car's set-up even after small changes during his pit stop.

He finished second again at the Nürburgring, this time behind Schumacher, before winning in Barcelona after the German driver experienced tyre problems. Coulthard posted an impressive second, despite having stepped out unharmed after the Learjet in which he'd been travelling crash-landed four days earlier. At Monaco DC dominated as Häkkinen fell victim to a gearbox problem and Schumacher's suspension broke. The Scot won again at Magny-Cours with Häkkinen

At Sepang for the Malaysian Grand Prix. the final race of the 2000 season, Mika Häkkinen came fourth and took the runner-up spot in the title race.

second and still complaining about his car. In Austria, however, a refreshed Häkkinen stormed through to win and to declare: "*We've solved our problems. I'm back to what I used to be and the Championship is not over yet.*"

With Schumacher failing to score both there and in Germany two weeks later, and with Häkkinen winning in Hungary as well as at Spa, he was not just back in contention but actually leading the Championship. Ferrari fought back with wins at Monza and Indianapolis, leaving Häkkinen trailing Schumacher by eight points with just two races left. He fought back hard at Suzuka but as the rain fell the advantage went to Schumacher. The German eventually won his first title with Ferrari, who also narrowly took the Constructors' World Championship, but the season had seen a classic battle between the two top teams.

The team had once again scored seven wins, and overall reliability had been much better with Häkkinen in the points for every race but three and Coulthard for all but four.

MODEL	McLaren-Mercedes MP4-15
TYPE/FORMULA	Formula 1
YEAR OF PRODUCTION	2000
DESIGNER	Adrian Newey/Neil Oatley
EXAMPLES BUILT	7
ENGINE	Mercedes-Benz FO 110J V10
CUBIC CAPACITY	2997cc
ELECTRONICS	STAR System (TAG-210)
POWER OUTPUT	795bhp

TRANSMISSION	McLaren semi-auto longitudinal 7-speed
CHASSIS	McLaren moulded carbon-fibre/honeycomb composite
BODY	Carbon-fibre single piece cockpit/engine cover & nose
FRONT SUSPENSION	Unequal length wishbone, push-rod & bell
	crank operating inboard torsion bar/damper
REAR SUSPENSION	Unequal length wishbone, push-rod & bell
	crank operating inboard torsion bar/damper
BRAKES F/R	Outboard carbon-fibre discs
WHEELS DIAMETER x WIDTH F/R	13x12/13x13.7in

TYRES F/R	Bridgestone
LENGTH	178in - 4521mm
WIDTH	70.9in - 1800mm
HEIGHT	40in - 1016mm
WHEELBASE	120.5in - 3061mm
TRACK F/R	55/55.5in - 1397/1408mm
WEIGHT	1322lb - 600kg
PRINCIPAL DRIVERS	Häkkinen, Coulthard
IDENTIFYING COLOURS	Silver/Anthracite/Black/Rocket Red

2001 MP4-16
FORMULA 1

The F1 regulations for 2001 effectively demanded a clean-sheet approach because, as Technical Director Adrian Newey acknowledged, while small they were highly significant.

The biggest was the requirement that the front wing be raised 50mm. "*That might seem modest,*" Newey said, "*but it has had quite a knock-on effect on the configuration of the remainder of the car. In addition, we have a much smaller rear wing; the upper wing section is now limited in depth and to a total of three elements, whereas at places like Monaco and Hungary teams have run seven or even eight elements in the past. So, there is a major reduction of downforce here.*"

At the same time the design of the MP4-16 had to accommodate a number of new structural safety features, including stronger roll-hoops and greater padding to provide protection for the drivers' legs. The sides of the car also had to be capable of absorbing more energy in T-bone incidents, which called for longer sidepods since impact tests on the carbon-fibre/aluminium composite chassis were carried out further forward along the cockpit.

Working closely as ever with Newey and the McLaren design team, Mercedes-Benz produced another new V10, the FO 110K, which delivered 800bhp through McLaren's longitudinal seven-speed semi-automatic gearbox. Unfortunately, Ferrari at this time almost certainly enjoyed a power advantage of around 20bhp. And the MP4-16 was not as reliable as it should have been, leading to problems in Australia, Spain, Monaco and Austria.

Mercedes-Benz's problems were made worse by the mid-season death of Ilmor co-founder Paul Morgan in a vintage aircraft accident, and by a ban on the use of beryllium as an engine material. Mario Illien had found it particularly useful as a hardening agent in alloys. Some of the team's problems also lay with the car itself, as Martin Whitmarsh admitted. In Melbourne the front suspension failed on Häkkinen's car, causing him to crash, while electronic faults in the traction

and launch control affected Coulthard in Spain and Monaco, and Häkkinen in Austria. In addition, there was an aerodynamic problem. "*When we first tried to run the car in Spain,*" Whitmarsh said, '*we were trying to analyse why we were having some different results when we ran on the circuit to what the wind tunnel had led us to expect.*"

There was a problem with the front wing, and it took time to identify what it was doing to the rest of the car, and to correct it. As a result, Whitmarsh later observed, "*By the time we got to the fifth race we were probably where we ought to have been at the start. From that point on we were into the normal race-to-race improvements with smaller aerodynamic increments.*"

Despite these problems the MP4-16 gave David Coulthard his best season so far in Formula 1, with a win in Brazil just days after his 30th birthday, and another in Austria. A second place in San Marino, and two thirds, in the US and Japan, left him second overall in the Drivers' World Championship with 65 points. Unfortunately, Häkkinen's performance was less impressive, and the Finn finished fifth overall with only 37 points. He had to wait until Silverstone in July before he won a race. Later, in Italy, he announced that having captured two World Championships, scored 19 race wins, set 26 pole positions and amassed a grand total of 420 points in his career, he would be taking a one-year sabbatical in 2002. Shortly afterwards, at Indianapolis, he added a 20th win to that tally, though at the time no one was to know it, this would actually be his last, as he never did return to F1.

Following the opening race of the 2002 season in Australia, Formula 1 veteran Jean Alesi, who had officially retired at the end of the previous year, made one final appearance in a Formula 1 car. Prior to the Malaysian Grand Prix at Sepang, and with the regular works drivers otherwise occupied, Jean spent three days testing a revised version of the 2001 car. Designated MP4-16B the car was fitted with a new transmission and, although the first day of the mammoth tyre test was blighted by wet and cold weather, by the time the test was over, Jean had run over 220 laps, more than four GP distances.

The 2997cc Mercedes-Benz FO 110K V10 engine had a cast aluminium alloy block with wet liners, a one-piece aluminium head and steel crankshaft.

The Austrian Grand Prix at the A1-Ring in May provided David Coulthard with his second Grand Prix win of the 2001 season.

MODEL	McLaren-Mercedes MP4-16	TRANSMISSION	McLaren semi-auto sequential longitudinal 7-speed	TYRES F/R	Bridgestone
TYPE/FORMULA	Formula 1	CHASSIS	Moulded carbon-fibre/aluminium honeycomb composite	LENGTH	181in - 4597mm
YEAR OF PRODUCTION	2001	BODY	Carbon-fibre single piece cockpit/engine cover & nose	WIDTH	70.9in - 1800mm
DESIGNER	Adrian Newey/Neil Oatley	FRONT SUSPENSION	Unequal length wishbone, push-rod & bell	HEIGHT	40in - 1016mm
EXAMPLES BUILT	7		crank operating inboard torsion bar/damper	WHEELBASE	122in - 3099mm
ENGINE	Mercedes-Benz FO 110K V10	REAR SUSPENSION	Unequal length wishbone, push-rod & bell	TRACK F/R	56/55in -1422/1397mm
CUBIC CAPACITY	2997cc		crank operating inboard torsion bar/damper	WEIGHT	1322lb - 600kg
ELECTRONICS	STAR System (TAG-210)	BRAKES F/R	Outboard carbon-fibre discs	PRINCIPAL DRIVERS	Häkkinen, Coulthard
POWER OUTPUT	810bhp	WHEELS DIAMETER x WIDTH F/R	13x12/13x13.7in	IDENTIFYING COLOURS	Silver/Anthracite/Black/Rocket Red

One Finn replaced another, as Mika Häkkinen's place on the team was taken by Kimi Räikkönen, who had made a stupendous impression in his rookie season in 2001 with Sauber-Petronas. He and David Coulthard were joined by new test driver Alex Wurz, as Olivier Panis used his impressive test performances as a springboard to a new race driver with Toyota.

They had a new West McLaren Mercedes to drive, the MP4-17. The biggest changes to the MP4-16 concerned the aggressively sculptured aerodynamic lower front wishbone mountings. These now extended dihedrally from the base of the chassis, an idea which had been tested on the previous season's car. Significantly, the new car benefited from its development time in the new wind tunnel. This had come on stream at McLaren's new state-of-the-art headquarters, which was still under construction in Woking not far from the existing factory in Albert Drive.

"The new wind tunnel has allowed us to do certain things that we couldn't in the previous facility," Adrian Newey revealed, without elaborating further.

A switch back to Michelin tyres was another reason why Newey had to redesign the suspension completely. *"Tyres can have a considerable effect on the weight of the steering, the aerodynamics and the whole balance of the car,"* he explained. *"Tyre characteristics are influenced by a great many variables... the condition of the asphalt on the track, the ambient temperature and the way the car is set up. As a result, they will respond in a very non-linear manner."*

There were difficulties in working with Michelin initially because the contract with Bridgestone did not expire until the end of 2001, but West McLaren Mercedes went into the new season full of optimism. Not all of it was justified, however. The car looked dramatic and its new, even smaller 90° V10 FO 110M Mercedes-Benz engine ran to more than 18,000rpm. But there was still a power deficit to Ferrari, and at the same time BMW-Williams had clearly raised its game, as had Honda and Cosworth. The FO 110M's reliability was at times poor, with Räikkönen suffering several engine failures and having to cut his revs dramatically at Suzuka in order to finish the race.

Not all of the problems were Mercedes-Benz's. Räikkönen's car broke a rear hub at Interlagos, and at Barcelona a broken exhaust and a manufacturing fault in the rear wing took him out of the race.

The season started well, however. On his debut for West McLaren Mercedes in Melbourne, Räikkönen finished on the podium after coming third. And development continued throughout the season with particular regard to cutting the overall weight and making a number of significant aerodynamic improvements. The rear end of the car was also altered considerably, with a new gearbox and suspension

set-up mid-year. Here the team fell victim to poor timing, Newey admitting to over-optimism in the way the new equipment was readied just in time for the August test ban. As a result, some of the changes were held over until the next year, and what would become the MP4-17D.

Over the course of the year both drivers turned in some memorable performances. There was just one victory, and that came courtesy of Coulthard at Monaco, his favourite circuit. But Räikkönen should have won in France, where he was heading Schumacher and had the Ferrari driver under control, until he was the first to encounter unflagged oil that had just been spilled by Allan McNish's broken Toyota. Räikkönen spun, handing the win to Schumacher. Coulthard was second in Canada, and took thirds in Brazil, France and the US, a couple of fifths, and a sixth. Räikkönen's highlight, meanwhile, was second in France after he recovered from his spin, thirds in Japan and the European Grand Prix at Nürburgring, and fourths in both Hungary and Canada.

A total of 65 points left the team third in the Constructors' World Championship behind Ferrari and BMW-Williams.

The 2002 Monaco Grand Prix would turn out to be the team's only win of the year. David Coulthard took the lead on the first lap and led all the way to the finish. Kimi Räikkönen (left) who joined at the start of the year dropped out on lap 44 after a coming together with Barrichello left him with severe handling problems.

MODEL	McLaren-Mercedes MP4-17A
TYPE/FORMULA	Formula 1
YEAR OF PRODUCTION	2002
DESIGNER	Adrian Newey/Neil Oatley
EXAMPLES BUILT	9
ENGINE	Mercedes-Benz FO 110M V10
CUBIC CAPACITY	2997cc
ELECTRONICS	STAR System (TAG-210)
POWER OUTPUT	825bhp

TRANSMISSION	McLaren longitudinal sequential auto 7-speed
CHASSIS	Moulded carbon-fibre/aluminium honeycomb composite
BODY	Carbon-fibre single piece cockpit/engine cover & nose
FRONT SUSPENSION	Unequal length wishbone, push-rod & bell
	crank operating inboard torsion bar/damper
REAR SUSPENSION	Unequal length wishbone, push-rod & bell
	crank operating inboard torsion bar/damper
BRAKES F/R	Outboard carbon-fibre discs
WHEELS DIAMETER x WIDTH F/R	13x12/13x13.7in

TYRES F/R	Michelin
LENGTH	183in - 4648 mm
WIDTH	70.9in - 1800mm
HEIGHT	40.5in - 1029mm
WHEELBASE	124in - 3150mm
TRACK F/R	55.5/55.5in - 1410/1410mm
WEIGHT	1322lb - 600kg
PRINCIPAL DRIVERS	Coulthard, Räikkönen
IDENTIFYING COLOURS	Silver/Anthracite/Black/Rocket Red

2002 MP4-T5 SOAPBOX

One of the less well-known recent McLaren single seaters was the MP4-T5. Its origins lay in the annual Goodwood Festival of Speed, an event traditionally supported by McLaren which over the years has taken a number of contemporary and historic cars to the Sussex venue.

The MP4-T5's success owed a good deal to Mark Childs, who joined McLaren from university in 2001 and brought with him the experience of building a contender for the Goodwood Gravity Racing Club Soapbox Challenge the previous year. Keen to repeat the experience once he had joined the Vehicle Development Department, where he was working on the Mercedes-Benz SLR McLaren, Childs admits to having pestered Gordon Murray for several months before the latter agreed to support an entry providing all the design and construction work was carried out in the evenings and at weekends.

The typically McLaren intention was to win the Soapbox Challenge, and the first task was to break down the engineering challenge to fundamental physics, identifying gravity as the only motive force, and aerodynamic drag and rolling resistance as the two key retarding forces. After minute study of the rules the team decided to enter the Streamliner rather than the Roadster class, the fully enclosed bodywork being then limited in terms of maximum length, width and mass, with a minimum driver eye-line height requirement. The budget was pegged by the rules at just £1000.

Thereafter the approach was typically McLaren: thorough and painstaking. The profile and corner radii of the Goodwood track were measured so that the data gathered could be used to build a mathematical model simulation to predict cornering forces and top speed. To minimise the

frontal area the team also had to find a driver of suitably small stature and the necessary skills, such as reaction times and courage, to conduct a machine capable of speeds in excess of 60mph. McLaren test driver Chris Goodwin stepped up to the challenge, and the MP4-T5 was designed around his jockey-sized frame.

Initially using a template cut to show the basic profile, the vehicle's layout was worked on to arrive at the optimum weight distribution, minimal drag, and the best handling characteristics for Goodwood. This was then 3D modelled using computer-aided design (CAD), after which a wooden mock-up was constructed to assist the integration of all elements of the mechanical design. With insufficient time for any wind tunnel testing, the overall shape was derived using various neutral wing profiles and calculated estimations.

Patterns were then hand-made, then moulds, and finally the vehicle's carbon composite monocoque was completed, with front and rear bulkheads being manufactured from the damaged floor of an F1 GTR to give increased chassis stiffness and better driver protection. Other components, such as rod ends, carbon material, ballast, a four-point racing harness and a Formula 1 steering rack were similarly sourced from within the Group, while the steering wheel was based on the design from Mika Häkkinen's MP4-16 race car.

Some features were naturally custom-made, such as the lightweight, fared-in wheels, its vacuum-formed featherweight screen, and the twin front rim brakes. The vehicle had an exceptionally comprehensive specification, with the monocoque boasting a high strength to low weight ratio with a variety of different core sizes being used to increase chassis stiffness in all its high-stress areas. It also featured deformable front and rear crash structures, and front and rear roll-hoops, the latter being carbon items fully integrated into the monocoque.

Built from pieces of a damaged F1 GTR chassis, the carbon-fibre composite monocoque of the MP4-T5 nears completion in the workshops of the Vehicle Development Department at Woking Business Park.

With Chris Goodwin at the controls, the MP4-T5 took to the track for its first test run on the Goodwood hill. It wasn't until Ron Dennis had seen the vehicle pictured in Auto Express that he gave his full and official blessing to the project.

For the first test day at Goodwood the team had no more to show than a few CAD drawings and some sketches, but by the second Childs and his colleagues had a fully operational machine. The day was spent setting it up adjusting various components to ensure it behaved as predicted and fine-tuning the handling. The car then adopted its own unique McLaren branding, Ron Dennis giving the project his official blessing.

With stiff competition expected from BMW/Rolls-Royce, Lotus, Bugatti, Prodrive, Jaguar, Ford and Bentley, the team was quietly confident that it had the fastest car. In the end the results spoke for themselves. The McLaren MP4-T5 not only registering the fastest time of any car in all categories, but also setting a new course record of 65.1 seconds.

The steering wheel, such as it was, was based on the one fitted to the 2001 MP4-16 Formula 1 car driven by Häkkinen and Coulthard, albeit with fewer electronic controls, (see page 200).

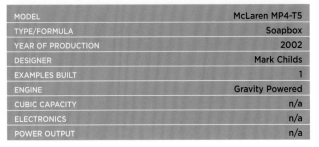

MODEL	McLaren MP4-T5
TYPE/FORMULA	Soapbox
YEAR OF PRODUCTION	2002
DESIGNER	Mark Childs
EXAMPLES BUILT	1
ENGINE	Gravity Powered
CUBIC CAPACITY	n/a
ELECTRONICS	n/a
POWER OUTPUT	n/a

TRANSMISSION	n/a
CHASSIS	Carbon-fibre composite monocoque/driver safety cell
BODY	Integral to chassis, carbon-fibre wheel covers and axle fairings
STEERING	Rack and pinion ex-McLaren Formula 1
FRONT SUSPENSION	Single axle, adjustable toe, castor and camber
REAR SUSPENSION	Single axle, adjustable toe and camber
BRAKES F/R	Twin front wheel rim brakes
WHEELS DIAMETER x WIDTH F/R	Custom 600x20mm

TYRES F/R	650 mm diameter road tyre (slicks)
LENGTH	76.8in - 1950mm
WIDTH	43.3in - 1100mm
HEIGHT - DRIVER EYELINE (regulation)	30.3in - 770mm
WHEELBASE (adjustable)	39.4in - 1000mm
TRACK F/R (adjustable)	51.2in - 1300mm
WEIGHT INC DRIVER MIN/MAX (regulation)	220/298lb - 100/135kg
PRINCIPAL DRIVERS	Chris Goodwin
IDENTIFYING COLOURS	Papaya

The West McLaren Mercedes MP4-18 was so keenly anticipated and discussed by the media that some pundits were moved to describe it as *"the most anxiously awaited F1 car of the year,"* yet it never actually raced.

The MP4-17A had failed to win the World Championship in 2002 but it was a great piece of high-speed sculpture and provided Adrian Newey and his team with a good starting point for 2003 as work continued simultaneously on the MP4-18. For the latter, Ron Dennis was quick to accept that a quantum leap in performance was necessary. *"Nothing else will do,"* he insisted.

Accordingly, as work proceeded on MP4-18, Mercedes-Benz designed a radical new V10, the FO 110P, to make up what some observers calculated as a seven per cent power deficit to its main rivals. The team pioneered a new 'quick change' installation on the car, to speed up engine changes. The new powerplant was mated to a new lowline transmission.

The MP4-18 boasted a new carbon composite monocoque which was designed to be not just stiffer and lighter but also have a lower centre of gravity. Externally, the car's nose structure was shorter and lower, while the packaging of the rear end was aggressively tight and a small dorsal fin-shape to the engine cover added to its purposeful looks.

Simulation tests at McLaren using a range of powerful new diagnostic tools showed the car indeed to have taken a dramatic step forward from the baseline '17D' in terms of performance. Design work had concentrated on a number of developments intended to improve the overall aerodynamic efficiency while paying even closer attention to details and to new materials. It was also the first McLaren designed specifically to maximise the performance of the new Michelin tyres.

Significantly, and in part because continued development of the MP4-17 meant it retained a high degree of competitiveness into the 2003 season, the team adhered to its decision to conceive, design and engineer the MP4-18 for as long as it took to get it right rather than be bound by the starting date for the season, or the date of any particular race thereafter. It was assisted here by a period of rule stability, which meant that the car could evolve in a less frantic environment, although Newey disclosed that the basic design had been fixed by mid-February.

Dennis continued to insist, *"The car will only run when we can be satisfied that it is better than the '17D' and as reliable."* As a result, it didn't make its first public appearance until May. By that time Kimi Räikkönen was making great use of the interim MP4-17D to fight for the lead in the Drivers' World Championship.

The new transmission used a carbon-fibre casing and boasted numerous innovations and was one reason why the car was late. The design demanded some innovative manufacturing techniques that had given rise to more problems than had been anticipated.

Test pilot Alexander Wurz was hugely enthusiastic about the car, keenly expressing his *"excitement to be driving the MP4-18A for the first time"* and confirming that everything about it *"feels great"*. Newey too expressed confidence that the car had what it took to take the battle to Ferrari, explaining that his design *"has probably had more research put into it than any other car I have worked on."*

There was talk of the MP4-18 making its long awaited race debut, albeit with the old transmission, at the British GP at Silverstone in July, but that didn't happen; nor did it appear on Mercedes-Benz's home turf for the European Grand Prix at the Nürburgring, which had also been widely anticipated. Instead, amid revelations that the tight packaging of its rear bodywork led to underbonnet fires within five fast laps, the MP4-17D was kept in service to the end of the season and the new car was kept in abeyance.

The MP4-18B (photographed here) run later in the year was fitted with revised exhaust outlets and re-designed rear bodywork that helped alleviate heat build-up around the engine. It eventually paved the way in terms of concept and new ideas for the cars that were to follow.

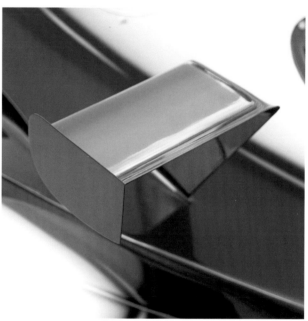

The team hoped that MP4-18 would be a huge leap forward in performance. In the end it never had the chance to race in a Grand Prix, but provided a solid stepping stone for the cars that followed in 2004 and 2005.

The monocoque on the radical MP4-18 was stiffer and lighter than the 2002 car's. With a lower centre of gravity, shorter nose and tighter rear end packaging it looked altogether more purposeful than its predecessor.

MODEL	McLaren-Mercedes MP4-18B
TYPE/FORMULA	Formula 1
YEAR OF PRODUCTION	2003
DESIGNER	Adrian Newey
EXAMPLES BUILT	3 (+ 3 monocoques)
ENGINE	Mercedes-Benz FO 110P V10
CUBIC CAPACITY	2997cc
ELECTRONICS	STAR System (TAG-210)
POWER OUTPUT	860bhp

TRANSMISSION	McLaren semi-auto sequential longitudinal 7-speed
CHASSIS	Moulded carbon-fibre/aluminium honeycomb composite
BODY	Carbon-fibre single piece cockpit/engine cover & nose
FRONT SUSPENSION	Unequal length wishbone, push-rod & bell
	crank operating inboard torsion bar/damper
REAR SUSPENSION	Unequal length wishbone, push-rod & bell
	crank operating inboard torsion bar/damper
BRAKES F/R	Outboard carbon-fibre discs
WHEELS DIAMETER x WIDTH F/R	13x12/13x13.7in

TYRES F/R	Michelin
LENGTH	182in - 4623mm
WIDTH	70.9in - 1800mm
HEIGHT	40in - 1016mm
WHEELBASE	122in - 3099mm
TRACK F/R	55/55in - 1397/1397mm
WEIGHT	1322lb - 600kg
PRINCIPAL DRIVERS	Coulthard, Räikkönen, Wurz
IDENTIFYING COLOURS	Silver/Anthracite/Black/Rocket Red

It was an indication of how seriously McLaren was taking its programme with the MP4-18A that it elected to start the 2003 season with a heavily revised 'D' version of the MP4-17.

The latter design was powered by an updated version of the Mercedes-Benz FO 110M engine rather than the all-new FO 110P being prepared for use in the newer car. The MP4-17D was thus an interim model but featured significant changes which included a revised transmission, internal chassis modifications, and improvements to the aerodynamics and suspension. The development work was a big success. David Coulthard won the opening race in Australia and was in contention in Malaysia too until suffering a spark box problem. Kimi Räikkönen, who had come third in Melbourne, scored his first Grand Prix triumph at Sepang to put himself at the head of the World Championship points table. He stayed there after just losing out to Giancarlo Fisichella's Jordan in a farcical wet Brazilian GP, and narrowly held on as Michael Schumacher finally put three consecutive wins together in his Ferrari.

Soon it became a three-way fight, as Ralf Schumacher and Juan Pablo Montoya pushed closer in their BMW-Williams cars, but victory for Michael Schumacher in Canada finally put him at the top of the table. One of the turning points for Räikkönen, who was sixth in Montreal after a qualifying mistake obliged him to start from the pitlane, came at the GP of Europe at Nürburgring. He was romping away from the field when his engine broke.

Third place for the Finn at Silverstone narrowed the gap to Schumacher to seven points, with race victor Montoya a similar number behind Kimi. But when Montoya won at Hockenheim where Räikkönen was the victim of a first-corner accident, the Colombian moved ahead. Then second

place in Hungary for Räikkönen, behind Alonso, left the scores as Schumacher 72, Montoya 71, Räikkönen 70.

Then came controversy at Monza, where a protest from Bridgestone (after Schumacher had finished a beaten and lapped eighth at the Hungaroring) led to the FIA reinterpreting its previous ruling on what constituted reasonable tyre wear. Michelin's front tyres, it decided, breached acceptable rates, obliging the French company at minimal notice to create new tyres for all of its teams, among them McLaren and Williams. Their momentum was seriously compromised as they acclimatised to the different characteristics of the new tyres, they lost valuable momentum. Schumacher, meanwhile, won in Italy and America, where Räikkönen was respectively fourth and second. The tide had turned. Going into the final round, Kimi was nine points behind Michael. Though the latter struggled to the eighth place he needed, second place for Räikkönen behind Schumacher's team-mate Rubens Barrichello left him second overall, two points shy.

Coulthard finished second in Germany, third in Japan, fourth in Brazil, fifth in San Marino, where Räikkönen had started from pole, and fifth again in Austria, France, Britain and Hungary. His 51 points put him seventh overall.

The MP4-17D may have been an interim car, but its tally of 142 points left it only two short of BMW-Williams and 16 off Ferrari's final score. And the introduction of various parts from the unraced MP4-18A, as the season developed, not only kept it in play but laid valuable groundwork for the MP4-19A which followed.

"The reality," Martin Whitmarsh reflected, "is that during the first third of the season we were distracted by concentrating on the new car, and by Canada it was clear that we needed to

apply more energy into the MP4-17D project in order to maintain its Championship assault. All the work done to it wasn't actually designed to help us close on the leaders; it was intended to help us keep up and not drop back further down the grid."

Nevertheless, with only slightly better fortune the MP4-17D could have joined its illustrious forebears as a title winner.

MODEL	McLaren-Mercedes MP4-17D	TRANSMISSION	McLaren semi-auto sequential longitudinal 7-speed	TYRES F/R	Michelin
TYPE/FORMULA	Formula 1	CHASSIS	Moulded carbon-fibre/aluminium honeycomb composite	LENGTH	183.5in - 4661mm
YEAR OF PRODUCTION	2003	BODY	Carbon-fibre single piece cockpit/engine cover & nose	WIDTH	70.9in - 1800mm
DESIGNER	Adrian Newey/Neil Oatley	FRONT SUSPENSION	Unequal length wishbone, push-rod & bell	HEIGHT	40.5in - 1029mm
EXAMPLES BUILT	6		crank operating inboard torsion bar/damper	WHEELBASE	124in - 3150mm
ENGINE	Mercedes-Benz FO 110M V10	REAR SUSPENSION	Unequal length wishbone, push-rod & bell	TRACK F/R	55/55.5in - 1397/1409mm
CUBIC CAPACITY	2997cc		crank operating inboard torsion bar/damper	WEIGHT	1322lb - 600kg
ELECTRONICS	STAR System (TAG-210)	BRAKES F/R	Outboard carbon-fibre discs	PRINCIPAL DRIVERS	Coulthard, Räikkönen
POWER OUTPUT	885bhp	WHEELS DIAMETER x WIDTH F/R	13x12/13x13.7in	IDENTIFYING COLOURS	Silver/Anthracite/Black/Rocket Red

2004 MP4-19A
FORMULA 1

The MP4-18A may never have felt the heat of competition but every lesson that McLaren learned in its design and construction went into its successor, the MP4-19A. The family resemblance was unmistakable.

The new car was ready for testing weeks before Christmas thanks to the head start bequeathed by the MP4-18A. It displayed a similar approach to its overall packaging, which was much tighter at the rear end, and a similar overall outline. But the internal architecture of the two monocoques was substantially different. *"Appearances can be misleading,"* Martin Whitmarsh said. *"While the MP4-18A and MP4-19A chassis look very similar in profile, they are completely different in terms of their structures under the skin."*

Brake developments, the launch control systems, and a number of engine-based refinements were carry-overs from the MP4-18, but there was plenty that was new too and personnel were at pains to point out that it would be unwise to underestimate how much technology and experience had been applied to the new project.

MP4-19A was stiffer and stronger without any weight penalty and boasted an even lower centre of gravity. It was powered by yet another new version of the Mercedes-Benz V10, designated FO 110Q, the focus of whose development had centred on a new FIA-mandated requirement that an engine had to last a whole Grand Prix weekend.

West McLaren Mercedes was bullish about the MP4-19A's chances. *"Our intention is to hit the ground running at the start of next season with a technical package that is capable of sustaining a consistent challenge for the World Championship from the very first race of the season,"* Ron Dennis said.

On the driving front there was further stability, with Kimi Räikkönen and David Coulthard paired together again, and Alex Wurz continuing to be supported on the test side by Spanish former Arrows and Jaguar racer, Pedro de la Rosa. There were changes in the sport itself, however, with two qualifying sessions being run back-to-back on each Saturday, and two new races, in Bahrain and China. Such was the schedule that the Monaco, European, Canadian, US, French and British Grands Prix were to be run within a hectic eight-week period.

In Australia Räikkönen retired after a loss of coolant from the radiator resulted in engine failure, and Coulthard was only eighth. Work was needed to rectify handling problems and an ongoing power deficit. Dennis pointed to the difficulty of maintaining grip in the faster corners with the Michelin tyres, owing to problems caused by unseasonably low temperatures, but there was no disguising how disappointed the team was.

The lack of performance in Melbourne was baffling, for in virtually every test session prior to the start of the season the MP4-19A had been about a second quicker than the MP4-17D. In a desperate run of results, Räikkönen finished

The opening race of the 2004 season wasn't a good one for the team. After qualifying 10th on the grid, Kimi Räikkönen (above) was out with engine failure by lap nine and David Coulthard who started 12th could only score a single point for eighth place, a lap down on the leader.

only fifth in Canada, sixth in America and eighth in Imola, whilst Coulthard could only manage sixth in Malaysia and Canada and seventh in America, to go with that eighth in Australia. Qualifying hadn't been much better either, with the best Räikkönen could manage being a fourth at the Nürburgring, and fifth at both Sepang and Monaco. The best Coulthard could manage was eighth place on the grid, also in the Principality. As the season neared its mid-point, a heavily revised version of the car, MP4-19B, could not come soon enough.

MODEL	McLaren-Mercedes MP4-19A	TRANSMISSION	McLaren semi-auto sequential longitudinal 7-speed	TYRES F/R	Michelin
TYPE/FORMULA	Formula 1	CHASSIS	Moulded carbon-fibre/aluminium honeycomb composite	LENGTH	181in - 4597mm
YEAR OF PRODUCTION	2004	BODY	Carbon-fibre single piece cockpit/engine cover & nose	WIDTH	70.9in - 1800mm
DESIGNER	Adrian Newey	FRONT SUSPENSION	Unequal length wishbone, push-rod & bell	HEIGHT	40in - 1016mm
EXAMPLES BUILT	5		crank operating inboard torsion bar/damper	WHEELBASE	122in - 3099mm
ENGINE	Mercedes-Benz FO 110Q V10	REAR SUSPENSION	Unequal length wishbone, push-rod & bell	TRACK F/R	55/56.5in - 1397/1435mm
CUBIC CAPACITY	2997cc		crank operating inboard torsion bar/damper	WEIGHT	1322lb - 600kg
ELECTRONICS	STAR2 System (TAG-310)	BRAKES F/R	Outboard carbon-fibre discs	PRINCIPAL DRIVERS	Coulthard, Räikkönen
POWER OUTPUT	895bhp	WHEELS DIAMETER x WIDTH F/R	13x12/13x13.7in	IDENTIFYING COLOURS	Silver/Anthracite/Black/Rocket Red

2004 MP4-19B
FORMULA 1

Following the disappointing debut of the MP4-19A the team rushed through a new version, MP4-19B, in time for the French Grand Prix at Magny-Cours. Kimi Räikkönen, David Coulthard and testers Pedro de la Rosa and Alex Wurz had amassed 600 laps in it during a three-day test in Jerez de la Frontera in Spain, and there was optimism that it was a significant step forwards.

The car was based around a further modified Mercedes-Benz V10 with an uprated lubrication system, and a new monocoque with revised rear-end aerodynamics. Newly profiled sidepods and repositioned barge boards necessitated a repositioning of the radiators and, together with a new position for the hot-air sidepod exhausts, the winglets on top of the sidepods now featured two, rather than one, elements. The engine cover was also subtly redesigned and now ran more horizontally back from the roll-over hoop.

One of the primary aims was to improve the balance during cornering by addressing the differential between front and rear tyre temperatures that the rendered the MP4-19A difficult to set up.

Ron Dennis was optimistic: *"The hard work of the whole team is leading us in the right direction. Both our chassis and engine performance have taken a positive step forward."*

The last eight Grands Prix of the 18-race season saw a steady improvement in performance for West McLaren Mercedes, brought on by both the chassis changes,

and much improved engine performance and reliability. Räikkönen and Coulthard finished sixth and seventh respectively in the French Grand Prix, after the Scot had been an encouraging third fastest in qualifying. Trying a new style of brake discs which featured transverse grooves and in theory offered more response, Räikkönen then took pole position at Silverstone. He led the British GP until the first round of pit stops on lap 11, and finished a close second, two seconds adrift of Schumacher's Ferrari.

Coulthard finished seventh at Silverstone and fourth in Germany, where Räikkönen went out after just 13 laps following an accident. In Hungary the Finn went the same distance before electrical problems in the injection system accounted for his MP4-19B; both drivers had relied on harder-compound Michelins for qualifying and been caught out by unusually low ambient and track temperatures which left them on the fifth and sixth rows of the grid. David Coulthard struggled home a lowly ninth. Then came Spa, and redemption.

As Coulthard qualified a promising fourth Räikkönen started only 10th, but in a straight fight came through to beat the dominant Schumacher. There was drama at the start as the Finn's car was hit by Felipe Massa's Sauber-Petronas, but he was able to keep going and moved up steadily as three safety car periods dictated the pace. He passed Schumacher at the first restart, then Coulthard, to take third place behind the Renault pair of Jarno Trulli and Fernando Alonso. He took the lead on the 12th lap, after Trulli made a pit stop and Alonso crashed, then maintained his advantage after his

own two pit stops to lead Schumacher home by 3.1s in one of the greatest turnaround victories in history.

It was his second win, McLaren's 138th, and a wonderful vindication for the new car. To rub it in, he also set the fastest lap. Coulthard sustained an early puncture, collided with Jaguar's Christian Klien after making up ground, and finished seventh after another recovery drive.

Monza brought sixth place for Coulthard and an engine failure for Räikkönen, and they were third and ninth in reversed order in the inaugural race in China. Sixth for the Finn and a collision with Rubens Barrichello for DC summarised Japan, but Räikkönen pushed Juan Pablo Montoya's winning BMW-Williams all the way in Brazil's finale to end a tough season on a bright note.

Räikkönen finished seventh in the Drivers' points table, Coulthard equal ninth with Ralf Schumacher. McLaren was fifth in the Constructors', its lowest position since 1981 and the first year of the MP4 dynasty. But the MP4-19B had shown the way forward.

An era ended as Coulthard left to join Red Bull for 2005 after nine seasons, 150 races, seven pole positions and a dozen wins for the Woking team, for whom he had first tested at Silverstone in November 1990. In his place came Montoya, who in Brazil had demonstrated his potential in the best possible way to his new employers.

In August Kimi Räikkönen took the only win of the year for the team. Having qualified 10th for the Belgian Grand Prix at Spa Francorchamps, he was up to fifth by the end of the first lap and in a straight fight, out-drove Michael Schumacher to claim his second GP victory.

MODEL	McLaren-Mercedes MP4-19B
TYPE/FORMULA	Formula 1
YEAR OF PRODUCTION	2004
DESIGNER	Adrian Newey
EXAMPLES BUILT	4
ENGINE	Mercedes-Benz FO 110Q V10
CUBIC CAPACITY	2997cc
ELECTRONICS	STAR2 System (TAG-310)
POWER OUTPUT	910bhp

TRANSMISSION	McLaren semi-auto sequential longitudinal 7-speed
CHASSIS	Moulded carbon-fibre/aluminium honeycomb composite
BODY	Carbon-fibre single piece cockpit/engine cover & nose
FRONT SUSPENSION	Unequal length wishbone, push-rod & bell
	crank operating inboard torsion bar/damper
REAR SUSPENSION	Unequal length wishbone, push-rod & bell
	crank operating inboard torsion bar/damper
BRAKES F/R	Outboard carbon-fibre discs
WHEELS DIAMETER x WIDTH F/R	13x12/13x13.7in

TYRES F/R	Michelin
LENGTH	182in - 4623mm
WIDTH	70.9in - 1800mm
HEIGHT	40in - 1016mm
WHEELBASE	122in - 3099mm
TRACK F/R	55/56.5in - 1397/1435mm
WEIGHT	1322lb - 600kg
PRINCIPAL DRIVERS	Coulthard, Räikkönen
IDENTIFYING COLOURS	Silver/Anthracite/Black/Rocket Red

2005 MP4-20A FORMULA 1

The new McLaren-Mercedes MP4-20A took a lot of its basic design from the unraced MP4-18A. *"We stuck to our guns,"* Neil Oatley said, *"because we had faith in it. We knew we had been too aggressive with the 18A, but that didn't make it a bad car. It made the choices wrong, but it didn't make the philosophy wrong."*

This aggressive approach led to a car that was a genuine leap forward, but which was too light and, as a result, insufficiently rigid. *"We didn't really understand how to trade stiffness against performance against strength."*

Now the latest car to bear the McLaren name incorporated all of the lessons that had been learned, from the MP4-18A and from the two iterations of the MP4-19. The MP4-20A looked quite different from its immediate predecessor, partly thanks to a change which was brought about by the new set of rules drawn up by the FIA for 2005. The front wing had to be raised another 50mm, the maximum height of the diffuser was restricted, and the rear wing had to be moved significantly forward, all in an attempt to reduce downforce. Changes were accordingly made in these areas, together with detail revisions to the deflectors and barge boards around and behind the front suspension. Technical Director Adrian Newey believed that downforce had been cut by as much as 28 per cent, according to wind tunnel data.

The suspension geometry was also revised, a large amount of work was carried out on the critical hydraulic systems, and there was a new version of the Mercedes-Benz V10, the FO 110R, which was required now to last for two GPs.

The early races were tough. Heavy rain during qualifying for the Australian opener left Räikkönen 10th and Montoya ninth on the grid and they worked up the field to finish eighth and sixth respectively. Montoya was fourth in Malaysia, but Räikkönen lost a possible victory. He was leading and had set fastest lap by the 24th tour, but a rear tyre deflation, due to a valve failure, forced him into a spin and then to crawl round for a replacement. He recovered to finish ninth.

Montoya injured himself prior to Bahrain and had to be replaced by Pedro de la Rosa - who finished fifth as Räikkönen made the podium with third place. Alex Wurz, standing in for Montoya, repeated that result in San Marino, where a driveshaft failure halted Räikkönen.

The big breakthrough came in Spain, where a dominant Räikkönen beat season pacesetter Fernando Alonso's Renault fair and square as a recovered Montoya bravely took seventh after a spin and problems with his refuelling rig. McLaren was back on track, as Räikkönen proved with another decisive win in Monte Carlo, where Montoya followed Alonso home with fifth place. The battle for the title was distilling into Alonso versus Räikkönen, with 49 and 27 points apiece.

A hat-trick was denied Kimi at Nürburgring when a calculated gamble to get to the finish with a flat-spotted and badly vibrating tyre backfired on the last lap, breaking the McLaren's right front suspension and forcing a non-finish as a grateful Alonso inherited victory. Montoya was seventh.

Räikkönen bounced back to win in Canada, then came the controversial US GP at Indianapolis where all the Michelin runners were forced to withdraw after the warm-up lap because of tyre problems. That was particularly galling for Kimi as he had qualified on the front row, and because a flypast win for Michael Schumacher brought him within three points of the Finn's 37. Alonso still led with 59. They finished in the order Alonso, Räikkönen, Schumacher in France, then Montoya won his first race for the team at Silverstone as Räikkönen completed the podium behind Alonso. Now the Spaniard had 77 points, the Finn 51. Alonso beat Montoya in Germany, with Räikkönen retiring after 35 laps with a hydraulic leak after leading from pole. With a 36-point advantage, Alonso looked safe until Kimi sliced away 10 by winning in Hungary, and another two by beating Alonso in the first Turkish GP. Now the gap was 24.

Montoya took a second victory to endorse the performance of the MP4-20A in Monza, where Alonso finished second and Räikkönen fourth after an engine failure in practice negated his pole position and obliged him to fight through from 11th place on the grid. At Spa he got his revenge, leading Alonso home as Montoya controversially crashed while lapping Antonio Pizzonia's Williams. Montoya then led a McLaren

Above and right: Juan Pablo Montoya scored his third win of the season in Brazil (top) and finished fourth in the Championship.

1-2 in Brazil. It was the team's 40th. Third place there was sufficient for Alonso to put the title beyond Kimi's reach, however, with 117 points to 94.

The Japanese and Chinese GPs remained. In the former Kimi drove the race of his life. Everything went wrong for the team in qualifying when both he and Montoya started from the back of the grid after sudden rain in qualifying rendered things a lottery. Kimi started 17th, Juan Pablo 18th. The consolation was that close rivals Michael Schumacher and Fernando Alonso were 14th and 16th. Montoya was eliminated in an accident on the first lap and Giancarlo Fisichella should have won for Renault, but Räikkönen drove a blistering race to catch and pass all of his rivals and deny the Italian literally at the beginning of the final lap.

Alonso bounced back to beat Räikkönen in China, with Montoya falling out after 24 laps. Thus, a gripping season of redemption for McLaren ended with 10 victories, Räikkönen in second place in the Drivers' World Championship with 112 points to Alonso's 133 and Montoya fourth on 60, and McLaren-Mercedes second to Renault in the Constructors' with 182 points to 191.

Despite taking seven wins during the 2005 season, including the Japanese Grand Prix (above), Kimi Räikkönen had to be content with second place in the title race.

MODEL	McLaren-Mercedes MP4-20A
TYPE/FORMULA	Formula 1
YEAR OF PRODUCTION	2005
DESIGNER	Adrian Newey
EXAMPLES BUILT	7
ENGINE	Mercedes-Benz FO 110R V10
CUBIC CAPACITY	2997cc
ELECTRONICS	STAR2 System (TAG-310)
POWER OUTPUT	920bhp

TRANSMISSION	McLaren semi-auto sequential longitudinal 7-speed
CHASSIS	Moulded carbon-fibre/aluminium honeycomb composite
BODY	Carbon-fibre single piece cockpit/engine cover & nose
FRONT SUSPENSION	Unequal length wishbone, push-rod & bell
	crank operating inboard torsion bar/damper
REAR SUSPENSION	Unequal length wishbone, push-rod & bell
	crank operating inboard torsion bar/damper
BRAKES F/R	Outboard carbon-fibre discs
WHEELS DIAMETER x WIDTH F/R	13x12/13x13.7in

TYRES F/R	Michelin
LENGTH	182in - 4623mm
WIDTH	70.9in - 1800mm
HEIGHT	41in - 1041mm
WHEELBASE	123in - 3124mm
TRACK F/R	55/56.5in - 1397/1435mm
WEIGHT	1322lb - 600kg
PRINCIPAL DRIVERS	Räikkönen, Montoya
IDENTIFYING COLOURS	Silver/Anthracite/Black/Rocket Red

2006 MP4-21A
FORMULA 1

Following its impressive recovery during the 2005 season, McLaren-Mercedes headed into a new era in 2006 as the FIA introduced new regulations in Formula 1, catering for 2.5-litre V8 engines.

Mercedes-Benz reacted with its all-new FO 108S V8 which weighed in at 95kg. During winter testing Räikkönen, Montoya and de la Rosa covered 8,692km in the new McLaren MP4-21 that was built to receive it, the equivalent of 28 Grands Prix. The lap times were competitive, and several times the V8 withstood the strain of two race weekends' worth of running and up to 50 per cent more, at Barcelona and Valencia and on the dynamometers.

The new car was an evolution of the MP4-20 with its carbon-fibre and aluminium honeycomb composite monocoque, but was unusual inasmuch as it retained a separate dashboard. This was tiny, 120mm wide and weighing less than 100gm, with 15 light-emitting diodes across the top which let the drivers know when the optimum point had been reached to change gear. According to head of vehicle electronics, Charlie Hawkins, this was crucial: "While the drivers have a tremendous feel for when to change gear, this gives them the all-important edge when it comes to precision."

While Fernando Alonso was again expected to be the primary opponent in his Renault, the news had broken the previous December that following discussions initiated by Ron Dennis immediately after the 2005 Brazilian GP, he had signed to join McLaren for 2007.

Optimism about the new car's capabilities seemed completely justified, but things went wrong for Räikkönen early in the season opener in Bahrain when a rear suspension failure during qualifying seriously damaged his car and left him at the back of the 22-car field. On race day, however, he fought through brilliantly to third place behind Alonso and Michael Schumacher, with Montoya in fifth.

In Malaysia Renault scored a 1-2, leaving Montoya to pick up fourth as Räikkönen was the victim of a first-lap accident. Kimi bounced back with another second to Alonso in Melbourne, albeit some way behind him but able to match his pace in the final stages. Montoya suffered a hydraulic failure. The Colombian was third in San Marino, the Finn fifth, as Michael Schumacher headed Alonso home.

McLaren made its 600th Grand Prix start in the GP of Europe at Nürburgring, but Räikkönen could only finish fourth, and Montoya's engine broke. Spain was similarly disappointing, with another fifth and a retirement respectively. It was abundantly clear that a Championship challenge was going to be unlikely, as Renault led Ferrari and McLaren with 78 points to 59 and just 42 for the Woking team.

At Monaco things improved. Räikkönen ran second behind Alonso on the opening lap, was displaced by Mark Webber's Williams on the second until he refuelled on the 22nd, then led briefly on the 24th as Alonso refuelled. His own stop dropped him back to third until overheating following a safety car period saw the car set fire on the 49th lap. Montoya, however, was a smooth runner-up to the Spaniard, 14.5s adrift. "We threw away Monaco," Martin Whitmarsh said trenchantly. "We undeniably had the best package, but the reality is that every element of our package needs to be better, so we're working hard to improve that situation."

The MP4-21, for example, shared its predecessor's admirable attribute of being able to preserve its rear tyres. But whereas such a quality had been invaluable in 2005, when a single set had to last the distance, the reintroduction of tyre changes in 2006 robbed the team of this important advantage. Now it was struggling to get enough heat into the rear tyres and hence decent traction, during qualifying. Alonso won again at Silverstone, where Schumacher finally got the better of Räikkönen after a great battle for second. Montoya was sixth.

Driver issues hit the headlines in Montreal, as speculation grew that Räikkönen was to leave the team. On the track the order of the top three was the same as at Silverstone, but Montoya was eliminated in an accident. The Colombian was under a lot of pressure by now, with four retirements in 10 races, and when he crashed into Räikkönen in the first corner of the US GP at Indianapolis the following week, his career with McLaren reached its conclusion. As he headed

After Kimi Räikkönen had chased Alonso's Renault for two-thirds of the Monaco Grand Prix, Juan Pablo Montoya inherited second place when the Finn retired.

off to pastures new in America's NASCAR series, Pedro de la Rosa was drafted in as his interim replacement. The Spaniard finished seventh first time out in France, two places behind Kimi. The Finn was third in Germany as de la Rosa's fuel pump malfunctioned, then Kimi crashed spectacularly while leading in murky conditions in Hungary. He admitted that it was his fault as he lost concentration lapping Liuzzi's Toro Rosso. De la Rosa took up the cudgels and resisted Schumacher, to finish an excellent second to first-time winner, Jenson Button.

An accident claimed Räikkönen early in Turkey, where de la Rosa was fifth, then Kimi finished nine seconds behind Schumacher at Monza as F1's 'second Spaniard' suffered early engine failure. It was Kimi's turn to go out early in China, with throttle problems, and Pedro's to finish fifth.

When Brazil brought just another fifth for Räikkönen and eighth for de la Rosa, a disappointing season ended with McLaren third on 110 points in the Constructors' World Championship, to Renault's 206 and Ferrari's 201. Räikkönen was fifth in the Drivers' on 65, Montoya eighth on 26, and de la Rosa 11th on 19. It was time to regroup for what would go down in history as one of F1's most dramatic and controversial seasons.

The hi-tech steering wheel
of the MP4-21A is a work of
technological art. The tiny LED
dashboard above it shows the
gear selected, the optimum
change point and other vital
information including lap times.

MODEL	McLaren-Mercedes MP4-21A	TRANSMISSION	McLaren semi-auto sequential longitudinal 7-speed	TYRES F/R	Michelin
TYPE/FORMULA	Formula 1	CHASSIS	Moulded carbon-fibre/aluminium honeycomb composite	LENGTH	185in - 4706mm
YEAR OF PRODUCTION	2006	BODY	Carbon-fibre single piece cockpit/engine cover & nose	WIDTH	70.6in - 1795mm
DESIGNER	McLaren Racing	FRONT SUSPENSION	Unequal length wishbone, push-rod & bell	HEIGHT	43.3in - 1100mm
EXAMPLES BUILT	7		crank operating inboard torsion bar/damper	WHEELBASE	124.4in - 3160mm
ENGINE	Mercedes-Benz FO 108S V8	REAR SUSPENSION	Unequal length wishbone, push-rod & bell	TRACK F/R	57/55.9in - 1448/1419mm
CUBIC CAPACITY	2400cc		crank operating inboard torsion bar/damper	WEIGHT	1322lb - 600kg
ELECTRONICS	STAR2 System (TAG-310)	BRAKES F/R	Outboard carbon-fibre discs	PRINCIPAL DRIVERS	Räikkönen, Montoya, de la Rosa
POWER OUTPUT	735bhp	WHEELS DIAMETER x WIDTH F/R	13x12/13x13.7in	IDENTIFYING COLOURS	Chrome/Anthracite/Rocket Red

2007 MP4-22 FORMULA 1

The Vodafone McLaren Mercedes MP4-22 was first seen in action in Valencia, Spain, in January 2007, following a lavish launch that featured the team's cars running on the city's streets in front of crowds of over 250,000. The event celebrated the arrival of Vodafone as title sponsor.

It represented the result of a painstaking review of no fewer than 11,000 individual components, and work on the design had been initiated well over a year before with discussions about the clutch and gearbox as early as December 2005 and initial sketches for a number of aerodynamic concepts being made around the same time. March 2006 saw these early ideas further developed using CAD software, after which the first of many computational fluid dynamic simulations were run. Work in the wind tunnel at the McLaren Technology Centre did not commence until May, eventually reaching a peak in mid-2007 by which time the tunnel was operating 19 hours a day testing and retesting a succession of developments of the 60 per cent scale model.

Over many months the steady development of the new design involved the generation of more than 4,500 component drawings, and 3,500 tooling drawings as the team left nothing to chance in its attempt to get back on top.

It was clear that an immense amount of work had gone into the hunt for novel aerodynamic solutions. The resultant shrink-wrapped style of the bodywork covering the revised Mercedes-Benz FO 108T V8 was reminiscent of MP4-18A.

The team of aerodynamicists had narrowed the airbox as much as possible, and the distinctive dorsal fin was necessary in order to meet yet another new bodywork regulation. The lower-revving engine which resulted from further rule changes also allowed for the sidepods to be fitted with smaller chimneys with trim under-sculpted air intakes.

Another major innovation was the pylon-mounted rear wing, replacing a more conventional endplate-mounted item. The front wing was radically different too; it was another triple-tiered assembly which was now vane-mounted so that its main plane, hanging freely, jutted steeply forward. Due to new crash-protection regulations the car featured completely new rear crash structures which were wider and blunter. An additional 6mm thick panel also had to be bonded to the side of the driver cell, to offer enhanced protection against penetration by debris in an accident.

"Many cars' rear crash structures were becoming more pointed," explained Martin Whitmarsh, *"so they were becoming quite good penetration tools. If a car spun and went into another, it could have been quite perilous."* Frontal protection was also enhanced after the regulations raised the velocity of impact in the mandatory crash tests from 14 to 15 metres per second.

The FO 108T motor now ran to 19,000rpm following an FIA-mandated reduction in revs, and internal revisions had resulted in a fatter torque curve and better cooling and were aimed to make the unit more driveable.

When the MP4-22 was first unveiled Whitmarsh made it clear that it was still far from finished aerodynamically. *"It is a snapshot taken some time ago,"* he revealed. *"We're finding new performance in the wind tunnel every day and will phase in a significant package of changes by week seven. You'll see the car sprouting a lot of new aero componentry."*

The other technical significant change, following Michelin's withdrawal at the end of 2006, was a switch back to Bridgestone rubber. Besides the interface of the vehicle with the road via the tyre contact patches, this also impacted on the aerodynamics as the front tyres affect the airflow over structures in their vicinity. Here CFD simulations relating to heat and fluid flow had allowed the car's designers and engineers to find the best way to accommodate the demands and benefits of the changes. The team was confident that the switch from Michelin would therefore not materially affect the suspension's operation and made the decision to stick with the previous year's keel arrangement.

Besides the Vodafone sponsorship, there was big news for the racing and marketing departments in the new driver line-up. It was a major boost for the team to welcome aboard double World Champion Fernando Alonso, who brought valuable experience and focus and proven race-winning ability. And a media furore was ignited when it was finally confirmed that his partner would be 22-year-old rookie Lewis Hamilton, who had been a member of the McLaren and Mercedes-Benz squad since his karting days.

It was expected that Hamilton would help Alonso to gather points in the campaign for the Constructors' World Championship as he gained experience, but his career got off to a sensational start in Melbourne when he ran ahead of the Spaniard for many laps before finishing third as Kimi Räikkönen, now with Ferrari, led them home.

In Sepang for the Malaysian GP, Hamilton backed up Alonso all the way. The champion took his first win for the marque with Lewis also beating the Ferraris and setting fastest lap as he helped the team to score a dominant 1-2.

In Spain, Hamilton led Fernando home, second and fifth, as Ferrari's Felipe Massa won. Hamilton was second again in Monaco, this time behind Alonso who scored McLaren's 150th victory.

No rookie in history had been the podium for his first five races, but Hamilton was far from finished. In North America in June he won in both Montreal and Indianapolis to increase a sensational lead in the World Championship table, and with Alonso finishing seventh and second respectively, each time beaten by his rookie team mate, McLaren led Ferrari in the Constructors' points table by 106 to 71.

Hamilton was third in France and Britain as Ferrari hit back, Alonso taking seventh and second again before taking a timely victory in the GP of Europe at Nürburgring. That was where the Brit's amazing record run of podiums finally came to a halt as various adventures in a race run in changeable conditions, which followed a nasty qualifying shunt when a wheel broke, left him ninth, out of the points for the first time. Now he led Alonso by just two.

Monaco 2007 saw the 150th Grand Prix win for the McLaren team. From Pole Position, Fernando Alonso led home Lewis Hamilton (above) in a fine 1-2 finish.

MODEL	McLaren-Mercedes MP4-22
TYPE/FORMULA	Formula 1
YEAR OF PRODUCTION	2007
DESIGNER	McLaren Racing
EXAMPLES BUILT	6
ENGINE	Mercedes-Benz FO 108T V8
CUBIC CAPACITY	2398cc
ELECTRONICS	STAR2 System (TAG-310)
POWER OUTPUT	765bhp

TRANSMISSION	McLaren semi-auto sequential longitudinal 7-speed
CHASSIS	Moulded carbon-fibre/aluminium honeycomb composite
BODY	Carbon-fibre single piece cockpit/engine cover & nose
FRONT SUSPENSION	Unequal length wishbone, push-rod & bell crank operating inboard torsion bar/damper
REAR SUSPENSION	Unequal length wishbone, push-rod & bell crank operating inboard torsion bar/damper
BRAKES F/R	Outboard carbon-fibre discs
WHEELS DIAMETER x WIDTH F/R	13x12/13x13.7in

TYRES F/R	Bridgestone
LENGTH	187in - 4749mm
WIDTH	70.6in - 1795mm
HEIGHT	43.3in - 1100mm
WHEELBASE	124.4in - 3160mm
TRACK F/R	57.2/55.9in - 1454/1419mm
WEIGHT	1322lb - 600kg
PRINCIPAL DRIVERS	Alonso, Hamilton
IDENTIFYING COLOURS	Chrome/Rocket Red

2008 MP4-23
FORMULA 1

The MP4-23, was unveiled at the Mercedes-Benz Museum in Stuttgart-Untertürkheim on January 7th 2008, Lewis Hamilton's 23rd birthday. The latest challenger from Woking was only completed the previous evening, and its debut coincided with the introduction of Finn Heikki Kovalainen as Fernando Alonso's replacement. He was joined on stage by Hamilton, Pedro de la Rosa and fellow test driver Gary Paffett. Just 48 hours later, two cars kicked off the winter's rigorous testing schedule at Spain's Circuito de Jerez de la Frontera – the first time in the team's history that it had completed two new chassis prior to the first test, and a source of considerable pride

The MP4-23 had begun life 10 months previously, detailed simulation and analysis work forming an integral part of the development process. The latter was, as usual, an ongoing process that would continue right up until that first race just 68 days later, and beyond. There were 150 engineers assigned to the project from the outset when initial wind tunnel tests had taken place in late May 2007, and the first chassis was ready for the autoclave in mid-November.

It represented a substantial evolution of the MP4-22, and although initially it was visually similar, as the season progressed upgrades to most of the aerodynamic surfaces, including wings, barge boards and additional bodywork components, endowed it with its own clear identity. The clearest visual departures focused around the roll-hoop assembly, which had been considerably tidied up to improve airflow to the top body, and the raised cockpit protection areas – mandatory for 2008.

The latest version of the 2.4-litre, eight-cylinder Mercedes-Benz FO 108V, a 90-degree unit conforming to the FIA-mandated 19,000rpm limit, and driving through McLaren's own seven-speed gearbox, was installed in a chassis that represented a familiar mix of McLaren moulded carbon-fibre/aluminium honeycomb composite technology incorporating the necessary crash structures and an integral safety fuel cell.

With two cars ready for the first day of testing in nearly perfect conditions at Jerez, Heikki Kovalainen was clearly delighted: "We have a comprehensive development schedule to work through over the next couple of months, but the performance today is definitely an encouraging starting point." Lewis Hamilton took his car out the following day, running 103 laps and describing the experience as "fantastic".

The gruelling test sessions paid off handsomely as Lewis kickstarted his 2008 title campaign in the best possible way, winning the Australian Grand Prix with ease from pole position and picking up another four points a fortnight later in Malaysia. A sublime victory around the streets of Monte Carlo followed in May, before the team hit its most competitive streak, winning three consecutive races in Great Britain. Germany and Hungary, the latter marking Kovalainen's maiden Formula 1 victory. The upturn in performance came courtesy of an intense mid-season testing programme that delivered a number of key aerodynamic improvements.

As the season progressed, the points continued to roll in, Hamilton scoring consistently in Valencia, Spa, Monza and Singapore. Into the last three races, Hamilton's over-exuberance in Japan cost him a strong finish after he flat-spotted his tyres at the first corner and was punted into a spin by Felipe Massa one lap later. The chastened Briton reinforced his title ambitions a week later, however, when he took a commanding victory in the Chinese Grand Prix. In both Fuji and Shanghai, Kovalainen also looked

increasingly competitive before an engine failure and a puncture respectively cost him strong finishes.

The title fight went to the final round in Brazil, with Hamilton arriving at the race with a seven-point lead. Around the sweeping circuit of Interlagos, Hamilton was crowned 2008 FIA Formula 1 World Champion. In one of the most dramatic finishes to a world championship ever, Lewis took the title by a single point after securing fifth position on the final corner of the final lap of the final race of the season. Hamilton finished the year with 98 points, one point ahead of Ferrari's Felipe Massa, who won his home race. At the age of just 23 years, 10 months and 26 days, Lewis Hamilton became the youngest champion in Formula 1 history.

The team continued to develop the MP4-23 right up until the end of the season, introducing an innovative four-deck front wing at Silverstone and fashionable nosebox winglets in Hungary. Attempts to race a dorsal fin engine cover were dropped after an inconclusive test at Hockenheim. Nonetheless, the development tap remained turned on until the final race, when the team introduced and raced a brand-new rear wing.

While Kovalainen's year was hurt by poorer reliability, the Finn nonetheless managed 11 points finishes and a final tally of 53 points, which saw him place seventh in the Drivers' Championship. Despite a late surge, the team finished second in the Constructors' title race, 21 points behind their Italian rivals.

Lewis Hamilton took the Drivers' title by a single point with a last-gasp fifth place in the Brazilian Grand Prix - one of the most dramatic conclusions to a championship ever. Heikki Kovalainen crossed the line in seventh, helping McLaren Mercedes to second in the Constructors' Championship.

MODEL	McLaren-Mercedes MP4-23
TYPE/FORMULA	Formula 1
YEAR OF PRODUCTION	2008
DESIGNER	McLaren Racing
EXAMPLES BUILT	6
ENGINE	Mercedes-Benz FO 108V V8
CUBIC CAPACITY	2398cc
ELECTRONICS	FIA Standard ECU (Microsoft MES)
POWER OUTPUT	765bhp

TRANSMISSION	McLaren semi-auto sequential longitudinal 7-speed
CHASSIS	Moulded carbon-fibre/aluminium honeycomb composite
BODY	Carbon-fibre single piece cockpit/engine cover & nose
FRONT SUSPENSION	Unequal length wishbone, push-rod & bell
	crank operating inboard torsion bar/damper
REAR SUSPENSION	Unequal length wishbone, push-rod & bell
	crank operating inboard torsion bar/damper
BRAKES F/R	Outboard carbon-fibre discs, Akebono calipers
WHEELS DIAMETER x WIDTH F/R	13x12/13x13.7in

TYRES F/R	Bridgestone
LENGTH	188in - 4775mm
WIDTH	70.6in - 1795mm
HEIGHT	43.3in - 1100mm
WHEELBASE	125.5in - 3188mm
TRACK F/R	57.2/55.9in - 1454/1419mm
WEIGHT	1322lb - 600kg
PRINCIPAL DRIVERS	Hamilton, Kovalainen
IDENTIFYING COLOURS	Chrome/Rocket Red

2009 MP4-24
FORMULA 1

Conceived in response to an almost unprecedented series of detail rule changes ahead of the 2009 season – including, most visibly, the welcome and much-heralded return of slick tyres – McLaren unveiled its latest contender for the FIA Formula One World Championship at its Woking headquarters on 16th January of that year.

The teams expectations for their defence of the 2008 title were characteristically very high. The new 2009 Vodafone McLaren Mercedes MP4-24 may have shared the same FO108W power unit, but in most other regards it represented a very significant departure from its world championship-winning predecessor. Designed to accommodate a series of new bodywork regulations, the new challenger looked radical and was, as well as housing a battery of new technologies under the skin, including McLaren's own highly sophisticated kinetic energy recovery system or KERS.

The company was bullish about its new car too, the fruit of more than 18 months of detail development and refinement being unveiled to the press as Ron Dennis announced he was handing over the reigns of Team Principal to Martin Whitmarsh.

Over that 18-month period, keen to ensure both the grip from its new slick tyres and its reduced aerodynamics were fully optimised, the team under Engineering Director Paddy Lowe and Design and Development Director Neil Oatley, had gone back to review every single element of the package. When they were finished the MP4-24 appeared to many industry observers to be more developed than its rivals, and likely to be able to exploit a number of different concepts in its highly advanced aerodynamics.

Expected to deliver up to half a second gain per lap, the aforementioned KERS was expected to be another game-changer. McLaren's system had been developed over a period of two years, working hand in hand with the team's partners at Mercedes-Benz High Performance Engines in order to recover energy under braking and to store it for later release.

With in-season testing outlawed, the MP4-24 underwent an intensive winter programme ahead of the Australian season-opener scheduled for March 29, its all-new monocoque (complete with distinctive drooping nose) making its first test run at the Autódromo Internacional do Algarve, with Pedro de la Rosa at the controls.

Of particular note, the front wing was a markedly more complex affair than previously, sporting no fewer than five fences and a two-element flap, the upper part of which was controlled via the steering wheel. The sidepods represented another major departure, being tall and slim to maximise the space between the rear wheels (for improved cooling) and with the exhaust outlets placed high and far back.

With serious concerns that the car was underperforming aerodynamically, the season got off to a challenging start in Melbourne when Lewis Hamilton was disqualified and Heikki Kovalainen retired. Round two in Malaysia was little better: torrential rain cut the race in half with another retirement for Kovalainen and an unspectacular seventh place

for Hamilton. Whitmarsh admitted his team *"had not done a good enough job"* and as work continued to improve the drivers' chances there was some improvement at Shanghai in April with the Finnish driver taking 5th place for some points and Hamilton coming in 6th despite flying off the track on several occasions.

At Sakhir for the Bahrain race there was another modest step forward, Hamilton missing the podium by one place while the Finn finished a distant 12th. Three more retirements were to follow for Kovalainen in the four subsequent rounds and he was to see little more to celebrate for the remainder of the season. His teammate eventually pulled off couple of very good results. A major upgrade package for the German GP brought a huge improvement in performance, and Hamilton took a memorable win at the Hungaroring. The first GP win for a KERS equipped F1 car.

Another win for Hamilton, from pole came in Singapore, followed by podium finishes in Japan and Brazil, but it was too little too late, and a deeply unsatisfactory season for the team.

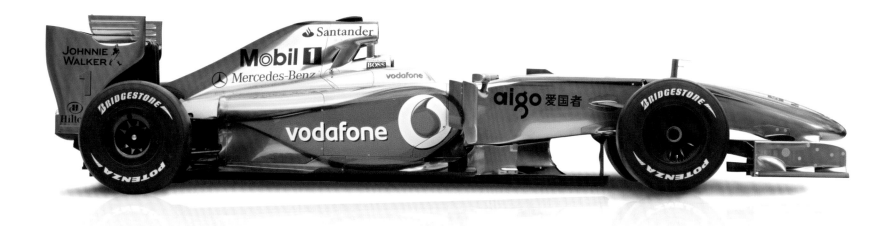

MODEL	McLaren-Mercedes MP4-24	TRANSMISSION	McLaren semi-auto sequential longitudinal 7-speed	TYRES F/R	Bridgestone
TYPE/FORMULA	Formula 1	CHASSIS	Moulded carbon-fibre/aluminium honeycomb composite	LENGTH	192.6in - 4892mm
YEAR OF PRODUCTION	2009	BODY	Carbon-fibre single piece cockpit/engine cover & nose	WIDTH	70.9in - 1800mm
DESIGNER	McLaren Racing	FRONT SUSPENSION	Unequal length wishbone, push-rod & bell	HEIGHT	37.4in - 950mm
EXAMPLES BUILT	5		crank operating inboard torsion bar/damper	WHEELBASE	124.8in - 3171mm
ENGINE	Mercedes-Benz FO 108W V8	REAR SUSPENSION	Unequal length wishbone, push-rod & bell	TRACK F/R	57.2/55.9in - 1454/1419mm
CUBIC CAPACITY	2398cc		crank operating inboard torsion bar/damper	WEIGHT	1334lb - 605kg
ELECTRONICS	FIA Standard ECU (Microsoft MESL)	BRAKES F/R	Outboard carbon-fibre discs, Akebono calipers	PRINCIPAL DRIVERS	Hamilton, Kovalainen
POWER OUTPUT	765bhp	WHEELS DIAMETER x WIDTH F/R	13x12.8/13x13.7in	IDENTIFYING COLOURS	Chrome/Rocket Red

CHAPTER
06

JENSON
BUTTON

Passion for motor racing runs in my family. My dad raced in rallycross; I was racing a kart before I was old enough to know what Formula 1 was. My first memories of watching F1 are from the mid-1980s, when one particular team and driver stood apart from the rest. That man was my dad's favourite driver and he soon became mine: Alain Prost.

I liked the striking red and white cars he drove – and the way he drove them. It set me on the path to becoming a successful driver in my own right. He wasn't just fast, he looked after the car and a he built a team around him. He was the most complete driver, driving for the most complete team.

So it was a privilege as well as a delight for me to carry the number one to McLaren in 2010 and join this fantastically successful family. For me the joy was twofold: not only was I now part of this frontrunning team with such a proud history, racing to win Grand Prix races, I was also able to drive their historic cars at events such as the Goodwood Festival of Speed.

I had already driven a McLaren F1 car as part of my prize for winning the McLaren Autosport BRDC Award in 1999. But that was just a test session. When you arrive at the McLaren Technology Centre as an F1 driver for the first time and see all those cars lined up on the Boulevard, that's when it hits you that you're now part of a great tradition.

I have many fond memories of my time as a McLaren F1 driver. Right from my first test, the MP4-25 felt good. We won the second race of the year, in Australia, and the fourth, in China. Both of them were challenging weekends in tough, mixed, changing conditions. What was really impressive was how the team coped with all that unpredictability, moment by moment, and backed me to make the right calls from the cockpit. It's times like those that bring home to you how much of that success is down to the team as much as the cars.

While we didn't win the championship together, I'd say two of my favourite victories came with McLaren. Canada 2011 was probably the most bizarre F1 race ever – over four hours from start to finish, including a two-hour stoppage for rain, and I came through the field from last to first, passing Sebastian Vettel for the lead on the final lap. We had some bumps along the way – I collided with my team-mate and got a drive-through penalty – but at no point did I sense that the team had given up, even when it seemed hopeless. Later that year, in Japan, I won from second on the grid, but under huge pressure in the final laps when Fernando Alonso and Vettel caught up as I began to run low on fuel. It was a special victory for me because I love racing in Japan and the atmosphere at Suzuka is always terrific.

If I have one regret about my time with McLaren it's that I proved to be too tall to fit in the cockpit of the 1988 MP4/4 when we ran one on track. To have driven one of the most successful Grand Prix cars of all time, one raced by Alain Prost and Ayrton Senna, would really have been the icing on the cake.

Jenson Button
2009 FIA Formula 1 World Champion

2010 MP4-25 FORMULA 1

Keen to set right the wrongs of the previous season, and with another set of regulations to meet, McLaren chose the UK headquarters of Vodafone to unveil the new car in which reigning World Champion Jenson Button and team-mate Lewis Hamilton would contest the 2010 FIA Formula 1 World Championship.

With a radical aerodynamic overhaul and a substantially larger fuel tank to take full advantage of the new rules, the MP4-25 was visibly a very different machine to the outgoing MP4-24. Mechanically it featured a subtly improved version of the double-World Championship winning Mercedes-Benz FO108X, 2.4-litre V8.

With Button and Hamilton, McLaren was the first team ever to field the sport's two most recent champions. To match such an illustrious pairing, McLaren was keen to underline the incredible pedigree of the team members behind the new car's design, individuals who could trace their involvement through an incredible seven Drivers' World Championships, five (out of eight) Constructors' World Championships and 112 of the team's 164 Grand Prix victories.

The new car represented the distillation of many years of expertise together with the benefit of many thousands of miles of racing experience and many tens of thousands of man-hours spent refining, improving, reworking and redefining the vehicle engineering and aerodynamics.

At the car's launch Engineering Director Paddy Lowe, responsible for all the engineering departments within McLaren, was quick to point out that "just about everything has changed on this car, compared with the MP4-24. We also had to get Jenson acclimatised to the team, make sure he was comfortable in the cockpit and work with him to find a brake pad construction he is happy with."

At the same time Chief Engineer Tim Goss was working on the detail specification and development of the new car, with special regards to recent clarifications of the regulations. In particular his brief included designing the MP4-25 "to take greater advantage of the aerodynamic benefits we can derive from the floor."

The interpretation led to a change in the layout of the rear of the car, making it longer than its predecessor, a result said Goss "of the additional fuel capacity. We've also lowered the chassis and bodywork while the removal of KERS has opened up opportunities on internal layout and weight distribution so that it is quite a different aerodynamic treatment to last year."

The larger fuel tank also required the repositioning of some of the car's internals. According to Goss, a key outcome of this was "a decision to move some of the car's cooling to sit centrally at the rear of the car. The new dorsal fin is partly to accommodate the additional cooling duct and partly a logical development of the high-downforce wing we ran last year."

Inevitably the new ban on in-race refuelling also affected the car's overall packaging, the width of the chassis being limited by the requirement to house the radiators in the sidepods and the team's clear determination not to compromise the outstanding aerodynamics of the car. The car made a good start with Hamilton scoring a podium finish at the season opener in Bahrain and new boy Button finish in 7th.

In Australia the running order was reversed, the reigning World Champion inheriting the lead and making good when Sebastian Vettel retired with brake problems. Malaysia however offered little for McLaren fans to get excited about.

The Chinese Grand Prix at Shanghai gave McLaren the first of three 1-2 finishes in 2010. Although they started fifth and sixth on the grid, Jenson Button (left) led Lewis Hamilton above) home in a dominant performance.

In Shanghai things changed decisively, with Button leading Hamilton over the line for a commanding McLaren 1-2, in a race in which the team never lost its dominant position. Spain saw another reversal, however, Hamilton exiting dramatically on the penultimate lap when a front wheel rim cracked and he blew a tyre. Button fared little better, but finished in the points, a disappointed fifth. Both qualified well in Turkey, with Hamilton demonstrating the car's enormously impressive straight-line speed and when, on lap 41, the two Red Bull cars collided, Hamilton stepped up smartly to take the lead, Button following him home for McLaren's second 1-2 finish of the season.

Canada saw a welcome repeat of this result – with Hamilton again leading his team mate – the two crossing the line in Valencia in the same order, albeit behind race winner Vettel of Red Bull Racing. Thereafter the results were less consistent than they might have been.

As the season drew to a close the McLaren duo were unable to find the outright speed needed to win races and take the drivers' title. Despite a strong performance at the final race in Abu Dhabi, with Hamilton second and Button third, McLaren finished second to Red Bull in the Constructors' title, with Hamilton fourth and Button fifth in the battle for the Drivers' Championship.

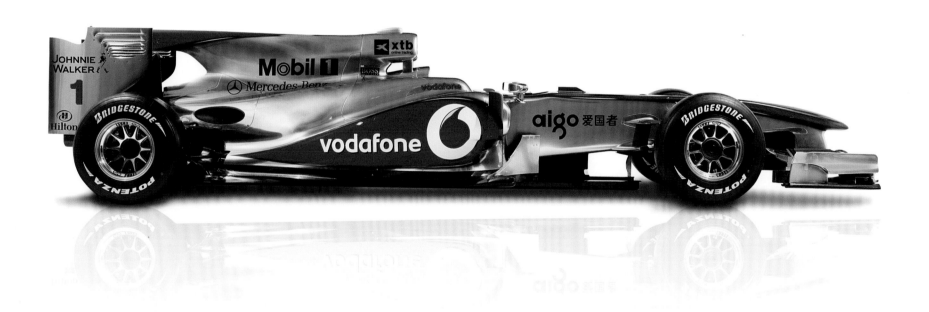

MODEL	McLaren-Mercedes MP4-25
TYPE/FORMULA	Formula 1
YEAR OF PRODUCTION	2010
DESIGNER	McLaren Racing
EXAMPLES BUILT	4
ENGINE	Mercedes-Benz FO 108X V8
CUBIC CAPACITY	2398cc
ELECTRONICS	FIA Standard ECU (Microsoft MESL)
POWER OUTPUT	765bhp

TRANSMISSION	McLaren semi-auto sequential longitudinal 7-speed
CHASSIS	Moulded carbon-fibre/aluminium honeycomb composite
BODY	Carbon-fibre single piece cockpit/engine cover & nose
FRONT SUSPENSION	Unequal length wishbone, push-rod & bell
	crank operating inboard torsion bar/damper
REAR SUSPENSION	Unequal length wishbone, push-rod & bell
	crank operating inboard torsion bar/damper
BRAKES F/R	Outboard carbon-fibre discs, Akebono calipers
WHEELS DIAMETER x WIDTH F/R	13x12/13x13.7in

TYRES F/R	Bridgestone
LENGTH	201.2in - 5111mm
WIDTH	70.8in - 1800mm
HEIGHT	37.4in - 950mm
WHEELBASE	136.3in - 3461mm
TRACK F/R	57.2/55.9in - 1476/1419mm
WEIGHT	1366lb - 620kg (with driver)
PRINCIPAL DRIVERS	Button, Hamilton
IDENTIFYING COLOURS	Chrome/Rocket Red

2011 12C
ROADCAR

In 2005, two years into production of the Mercedes-Benz SLR McLaren road car, Ron Dennis took the decision to create the first full production sports car under the McLaren name.

The legendary McLaren F1 had been a world-beater, true, but that was a supercar produced in (very) limited numbers. The SLR had been a step-change, with 2,153 made over seven years. The vision for the new company, McLaren Automotive, was that it would be producing around 4,000 cars per year, all wholly designed and constructed in-house. This was to be no side project; this would be the first volume performance car company to launch in the UK in decades, with a plan for a full range of vehicles and variants and a full global network of dealerships.

Performance was the watchword. The new car was to be, according to Dennis, not a supercar, but a performance vehicle. "Performance," he said, "means efficiency, low aerodynamics, drag and weight and the lowest CO_2 output per horsepower of any car ever made." These were the values that McLaren Automotive would take on board and would result in the MP4-12C, a vehicle conceived entirely by the team in Woking, that became the focus of the new era.

But there was to be no rushing in to build a car. A period of two years was spent studying benchmark brands, conducting feasibility studies and customer research before the design stage was even begun. This was, according to Dennis, to avoid committing before everything was in place - what he called "stepping on to the roundabout". "Once we've made one car, then we have to make another and then we're a car brand. So it was important to do that work."

When design work started it was under the eye of Frank Stephenson, one of the most influential automotive designers of our time, having designed the new Mini for BMW, the re-imagining of the Fiat 500, the Ferrari F430 and 612 Scaglietti and the Quattroporte and MC12 for Maserati.

The brief from Dennis to Stephenson and McLaren Automotive MD Antony Sheriff, who had left his position as director of product development for Fiat, Alfa Romeo and Lancia to join McLaren back in 2003, was clear: launch a car that outperforms the competition in all aspects - speed, emissions and dynamics. Sheriff's interpretation of the brief was equally succinct. The McLaren MP4-12C would be the 'and' car. "Compared to our main rivals," he said, "it has better performance 'and' is more fuel efficient; it is lighter

MODEL	12C
TYPE/FORMULA	Roadcar
YEAR OF PRODUCTION	2011-2015
DESIGNER	McLaren Automotive design team
EXAMPLES BUILT	Production numbers not released
ENGINE	McLaren M838T V8
CUBIC CAPACITY	3799cc
INDUCTION	Twin turbocharged
POWER OUTPUT	441kW/600PS/592bhp

TRANSMISSION	7-speed McLaren Seamless Shift
CHASSIS	One-piece carbon-fibre MonoCell
BODY	Low density composite and aluminium alloy panels
FRONT SUSPENSION	McLaren ProActive Chassis Control,
	double wishbone independent suspension
REAR SUSPENSION	McLaren ProActive Chassis Control,
	double wishbone independent suspension
BRAKES F/R	Cast iron disc with forged aluminium bell design
WHEELS DIAMETER x WIDTH F/R	19x8.5/20x11in

TYRES F/R	Pirelli P ZERO (McLaren spec)
LENGTH	177.5in - 4509mm
WIDTH	75.1in - 1908mm
HEIGHT	47.2in - 1199mm
WHEELBASE	105.1in - 2670mm
TRACK F/R	65.2/62.3in - 1656/1583mm
DIN WEIGHT	2868lb - 1301kg
PRINCIPAL DRIVERS	n/a
IDENTIFYING COLOURS	n/a

'and' stronger, safer 'and' fully equipped; it is smaller in its exterior dimensions 'and' spacious inside; it has better handling 'and' is more comfortable. "As for the 12C's performance, efficiency was a key aim. It's the most powerful car in its class, yet with CO2 figures of just 279g/km, each horsepower is produced more efficiently than virtually any other car on sale today featuring a petrol, diesel or hybrid engine."

At the heart of the MP4-12C was the McLaren MonoCell chassis. Thirty years on from the MP4/1 F1 car, which was the first in the sport to use a carbon-fibre 'tub', the basis of 12C is a monocoque that weighs just 75kg and makes it the first car in its segment of the market to feature a carbon-fibre chassis, giving it unsurpassed structural integrity matched with low weight.

Times change however. Back when the McLaren F1 was being built in the 1990s, it took 3,000 hours to make its carbon-fibre chassis. The chassis for the SLR took 300 hours. The

monocoque for the 12C takes just four hours. "The principle," says Sheriff, "is pure Formula 1: a rolling chassis with non-structural bodywork draped over it. The construction of this car is truly different to any other car that's ever been built."

The 12C bristles with innovation. Under a glass cover, displayed in all its glory, is the M838T 3.8-litre, twin-turbo V8 engine, pumping out 592bhp at 7000rpm. Developed by McLaren with input from Ricardo Engineering, it weighs just 199kg and features a dry sump lubrication system along with a flat plane crankshaft, meaning the engine can be mounted extremely low in the car's chassis.

Mated to the engine is a dual clutch, seven-speed 'SSG' transmission, which can be switched through three different settings: Normal, Sport and Track. It also features a "Pre-Cog" function, which allows the driver to pre-select gears for near-instantaneous gearshifts. The gearbox also features an auto-matic mode for relaxed cruising, a launch control mode for fast starts, and a winter mode to aid grip in tricky conditions.

A brand-new suspension system was designed from the ground up to make the car ride like an executive saloon and handle like a well-honed circuit racer at the same time. The result was ProActive Chassis Control, which featured adaptive damping and was based on double wishbones with coil springs. Roll control was made driver-adjustable, replacing mechanical anti-roll bars. This allows the car to maintain precise roll control under heavy cornering while decoupling the suspension in a straight line for uncompromised performance.

Another application of McLaren's Formula 1 expertise couldbe seen in the 12C's braking system – Brake Steer was a variation of the electronic driver aid used successfully on the 1997 McLaren MP4-12 Formula 1 car and developed for the 12C as a control system to prevent wheel spin and improve traction.

For all the bespoke engineering the 12C remained impressively light, tipping the scales at just 1,301kg, while the performance figures spoke for themselves. The car could achieve 100km/h in 3.1s or 200km/h in 8.9s on optional tyres, and tops out at 330km/h.

Crucially, however, the 12C was not designed around either the innovative engine and transmission or the carbon-fibre chassis. It was designed around pure function and the two most important 'components' - the driver and passenger. Sight lines dictated the position of the driving seat (not centrally located as in the McLaren F1, however

the driver and passenger sit closer to the mid-point of the car), thumb scallops on the steering wheel were built to the exact dimensions of those on Lewis Hamilton's F1 car and there are controls on either side of the driver, in a nod to the McLaren F1 DNA that runs through the car. There is no wasted space, no vent or hole or line on the car that does not serve a purpose.

By the autumn of 2009 McLaren Automotive were ready to go public with the first official pictures of the car and to reveal the full scale of the plans for McLaren Automotive. A new car company with a much bigger volume demanded a new production facility. Foster and Partners, who had designed the McLaren Technology Centre, were engaged to create the McLaren Production Centre (MPC), to be built adjacent to the McLaren Group's headquarters on the Woking site. Its opening would mark a new era for the McLaren Group.

In the summer of 2010 the car was seen in public for the first time, at the Goodwood Festival of Speed in England, when Lewis Hamilton and Jenson Button drove it up the Hill. On the other side of the Atlantic, the car made an appearance at the Pebble Beach Concours d'Elegance where it again attracted all the attention.

When the world's motoring press finally got to drive the 12C

themselves, at the Autodromo Interancional do Algarve in Portugal in March 2011, the verdict was unanimous. "Quite simply," wrote Car magazine, "this is the most complete supercar the world has ever seen," while Top Gear magazine said: "When you put your foot down, it feels like no other car. It feels better. More alive. Just absolutely, totally brilliant." After almost six years of preparation Dennis, and McLaren Automotive, had stepped on to the roundabout.

2011 MP4-26
FORMULA 1

In a highly unusual and unusually public unveiling, February 4th saw McLaren's 2011 contender making its debut on Berlin's historic Potsdamer Platz. The car itself gradually materialised before a huge crowd, assembled using components brought to the site by Vodafone competition-winners, fans and customers before the team's two world championship-winning drivers put the final pieces into place, to complete the new MP4-26.

Immediately it was obvious that new car represented a radical departure from its predecessor, particularly in respect of its longer wheelbase, high flat nose, and innovative raised U-shape sidepods. Following the ban on the use of double-diffusers, the latter were clearly intended to feed as much clean air as possible to the lower plane of the rear wing and to the floor of the car, in order to recover lost downforce and get the rear-end working as well as possible.

At the same time the new car saw the introduction of a novel active rear-wing drag-reduction system, configured to futher increase the potential for overtaking, and an all-new electric KERS hybrid system. Of course in 2009, with engine partner Mercedes-Benz High Performance Engines, it had been Vodafone McLaren Mercedes who first posted a grand prix win using such a hybrid device, so hopes were naturally high that this new development would further sharpen what was already looking like a winning package.

A third year in succession of major regulation changes – particularly with regards aerodynamics – had forced a number of new challenges on the team and, at the same time a new tyre supplier in Pirelli underlined the urgent need to establish the correct balance between car and tyre, and to explore new ways to get the most out of this new configuration. Quietly confident in the face of so much change, Director of Engineering Tim Goss was nevertheless keen to stress that during forthcoming testing at Jerez and

Barcelona, the team would be concentrating on optimising the new car's reliability before chasing performance. Thereafter, he said, "by the time we get to the first race of the 2011 season, the focus will change to delivering a considerable performance upgrade package."

Typical of McLaren's innovative approach with the new car was the decision to wait until after the first pre-season test to unveil the MP4-26, and to use an interim MP4-25 chassis to focus on tyre development and understanding. Such a decision may have given key rivals an additional three days of running their own cars, but arguably it also gave the Woking team a useful competitive edge by allowing both drivers and designers more time to get to grips with the specific demands of the new Pirelli tyres.

For rival teams much of the additional time will almost certainly have been spent on KERS development work, something of which McLaren already had a very deep understanding. But whilst their knowledge and experience of the technology remained second-to-none, numerous detail changes were required for the new car. For example the entire system was now a single integrated unit, located within the survival cell, beneath the fuel-tank and with its cooling intake below the main roll-hoop intake — whereas in 2009 the majority of KERS componentry was housed in the sidepods.

Clearly getting KERS back into the car had been a substantial task for the team, as indeed was the need to package the systems in such a way as to allow more fuel to be carried. Equally clear is that meeting the new challenges was only made possible by radically restructuring the way in which senior personnel worked within their respective departments, management changes which also made it possible to liberate what Goss refers to as the "horsepower within the design department."

That said, one of the most remarkable things about McLaren's Berlin debut is how such a public event was organised in such a way as to conceal so much of what was actually going on beneath the skin of the beast. Such a decision is not hard to defend, it's a competitive business. Neither was team principal Martin Whitmarsh remotely apologetic when he declared at a media conference following the reveal, "Be warned, you haven't seen it all. I think there are some really interesting bits on the car that you can see. But there are some bits we have hidden from you and our competition."

He was, he said, "brimming with excitement, I think it's a fantastic car [and] it never ceases to amaze me that even though the regulations are much more constrictive, especially around the diffuser area, it just drives creativity." If nothing else the mystery, whilst frustrating to seasoned industry watchers, was quickly seen to heighten excitement in the new season, demonstrating what Whitmarsh calls "the enthusiasm within Vodafone McLaren Mercedes to engage the general public; to show them that our sport is intense and exciting, and that we're very keen to showcase Formula 1 to the wider world."

The new technical challenges, combined with very different tyre characteristics, made the opening races of the 2011 season gripping and unpredictable. Vodafone McLaren Mercedes was right at the forefront: Hamilton and Button took second place in the two opening races, then Hamilton went one better in China, seizing the lead on lap 52 and pushing on to take the teams 170th Grand Prix win.

At the first race of the season in Melbourne, Lewis Hamilton took second place, but three weeks later he went one better and scored the first victory for the MP4-26 at the Chinese GP (left), where team-mate Jenson Button was fourth.

MODEL	McLaren-Mercedes MP4-26	TRANSMISSION	McLaren semi-auto sequential longitudinal 7-speed	TYRES F/R	Pirelli
TYPE/FORMULA	Formula 1	CHASSIS	Moulded carbon-fibre/aluminium honeycomb composite	LENGTH	203in - 5160mm
YEAR OF PRODUCTION	2011	BODY	Carbon-fibre multi-piece cockpit/engine cover & nose	WIDTH	71.2in - 1810mm
DESIGNER	McLaren Racing	FRONT SUSPENSION	Unequal length wishbone, push-rod & bell	HEIGHT	37.4in - 950mm
EXAMPLES BUILT	4		crank operating inboard torsion bar/damper	WHEELBASE	138.2in - 3510mm
ENGINE	Mercedes-Benz FO 108Y V8	REAR SUSPENSION	Unequal length wishbone, pull-rod & bell	TRACK F/R	58.8/56.6in - 1494/1439mm
CUBIC CAPACITY	2398cc		crank operating inboard torsion bar/damper	WEIGHT	1410lb - 640kg
ELECTRONICS	FIA Standard ECU (Microsoft MESL)	BRAKES F/R	Outboard carbon-fibre discs, Akebono calipers	PRINCIPAL DRIVERS	Button, Hamilton
POWER OUTPUT	765bhp	WHEELS DIAMETER x WIDTH F/R	13x12/13x13.7in	IDENTIFYING COLOURS	Chrome/Rocket Red

2011 12C GT3
RACECAR

In May 2011 McLaren announced a race version of the 12C, the 12C GT3 and by July, just two months later, was ready to go endurance sports car racing for the first time since its F1 GTR-dominating days nearly two decades prior. Martin Whitmarsh, McLaren Group Chief Executive Officer said: "McLaren has racing in its blood and it was a natural step to take our 12C road car and turn it into the most reliable, efficient and easy to drive GT3 car."

Designed to compete in the GT3 class of the FIA GT series, the 12C GT3 was the first purpose-built McLaren-badged GT racer since the McLaren F1. The 12C GT3's pilot program was set to field a car during the second half of the 2011 season, fine-tuning it for delivery to privateer teams in 2012, and the 12C GT3 debuted in 2011 as a single-car entry at the Spa Francorchamps British GT Championship round, ahead of a three-car entry into the gruelling 24 Hours of Spa. Over the next year or more, the 12C GT3 would go on to score multiple titles and more than 50 race wins worldwide.

With the road-going version of the 12C using technology derived from Formula 1, it made sense that the 12C GT3 racecar would too. Just as with the 12C road car, the 12C GT3 utilised a full carbon-fibre monocoque chassis. Unlike the road car though, the racecar added a wind tunnel-honed, GT3 class-compliant all-carbon-fibre aerodynamics package, which included an adjustable rear wing, front splitter, front fender louvres and rear diffuser.

The twin-turbocharged 3.8-liter V8 used in the production 12C (known internally as the M838T) also appeared in the

GT3. Although it was largely unmodified, in line with FIA GT3 regulations the engine was detuned from 592bhp to around 493bhp. McLaren claimed that detuning the engine actually optimized power output for the track and provided a better performance balance for the car. Replacing the seven-speed Seamless Shift dual-clutch transmission was a newly developed six-speed sequential racing transmission. Featuring lightweight construction, this transmission reduced weight at the rear of the car and moved the car's center of gravity further forward, improving the drive wheels' tyre grip as well as the car's braking ability and overall handling performance.

For the braking system, McLaren contacted the brake manufacturer who had supplied the braking setup for McLaren's Formula 1 program. Six-piston monoblock calipers clamped down on 15-inch ventilated brake discs at the front, while four-piston calipers put the squeeze on 14-inch discs in the rear. As you would expect, the 12C GT3's suspension was tuned for racing, and came with adjustability for ride height, camber and toe on all corners. The steering wheel was taken right out of the earlier McLaren-Mercedes MP4-24 Formula 1 car, and offered setting and set-up changes through a variety of buttons and switches.

An initial 20 cars were scheduled to be produced for customer teams, and there was significant interest from potential buyers. By the end of production, the team had built 25 examples of the 12C GT3. Prior to being configured in GT3 spec, the final car, chassis no. 025, served as the launch platform for the newly announced 12C GT Cam-Am

Edition. The 12C GT Can-Am edition was a track-only design concept that featured increased engine performance of up to 630bhp and added downforce.

Despite being based on the GT3, the 12C GT Can-Am Edition was free from the restrictions of racing regulations and was envisioned as the 'ultimate track car.' With a few subtle engine modifications, it became the most powerful 12C derivative.

MODEL	12C GT3	TRANSMISSION	7-speed Seamless-Shift Gearbox (SSG)	TYRES F/R	Pirelli P ZERO
TYPE/FORMULA	Racecar	CHASSIS	One-piece carbon-fibre MonoCell	LENGTH	177.4in - 4507mm
YEAR OF PRODUCTION	2011	BODY	Carbon-fibre over aluminium front and rear frames	WIDTH	78.5in - 1995mm
DESIGNER	McLaren Automotive design team	FRONT SUSPENSION	McLaren ProActive Chassis Control,	HEIGHT	45.1in - 1145mm
EXAMPLES BUILT	Production numbers not released		double wishbone independent suspension	WHEELBASE	105.1in - 2670mm
ENGINE	McLaren M838T V8	REAR SUSPENSION	McLaren ProActive Chassis Control,	TRACK F/R	
CUBIC CAPACITY	3799cc		double wishbone independent suspension	WEIGHT	
INDUCTION	Twin turbocharged	BRAKES F/R	Outboard Ventilated Akebono Discs, 14.9/14.0in	PRINCIPAL DRIVERS	n/a
POWER OUTPUT	368KW/500PS/493bhp	WHEELS DIAMETER x WIDTH F/R	18x10/18x12in	IDENTIFYING COLOURS	n/a

2012 MP4-27 FORMULA 1

On Wednesday, February 1 Jenson Button and Lewis Hamilton pulled the covers off the new Vodafone McLaren MP4-27, the 2012 Formula 1 challenger that the team hoped would deliver them back to the top of the rostrum in both the Driver's and Constructor's Championships.

The mid-morning technical presentation of the MP4-27 at the McLaren Technology Centre showcased a natural evolution of the previous year's car, winner of six races, and underlined the message that the new season was very much one of growth through strength and continuity.

After finishing second in both the Drivers' and Constructors' Championships in 2011, the aim of McLaren for the new season was to fight for both world titles from the very start of the campaign.

While the all-new MP4-27 closely resembled the 2011 multiple race-winning car, the 2012 chassis was substantially revised from the ground up, with all major systems updated or re-designed for the new season. The most evident visual differences included more tightly waisted rear bodywork, developed to improve airflow to the rear of the car, and a revised cooling system, which re-sited the gearbox oil-cooler. The U-shaped sidepods from the MP4-26 were also re-designed – a legacy of the FIA's new exhaust regulations that redefined the shape of the rear bodywork.

Maintaining the same driver partnership into a third successive season, along with the belief in the validity of strengthened continuity, McLaren were the only team in Formula 1 whose driver line-up consisted of two world champions: Jenson Button and Lewis Hamilton, who, between them had already scored 22 grand prix victories for Vodafone McLaren Mercedes and were without doubt the strongest and most consistent driver line-up in the sport.

On the technical front, engineering trio Tim Goss (director of engineering), Paddy Lowe (technical director) and Neil Oatley (director of design and development programmes) once more superintended the drawing office.

Commenting on the MP4-27 Tim Goss said, "I think the most obvious change is the loss of the U-shaped sidepod, which we pioneered on last year's car. We reverted to a more conventional sidepod shape for this season because the U-shape was less suited to the new exhaust geometry restrictions. For 2012, the exhaust tailpipes now have to exit along the U-channel – so that particular feature was no longer really viable due to the new geometry restrictions. As a result, we decided to adopt a different approach to the way we feed the rear of the car. We have cleaned up the roll-hoop area and now have much tighter rear bodywork."

After demonstrating early promise in testing, the team headed to Australia for the season opener in Melbourne with high hopes. They were not to be disappointed. After a front

row lock-out in qualifying (Hamilton ahead of Button) Jenson took the lead at the start won the race in style with Hamilton finishing third. The car showed exceptional pace once again in Malaysia, as Hamilton and Button qualified 1-2, but rain disrupted the race and both drivers dropped back from their strong positions. Hamilton managed to hang on to finish third, but a collision with a backmarker dropped Button out of the points.

In China, Button and Hamilton finished second and third behind maiden winner Nico Rosberg, but then a string of pit-stop dramas held them back in what was proving to be one of the most unpredictable seasons in F1 history. Six different drivers won the first six races and then, in Montreal, Hamilton was at his brilliant best and made it seven out of seven.

After another short run of disappointing races the team bounced back with a second for Button in Germany and then scored three terrific race wins in a row in Hungary, Belgium and Italy, for Hamilton, Button and Hamilton respectively. Jenson's win from pole position in Spa was as resounding a victory as anyone delivered all season.

Following a major upgrade for the German Grand Prix at Hockenheim, the MP4-27 was effectively in a 'B' specification. Tighter rear bodywork that significantly increased the Coke-bottle profile, along with new sidepods and an accompanying new floor meant that, in the words of Paddy Lowe, "about 80 percent of the surface of the car was new."

The MP4-27 continued to be among the fastest of the cars on the grid, but reliability problems cost Hamilton a couple of victories in the second half of the season. He dominated in Singapore before a gearbox failure let Vettel through to win, and in Abu Dhabi, after taking pole and leading comfortably, Hamilton was denied what would have been his fourth win of the season when he retired with a loss of fuel pressure. Hamilton did win the US Grand Prix, though – the first race to be held in Austin, Texas – and when Button claimed the last race of the season in Brazil the MP4-27 had added seven to McLaren's total of GP victories, taking the figure to 182.

MODEL	MP4-27
TYPE/FORMULA	Formula 1
YEAR OF PRODUCTION	2012
DESIGNER	McLaren Racing
EXAMPLES BUILT	4
ENGINE	Mercedes-Benz FO 108Z V8
CUBIC CAPACITY	2398cc
INDUCTION	FIA Standard ECU (Microsoft MESL)
POWER OUTPUT	785bhp

TRANSMISSION	McLaren seamless shift hand-operated 7-speed
CHASSIS	Moulded carbon-fibre composite
BODY	Carbon-fibre composite engine cover, sidepods and floor
FRONT SUSPENSION	Inboard torsion bar/damper system operated by pushrod and bell crank with a double wishbone arrangement
REAR SUSPENSION	Inboard torsion bar/damper system operated by pushrod and bell crank with a double wishbone arrangement
BRAKES F/R	Outboard carbon-fibre discs, Akebono calipers
WHEELS DIAMETER x WIDTH F/R	13x12/13x13.7in

TYRES F/R	Pirelli
LENGTH	201.2in - 5111mm
WIDTH	70.8in - 1798mm
HEIGHT	37.4in - 950mm
WHEELBASE	136.2in - 3459mm
TRACK F/R	58.8/56.6in - 1494/1439mm
WEIGHT	1246lb - 565kg
PRINCIPAL DRIVERS	Button, Hamilton
IDENTIFYING COLOURS	Chrome/Rocket Red

MODEL	12C Spider	TRANSMISSION	7-speed Seamless-Shift Gearbox (SSG)	TYRES F/R	Pirelli P ZERO
TYPE/FORMULA	Roadcar	CHASSIS	One-piece carbon-fibre MonoCell	LENGTH	177.5in - 4509mm
YEAR OF PRODUCTION	2012-2014	BODY	Carbon-fibre over aluminium front and rear frames	WIDTH	82.4in - 2093mm
DESIGNER	McLaren Automotive design team	FRONT SUSPENSION	McLaren ProActive Chassis Control,	HEIGHT	47.4in - 1203mm
EXAMPLES BUILT	Production numbers not released		double wishbone independent suspension	WHEELBASE	105.1in - 2670mm
ENGINE	McLaren M838T V8	REAR SUSPENSION	McLaren ProActive Chassis Control,	TRACK F/R	65.2/62.3in - 1656/1583mm
CUBIC CAPACITY	3799cc		double wishbone independent suspension	WEIGHT	3033lb - 1376kg
INDUCTION	Twin turbocharged	BRAKES F/R	Cast iron discs with forged aluminium hubs	PRINCIPAL DRIVERS	n/a
POWER OUTPUT	616bhp	WHEELS DIAMETER x WIDTH F/R	19x 8.5/20x11in	IDENTIFYING COLOURS	n/a

2013 MP4-28 FORMULA 1

Although the MP4-27 had set the pace at the beginning of 2012, in the middle, and again at the end, and won a total of seven of the 20 races, McLaren opted for more than just evolution in the design of the MP4-28 for 2013.

The design team pursued an aggressive development philosophy in the final season of the 2.4-litre, normally aspirated V8 era, aiming to make greater progress than their rivals. The key change was the switch to an ambitious pullrod front suspension concept, which was expected to unlock greater performance from the Pirelli tyres.

And when Jenson Button lapped the Jerez de la Frontera circuit in 1m 18.861s on the first day of official 2013 F1 testing, jaws dropped up and down the pit lane. Mark Webber was his closest challenger, and had managed only 1m 19.709s for Red Bull. The next day Button's new team-mate Sergio Perez settled in very quickly, looking strong in long-run evaluations. The decision to do more than just warm over the winning MP4-27 already seemed to be paying off.

It transpired, however, that the new car was very sensitive to changes in ambient and track temperatures. Button and Perez had set their fast laps in cool conditions, and when the car ran in warmer climes it became inconsistent as they struggled to find its sweet spot every time. Both drivers frequently reported that they had trouble understanding their new mount.

The performance was therefore compromised in the opening races, in Australia and Malaysia, but the team remained confident that the MP4-28 had much greater development potential than the majority of its rivals. Thus they decided not to revert to the proven MP4-27, keeping the faith that the MP4-28 would become stronger still once they uncovered its secrets. But things didn't work out that way.

When ride-height problems kept Button to a ninth place finish in bumpy Melbourne, there were suggestions that the innovative front suspension arrangement was the source, but team boss Martin Whitmarsh said there was no evidence in the data to support that conclusion. In what became a year of disappointment, Button's best result was fourth in Brazil, with fifth in China and sixth in Monaco, while Perez's fifth in India was the apogee of his first season with a top team. McLaren were fifth in the Constructors' World Championship, scoring 122 points to the dominant Red Bull team's 397.

The underlying weakness of the MP4-28 centred on the aggressive design revisions to the rear end of the car, which had prevented the team running an optimal ride height in Melbourne, while the other primary shortcomings were generally judged internally to be aerodynamic. The engineers sought to change the way the entire platform of the car worked and introduced major revisions in Spain, including significantly modified rear bodywork, sidepods and rear wing, but they proved insufficiently transformative.

"The car wasn't quick enough and we've made some changes and it probably still isn't quick enough," Whitmarsh was moved to say on more than one occasion. "But it's not quick enough by one percent. Yes, we're a big team so it's right to be hard on us over that. But if you step back and people use words such as 'profound' to describe our problems, I think they are misplaced. The car doesn't have enough downforce, there's no secret to it. We've got to work harder to improve it."

Like all top F1 teams, McLaren are highly self-critical. The technical team – led by former Williams designer Sam Michael and joined by former Sauber technical director Matt Morris – kept pushing all through the season.

"We were greedy and over-ambitious technically," Whitmarsh admitted, as McLaren set about an intensive analysis of the car's problems while honing the design of the upcoming MP4-29, which would be the last Mercedes-engined car from the Woking factory. "I don't like it if we aren't competitive enough, and coming racing when you don't have a realistic chance of winning a race."

MODEL	MP4-28
TYPE/FORMULA	Formula 1
YEAR OF PRODUCTION	2013
DESIGNER	McLaren Racing
EXAMPLES BUILT	4
ENGINE	Mercedes-Benz FO 108F V8
CUBIC CAPACITY	2398cc
ELECTRONICS	FIA Standard ECU (Microsoft MESL)
POWER OUTPUT	790bhp

TRANSMISSION	McLaren seamless shift hand-operated 7-speed
CHASSIS	Moulded carbon-fibre composite
BODY	Carbon-fibre composite engine cover, sidepods and floor
FRONT SUSPENSION	Inboard torsion bar/damper system operated by pushrod and bell crank with a double wishbone arrangement
REAR SUSPENSION	Inboard torsion bar/damper system operated by pushrod and bell crank with a double wishbone arrangement
BRAKES F/R	Outboard carbon-fibre discs, Akebono calipers
WHEELS DIAMETER x WIDTH F/R	13x12/13x13.7in

TYRES F/R	Pirelli
LENGTH	199.6in - 5071mm
WIDTH	70.8in - 1798mm
HEIGHT	37.4in - 950mm
WHEELBASE	134.6in - 3419mm
TRACK F/R	58.8/56.6in - 1494/1439mm
WEIGHT	1250lb - 567kg
PRINCIPAL DRIVERS	Button, Perez
IDENTIFYING COLOURS	Chrome/Rocket Red

2013 McLAREN P1 ROADCAR

The McLaren P1 which debuted in production form at the 2013 Geneva Motor Show, had a clear goal – to be the best driver's car in the world both on the road and on the track. To achieve this objective, McLaren used all of its 50 years of racing experience and success, especially in the fields of aerodynamics and lightweight carbon-fibre technology.

The result is a true superhero amongst supercars, both supermodel shapely and heroically powerful. A car that has an unprecedented amount of downforce for a road vehicle: similar levels to a GT3 racing car and yet with even greater ground effect. This downforce not only boosted cornering and braking performance, it also helped balance, stability and driveability at all speeds.

If the P1 was intended to be the best driver's car in the world then it needed to have exceptional straight-line performance and instant throttle response. To deliver this, the P1 used an innovative IPAS petrol-electric powertrain comprising of a substantially revised 727bhp, 3.8-litre twin-turbo V8 petrol engine, coupled to a 177bhp, single electric motor, that was collectively known as M838TQ. Although the combined power output was a massive 903bhp, as important as absolute power was the electric motor's ability to provide instant torque, making the powertrain superbly responsive.

The P1 was also amazingly efficient and could return 34.0mpg on the EU combined cycle, with CO_2 emissions of just 194g/km. In addition, the electric motor offered a range of almost 7 miles in full electric mode on the NEDC cycle, where emissions drop to

zero. Top speed was electronically limited to 217mph, with the 0-62mph standing start acceleration taking just 2.8 seconds. The braking figures provided by the P1's bespoke system were equally as impressive. The specially formulated carbon ceramic discs, coated in silicon carbide, could bring the McLaren P1 to a halt from 62mph in a distance of just 30.2 metres.

The astonishing technology developed for the McLaren P1 included active aerodynamics and adjustable suspension — both of which were, by 2012, banned in Formula 1 due to the inherent performance advantage. Airflow was optimised around the body through the use of an active wing and underbody devices. The adjustable rear wing could extend from the bodywork by 120mm on road, and up to 300mm on the race track, maximising the levels of downforce. The wing was directly inspired by Formula 1 design, with the

intersection of the double element rear wing and design of the endplates being the same as that on the 2008 championship winning MP4-23.

In addition, and as part of the all new hydro-pneumatic suspension system, the McLaren P1 also featured adjustable ride height. To produce additional ground effect aerodynamic, the revolutionary RaceActive Chassis Control (RCC) could lower the car by 50mm in Race mode. The P1 also featured adaptive spring rates, roll control, pitch control and damping, all providing a huge range of adjustment on a devastatingly quick car, that in 2013 had upped the Hypercar stakes to a totally new and unprecedented level.

MODEL	P1
TYPE/FORMULA	Roadcar
YEAR OF PRODUCTION	2013-2016
DESIGNER	McLaren Automotive design team
EXAMPLES BUILT	375
ENGINE	McLaren M838TQ IPAS (V8 + electric)
CUBIC CAPACITY	3799cc
INDUCTION	Twin turbocharged
POWER OUTPUT	903bhp (747bhp +176bhp)

TRANSMISSION	7-Speed Seamless-Shift Gearbox (SSG)
CHASSIS	One-piece carbon-fibre MonoCell
BODY	Carbon-fibre over aluminium front and rear frames
FRONT SUSPENSION	McLaren ProActive Chassis Control, double wishbone independent suspension
REAR SUSPENSION	McLaren ProActive Chassis Control, double wishbone independent suspension
BRAKES F/R	Akebono carbon ceramic discs
WHEELS DIAMETER x WIDTH F/R	19x9/20x11.5in

TYRES F/R	245/35 R19 - 315/30 R20
LENGTH	180.6in - 4588mm
WIDTH	76.6in - 1946mm
HEIGHT	46.8in - 1188mm
WHEELBASE	105.1in - 2670mm
TRACK F/R	65.3/63.1in - 1658/1604mm
WEIGHT	3,075lb - 1,395kg
PRINCIPAL DRIVERS	n/a
IDENTIFYING COLOURS	n/a

2012 12C SPIDER ROADCAR

The new McLaren 12C Spider unveiled at Pebble Beach "Car Week" in 2012, was set to become the second vehicle in the growing range of high performance sports cars from McLaren Automotive. This lightweight, mid-engine open-top sports car combined the astonishing performance of the 2011 model year 12C, with the increased exhilaration of roof-down motoring. Unlike the majority spiders or convertibles from other manufacturers, the 12C Spider managed to offer the same performance, handling and driver enjoyment as the fixed-roof coupé version.

Developed alongside the 12C Coupé as a 'pure McLaren' driver-focused sports car, the 12C Spider featured the same mechanical specification as the recently announced, 2013 Model Year 12C. This included the revised 3.8-litre V8 twin-turbo engine set into the rear of the by now well proven, industry-leading, carbon-fibre MonoCell built in Woking. The MonoCell in the 12C, which was designed from the outset with a convertible version in mind, needed no extra strengthening to provide the necessary rigidity for the conversion to an open roof car, ensuring it continued to offered the exemplary handling and safety that the 12C had become renowned for since its launch almost two years earlier.

The 12C Spider was mechanically identical to the 12C, but with an engine upgraded that delivered a 24bhp bump and now gave out 616bhp. Acceleration from 0-62mph (100 km/h) (when fitted with Pirelli P Zero Corsa tyres) was quoted as the same as for the coupé, just 3.1 seconds. Fuel consumption and emissions also remained the same, with the Spider returning 24.2 mpg (11.7 l/100km) on the combined cycle and 279g/km. The figures were of course significantly better than the majority of high performance convertible sports cars, in keeping with McLaren's commitment to class-leading fuel efficiency. Maximum speed was quoted at 204mph (329km/h).

The two-piece retractable hard top on the Spider could be raised or lowered in less than 17 seconds and on the move at speeds up to 30 km/h (19mph). When lowered, the roof stowed cleverly beneath a body coloured hard tonneau cover which incorporated twin buttresses. With the roof raised, the area beneath the tonneau cover could be used as additional luggage space.

The 12C Spider featured a heated glass rear window, which could be operated independently of the roof. With the roof down, the rear window moved automatically to an 'aero'

position to minimise buffeting. Additionally, with the roof up, the window could be lowered to give direct access to the sound of the twin-turbo 3.8-litre V8 engine mounted directly behind the cabin.

The roll over protection system fitted included a steel structure within each of the rear buttresses to absorb any impact and protect occupants. However, an 'active' pop-up system was ruled out as it would have added weight. The overall weight of the Spider increased by just 88lb (40kg) over the coupé, mainly due to its retractable roof panels (constructed from the same lightweight composite as the body) and a new exhaust system.

The detail changes of the 12C Spider extended to both the audio and climate control systems. The audio output changes when the roof is open — to compensate for the change in environment — while the climate control adapts when the roof is lowered.

The 12C Spider also used the same ProActive Chassis Control that had proved such a revelation with the 12C coupé. The suspension which was based on double wishbones and coil springs, similar to a current Formula 1 car featured innovative adaptive dampers, interconnected hydraulically and linked to a gas-filled accumulator, provide pro-active responses, depending on road conditions and driver preferences. Normal, Sport and Track settings were available which operated independently of the transmission settings.

2014 MP4-29
FORMULA 1

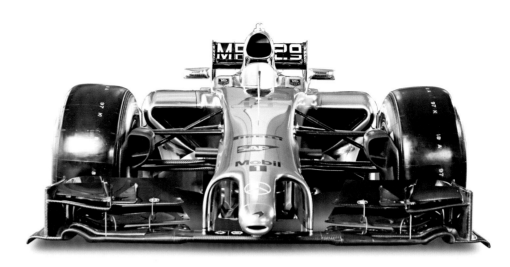

The disappointing performance of the MP4-28 had far-reaching consequences, as Ron Dennis took back control of running the race team from Martin Whitmarsh, who left the company during the pre-season shake-up, and Eric Boullier was recruited from Lotus as racing director.

Formula 1 faced a dramatic new scene after the greatest rules upheaval in its long history, and as Dennis began a root-and-branch reform of each department in search of the team's mojo, he made a 20-minute address to the staff at the factory on January 16th. "There will be changes," he pledged. "We will win again."

Most rule changes over the years have focused on aerodynamics and engine capacity. But this time the whole powertrain was new: 90-degree, 1.6-litre turbocharged V6s capped at 15,000rpm and augmented by hybrid systems. The purpose was to realign F1's powertrain philosophy to be more in keeping with, and more relevant to, emergent roadcar technologies. Accordingly, and befitting the nature of F1 as a valuable development crucible, these power units were much more complex and were boosted at 3.5bar (50psi) via the return of the turbocharger for the first time since 1988. Direct fuel injection also offered greater efficiency. But the power units also used two forms of energy recovery system – an MGU-K (K for kinetic energy) and MGU-H (H, for heat) that dramatically increased efficiency by harvesting energy dissipated as heat not just from the brakes, but also from the turbocharger itself.

The basic V6 engine produced around 447kW (600bhp), but with the extra 120kW (160bhp) generated by the ERS it had similar power to the previous generation of 2.4-litre naturally aspirated V8s, but much better fuel efficiency. This was crucial because of another key change: the amount of fuel permitted for a race was cut dramatically. Where the V8s used up to 160kg (225-litres) of fuel flowing at 170kg/hour during each race (typically 90 minutes long), teams were now only allowed 100kg (140-litres), with a maximum flow rate of 100kg/hour.

On the aerodynamics front, exhaust-blown diffusers were banned, and there were other stringent measurements governing the front and rear wings. Minimum chassis weight was increased from 642kg to 690kg in order to accommodate the greater heft of the hybrid systems.

McLaren's technical department produced another all-new car to package all of this technology. The MP4-29 was powered by the Mercedes PU106A V6, which would prove

far the best engine of the season, and there was a switch back to pushrod front suspension after all the trouble with pullrods the previous year. Pullrod suspension was retained at the rear, however.

So dramatic were the changes that nobody knew what to expect at the first race, in Melbourne. Nico Rosberg won for Mercedes from Daniel Ricciardo's Red Bull. Reigning World Series by Renault champion Kevin Magnussen, whose father Jan had raced once in F1 in 1995 for McLaren, brought his McLaren home third on his F1 debut but was promoted to second when the Red Bull was disqualified for irregular fuel flow. Jenson Button, whose season began in the most tragic circumstances when his much-loved father John succumbed to a heart attack in January, moved up to third. But McLaren's great start proved to be a false dawn.

Button said that the MP4-29 had an inherently good feel to it, much better than the MP4-28's, but although that initial success put McLaren into the lead of the Constructors' World

MODEL	MP4-29
TYPE/FORMULA	Formula 1
YEAR OF PRODUCTION	2014
DESIGNER	McLaren Racing
EXAMPLES BUILT	4
ENGINE	Mercedes-Benz PU 106A V6 hybrid
CUBIC CAPACITY	1598cc
ELECTRONICS	FIA Standard ECU (Microsoft MESL)
POWER OUTPUT	780bhp

TRANSMISSION	McLaren seamless shift hand-operated 8-speed
CHASSIS	Moulded carbon-fibre composite; cockpit controls and fuel cell
BODY	Carbon-fibre composite engine cover, sidepods, floor, nose, wings
FRONT SUSPENSION	Carbon-fibre wishbone and pushrod suspension elements operating inboard torsion bar and damper system
REAR SUSPENSION	Carbon-fibre wishbone and pushrod suspension elements operating inboard torsion bar and damper system
BRAKES F/R	Outboard carbon-fibre discs, Akebono calipers
WHEELS DIAMETER x WIDTH F/R	13x12/13x13.7in

TYRES F/R	Pirelli
LENGTH	207in - 5257mm
WIDTH	70.8in - 1798mm
HEIGHT	37.4in - 950mm
WHEELBASE	136.2in - 3460mm
TRACK F/R	58.8/56.6in - 1494/1439mm
WEIGHT	1356lb - 615kg
PRINCIPAL DRIVERS	Button, Magnussen
IDENTIFYING COLOURS	Chrome

Championship, it soon became clear that the MP4-29 lacked the Mercedes' race-winning pace and the team never looked as strong again. They lost ground to Red Bull, Ferrari and Williams in the pursuit of Mercedes, finishing fifth overall.

2014 was, then, a transitional year as the Woking team wound down its association with Mercedes after 20 seasons and looked ahead to a new relationship with Honda. Dennis put some of the performance deficit down to running Mobil fuel rather than the bespoke Petronas brew that had been specifically developed for the Mercedes engine by the Malaysian company, a sponsor of the works team. It was reckoned to be worth another 40bhp.

By the end of the season aerodynamic development had enhanced the MP4-29's front-end grip and left engineers feeling confident about the upcoming Honda-engined MP4-30, and Dennis and engine programme leader Yasuhisa Arai spoke of winning races in 2015. In the meantime, McLaren also started the lengthy process of dismantling their matrix management system in favour of a more conventional arrangement with heads of department reporting to a technical director. There was also a focus on giving engineers from the younger generation more of a voice in the development process.

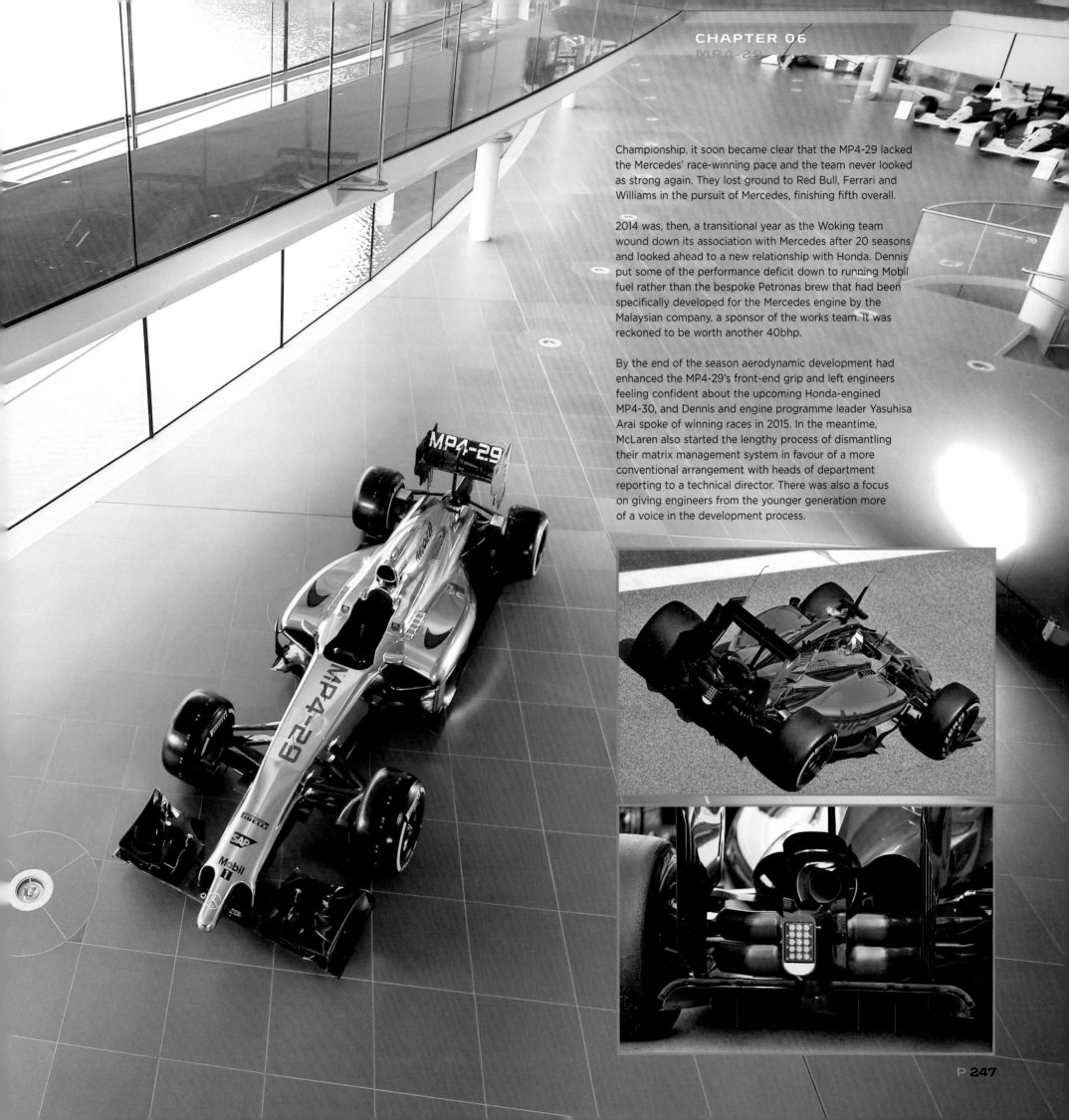

2014 650S SPIDER ROADCAR

With the end of production of the 12C and 12C Spider in early 2014, by April, McLaren Automotive had announced their replacement, the 650S. The new 650S model would be available from the outset in both Coupé and Spider body styles. The McLaren 650S Coupé had a fixed roof and glass engine cover, while the Spider featured a two-piece Retractable Hard Top (RHT) that could be automatically raised or lower in less than 17 seconds.

The 650S badge designation referred to the power output of 650PS (641bhp) from the unique British-built McLaren M838T twin turbo V8 engine. 'S' stood for 'Sport', underlining the focus and developments made to handling, transmission, drivability and engagement.

The 650S Spider was mechanically identical to the 650S Coupé, offering the same performance, handling and driver enjoyment. As with the 12C, the secret of success for the 650S was its industry-leading, Formula 1-inspired, carbon-fibre MonoCell chassis (weighing just 75kg), and front and rear aluminium subframes it shared with its predecessor. This set-up needed no extra strengthening to provide the necessary rigidity or safety when developing a convertible and kept any weight increase to a minimum, meaning the 650S Spider offered all the enjoyment and driver appeal of the fixed-roof sibling – but with the added appeal of wind-in-the-hair top-down driving. At 1,370kg (dry), overall weight, the Spider was only marginally higher (40kg) than the Coupé and less than any other car in its class. As you would expect, the additional weight came from the Retractable Hard Top and roof mechanism.

The design of the 650S was inspired by the McLaren P1 and showcased a new family design language for the brand. More importantly, the new look followed the McLaren design ethos of 'form follows function', with the front bumper providing a dramatic, yet clean, appearance while the integrated front splitter contributed to increased levels of downforce. This offered a greater level of steering feeling and confidence to the driver on turn-in, while also adding to the agility and handling balance. Unique door blades behind the front wheels, on the leading edge of the dihedral doors, directed air from the trailing edges of the front splitter, further benefiting front-end grip and vehicle balance.

Both 650S models used a unique version of the award-winning M838T engine. New pistons and cylinder heads provided a boost in engine power and torque, and these were combined with new exhaust valves and revised cam timing. Further advances were made to the transmission software to allow faster and crisper gearshifts which all added to the aural drama in 'Sport' mode which employed 'cylinder cut' technology. The system produces an exhaust flare on upshifts which is achieved by momentarily interrupting the spark and 'popping' the fuel on re-ignition. This gives a distinctive engine note, as exhaust sound is amplified, without any loss in performance.

The 0-100 km/h (62mph) sprint took 3.0 seconds, for both Spider and the Coupé, and the Spider could reach

2014 650S ROADCAR

200km/h (124mph) in 8.6 seconds, only 0.2 seconds shy of the fixed-head model. Maximum speed for both cars was quoted as 329km/h (204mph). Fuel consumption and emissions were the same for both the Coupé and the Spider, both returning 24.2mpg (11.7 l/100km) on the EU combined cycle and 275 g/km.

As with the 12C Spider, the 650S Spider used a heated glass rear window, operating independently of the roof. With the roof down, the rear window could act as a wind deflector, reducing cabin buffeting. Roof up, the rear screen could be lowered to allow more engine noise – and driving drama – into the cabin, and for a semi-open top driving experience even when was raining. When down, the roof was stowed beneath a body-coloured hard tonneau cover incorporated in the twin rear buttresses. With the roof raised, the area beneath the tonneau cover could be used as additional luggage space. The roll over protection system on the 650S included a steel structure within each of the rear buttresses to absorb any impact and protect occupants. An 'active'

pop-up system was ruled out as it would have added weight.

Inside the cabin, the detail changes of the McLaren 650S Spider extend to both the audio and climate control systems. Audio output was set to change when the roof was open — to compensate for the change in environment — while the climate control adapts when the roof is lowered. The audio system, developed by bespoke British hi-fi specialists Meridian, optimised the music output depending whether driving with the roof in place, or stowed. Meridian was involved throughout the development of the audio system to ensure optimised audio quality. The recalibrated Automatic Volume Control (AVC) and Automatic Tone Control (ATC) systems, first shown in the 12C Spider, were present in the McLaren 650S Spider, whereby Individual speakers are automatically adjusted to take into account increases in external sound.

Other technologies with links back to the company's Formula 1 rich heritage included full wishbone suspension, mid-engine

architecture, Brake Steer for enhanced agility, carbon ceramic disc brakes (standard on the McLaren 650S) and active aerodynamics. The McLaren Airbrake, originally fitted to the 12C and 12C Spider and designed to offer optimised levels of downforce on the rear of the car, now worked with greater levels of functionality, and offered a greater degree of stability in a wider range of conditions.

"Everything we have learnt from the McLaren P1 and the 12C has gone into the McLaren 650S. The result is a car that's faster, more fun and thrilling to drive, yet also more comfortable, luxurious and even easier to enjoy, day-to-day" said McLaren Automotive CEO Mike Flewitt. "At McLaren, we are a fast moving company, continually striving for improvements and technical advantages. We always want to push, to improve. That's our Formula 1 heritage and mentality shining through. Always seeking to innovate, to be the class-leaders, to bring new technologies to market as fast as possible."

MODEL	650S Spider and 650S	TRANSMISSION	7-speed Seamless-Shift Gearbox (SSG)	TYRES F/R	Pirelli P ZERO Corsa
TYPE/FORMULA	Roadcar	CHASSIS	One-piece carbon-fibre MonoCell	LENGTH	177.6in - 4512mm
YEAR OF PRODUCTION	2014-2016	BODY	Carbon-fibre over aluminium front and rear frames	WIDTH	82.4in - 2093mm
DESIGNER	McLaren Automotive design team	FRONT SUSPENSION	McLaren ProActive Chassis Control,	HEIGHT	47.4in - 1203mm/47.2in - 1199mm
EXAMPLES BUILT	Production numbers not released		double wishbone independent suspension	WHEELBASE	105.1in - 2670mm
ENGINE	McLaren M838T V8	REAR SUSPENSION	McLaren ProActive Chassis Control,	TRACK F/R	65.2/62.3in - 1656/1583mm
CUBIC CAPACITY	3799cc		double wishbone independent suspension	WEIGHT	3020lb - 1370kg
ELECTRONICS	Twin turbocharged	BRAKES F/R	Carbon Ceramic Discs with Forged Aluminium Hubs	PRINCIPAL DRIVERS	n/a
POWER OUTPUT	641bhp	WHEELS DIAMETER x WIDTH F/R	19x8.5/20x11in	IDENTIFYING COLOURS	n/a

2014 650S GT3
RACECAR

Born from the highly successful McLaren 12C GT3 which had won multiple titles and scored over 50 race wins following its launch in 2011, the McLaren 650S GT3 racecar, wearing McLaren's historic number 59 livery, was officially revealed at the 2014 Goodwood Festival of Speed. Fifteen examples of the 650S GT3 race car were scheduled to be produced and delivered to customer teams by the beginning of the 2015 race season.

Designed and built to contest GT3 championships the world over, the 650S GT3 was the latest generation of track-focused racers coming out of Woking. Offering optimised aerodynamics and enhanced levels of driver engagement and set to make its competitive debut with customer teams from early 2015 the GT3 improved upon just about every aspect of its elder brother, from drivability, to aerodynamics and serviceability.

After completing a development season in 2014 and as the final stage of development, the 650S GT3 hit the ground running with an impressive podium finish on its debut at that year's Gulf 12-hour race at Yas Marina in December. The car would make its competitive debut with customer teams in early 2015, and by the end of the season the 650S GT3 has claimed multiple championships and race wins worldwide, becoming one of the most successful GT3 cars to date.

As a GT3 class car the 650S GT3 was eligible to compete in a incredible variety of international and national series and events worldwide and proved itself to be competitive across the globe, winning the Blancpain Endurance Cup, Bathurst

12-Hour, Asian Le Mans Series and Pirelli World Challenge, as well as scoring race wins in many other series. Both professional and non professional drivers alike found success with the car's versatility, staying competitive on every type of circuit and in a variety of weather conditions.

The McLaren 650S GT3 featured the same award-winning 3.8-litre M838T V8 twin-turbo engine, and carbon-fibre MonoCell chassis as the road-going 650S, making it one of the most technically advanced, safe and sophisticated GT3 cars on the track. The fully race-prepared twin-turbo engine churned out 493bhp and included a purpose-built ECU offering better functionality for turbo boost and gearshifts. Owing to GT racing regulations though, that power output was, ironically, lower than the roadgoing 650S's. However, as befits a hardcore GT3-spec racer, many of the components were unrecognisable from the road car. The engine was mated to a new six-speed sequential motorsport gearbox while the brakes featured six-pot callipers at the front and four-piston items at the rear, all grabbing huge 380mm ventilated discs.

Large air intakes and a massive front splitter dominated the new car's front end, giving it a more aggressive look while new lightweight carbon-fibre bodywork wrapped around redesigned air intakes for better cooling. A massive carbon-fibre wing worked together with the carbon front splitter to manage the airflow keeping the 650S GT3 on the track. A 52mm wider track, revised suspension geometry and upgraded components were claimed to give the car greater drivability and adjustability for all types of drivers wanting to go GT racing.

The first race for the 650s GT3 was the Gulf 12-hours at Yas Marina, where two cars were entered as the final stage of the development programme. The Pro entry of Rob Bell, Kevin Estre and Alvaro Parente secured a podium finish, while the Pro-Am entry Peter Kox, Nico Pronk and Gilles Vannelet finished 12th. The result underlined the performance and reliability of the car while also underlining the drivability for a range of driver abilities.

The cabin was certainly driver-focused, with the new McLaren GT-developed race seat with a six-point harness as standard, bolted directly to the chassis and the steering wheel and pedal box fully adjustable to suit the driver. Driver protection was provided by an additional FIA-approved rollcage, which afforded a greater degree of comfort with more head and leg room. A bespoke motorsport digital dash greeted the driver behind the unique steering wheel, itself inspired by the McLaren Mercedes Formula 1 car's helm.

MODEL	650S GT3	TRANSMISSION	6-Speed sequential motorsport transmission	TYRES F/R	Pirelli P ZERO
TYPE/FORMULA	Racecar	CHASSIS	Carbon-fibre MonoCell, aluminium f&r sub frames	LENGTH	177.4in - 4507mm
YEAR OF PRODUCTION	2014	BODY	Bespoke lightweight carbon-fibre/composite body panels	WIDTH	78.5in - 1995mm
DESIGNER	McLaren Automotive design team	FRONT SUSPENSION	Fully adjustable double wishbone adjustable	HEIGHT	45.1in - 1145mm
EXAMPLES BUILT	15		4-way dampers with coil over springs	WHEELBASE	105.1in - 2670mm
ENGINE	McLaren M838T V8	REAR SUSPENSION	Fully adjustable double wishbone adjustable	TRACK F/R	
CUBIC CAPACITY	3799cc		4-way dampers with coil over springs	WEIGHT	2952lb - 1330kg
ELECTRONICS	Twin turbocharged	BRAKES F/R	Monoblock calipers with ventilated discs	PRINCIPAL DRIVERS	n/a
POWER OUTPUT	368KW/500PS/493bhp	WHEELS DIAMETER x WIDTH F/R	18x12.5/18x13in	IDENTIFYING COLOURS	n/a

2015 MP4-30 FORMULA 1

Despite the optimism and enthusiasm with which McLaren embraced its new relationship with Honda, 2015 was destined to be a difficult and disappointing season.

Once Mercedes elected to start their own team, Honda was the clear choice, especially given their past relationship with McLaren which had yielded so much success with Ayrton Senna, Alain Prost and Gerhard Berger.

The new MP4-30 retained the MP4-29's basic pushrod front and pullrod rear suspension platform, but elsewhere broke fresh ground with its elegant shrink-wrapped bodywork, which itself was facilitated by the tiny size of Honda's first Formula 1 power unit since 2008. Both companies had worked to a 'size zero' engineering philosophy.

The package looked good when it was first revealed, and had the neatest rear end in the quest for perfect aerodynamic performance. But it would transpire that the small size of the Honda engine would be its downfall, and it proved underpowered and unreliable. Some believed that the company had been persuaded to return to the sport a year sooner than they wanted to.

The team conducted the first track test of the engine in Abu Dhabi in December 2014, and it became clear there were difficulties. These came into even sharper focus during the pre-season tests, first in Jerez and then in Barcelona, as the power unit was beset by persistent and varied teething troubles.

There were ongoing issues with seals on the MGU-K component in the energy recovery system. But hydraulic leaks and sensor problems in the final test also severely limited mileage, and McLaren's tally over all three sessions was only 1087 miles. Racing director Eric Boullier admitted that the team was "50 percent" down on where they had expected to be at that stage.

Then new signing Fernando Alonso, returning to McLaren for the first time since 2007, was injured in a freak accident that generated a media frenzy and required Kevin Magnussen to be recalled for the opening race in Australia when doctors advised Alonso not to race.

There were positive aspects, however. Magnussen was enthusiastic and agreed with Alonso that McLaren's new

technical direction, formed partly by the arrival of aerodynamicist Peter Prodromou in late 2014, was the right one. Rather than trying to maximise downforce, McLaren had now aimed to generate consistent and predictable loads on the car which could be exploited at all times.

Though Magnussen completed relatively few miles between stoppages, he reported that on first acquaintance the MP4-30 felt like a completely different car to the unpredictable MP4-29. It was very consistent, stable, and threw few surprises at the driver.

He also commented that while Honda's engine was still at an early stage of its development as a race unit, the torque delivery and upshifts compared well with the title-winning Mercedes power unit they had used in 2014. "Although there is still some way to go, I was pleasantly surprised how smooth it was," he said.

Dennis had huge faith in Honda's state-of-the-art technical facilities and its understanding of energy harvesting. But through a series of technical misadventures, as Honda understandably struggled to match rival manufacturers who had a considerable head start, McLaren endured one of the toughest seasons in their history.

It took until Monaco, the sixth round, before Jenson Button

guided his car home eighth, for two points, and much of the time the MP4-30s failed to get through the first session of qualifying or had to take grid penalties when engine components needed to be replaced.

The problems were manifold, and inter-linked. The internal combustion engine was unreliable, and the control systems that integrated the power contribution of the hybrid systems needed more development. The ERS system, packaged within the engine's vee to help McLaren shrink-wrap the rear bodywork, failed to deliver sufficient power, deployed it erratically, and was also unreliable.

The engine problems made it hard to see how much progress McLaren was really making on the chassis side, though the Prodromou-inspired search for useable rather than peak downforce continued to yield fruit. "I think the chassis is actually pretty good and that we will be able to do a much better job once we get some power that we can use," Alonso said during the Brazilian Grand Prix weekend.

Both Alonso and Button drove as hard as they could, while having to watch their mirrors constantly for much faster rivals. They could not be faulted for the way they handled the difficult situation, conducting themselves with dignity and resolve as McLaren finished ninth overall with 27 points from five scoring races.

MODEL	MP4-30
TYPE/FORMULA	Formula 1
YEAR OF PRODUCTION	2015
DESIGNER	McLaren Racing
EXAMPLES BUILT	4
ENGINE	Honda RA615H V6 hybrid
CUBIC CAPACITY	1598cc
ELECTRONICS	MAT (McLaren Applied Technologies)
POWER OUTPUT	760bhp

TRANSMISSION	McLaren seamless shift hand-operated 8-speed
CHASSIS	Moulded carbon-fibre composite; driver controls and fuel cell
BODY	Carbon-fibre composite engine cover, sidepods, floor, nose, wings
FRONT SUSPENSION	Carbon-fibre wishbone and pushrod suspension elements operating inboard torsion bar and damper system
REAR SUSPENSION	Carbon-fibre wishbone and pushrod suspension elements operating inboard torsion bar and damper system
BRAKES F/R	Outboard carbon-fibre discs, pads with Akebono calipers
WHEELS DIAMETER x WIDTH F/R	13x12/13x13.7in

TYRES F/R	Pirelli
LENGTH	209.3in - 5316mm
WIDTH	70.8in - 1798mm
HEIGHT	37.4in - 950mm
WHEELBASE	138.5in - 3519mm
TRACK F/R	58.8/56.6in - 1494/1439mm
WEIGHT	1383lb - 627kg
PRINCIPAL DRIVERS	Button, Alonso, Magnussen
IDENTIFYING COLOURS	Chrome/Black

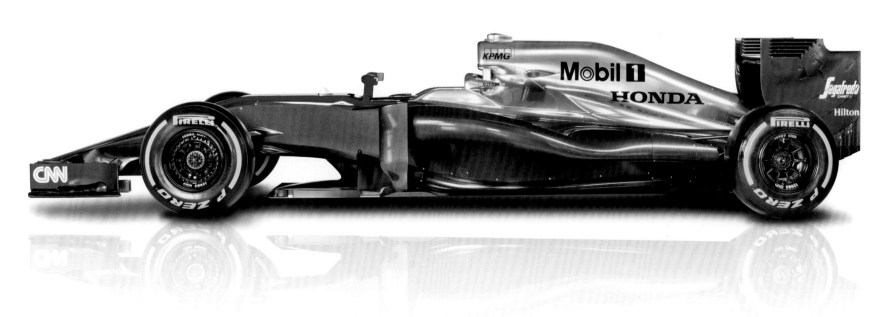

2015 675LT ROADCAR

The new 675LT model which debuted in production form at the 2015 Geneva Motor Show, was the lightest, most powerful, fastest and most track-focused, yet road legal, model in the McLaren Super Series and resurrected one of the most revered names in modern-day GT racing — the 'Longtail'. With confirmation that just 500 of the 675LT Coupé would be produced, all 500 were sold before the first cars were delivered to customers in July of 2015.

The 675LT, the first McLaren in nearly two decades to wear the LT — or 'Longtail' — name, stayed true to the spirit of its iconic predecessor with aerodynamically optimized, dramatically enhanced styling that results in 40% more downforce than the 650S it sat alongside in the McLaren Super Series.

"The Longtail is a famous name in the history of McLaren, first used on the fastest version of the iconic McLaren F1," explained Mike Flewitt, McLaren Automotive CEO. "The McLaren F1 GTR 'Longtail' was the final highly successful iteration of the F1 and it is an appropriate name for the most exhilarating and driver-focused version of the Super Series. The 675LT is the purest distillation of what McLaren stands for — pure driving pleasure."

The main focus for the 675LT was clear: to deliver maximum performance, engagement and excitement. To achieve this, overall weight was reduced by 220.4lbs (100kg) through the increased usage of carbon-fibre — by now the signature material of McLaren — and by numerous lighter components throughout, including newly developed suspension geometry derived from the McLaren P1, resulting in an increased track of 20mm. Power from the newly-developed M838TL 3.8-liter twin-turbocharged V8 engine was quoted as 666bhp at 7,100rpm, with a torque figure of 516lb.ft. at 5,500-6,500 rpm.

These extreme weight saving measures left the 675LT with a dry weight of just 2,712lbs (1,230 kg), meaning a power-to-weight ratio of 541bhp per ton. The sprint from 0-62mph (0-100 km/h) took just 2.9 seconds, with controlled torque delivery ensuring optimized traction off the line. Acceleration continued at relentless pace, with the 124mph (200km/h) barrier broken in 7.9 seconds, on to a top speed of 205mph (330km/h). Despite these remarkable performance figures, the 675LT was able to return 24.2mpg and the same CO2 emissions (275g/km) as the other cars in McLaren's Super Series of models. Though noticeably faster, the 675LT also retained much of the usability and practicality seen on the 650S.

New carbon-fibre bodywork driven by aerodynamic needs, helped minimise the overall weight and optimise aerodynamic performance with the addition of a newly designed front splitter, Formula 1-style nose end-plates and a larger 'Longtail' Airbrake. Additionally, the rear deck was also new. These bodywork changes contributed to a significant increase in downforce levels, up 40 percent over the already extremely aerodynamically-efficient 650S.

The 675LT was fitted with adjustable settings for both handling and powertrain through the Active Dynamics Panel rotary switches. While this system was shared with other models in the McLaren range, the Normal, Sport and Track settings were uniquely calibrated to the 675LT and were designed to provide the most engaging and track-focused experience. Front ride height was reduced and the track was widened. Fitted as standard, the Ultra-Lightweight 10-spoke forged alloy wheels were the lightest design ever offered by McLaren, saving a combined 1.75lbs (800g) over the lightest wheel design previously offered.

The driver-focused and minimalist environment of the 675LT was designed to be ergonomically optimized with minimal distractions for the driver. The uncluttered driver zone was void of steering wheel-mounted switches, with clear and concise displays on either side of the larger rev counter. Inspired by those fitted to the P1, the extended carbon-fibre gearshift paddles (the first time this material was used for this application on the Super Series) were mounted on a rocker behind the steering wheel. The cabin was upholstered in lightweight Alcantara and featured a four-speaker Meridian hi-fi, Sirius satellite radio and a satellite navigation system as standard. In the pursuit of minimal weight and to suit its purposeful intent, air conditioning was removed from the standard package, but could be specified as a no cost option.

The 675LT's pair of lightweight carbon-fibre seats were modelled on those in the McLaren P1 and were upholstered in Alcantara and embossed leather. These reduce weight by 33lbs (15kg) and in a further effort to reduce weight, carpet and sound deadening materials were in limited supply within the cabin.

"The 675LT is the closest thing there is to a McLaren P1," explained Mike Flewitt. "It is always so engaging and dramatic, and alongside the McLaren P1, it's the most extreme expression yet of McLaren road car engineering. Though brilliant on the track — and likely to be extensively used on track days — the extra engagement and performance is immediately obvious when driving on the road, even at low speeds."

MODEL	675LT	TRANSMISSION	7-speed Seamless-Shift Gearbox (SSG)	TYRES F/R	Pirelli P ZERO
TYPE/FORMULA	Roadcar	CHASSIS	One-piece carbon-fibre MonoCell	LENGTH	179in - 4546mm
YEAR OF PRODUCTION	2015-2016	BODY	Carbon-fibre over aluminium front and rear frames	WIDTH	82.5in - 2095mm
DESIGNER	McLaren Automotive design team	FRONT SUSPENSION	McLaren ProActive Chassis Control,	HEIGHT	46.7in - 1188mm
EXAMPLES BUILT	500		double wishbone independent suspension	WHEELBASE	105.1in - 2670mm
ENGINE	McLaren M838TL V8	REAR SUSPENSION	McLaren ProActive Chassis Control,	TRACK F/R	65.2/62.3in - 1656/1583mm
CUBIC CAPACITY	3799cc		double wishbone independent suspension	WEIGHT	2712lb - 1230kg
INDUCTION	Twin turbocharged	BRAKES F/R	Carbon Ceramic discs with forged aluminium hubs	PRINCIPAL DRIVERS	n/a
POWER OUTPUT	666bhp	WHEELS DIAMETER x WIDTH F/R	19x8/20x11in	IDENTIFYING COLOURS	n/a

2015 570S
ROADCAR

The McLaren 570S Coupé was the first model to be launched in the 'McLaren Sports Series'. Following its global debut at the New York International Auto Show in April 2015, the new model range marked the entry of McLaren into the luxury sports car market, introducing race-derived technologies and supercar performance in a package which was very much a pure McLaren.

The McLaren Sports Series was the third and final product family to join the three-tier model range from McLaren Automotive announced in 2014. A pure McLaren from the ground up, the Sports Series launched in coupé body style with the 570S. This model completed the range alongside the Ultimate Series, which in 2015 comprised of the McLaren P1 and McLaren P1 GTR, and the Super Series, which was the core McLaren range which at that time featured the 650S, (available as both a Coupé and a Spider), and the 675LT.

"The Sports Series is aimed at a new audience for McLaren," explained Mike Flewitt, CEO of McLaren Automotive "It is the first time we've competed in the sports car as opposed to the supercar market. As with all McLaren models, we have prioritized performance, driving engagement and exhilaration. It is a totally driver-focused car, with excellent ergonomics and visibility, and a class-leading driving position. This is also the most day-to-day usable, practical and attainable McLaren we've ever made. It is a dramatic and beautiful sports car."

Chris Goodwin, McLaren Chief Test Driver added, "For the Sports Series we wanted to offer a real sports car feel. Ultimately, it means a car that feels nimble, agile and it must also possess a lightness and directness of response

to a driver's inputs. Certainly for us, a sports car really needs to engage the driver, at any speed."

The 570S Coupé demonstrates five key characteristics – aerodynamics and design, minimized weight, craftsmanship, day-to-day usability and driving involvement – to create the most attainable McLaren model to date.

The Sports Series introduced the McLaren design language to the sports car segment for the first time, with tense, 'shrink wrapped' body lines marking it out from the competition. Design cues and learnings from models in the Ultimate and Super Series ensured that the Sports Series cars looked every part a true McLaren, but with a clear identity of its own. Key design features included elegant flying buttresses, new thinner B-pillars, dihedral doors and a concave rear window to bring a new, unique and exciting look to the sports car segment. The Sports Series was the most usable and attainable model ever to wear a McLaren badge, but it retained the core design and dynamic focus that ensures it was still worthy of the iconic name.

The final design of the 570S Coupé was closely matched to the initial design sketches first proposed by Chief Designer Rob Melville and his team at the outset of the project. Clean, sweeping lines, and an uncluttered exterior gave a clear focus on the way air flowed over the sculpted panels, channeling air around the tightly packaged glasshouse, over and, in some areas, through the bodywork. Dynamic styling provides visual presence and is based around functional elements. This approach combines fluid surfaces and strong features to deliver a final aerodynamic shape designed to optimize air flow management in, out and around the vehicle. Weight is

minimized through the layering of panels, designed to float above aerodynamic surfaces along with suspended members, supporting the potency of this compact sports car.

Weighing in at 2,895lbs (1,313kg), thanks in part to the unique lightweight carbon-fibre MonoCell II chassis, the Sports Series 570S is almost 331lbs (150kg) lighter than its closest rival on the market. Power was provided by an evolution of the 3.8-litre twin-turbo V8 engine featuring 30 percent new components, ensuring electrifying performance and boasting a class-leading power-to-weight figure of 5lbs per hp (434PS per ton). At the same time, the interior was more tailored around day-to-day usability, with optimized access, greater levels of stowage space and more refinement.

MODEL	570S		TRANSMISSION	7-speed Seamless-Shift Gearbox (SSG)		TYRES F/R	Pirelli P ZERO
TYPE/FORMULA	Roadcar		CHASSIS	One-piece MonoCell		LENGTH	178.3in - 4530mm
YEAR OF PRODUCTION	2015		BODY	Carbon-fibre MonoCell II, aluminium front and rear frames		WIDTH	82.5in - 2095mm
DESIGNER	McLaren Automotive design team		FRONT SUSPENSION	Adaptive dampers and		HEIGHT	47.3in - 1202mm
EXAMPLES BUILT	Production numbers not released			double wishbone suspension		WHEELBASE	105.1in - 2670mm
ENGINE	McLaren M838TE V8		REAR SUSPENSION	Adaptive dampers and		TRACK F/R	65.9/67.3in - 1673/1618mm
CUBIC CAPACITY	3799cc			double wishbone suspension		WEIGHT	2895lb - 1313kg
INDUCTION	Twin turbocharged		BRAKES F/R	Carbon Ceramic Discs with Forged Aluminium Hubs		PRINCIPAL DRIVERS	n/a
POWER OUTPUT	562bhp		WHEELS DIAMETER x WIDTH F/R	19x8/20x10in		IDENTIFYING COLOURS	n/a

2015 McLAREN P1 GTR RACECAR

The fact that so many McLaren supercar owners were demanding an even more powerful version of the P1 was all the justification McLaren needed to announce in late 2014 that they would be building a track-dedicated spin-off of the supercar that was possibly amongst the best vehicles on the road in 2015. Celebrating 20 years since their victory in the 1995 24 Hours of Le Mans, McLaren announced that they would resurrect the GTR name by naming the track-only version of the P1, the P1 GTR.

The concept car made its debut at the 2014 Pebble Beach Concours d'Elegance in August of 2014 and the P1 GTR production model was officially unveiled at the 2015 Geneva Motor Show. The P1 GTR was initially only available to current P1 owners and the price quoted of £1.98 million included participation in a worldwide owners track day series; the chance to take part in at least six drive events at Formula 1 circuits.

The P1 GTR went into production in 2015, after all the 375 standard P1's had been built and were built, maintained and run by McLaren Special Operations. Initially McLaren didn't release figures on how many cars it would build, but said production will be "strictly limited."

The P1 GTR's hybrid engine was rated at a total power output of 1,000PS (986bhp), representing an 84PS or 83bhp increase over the standard production P1. With 800PS (789bhp) being delivered from the V8 internal combustion engine at 7,250rpm an additional 200PS (197bhp) came from its electric motor. McLaren did not disclose how the overall power increase over the P1 was achieved from the electric motor and the twin-turbocharged 3.8-litre V8.

Performance figures remained unconfirmed by McLaren at the time the GTR was launched, but the P1 GTR was rumoured to reach 60mph in around 2.5 seconds on the way to a top speed of 225mph, although officially this was electronically limited to 217mph. The GTR could reportedly launch itself from a standstill to 186mph in 17 seconds. The McLaren F1, once the world's fastest production car, did that in 22 seconds.

With an all up kerb weight of 1,440kg (3,175lb) which included the weight of the batteries, the P1 GTR was 50kg (110lb) lighter than the P1, achieving a power-to-weight ratio of 687bhp per tonne. Aside from the power hike, the P1 GTR also featured a wider track, racing slicks, and a tweaked exterior design to improve aerodynamics on the track. A titanium-alloy exhaust system ensured the twin-turbo V8 howled far louder than the standard road car, too. Designated as 'Track Only' the car of course featured slick Pirelli P-ZERO tyres, and had greater levels of performance,

grip, aerodynamics and downforce in comparison to the road car. Featuring a fixed ride height on race-prepared suspension, a fixed rear wing capable of using DRS, as well as the exclusively designed exhaust made of titanium and inconel. Due to that enormous fixed rear wing, the GTR generated ten percent more downforce than the road legal P1 and was also able to brake from 60mph to zero in 85ft.

Inside, the P1 GTR was certainly all business. Bare carbon-fibre was everywhere; however, it was the detachable steering wheel with its slew of toggles, switches, and buttons and the sliding Lexan side windows that cemented the GTR's racing pedigree. There are plenty of cars that blur the fine line between road car and race car, and plenty of automakers that like playing in that space, too. McLaren did that with the P1 and P1 GTR.

With the production run of the P1 GTR complete, and prompted by their efforts in converting track-only P1 GTRs to road-legal specification, Lanzante Motorsport commissioned McLaren Special Operations division to build a further total of six new P1 GTRs for them to develop into road-legal P1 LM variants. Of this production run, five P1 LMs were sold and the sixth, the prototype P1 LM codenamed 'XP1 LM,' was retained and used for development and testing of future models.

MODEL	P1 GTR	TRANSMISSION	7-Speed Seamless-Shift Gearbox (SSG)	TYRES F/R	Pirelli P ZERO
TYPE/FORMULA	Racecar	CHASSIS	One-piece carbon-fibre MonoCell	LENGTH	
YEAR OF PRODUCTION	2015-2016	BODY	Carbon-fibre over aluminium front and rear frames	WIDTH	
DESIGNER	McLaren Automotive design team	FRONT SUSPENSION	McLaren ProActive Chassis Control,	HEIGHT	
EXAMPLES BUILT	58		double wishbone independent suspension	WHEELBASE	
ENGINE	McLaren M838TQ IPAS (V8 + electric)	REAR SUSPENSION	McLaren ProActive Chassis Control, double	TRACK F/R	
CUBIC CAPACITY	3799cc		wishbone independent suspension	WEIGHT	3175lb - 1440kg
INDUCTION	Twin turbocharged	BRAKES F/R	Akebono carbon ceramic discs	PRINCIPAL DRIVERS	n/a
POWER OUTPUT	986bhp	WHEELS DIAMETER x WIDTH F/R	19x 8.5/20x11in	IDENTIFYING COLOURS	n/a

2016 MP4-31 FORMULA 1

There was good reason for optimism in the 2016 season: Fernando Alonso had said in Brazil the previous year that he thought the McLaren MP4-30 chassis was really strong, and the 2016 MP4-31 was an evolution of it.

Honda had made considerable changes both to their engine and to the management of their programme. Yusuke Hasegawa – who had been one of Gerhard Berger's engineers during Honda's last partnership with McLaren — came in as executive chief engineer and head of the F1 project. Yasuhisa Arai was replaced by Yoshiyuki Matsumoto as senior managing officer and director, supervising director of the F1 project, and president, chief executive officer and representative director of R&D.

The RA616H power unit demonstrated solid progress in all areas, notably its energy recovery system. Development had focused on improving energy harvesting and deployment, and on achieving a broad band of usable horsepower rather than narrow peaks. A complete redesign of the turbo compressor and turbine facilitated much better energy harvesting and cured one of the previous season's problems, that of electrical energy running out well before the end of the straights on some circuits.

The unit retained the turbo-in-vee design of the RA615H, however, in the interests of space utilisation, weight and throttle lag control, and that created associated limitations. Hasegawa reckoned each of F1's four engines was separated by around 40bhp. Mercedes set the benchmark with around 1000bhp, that meant that the Ferrari had 960, the Renault

920 and the Honda 880. Back in Tochigi the focus was always on working to make up that deficit for 2017, when McLaren were expecting to challenge for podiums, if not wins.

The MP4-31 was an evolution of the MP4-30, still with a 'blown' front axle and an S-duct, but while the rear end was still very tightly packaged the rear suspension had been both strengthened and simplified, and the engine cover was higher to facilitate better airflow and thus engine breathing. Racing director Eric Boullier made progress at the factory in getting engineers - such as Tim Goss, Matt Morris and Neil Oatley, and aerodynamicist Peter Prodromou and their respective departments - to bring a more pragmatic engineering approach to bear. This had already started with the successful abandonment of the search for peak downforce figures and instead generating usable aero 'grunt' which, in 2015, had translated into attainable and reasonably competitive lap times.

This all generated a good step forward, and a base on which the McLaren-Honda partnership could continue to build. In pre-season tests the new car was troubled by understeer and niggling little problems. But reliability was much better and both Alonso and Jenson Button liked its enhanced rear-end stability and managed more than 2000 miles of running.

The MP4-31 proved to be reasonably competitive at many tracks, and from the start of the European season in May was a regular visitor to the final knock-out stages of qualifying. Fernando Alonso bounced back well from a massive shunt in the season-opening Australian GP, despite

having to miss Bahrain too, and was a strong team leader who contributed 54 of the team's 76 points, courtesy of sixth in Russia, fifth in Monaco, sevenths in Hungary, Belgium, Singapore and Malaysia, fifth in America and tenth place finishes in both Brazil and Abu Dhabi.

By contrast, Jenson Button had a less satisfactory season as he headed into semi-retirement, often complaining of handling difficulties and scoring only 21 of those points with sixth in Austria, eighth in Germany, ninths in Spain, Monaco, Malaysia and America and tenth in Russia. When the car felt good, though, the 2009 champion was every bit as fast as he had been in his heyday.

The remaining point came via Stoffel Vandoorne, who took tenth on his debut in Bahrain when he substituted for Alonso. The Belgian GP2 star gave an accomplished account of himself, and was the driver who identified a 'dead' spot in the front wing's performance when it appeared to stall at a certain angle. That, and the engine's lack of pure grunt — which hurt the car's straightline speed – remained the MP4-31's abiding limitations.

If 2015 had been a massive disappointment 2016 proved to be a season of upward movement, but further changes behind the scenes were to come the following year. Ron Dennis, who had so brilliantly led the team to many of its World Championship successes, left the company after reaching an agreement with his fellow shareholders in McLaren Technology Group and McLaren Automotive to sell his shareholding in both companies.

MODEL	MP4-31	TRANSMISSION	McLaren seamless shift hand-operated 8-speed	TYRES F/R	Pirelli
TYPE/FORMULA	Formula 1	CHASSIS	Moulded carbon-fibre composite; driver controls and fuel cell	LENGTH	201.9in - 5129mm
YEAR OF PRODUCTION	2016	BODY	Carbon-fibre composite engine cover, sidepods, floor, nose, wings	WIDTH	70.8in - 1798mm
DESIGNER	McLaren Racing	FRONT SUSPENSION	Carbon-fibre wishbone and pushrod suspension	HEIGHT	37.4in - 950mm
EXAMPLES BUILT	4		elements operating inboard torsion bar and damper system	WHEELBASE	139.0in - 3531mm
ENGINE	Honda RA616H V6 hybrid	REAR SUSPENSION	Carbon-fibre wishbone and pushrod suspension	TRACK F/R	58.8/56.6in - 1494/1439mm
CUBIC CAPACITY	1598cc		elements operating inboard torsion bar and damper system	WEIGHT	1427lb - 647kg
ELECTRONICS	MAT (McLaren Applied Technologies)	BRAKES F/R	Outboard carbon-fibre discs, pads, Akebono calipers	PRINCIPAL DRIVERS	Button, Alonso, Vandoorne
POWER OUTPUT	860bhp	WHEELS DIAMETER x WIDTH F/R	13x12/13x13.7in	IDENTIFYING COLOURS	Grey

2016 540C
ROADCAR

Less than a month after announcing the first car in their 'Sports Series', the 570S Coupé in New York, McLaren showed off the second car in the series, the 540C, at the 2015 Shanghai Auto Show. The most attainable McLaren yet, the 540C Coupé joined the 570S to brings its race derived DNA to a new audience and segment.

Technically, the 540C could be regarded as McLaren's entry-level car, although that classification seemed more than a little unfair. While it was certainly the cheapest car the company offered, it still got the same mid-mounted 3.8-litre twin-turbocharged V8 like almost every other McLaren on sale. Although in the case of the 540C the power output was capped at 533bhp compared to the 562bhp of the 570S.

The 540C continued to sit with the 570S in McLaren's entry-level Sports Series range, the 625C (for the Asian market only), 650S and 675LT continued in the mid-range Super Series, while the P1 and its P1 GTR track variant were still part of the ultra-exclusive Ultimate Series.

At the heart of the 540C, as with the 570S, was the unique carbon-fibre MonoCell II chassis which featured new design updates with a greater focus on day-to-day usability, offering improved ingress to and egress from the cabin, along with class-leading occupant protection and safety. A dry weight of as low as 1,311kg (2,890lb) for the 540C was achieved as a result of this lightweight structure as well as the use of aluminium body panels. This figure saw the 540C almost 150kg lighter than its closest competitor.

Power was, as on most models in the McLaren range, delivered through the rear wheels via the now customary seven-speed seamless shift gearbox (SSG) which, aided by the low weight of the 540C, saw the 0 to 100km/h (62mph) sprint completed in 3.5 seconds, 0 to 200km/h (124mph) in just 10.5 seconds, and a top speed of 320km/h (199mph).

A subtly revised aerodynamic package and a dedicated wheel design marked out the 540C Coupé against the more powerful 570S Coupé. Unique aero blades below the front bumper channeled cold, clean air through the lower bodywork and up over the sculpted bonnet, flanked by large

LED headlamps. At the rear, the diffuser sat between the twin exhausts which exited below the rear bumper. The aerodynamically-led styling of the Sports Series Coupé featured intricately designed dihedral doors which included an elegant floating door tendon.

The 540C featured a newly-developed suspension system ensuring enhanced levels of driver engagement and refinement on both road and track. The system used front and rear anti-rollbars, Formula 1-style dual wishbones and independent adaptive dampers. The damper tuning was revised on 540C, compared to the 570S, with more focus on day-to-day road driving. Adaptive dampers offered control over bump and rebound settings using the familiar McLaren 'Normal', 'Sport' and 'Track' handling settings.

Inside the cabin, the 540C Coupé was luxuriously appointed with leather upholstery to the seats, dashboard and lower doors as standard. The 'floating' centre console featured a seven-inch IRIS touchscreen which controlled all elements of the infotainment system. The air conditioning controls were also incorporated, as first seen on the McLaren P1, minimising switchgear in the cabin. The touchscreen also controlled the standard satellite navigation, Bluetooth telephony and media streaming, voice activation and the audio media player.

MODEL	540C
TYPE/FORMULA	Roadcar
YEAR OF PRODUCTION	2016
DESIGNER	McLaren Automotive design team
EXAMPLES BUILT	Production numbers not released
ENGINE	McLaren M838TF V8
CUBIC CAPACITY	3799cc
INDUCTION	Twin turbocharged
POWER OUTPUT	533bhp

TRANSMISSION	7-speed Seamless-Shift Gearbox (SSG)
CHASSIS	One-piece carbon-fibre MonoCell
BODY	Carbon-fibre over aluminium front and rear frames
FRONT SUSPENSION	Adaptive dampers
	and double wishbone suspension
REAR SUSPENSION	Adaptive dampers
	and double wishbone suspension
BRAKES F/R	Carbon discs withcast iron aluminium calipers
WHEELS DIAMETER x WIDTH F/R	19x8.5/20x11in

TYRES F/R	Pirelli P ZERO
LENGTH	178.3in - 4530mm
WIDTH	82.5in - 2095mm
HEIGHT	47.3in - 1202mm
WHEELBASE	105.1in - 2670mm
TRACK F/R	65.2/62.3in - 1656/1583mm
WEIGHT	2890lb - 1311kg
PRINCIPAL DRIVERS	n/a
IDENTIFYING COLOURS	n/a

2016 570GT
ROADCAR

In late 2016 McLaren Automotive expanded the Sports Series with another new model, the third in the range — the McLaren 570GT. Practical enough for everyday use, the two-seat, mid-engined 570GT was the most refined and road-biased McLaren yet to emerge from Woking. Designed with a focus on day-to-day usability and long distance comfort, it offered increased levels of practicality while remaining a true McLaren sports car.

The McLaren 570GT joined the 570S Coupé and 540C Coupé (540C not sold in the US) as the third model in the recently announced Sports Series family. The clean lines of the revised glasshouse gave the 570GT a sleek and refined silhouette – the second of three bodystyles which would eventually complete the Sports Series. A glass panoramic roof provided a bright, open cabin which extended through the large rear glass hatch to create a luxurious and relaxing driving environment. Craftsmanship throughout the interior of the 570GT was, as one would expect, of the highest level,

upholstered and specified with quality materials and the latest technologies throughout. Under the skin, the 570GT was developed with its own unique setup to reflect its position in the Sports Series range, while retaining the supercar levels of engagement experienced on the 570S Coupé.

Sharing the newly developed suspension system with the other models in the Sports Series, the 570GT emphasised long distance comfort through a reduction in the spring rates — 15 percent at the front and 10 percent at the rear. Independent adaptive dampers could be dynamically adjusted through Normal, Sport and Track settings, and were coupled to front and rear anti-roll bars. The overall set up of the 570GT was been calibrated to enhance road and motorway driving, and aid ride quality over poor road surfaces. The electro-hydraulic steering system is retained from the 570S Coupé, but with a two percent reduced ratio that smoothens driver inputs at high speed.

MODEL	570GT		TRANSMISSION	7-speed Seamless-Shift Gearbox (SSG)		TYRES F/R	Pirelli P ZERO
TYPE/FORMULA	Roadcar		CHASSIS	One-piece carbon-fibre MonoCell		LENGTH	178.3in - 4530mm
YEAR OF PRODUCTION	2016-19		BODY	Carbon-fibre over aluminium front and rear frames		WIDTH	82.5in - 2095mm
DESIGNER	McLaren Automotive design team		FRONT SUSPENSION	McLaren ProActive Chassis Control,		HEIGHT	47.2in - 1201mm
EXAMPLES BUILT	Production numbers not released			double wishbone independent suspension		WHEELBASE	105.1in - 2670mm
ENGINE	McLaren M838TE V8		REAR SUSPENSION	McLaren ProActive Chassis Control,		TRACK F/R	65.9/67.3in - 1673/1618mm
CUBIC CAPACITY	3799cc			double wishbone independent suspension		WEIGHT	2976lb - 1350kg
INDUCTION	Twin turbocharged		BRAKES F/R	Carbon Ceramic discs with forged aluminium hubs		PRINCIPAL DRIVERS	n/a
POWER OUTPUT	562bhp		WHEELS DIAMETER x WIDTH F/R	19x8/20x10in		IDENTIFYING COLOURS	n/a

The 570GT was fitted with the McLaren-developed, 3.8-litre twin turbo V8 M838TE engine, which debuted in the 570S Coupé. Power and torque remained at 562bhp (570PS) and 443lb.ft (600 Nm). Power was delivered to the rear wheels via a seven-speed seamless-shift transmission, and featured adjustment through Normal, Sport and Track settings to produce the expected, rewarding and engaging driving experience. These settings include bespoke gearchange calibrations from comfort (Normal mode), Cylinder Cut (Sport mode) and Inertia Push (Track mode).

The revised design of the 570GT saw the glasshouse with clean and sleek lines leading to the rear of the car. The styling concepts on 570GT meant that it would, of course, never be seen in 'Spider' form.

The 570GT was probably the most practical model ever launched by McLaren Automotive, and targeted towards longer journeys and weekends away. As with all Sports Series models, ingress and egress were optimized through a lower and narrower door sill, while the signature dihedral doors opened with a more upward arc. Within the ergonomically-optimized cabin, the pair of eight-way electrically adjustable sports seats were upholstered in high quality leather as standard. The control interface for the automotive climate control, infotainment, and navigation systems were managed through the centrally-mounted touchscreen, while vehicle setup parameters could be viewed on the TFT instrument cluster.

The standard fixed glass Panoramic Roof glass was treated with 18 percent transmission tint – the same as the glass roof of the McLaren P1 – and also featured SSF (Sound & Solar Film) to absorb solar radiation while providing additional noise insulation. With the increased glass area of the 570GT, cabin temperatures were regulated and maintained by an enhanced dual-zone air conditioning system. This system allowed fully automatic and independent settings for both passenger and driver. A two-stage Automatic function — 'Auto' and 'Auto Lo' — allowed a desired temperature to be obtained, with the latter setting limiting speed of the fans to minimize noise within the cabin.

The front luggage area remained unchanged from the 570S Coupé at 5.3 cubic feet (150-litres) of space, while the 570GT added a further 7.8 cubic feet (220-litres) of storage on the leather-lined Touring Deck. This area could be accessed via the side opening glass hatch, and brought total storage capacity of the 570GT to 13.1 cubic feet (370-litres). The glass hatch opened on the curbside (whether left-hand or right-hand drive) and was framed by carbon-fibre which provided significant torsional rigidity.

Refinement and day-to-day usability were further enhanced through the latest tyre technology from McLaren Automotive technical partner, Pirelli who supplied specially developed Pirelli P ZERO tires which reduced in-cabin road noise by up to three decibels thanks to the innovative Pirelli Noise Cancelling System (PNCS): a new technology patented by Pirelli for reducing road noise.

2016 675LT SPIDER ROADCAR

In response to significant customer demand, in New York on December 3rd 2015, McLaren Automotive revealed the most recent chapter in the history of the iconic 'Longtail' name, with confirmation of a new model, the 675LT Spider. Strictly limited to just 500 examples worldwide, and nearly 20 years after McLaren had first used the name on the 1997 F1 Longtail, the 675LT would be the second model in the Super Series to wear the LT badge.

The 675LT Coupé focused on light weight, enhanced aerodynamics, increased power and track-focused dynamics, and this limited-run model quickly sold out, even before the first deliveries commenced.

The 675LT Spider was the fifth new model debuted by McLaren Automotive in 2015 in what had become a defining year for the British brand. This latest model joined the McLaren P1 GTR, 570S Coupé. 540C Coupé and the fixed-head 675LT Coupé new to the line-up, and further strengthened the Super Series range.

Under the skin of the 675LT Spider sat the heavily revised 3.8-litre twin-turbo V8 powertrain seen in its Coupé sibling, ensuring performance figures are worthy of the LT – or 'Longtail' – badge. The power output and torque figures remain unchanged, with 666bhp (675PS) delivered at 7,100rpm and 516lb.ft (700Nm) available between 5,000-6,500rpm. The changes to the powertrain saw more than 50 percent of the components replaced to ensure optimized levels of power, torque and drivability. These include new, more efficient turbos, detail design changes to the cylinder heads and exhaust manifolds, new camshaft and lightweight connecting rods, and a faster-flowing fuel pump and delivery system. In addition, the newly developed deep golden color,

Solis — which derives its name from the Latin for sun — was a bespoke color only available on the open-top 675LT Spider.

Staying true to the 'Longtail' ethos, established by the McLaren F1 in the late 1990s, the 675LT Spider was developed with a focus on light weight and optimized aerodynamic performance. The special nature of the model was supported by the extensive use of carbon-fibre for the bodywork. As with the 675LT Coupé, the front bumper with larger splitter and end plates, front under body, side skirts, side intakes, lower side intakes, rear bodyside lower, rear fenders, rear deck, rear bumper, diffuser and 'Longtail' Airbrake were all carbon-fibre.

The dramatic styling and purposeful stance of the 675LT was retained within the Spider variant, with the extended front splitter flanked by front wing end plates, each working the airflow harder and increasing downforce. Sculpted carbon-fibre door sills run along the lower edge of the bodywork, flowing in to a smaller air intake ahead of the rear wheels. This sits below the more pronounced side intake, with both feeding clean, cool air into the side radiators which are more prominent to offer increased cooling. The retractable hard top stows below a color-coded tonneau cover, and the engine remains visible through a lightweight vented polycarbonate engine cover. At the rear, the lightweight titanium crossover twin exhausts exit below the active 'Longtail' Airbrake which is 50 percent larger than other Super Series models. This is integrated into the design of the flowing rear wings and despite the larger size, carbon-fibre construction ensures weight is actually reduced. Exposed bodywork across the rear deck and below the rear wing aids engine cooling, while louvers in the flared rear bumper optimize pressure levels.

Lightweight components were also found throughout the powertrain and chassis, all contributing to a dry weight of just 2,800lb (1,270kg). This weight is a full 220lb (100kg) lighter than the already lightweight 650S Spider, and gives a power-to-weight figure of 4.2lb per bhp. Due to the inherent strength of the carbon-fibre MonoCell chassis, no further strengthening – and associated weight increase – was added through the removal of the roof, and the 675LT Spider was only 88lb (40kg) heavier than the Coupé, all due to the retractable roof system.

MODEL	675LT Spider
TYPE/FORMULA	Roadcar
YEAR OF PRODUCTION	2016
DESIGNER	McLaren Automotive design team
EXAMPLES BUILT	500
ENGINE	McLaren M838T V8
CUBIC CAPACITY	3799cc
INDUCTION	Twin turbocharged
POWER OUTPUT	666bhp

TRANSMISSION	7 Speed Seamless-Shift Gearbox (SSG)
CHASSIS	One-piece carbon-fibre MonoCell
BODY	Carbon-fibre over aluminium front and rear frames
FRONT SUSPENSION	McLaren ProActive Chassis Control, double wishbone independent suspension
REAR SUSPENSION	McLaren ProActive Chassis Control, double wishbone independent suspension
BRAKES F/R	Carbon Ceramic discs with forged aluminium hubs
WHEELS DIAMETER x WIDTH F/R	19x8/20x11in

TYRES F/R	235-35 ZR19/308-30 ZR20
LENGTH	178.9in - 4546mm
WIDTH	78.9in - 2095mm
HEIGHT	46.9in - 1192mm
WHEELBASE	105.1in - 2670mm
TRACK F/R	65.2/62.3in - 1656/1583mm
WEIGHT	2800lb - 1270kg
PRINCIPAL DRIVERS	n/a
IDENTIFYING COLOURS	n/a

2016 570S GT4 RACECAR

In 2015, McLaren debuted the new Sports Series, a family of sports cars that slotted below the Super Series and was aimed at cars such as the Porsche 911 Turbo. Having already launched three models, the 570S, 540C, and 570GT, in 2016 McLaren pushed the Sports Series into motorsport territory with the announcement of a track-only version called the 570S GT4. As the name suggests, the race-bred coupe was developed to GT4 specifications, which made it eligible for an array of US and European racing championships, including the GT4 European series.

The 570S GT4, developed by McLaren GT — the motorsport division of the McLaren Automotive — was set to enter an intensive season-long development programme in the British GT championship ahead of customer deliveries in 2017.

"The launch of the Sports Series has broadened McLaren to a new audience, introducing technologies to the sports car market and to a new group of customers. The 570S GT4 is doing the same in the motorsport world, and will bring the opportunity to own and race a McLaren — previously limited to a very small number of people — to a much wider group," said Mike Flewitt, CEO of McLaren Automotive.

The track-only 570S GT4 shared the carbon-fibre MonoCell II chassis architecture with the other models in the Sports Series and marked the first time the technology had been made available in the GT4 category. The race-derived material with it's inherent strength and light weight is of clear benefit in racing applications. Driver protection was further enhanced with the addition of an FIA-approved rollcage and fire extinguisher system. Carbon-fibre and aluminium were used for the reprofiled bodywork, which was formed over wider track both front and rear to accommodate centre-locking lightweight cast magnesium alloy wheels shod with slick Pirelli racing tyres. Two-way adjustable motorsport dampers with coil-over springs were fitted front and rear, and an on-board air jacking system fitted as standard.

With a pure focus on lap times, the 570S GT4 featured a unique aerodynamic package which included a GT4-specification high level rear wing, mounted on aluminium pylons, a larger front splitter and reprofiled floor assembly. An additional front centre high temperature radiator sat below a GT3-inspired bonnet with radiator exit ducts. These upgrades were designed to optimise the aerodynamic performance and cooling of the 570S GT4 and to ensure it was able to perform in the harshest race conditions globally.

Inside is where the biggest differences lie. Where the road car is all about keeping passengers comfy, the race car is stripped bare. A few details from the road car did survive – electric windows, for example, and the infotainment screen was still present as well, although it showed track data rather than your playlist. The familiar engine start was also present.

The McLaren designed and developed 3.8-litre twin turbo V8 M838TE engine was carried over from the road-going Sports Series model. The seven-speed seamless shift gearbox also familiar to the other models in the range, transferred power to the track via the rear wheels. In unrestricted form, the driver could expect 562bhp and 443lb-ft of torque, but this was of course dramatically decreased when race restrictions were added. For both the IMSA and Pirelli World Challenge series' cars were limited 440bhp.

Pricing for the 570S GT4 started from £159,900 (about $215,000), a price that made it the most expensive in the Sports Series. For reference, the road-going 570S was listed at £143,250 (around $202,000) before options. The 570S GT4 was though significantly cheaper than the 650S GT3, which at the time was selling for £330,000 ($467,000).

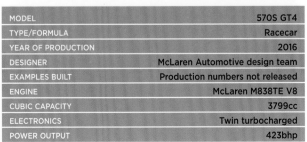

MODEL	570S GT4
TYPE/FORMULA	Racecar
YEAR OF PRODUCTION	2016
DESIGNER	McLaren Automotive design team
EXAMPLES BUILT	Production numbers not released
ENGINE	McLaren M838TE V8
CUBIC CAPACITY	3799cc
ELECTRONICS	Twin turbocharged
POWER OUTPUT	423bhp

TRANSMISSION	7-speed Sequential Shift Gearbox (SSG)
CHASSIS	Carbon-fibre MonoCell II
BODY	Aluminium and carbon-fibre panels
FRONT SUSPENSION	Motorsport adjustable dampers, coil-over springs and dual wishbones
REAR SUSPENSION	Motorsport adjustable dampers, coil-over springs and dual wishbones
BRAKES F/R	Cast Iron Discs with Forged Aluminium Hubs
WHEELS DIAMETER x WIDTH F/R	18x9/18x11in

TYRES F/R	Pirelli racing tyres: 265-645 R18/305-680 R18
LENGTH	181.3in - 4606mm
WIDTH	78.9in - 2095mm
HEIGHT	47.3in - 1202mm
WHEELBASE	105.3in - 2674mm
TRACK F/R	64.8/62.2in - 1647/1581mm
WEIGHT	3150lb - 1429kg
PRINCIPAL DRIVERS	n/a
IDENTIFYING COLOURS	n/a

2017 MCL-32 FORMULA 1

A new McLaren team faced the world in 2017: Zak Brown took over as Executive Director, with McLaren Group stalwart Jonathan Neale as Chief Operating Officer.

The internal changes had two external manifestations. The new car for the season appeared in an orange hue intended to reflect Bruce McLaren's influence on the team's rich history, along with a new type number to signify a new identity. Gone was the MP4 designation (which had originally stood for Marlboro Project 4) and in its place came MCL.

New technical rules dictated wider, more purposeful-looking cars, running wider tyres. Chief Technical Officer Tim Goss focused on saving weight as much as possible (even though the regulatory minimum weight went up from 1547lbs/702kg to 1602lbs/728kg) and lowering the centre of gravity, while Peter Prodromou addressed the front wing stall problem that had hampered the MP4-31. He also created distinctive gills on either side of the wing mounts, to enhance undercar airflow, and stuck with his philosophy of running the car at an aggressive rake angle.

Honda felt they had taken their existing internal combustion engine concept to its limits and therefore conducted a major redesign, which included catering for a new fuel limit upped to 105kg/hr from 100. The new RA617H, as expected, placed a larger-diameter IHI turbocharger outside the vee and drove it via a shaft, Mercedes-style. This should have boosted the power, but resonance issues and a mismatch between turbo and combustion chamber negated the potential gain.

Pre-season testing was beset by setbacks, and felt very much like 2015 all over again. The first failures were traced to a problem in the manufacture of the oil tank, but there was also an internal engine-related issue. Later there were electrical problems.

When testing had finished Mercedes had covered more

than six times the distance McLaren had completed. As the German team recorded over 2500 laps with their three teams, Ferrari over 2300 and Renault over 1700, during the eight days, McLaren were limited to 425. The longest run had been just 13 laps.

Lack of running had a knock-on effect on the flow of aerodynamic upgrades since the team hadn't completed enough distance to evaluate the launch spec properly. Exacerbating this was an ongoing spate of unreliability at races which led to Fernando Alonso and Stoffel Vandoorne frequently having to take penalties associated with power unit components – mostly notably the MGU-H — and starting from the back of the grid.

By the end of the season, the myriad power unit issues placed McLaren at the top of the chart for grid penalties, with 390. Vandoorne had 215, Alonso 160, Jenson Button (who substituted for Alonso in Monaco) 15, while the 18 other drivers who picked up similar penalties amassed 440 between them.

Lack of power meant the car had to be driven aggressively, often to the detriment of its tyres. One speed trap, at Barcelona in May, revealed that while Sebastian Vettel's Ferrari was reaching 326.5 kmh in qualifying, Daniel

Ricciardo's Renault-powered Red Bull 323.0, and Lewis Hamilton's Mercedes 322.7, Alonso's McLaren-Honda was peaking at 310.2.

Poor results were having a detrimental effect on Brown's quest for sponsorship and the team's overall position, and therefore its FOM earning power. They were bad, too, for morale. By Singapore a divorce had been thrashed out. Under its terms, McLaren would switch to Renault power units for 2018, while Honda would supply Toro Rosso, and then both Toro Rosso and Red Bull from 2019.

Throughout all the turmoil and despite his commitment to run at the Indianapolis 500, Alonso never gave less than his best. His late-season drives in particular, notably against Lewis Hamilton in Mexico, underlined yet again his determination. Vandoorne struggled initially, but later came good and at times matched the Spaniard's pace in what was a very difficult rookie season.

Alonso's best result was sixth with fastest lap in Hungary, while Vandoorne took a brace of sevenths in Singapore and Malaysia. In one of their toughest-ever seasons, McLaren finished ninth overall with 30 points.

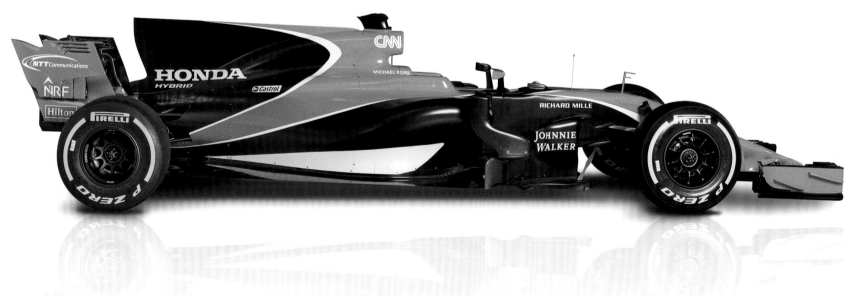

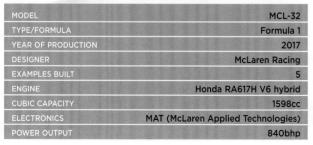

MODEL	MCL-32	TRANSMISSION	McLaren seamless shift hand-operated 8-speed	TYRES F/R	Pirelli
TYPE/FORMULA	Formula 1	CHASSIS	Moulded carbon-fibre composite; driver controls and fuel cell	LENGTH	213.7in - 5429mm
YEAR OF PRODUCTION	2017	BODY	Carbon-fibre composite engine cover, sidepods, floor, nose, wings	WIDTH	78.7in - 1998mm
DESIGNER	McLaren Racing	FRONT SUSPENSION	Carbon-fibre wishbone and pushrod suspension	HEIGHT	37.3in - 948mm
EXAMPLES BUILT	5		elements operating inboard torsion bar and damper system	WHEELBASE	138.6in - 3520mm
ENGINE	Honda RA617H V6 hybrid	REAR SUSPENSION	Carbon-fibre wishbone and pushrod suspension	TRACK F/R	65.1/61.3in - 1653/1558mm
CUBIC CAPACITY	1598cc		elements operating inboard torsion bar and damper system	WEIGHT	1440lb - 653kg
ELECTRONICS	MAT (McLaren Applied Technologies)	BRAKES F/R	Outboard carbon-fibre discs, pads Akebono calipers	PRINCIPAL DRIVERS	Button, Alonso, Vandoorne
POWER OUTPUT	840bhp	WHEELS DIAMETER x WIDTH F/R	13x13.7/13x16.9in	IDENTIFYING COLOURS	Black/Orange

MODEL	720S	TRANSMISSION	7-speed Seamless-Shift Gearbox (SSG)	TYRES F/R	Pirelli P ZERO
TYPE/FORMULA	Roadcar	CHASSIS	One-piece carbon-fibre MonoCell II	LENGTH	179in - 4543mm
YEAR OF PRODUCTION	2017	BODY	Carbon-fibre over aluminium front and rear frames	WIDTH	76in - 1930mm
DESIGNER	McLaren Automotive design team	FRONT SUSPENSION	Independent adaptive dampers, dual wishbones,	HEIGHT	47in - 1196mm
EXAMPLES BUILT	Currently in production		Proactive Chassis Control II (PCC II)	WHEELBASE	105.1in - 2670mm
ENGINE	McLaren M840T V8	REAR SUSPENSION	Independent adaptive dampers, dual wishbones,	TRACK F/R	65.9/64.2in - 1674/1629mm
CUBIC CAPACITY	3994cc		Proactive Chassis Control II (PCC II)	WEIGHT	2828lb - 1283kg
INDUCTION	Twin turbocharged	BRAKES F/R	Carbon Ceramic discs	PRINCIPAL DRIVERS	n/a
POWER OUTPUT	710bhp	WHEELS DIAMETER x WIDTH F/R	19x9/20x11in	IDENTIFYING COLOURS	n/a

McLaren Automotive began 2017 by announcing the introduction the first car in second-generation of their Super Series, the product family at the heart of the McLaren brand, the 720S. The new mid-engined, rear-wheel-drive supercar successor to the 650S Coupé was set to mark the dawn of a new era for the McLaren.

Lighter, faster, and even more dynamically capable than its predecessor and with unparalleled levels of interior space and sophistication, McLaren felt the new 720S had a breadth and depth of abilities that would involve and satisfy a driver in a way that no other car could. Deliveries were set to start in May of 2017.

"Super Series is the core of the McLaren business and personifies the blend of extreme performance, crafted luxury and unparalleled driver involvement that is the McLaren heartland. This is the first time we have replaced a product family and the new 720S is absolutely true to McLaren's pioneering spirit in being a revolutionary leap forwards, both for our brand and the supercar segment" commented Mike Flewitt, CEO at McLaren Automotive.

McLaren's expertise in carbon-fibre structures – every road car built by the British manufacturer since the McLaren F1 in 1993 has had a carbon-fibre chassis — underpinned the construction of the new 720S; the architecture of the car was based around a new carbon-fibre 'tub' and upper structure, the McLaren Monocage II. This technology delivers extreme strength and rigidity in a lightweight structure — the ideal base for any supercar. A range of aluminium alloys are also used extensively in the chassis, as well as for some body panels. This familiar central structure was key to the 720S' 2,828lb (1283kg) amazingly light weight and the unparalleled interior space and visibility of the 720S.

One of the key points in the design of the new 720S was the absence of radiator intakes on the side of the car. This function was now carried out by the new unique 'double-skin' aerodynamic form of the dihedral doors, which channelled air to the high-temperature radiators that cooled the revised, enlarged capacity, mid-mounted engine.

The new M480T engine powering the 720S continued the lineage of McLaren's multiple-award-winning, twin-turbocharged V8 engine series. Now pushed out to a full 4-litres, the engine generated a maximum of 710bhp and up to 568lb/ft of torque, delivering truly astonishing levels of performance. From standstill to 62mph (100kph) took less than three seconds and just five seconds later the car was able to pass the 124mph (200kph) mark. Maximum speed was quoted at 212mph (341kph). Braking was equally impressive, the new 720S coming to a halt from 124mph in just 4.6 seconds, covering 383ft.

Owners of the new 720S were set to benefit from the most involving driver experience ever from a McLaren Super Series car — an incredibly impressive benchmark in its own right — calling on huge reserves of grip, balance, and performance to enjoy the car to its full potential. Double the aerodynamic efficiency of the 650S and a new generation of McLaren's Proactive Chassis Control combined with new suspension and the established excellence of McLaren's power-assisted, electro-hydraulic steering to deliver a driving experience that was unmatched in terms of sheer breadth of capability. All of this, while completely at ease in a cabin environment that

McLaren felt established new standards in the supercar segment for visibility, space and comfort.

Together with a full complement of advanced convenience technologies, these attributes gave the new McLaren 720S an incredible degree of usability and validated its claim to be the most complete supercar on sale. "The 720S is a new chapter in the development of McLaren's design language; it has perfect proportions that bring our key design pillar of 'Everything for a Reason' together in one pure, aerodynamic-ally shrink-wrapped and sophisticated whole. McLaren is always brave in its approach and this car is the perfect expression of that innovative culture," said Rob Melville, Chief Designer of the McLaren Super Series.

2017 570S SPIDER ROADCAR

Unveiled to the public in July of 2017, three new exterior colors and an all-new, 10-spoke lightweight forged alloy wheel design, celebrated the launch of the 570S Spider. The two-piece retractable hardtop roof finished in any of these new body colors or contrasting Dark Palladium grey, fully enabled the Spider's lightweight, aluminium bodywork and beautifully-sculpted surfaces to maintain the design purity of Coupé when closed, and introduced a dramatic visual signature when open, accentuating the way in which the aluminium body panels 'wrap around' the cabin.

The breathtaking body design was enhanced by a rear spoiler, finished in Dark Palladium grey (a visible carbon fiber finish is available at additional cost via McLaren Special Operations) and the same aerodynamics as the 570S Coupé. The headlights referenced McLaren's Speedmark logo, sweeping dramatically around the light clusters and down into aggressive aero blades either side of the front splitter.

Electrically operated from the driver's seat using one simple control, the roof folded effortlessly to stow beneath a beautifully crafted tonneau cover that rose automatically to accommodate the lowered panels and returns to its closed position with the assistance of soft-close technology. The roof could be opened or closed in just 15 seconds, even at vehicle speeds of up to 25mph.

A glazed wind deflector could also be electrically closed or lowered at the push of a button, providing further versatility with the roof up or down. The deflector reduced wind-buffeting when the roof was down and if desired could be lowered when the roof was closed to allow additional sound and fresh air into the cabin. Owners wanting to enjoy even more of the distinctive exhaust note of the new Spider could specify an optional sports system that channelled exhaust sound towards the cabin, via the area beneath the tonneau cover.

The retractable hardtop was designed to withstand the severest conditions and is significantly more weather and fade resistant than fabric, yet with its operating mechanism added just 101lbs to the weight of the Spider; this was the only variance in weight between the new convertible and the 570S Coupé.

The new Spider employed racecar-style, double-wishbone suspension all-round, with steel springs, twin-valve adaptive dampers and anti-roll bars calibrated to the same specifications as the 570S Coupé. Body control was certainly exceptional

and the overall drive incredibly pure and rewarding, while retaining and impressive level of comfort. Accessing the Active Dynamics Panel added another level of personal choice, allowing the driver to choose from Normal, Sport or Track modes for progressively softer or firmer suspension. This versatility ensured that the Spider was as at ease in everyday use on the road as it was on the track.

Rob Melville, Design Director at McLaren Automotive was pleased with the results of the 570S Spider project. "Maintaining the purity of the Sports Series' form language was crucial when designing the 570S Spider and a retractable hardtop rather than a fabric roof was key to achieving this. The Spider has a purposeful, dramatic silhouette, roof up or down, but with the roof lowered beneath the tonneau deck the car also has a real sense of fun that perfectly captures and reflects the way it drives."

MODEL	570S Spider	TRANSMISSION	7-speed Seamless-Shift Gearbox (SSG)	TYRES F/R	225-35 R19/285-35 R20
TYPE/FORMULA	Roadcar	CHASSIS	One-piece carbon-fibre MonoCell II	LENGTH	178.3in - 4530mm
YEAR OF PRODUCTION	2017	BODY	Carbon-fibre over aluminium front and rear frames	WIDTH	76in - 1930mm
DESIGNER	McLaren Automotive design team	FRONT SUSPENSION	Independent adaptive dampers, and dual wishbones	HEIGHT	47.3in - 1202mm
EXAMPLES BUILT	Currently in production			WHEELBASE	105in - 2670mm
ENGINE	McLaren M838TE V8	REAR SUSPENSION	Independent adaptive dampers and dual wishbones	TRACK F/R	65.9/63.7in - 1674/1618mm
CUBIC CAPACITY	3799cc			WEIGHT	2895lb - 1359kg
INDUCTION	Twin turbocharged	BRAKES F/R	Carbon Ceramic discs, aluminium calipers	PRINCIPAL DRIVERS	n/a
POWER OUTPUT	562bhp	WHEELS DIAMETER x WIDTH F/R	19x8/20x10in	IDENTIFYING COLOURS	n/a

If 2017 signalled a rebirth of McLaren in company management terms, 2018 brought similar change in terms of technical partnership. For the first time ever a McLaren F1 car carried Renault logos.

Installing the Renault power unit in an evolution of the MCL32 brought its own challenges, since the design of the car had been well under way before the swap from Honda was confirmed. But after a troubled start the team enjoyed a relatively promising spell, which ultimately cushioned it later in the year when performance and reliability dipped.

Testing proved problematic once again as a number of small issues – ranging from an improperly secured rear wheel to cooling, battery and turbo problems – hampered progress on the opening day. The team put this down to the lateness of the switch from Honda to Renault power, which meant the car had been completed later than hoped. However, Fernando Alonso's performance on the final day, when he set a time half a second off Raikkonen's Ferrari on the same Pirelli hypersoft tyres, provided a much-needed boost.

The MCL33, which featured a livery that was a more faithful reflection of Bruce McLaren's papaya orange than its forerunner's, was what the team called an "ambitious" car. It retained the MCL32's relatively short wheelbase, high rake and front-end design, but featured novelties in the rear suspension, and the shrink-wrapped rear bodywork was an aggressive indicator that in their new engine partnership the team had not settled for safe conservatism. The absence of compromise also made it likely that issues would crop up initially, so it might be a while before the car started to show its true potential.

"We had minor issues but I think that was because we didn't do a good enough job to prepare the car," Boullier admitted candidly after the tests. "We were a little bit stretched in terms of lead time and delay — but these are our issues.

Very quickly we are going to get back to normal. And if you want to be competitive you have to be a bit aggressive and ambitious."

McLaren went to the first race in Melbourne expecting the reliability to be suspect, given the lack of testing mileage. "Not 100%," Boullier said, "because we have not run as much as we wanted, so there will be a higher risk of failure somewhere. Nevertheless, we had only minor issues, which were all different. A good rebuild of the car for Australia will help us to fix them."

And, indeed, it did. Alonso finished fifth and Vandoorne ninth in Australia. The Spaniard then took three sevenths and an eighth in the following races, before enduring a spate of unreliability. The MCL33 was sometimes a match for the Renault R.S.18, which of course used the same R.E.18 power unit, but over the season it was no match for the similarly propelled Red Bull RB14.

By Canada it had been revised, with new and distinctive 'crocodile' intakes on the modified nose, but its high rake hampered its straightline speed, and the abiding problem was the lack of understanding and optimal management of the wake flow off the front wheels. This meant the car was unable to maintain its levels of downforce in cornering. It took until mid-season to analyse and identify the problem, and by then the team realised there was no way to do anything meaningful about it with the existing chassis design. They were thus forced to run a bigger than necessary rear wing, adding drag which slowed the car in a straight line.

The points garnered early on would prove crucial in securing the team sixth overall with 62 points. Not even the driving skills of Alonso and Vandoorne could compensate as other teams added performance with new developments, while McLaren had to focus on understanding why their own upgrades hadn't delivered the anticipated results.

Senior engineers Tim Goss and Matt Morris left the team along with racing chief Eric Boullier mid-season, and McLaren announced the recruitment of Toro Rosso's James Key as new Technical Director — though he would have to serve gardening leave until early 2019. Indianapolis 500 winner Gil de Ferran joined as Sporting Director, while former Benetton, McLaren, Ferrari and Manor stalwart Pat Fry joined on a consultancy basis to bring a fresh perspective to the design programme.

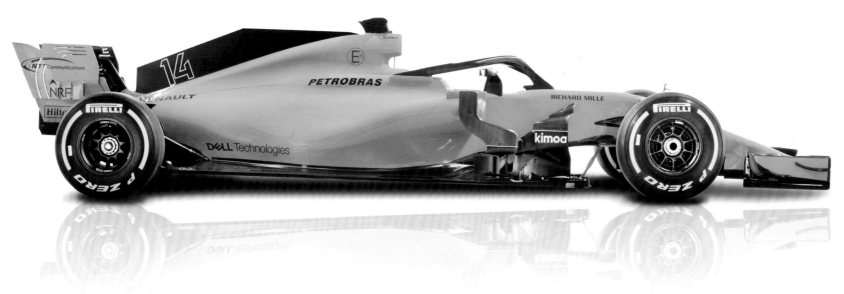

MODEL	MCL-33
TYPE/FORMULA	Formula 1
YEAR OF PRODUCTION	2018
DESIGNER	McLaren Racing
EXAMPLES BUILT	4
ENGINE	Renault RE18 V6 hybrid
CUBIC CAPACITY	1598cc
ELECTRONICS	MAT (McLaren Applied Technologies)
POWER OUTPUT	860bhp

TRANSMISSION	McLaren seamless shift hand-operated 8-speed
CHASSIS	Moulded carbon-fibre composite; driver controls and fuel cell
BODY	Carbon-fibre composite engine cover, sidepods, floor, nose, wings
FRONT SUSPENSION	Carbon-fibre wishbone and pushrod suspension elements operating inboard torsion bar and damper system
REAR SUSPENSION	Carbon-fibre wishbone and pushrod suspension elements operating inboard torsion bar and damper system
BRAKES F/R	Outboard carbon-fibre discs, pads, Akebono calipers
WHEELS DIAMETER x WIDTH F/R	13x13.7/13x16.9in

TYRES F/R	Pirelli
LENGTH	215.6in - 5477mm
WIDTH	78.7in - 1998mm
HEIGHT	37.3in - 948mm
WHEELBASE	140.5in - 3568mm
TRACK F/R	65.1/61.3in - 1653/1558mm
WEIGHT	1410lb - 640kg
PRINCIPAL DRIVERS	Alonso, Vandoorne
IDENTIFYING COLOURS	Papaya

2018 600LT
ROADCAR

Available to order from the summer of 2018, the 600LT Spider fully embodied the McLaren Longtail philosophy of increased power, reduced weight, optimized aerodynamics, track-focused dynamics and limited availability. In addition, it brought a new dimension of excitement over the 600LT Coupé, without compromise to the dynamic purity of the most performance-focused car in the Sports Series line-up: a retractable hardtop to give the choice of open-air driving.

Inspired by the McLaren 675LT models and their iconic 'Longtail' McLaren F1 GTR racing predecessor, the new addition to the LT family had all the physical hallmarks of a true McLaren 'Longtail', including an extended front splitter, lengthened rear diffuser, fixed rear wing and elongated silhouette – in this case by 2.9-inches, compared to the 570S Coupé.

A significant contributor to the 600LT's excellence on a track was the unique bodywork optimised aerodynamic performance, working in conjunction with a flat carbon-fibre floor to produce 220lbs of downforce at 155mph, that generated the increased grip and greater high-speed stability.

The 600LT epitomised the McLaren philosophy of producing lightweight super-sportscars that deliver extreme performance and are exceptionally rewarding to drive. With the engine management system of the 3.8-litre twin-turbocharged V8 recalibrated and reduced back pressure from a top-exit exhaust system that was even shorter and more extreme than that of the soon to be released McLaren Senna, allowing the engine to breathe more freely, the 600LT could call on peak power of 592bhp (600PS) at 7,500rpm and a maximum torque output of 457lb ft at 5,500-6,500rpm. These outputs again delivered astonishing levels

of performance: 0-62mph took just 2.9 seconds, matching the acceleration of the revered McLaren 675LT (with 0-60mph in 2.8 seconds). The 0-124mph figure could be achieved in a remarkable 8.2 seconds and the 600LT could continue gathering speed to a maximum of 204mph.

Bespoke P ZERO Trofeo R tires – developed with McLaren Technical Partner, Pirelli – were featured for the first time in the McLaren Sports Series. This unique track-focused tyre was a crucial element in the enhanced dynamic abilities of the 600LT. Tuned to help deliver the immediacy and steering feel for which McLaren was unquestionably renowned, as well as excellent rear-axle stability, the ultra-high-performance tyre featured a softer sidewall structure than was usual to improve compliance and thereby grip levels by ensuring the contact patch with the ground was maintained, even on less-than-perfect surfaces. By contrast, the belt construction of the Trofeo R tyre was stiffer than on any previous Sports Series tyre, to enhance lateral acceleration and improve cornering ability.

Combining with the new tyres were two new designs of forged Ultra-Lightweight aluminium alloy wheels — 10-spoke as standard and a 5-spoke alternative as a cost-option — which were the lightest wheels ever fitted to a Sports Series model, the reduction in unsprung weight bringing a tangible benefit to the dynamic qualities of the car.

Availability of the 600LT was set to be strictly limited, and the carbon-fibre body panels that required specialist tooling were just one of the reasons that the new 'Longtail' would be a rarer beast than the other models in the Sports Series.

The remit of any McLaren 'Longtail' was to engage and excite

to the absolute maximum, encouraging and enabling a driver to fully exploit the dynamic performance inherent in the car. The ethos underpinning every aspect of the development of the 600LT was a determination to deliver the purest possible connection between car and driver. To this end, the car had lighter and stiffer suspension components from the McLaren Super Series, the adoption of the forged aluminium double wishbones and uprights not only improving dynamic capabilities but also reducing weight by 22.5lbs. Ride height was reduced by 8mm and front track increased by 10mm, to deliver a more precise driving experience. The independent, continuously variable adaptive dampers and front and rear anti-roll bars that feature on all McLaren Sports Series models were retained but were significantly re-engineered to work with the new suspension geometry and deliver the track-focused performance demanded of the new 600LT.

The adoption of the braking system from the Super Series, which featured lightweight aluminium calipers and stiffer carbon ceramic discs, reduced weight by 8.8lbs. Working in conjunction with an all-new brake booster developed for the McLaren Senna, the result was incredibly responsive and progressive pedal feel during braking.

Rob Melville, Design Director at McLaren Automotive commented. "To stay true to its iconic race-bred predecessor, enhanced downforce and aerodynamics are at the heart of the McLaren 600LT. The 'Longtail' name gave us the freedom to push the envelope on the most extreme road-legal model in the Sports Series. We've been brave in creating the top-exit exhausts, but as well as their unique sound and visual appearance, this delivered tremendous opportunities to enhance aerodynamic performance because our aesthetic and technical designs are integrally linked."

MODEL	600LT	TRANSMISSION	7-speed Seamless-Shift Gearbox (SSG)	TYRES F/R	Pirelli P ZERO Trofeo R
TYPE/FORMULA	Roadcar	CHASSIS	Carbon-fibre monocoque, aluminium front/rear crash structures	LENGTH	181.3in - 4605mm
YEAR OF PRODUCTION	2018	BODY	Carbon-fibre over front and rear frames	WIDTH	76in - 1930mm
DESIGNER	McLaren Automotive design team	FRONT SUSPENSION	Independent adaptive dampers,	HEIGHT	47in - 1194mm
EXAMPLES BUILT	Production numbers not released		aluminium dual wishbones	WHEELBASE	105in - 2670mm
ENGINE	McLaren M838TE V8	REAR SUSPENSION	Independent adaptive dampers,	TRACK F/R	66.1/62.6in - 1679/1590mm
CUBIC CAPACITY	3799cc		aluminium dual wishbones	WEIGHT	2749lb - 1247kg
ELECTRONICS	Twin turbocharged	BRAKES F/R	Carbon Ceramic discs	PRINCIPAL DRIVERS	n/a
POWER OUTPUT	592bhp	WHEELS DIAMETER x WIDTH F/R	19x8/20x10in	IDENTIFYING COLOURS	n/a

2018 McLAREN SENNA
ROADCAR

Bearing the name of legendary McLaren, Williams, Lotus and Toleman Formula 1 driver, Ayrton Senna, and befitting its status as the ultimate McLaren road-legal track car, The McLaren Senna was designed, engineered and developed with single-minded purpose: to be the ultimate McLaren track car for the road. Legalized for road use, but not sanitized to suit it, the Senna was the second car in the 'Ultimate Series' that deliberately compromised McLaren's trademark breadth of supercar daily usability to deliver the most intense circuit experience of any road McLaren.

True to the legendary abilities of one of McLaren's greatest racers, every element of the McLaren Senna was an uncompromising performance ethos and a raw focus that delivered the purest connection between driver and car; this was the most responsive and engaging road-going McLaren ever. To this end, the appearance of the car was deliberately aggressive; organic shapes have gave way to a design language that was purposely fragmented in its pursuit of absolute performance, with downforce and aerodynamic balance the guiding principles. The McLaren Senna was the strongest expression yet of McLaren's 'form follows function' philosophy.

At the launch of the Senna at the 2018 Geneva Motor Show, Mike Flewitt, CEO at McLaren Automotive commented "The McLaren Senna is a car like no other: the personification of McLaren's motorsport DNA, legalized for road use but designed and developed from the outset to excel on a circuit. Every element of this new Ultimate Series McLaren has an uncompromised performance focus, honed to ensure the purest possible connection between driver and machine and deliver the ultimate track driving experience in the way that only a McLaren can."

The carbon structure at the core of the McLaren Senna, the McLaren Monocage III, was the perfect complement to the aerodynamics and powertrain. This strongest monocoque that McLaren had ever built for a road legal vehicle, Monocage III combined with an all-carbon body and uncompromising lightweight engineering throughout to make the McLaren Senna the lightest McLaren since the iconic F1.

The weight of 2,641lbs and the 789bhp power output from 4.0-liter twin-turbo V8, the most powerful McLaren road car internal combustion engine ever, gave the McLaren Senna a power-to-weight ratio of 659bhp-per-ton and truly savage performance: 124mph in just 6.8 seconds, with 62mph achieved in 2.8 seconds and 186mph in 18.8 seconds.

In the pursuit of even lighter weight, the airbags, infotainment screen and folding driver display were all removed, and the car was been fitted with a race-style steering wheel. However, the car did retain air conditioning, something owners probably appreciated during high-adrenaline track driving.

McLaren's designers went to extremes, visually and functionally cutting open the shrink-wrapped body to reduce weight. Proportionally, this is recognisably a McLaren but its hard to follow a single line from the front to the rear without it passing through a functional intake or vent. Airflow hitting the nose of the McLaren Senna met with four different surfaces, and was turned by each element in sequence: the front splitter; the active aero blades: secondary fixed aero blades and the slot-gaps located between the headlights and daytime running lights.

The leading edge of the Senna is a front splitter that was nearly six inches longer than the front splitter on the McLaren P1 and three inches longer than front splitter on the McLaren P1 GTR. It jutted out into the free-stream airflow, optimizing downforce not only in a straight line, but also during cornering. The carbon-fibre splitter was engineered to be as thin as possible, minimizing its intrusion into the airflow, while still meeting all legislative requirements. The front section could also be easily removed and replaced, meaning any damage caused by large curbs at race circuits could be rectified without having to change the entire splitter.

An innovative new hydraulic suspension system developed for the Senna, RaceActive Chassis Control II, worked in harmony with the active aerodynamics and sacrificed daily usability for circuit pre-eminence. Selecting Race mode brought the uncompromising nature of the McLaren Senna to the fore, the hydraulic suspension increasing roll stiffness and reducing ride height to lower the center of gravity and further improve aerodynamic performance. Aerodynamic control is fundamental and the cars Active front and rear aerodynamics helped endow the Senna with up to 1,763.7lbs (800kg) of total downforce and truly astonishing dynamic performance and circuit lap times.

"The McLaren Senna honors my uncle because it is so utterly focused upon the driver, and their absolute connection with the vehicle. This engagement, these sensory cues that the driver responds to and relies upon, the whole immersive experience, has been at the heart of the development from the very start," said McLaren ambassador Bruno Senna, the racing driver, nephew of Ayrton Senna.

MODEL	Senna
TYPE/FORMULA	Roadcar
YEAR OF PRODUCTION	2018-2019
DESIGNER	McLaren Automotive design team
EXAMPLES BUILT	500
ENGINE	McLaren M840TR V8
CUBIC CAPACITY	3994cc
INDUCTION	Twin turbocharged
POWER OUTPUT	789bhp

TRANSMISSION	7 Speed Seamless-Shift Gearbox (SSG)
CHASSIS	Carbon-fibre Monocage III
BODY	Carbon-fibre MonoCage, Aluminium Front and Rear Frames
FRONT SUSPENSION	McLaren RaceActive Chassis Control II, double wishbones independent interconnected hydraulic dampers
REAR SUSPENSION	McLaren RaceActive Chassis Control II, double wishbones independent interconnected hydraulic dampers
BRAKES F/R	CCM-R carbon ceramic discs with machined cooling vanes
WHEELS DIAMETER x WIDTH F/R	19x8/20x10in

TYRES F/R	245-35 R19/315-30 R20
LENGTH	186.8in - 4745mm
WIDTH	76.5in - 1950mm
HEIGHT	47.1in - 1195mm
WHEELBASE	105in - 2670mm
TRACK F/R	65.3/63.1in - 1658/1604mm
WEIGHT	2641lb - 1198kg
PRINCIPAL DRIVERS	n/a
IDENTIFYING COLOURS	n/a

2018 720S GT3 RACECAR

In November 2017, McLaren Automotive confirmed plans for a GT3 version of the 720S which would test throughout 2018 and launch with customer teams for the 2019 season. Following an extensive development programme for the new model over the course of 2018, the new 720S GT3 made its public debut at the Bahrain GT Festival almost a year-to-the-day later, ahead of its maiden competitive appearance at the Gulf 12-Hours race in Abu Dhabi.

The 720S GT3 was the first car designed and built by McLaren Customer Racing – the in-house motorsport department of McLaren Automotive – and ahead of initial deliveries to customer teams for the 2019 season, the new car ran at the Pure McLaren customer event held at the Bahrain International Circuit before making its public debut during the Bahrain GT Festival. The car was demonstrated on track, and formed a central attraction on display in the paddock during the event, which incorporated the inaugural FIA GT Nations Cup and SRO GT4 International Cup.

Following this appearance, the 720S GT3 then faced its most demanding challenge at the Gulf 12-Hours event on 13-15 December. One car, entered by McLaren Customer Racing, lined up on the grid at the Yas Marina circuit, home of the Abu Dhabi Grand Prix, for the final important stage of the development test programme before customer team deliveries. On its competitive debut, after leading the race for 10-hours, the end result saw the 720S GT3 cross the line an impressive fifth in the GT3 Pro class and eighth overall. More importantly, the 720S GT3 showed impressive race pace, and provided the team with valuable race data.

"It has been a great start to the competitive life of the 720S GT3, which has proven itself against a world-class field and just as importantly, successfully progressed the development programme. I am incredibly proud of the efforts of the team at the circuit and back in Woking, who have achieved this result against world-class opposition.

"The experience of going wheel-to-wheel with the teams and cars that our customers will be aiming to beat with the 720S GT3 in the future has proved invaluable as we continue to learn lessons about how to get the very best from the car. Add that experience to the vast amount that we have learned during the design, build, testing and development with the 720S GT3 so far, and we are growing in confidence about the prospects for the newest racing member of the McLaren family", said Dan Walmsley, McLaren Automotive, Motorsport Director.

Around 90 percent of the 720S GT3 was bespoke or had been enhanced from the 720S road car on which it was based. Importantly, at its core remained the same carbon-fiber monocoque chassis. A race-prepared version of the road car's 4.0-liter twin-turbo V8 made its debut, but instead of being paired to a dual-clutch transmission, it got power to the wheels via a six-speed sequential motorsport gearbox. The 720S GT3 also received a host of changes inside and out to comply with 2019 FIA GT3 regulations. The cabin featured a newly developed roll cage, fixed carbon-kevlar racing seat,

six-point harness, roof hatch extraction system, and side-impact protection. And a whole lot of new aerodynamics. The front and the rear were designed for maximum aerodynamic efficiency using computational fluid dynamics (CFD). Like wind-tunnel development, CFD helps make sure air travels around the car as smoothly as possible, but it is a much more efficient process. The 720S GT3 also featured new suspension geometry with four-way adjustable dampers and coil-overs, as well as an air-jack system and driver-adjustable traction control and ABS.

A main focus during the design and development of the 720S GT3 was to make a more accessible for teams and drivers – importantly in terms of drivability, but also from financial and serviceability perspectives as well. Fuel efficiency and tyre management were also a key focus area during the development progamme, too, working with Pirelli to run several endurance tests ahead of the 2019 season. And it paid off straight from the start. On the car's customer team debut, the 720S GT3 made history at the Albert Park circuit in Melbourne by claiming pole position and race victory.

MODEL	720S GT3	TRANSMISSION	6-Speed sequential	TYRES F/R	Pirelli P ZERO
TYPE/FORMULA	Racecar	CHASSIS	McLaren carbon-fibre MonoCage II	LENGTH	183.6in - 4664mm
YEAR OF PRODUCTION	2018	BODY	Bespoke lightweight carbon-fibre composite panels	WIDTH	80.3in - 2040mm
DESIGNER	McLaren Automotive design team	FRONT SUSPENSION	Motorsport adjustable dampers,	HEIGHT	47.3in - 1202mm
EXAMPLES BUILT	Production numbers not released		coil-over springs and dual wishbones	WHEELBASE	106.1in - 2696mm
ENGINE	McLaren M840T V8	REAR SUSPENSION	Motorsport adjustable dampers,	TRACK F/R	68.7/67.6in - 1745/1716mm
CUBIC CAPACITY	3994cc		coil-over springs and dual wishbones	WEIGHT	3150lb - 1429kg
INDUCTION	Twin turbocharged	BRAKES F/R	Cast Iron Discs with Forged Aluminium Hubs	PRINCIPAL DRIVERS	n/a
POWER OUTPUT	710bhp	WHEELS DIAMETER x WIDTH F/R	12.5x18/13x18in	IDENTIFYING COLOURS	n/a

2019 McLAREN SENNA GTR RACECAR

The McLaren Senna GTR, the track-only McLaren Hypercar that had debuted in concept form at the Geneva International Motor Show in March of 2018 and sold-out in the same month, actually began dynamic testing before the end of the year, ahead of its official launch just twelve month later at the 2019 edition of the same event in Switzerland.

"The McLaren Senna GTR is a perfect example of our determination to bring our customers the Ultimate expression of track driving performance and excitement. The McLaren Senna was designed from the outset to be an extreme track car, but the 2018 McLaren Senna GTR Concept suggested how much more further we could go and now, free from the constraints of road car legislation and motorsport competition rules, we have pushed the limits of what is technically possible to advance circuit driving capability to another level entirely" CEO of McLaren Automotive Mike Flewitt told journalists at that initial 2018 announcement.

With production of this even more extreme version of the road-legal McLaren Senna capped at 75 examples, and priced at around $1.4 million plus taxes (dependent on customer specifications), all 75 were sold well before the first cars which joined the McLaren Senna and McLaren Speedtail in the brand's Ultimate Series, were delivered to customers in September of 2019.

Each Senna GTR offered its owner virtually unlimited opportunities for personalization by McLaren Special Operations Options, from paint colors in the MSO Defined portfolio to unique, multi-hued liveries as an MSO Bespoke commission that imagined a wholly individual expression of track car artistry.

The McLaren Senna GTR is powered by the most extreme version yet of McLaren's 4.0-liter twin turbocharged V8 engine. The M840TR unit, with electronically controlled twin-scroll turbochargers, produces 814bhp with 590lb ft of torque. The extra 25bhp over the engine in the McLaren Senna has been achieved by engine control recalibration and removing the secondary catalyst to reduce back pressure. Removing the catalyst also heightens the aural experience of driving the McLaren Senna GTR. The dry weight of 2,619lbs meant the Senna GTR had a power-to-weight ratio of 694bhp-per ton.

The exhaust system of the concept car shown here, which actually exited through side pipes just ahead of the rear wheels, was replaced with a more conventional rear exit system on the production cars, with the pipes emerging from the rear deck under the rear wing in the same location as on the road-legal Senna. The change was made for the purest of engineering reasons: the side exit pipes may have looked the part, but the rear exit pipes provided the shortest, quickest route for exhaust gases to exit, saving weight and reducing complexity.

Three powertrain modes were available to the McLaren Senna GTR driver: Wet, Track and Race. The newly devised Wet setting, provided greater support from the ESP and ABS electronic systems and was particularly intended for use with wet tires. The transmission, which included a new Launch Control function, was the same, 7-speed plus reverse Seamless Shift Gearbox (SSG) that featured in the road-legal McLaren Senna.

Compared to the standard McLaren Senna wing fitted to the 2018 GTR Concept, the wing of the production McLaren Senna GTR was reprofiled and relocated, pushed backwards so that its trailing edge was now outside the car's footprint. This new, 'free of road car restrictions' position allowed the wing to be coupled to the diffuser, making best use of the air flowing over the rear of the car.

Like the road-legal McLaren Senna, the McLaren Senna GTR of course featured active aerodynamics in the shape of the active aero blades flanking the Low Temperature Radiator and an articulated rear wing – elements that were not currently permitted in GT3 racing but bring significant aero advantages. The wing could be 'stalled' for maximum speed thanks to a driver activated drag reduction system (DRS).

The McLaren Senna GTR was 22lbs lighter than even the McLaren Senna, already a paragon of race-bred leanness. And this is despite the track car's wider track, extended body and the fitment of essential track equipment including pneumatic air jacks, pit radio, fire extinguishing system and data logger. Many of the creature comforts fitted to the McLaren Senna were deleted for the McLaren Senna GTR, including touch screens and the audio system, air-conditioning was however retained. As with the road-legal Senna, the engine start button is mounted in the roof. And when that big red button is pressed, the McLaren Senna GTR snarls into life, ready to deliver Ultimate thrills on the track.

MODEL	Senna GTR	TRANSMISSION	7-speed Seamless-Shift Gearbox (SSG)	TYRES F/R	Pirelli P ZERO
TYPE/FORMULA	Racecar	CHASSIS	Carbon-fibre Monocage III	LENGTH	
YEAR OF PRODUCTION	2019	BODY	Carbon-fibre MonoCage, Aluminium Front and Rear Frames	WIDTH	
DESIGNER	McLaren Automotive design team	FRONT SUSPENSION	McLaren RaceActive Chassis Control II,	HEIGHT	
EXAMPLES BUILT	75		double wishbones independent interconnected hydraulic dampers	WHEELBASE	105in - 2670mm
ENGINE	McLaren M840TR V8	REAR SUSPENSION	McLaren RaceActive Chassis Control II,	TRACK F/R	68.2/66.4in - 1732/1686mm
CUBIC CAPACITY	3994cc		double wishbones independent interconnected hydraulic dampers	WEIGHT	2619lb - 1188kg
INDUCTION	Twin turbocharged	BRAKES F/R	Cast Iron Discs with Forged Aluminium Hubs	PRINCIPAL DRIVERS	n/a
POWER OUTPUT	814bhp	WHEELS DIAMETER x WIDTH F/R	18x10/18x12in	IDENTIFYING COLOURS	n/a

2019 MCL-34
FORMULA 1

Following Fernando Alonso's decision to retire from F1 and race elsewhere, McLaren rallied again around a heavily revised new car and a new driver pairing: Carlos Sainz and promising British rookie Lando Norris.

2018 had provided a hard lesson to those who believed the Renault engine would solve everything that had been perceived to be wrong when Honda were supplying McLaren's power units. The result of this humbling was a great deal of soul-searching. Many practices within the company were examined and revised, notably how tools such as the wind tunnel and computational fluid dynamics were applied in the research and development department. The MCL33 had taught the engineers that if an inherent flaw escaped notice early in the process, it would remain a fundamental shortcoming no matter how much development they subsequently threw at it.

While Peter Prodromou worked on solving the inherent aerodynamic riddles, and making changes for new rules which demanded simplified front and rear wings, Pat Fry brought his own brand of pragmatism to the chassis side. Renault upgraded their engine to give even more power and to cope with a revised fuel flow limit of 110kg/hr. The new car looked reasonable in testing, and reliability was good.

Necessarily, 2019 was a rebuilding year in which McLaren had to lay the new groundwork for their future while trying to make as much progress as possible.

New technical director James Key was able to come on board sooner than expected, in Bahrain in April, while Andreas Seidl – the Team Principal joining from Porsche's World Endurance Championship programme – was announced in January and arrived in May. Both brought an air of calm technical ability with them that helped to boost spirits further, and development of the MCL34 kept pace with rivals as McLaren became embroiled in the tight midfield battle where lap times were close and two or three teams could be bracketed within half a second.

Norris qualified eighth on his debut in Australia and should have scored points, but was one of several drivers who visited the pits early for scheduled stops and ended up in a queue behind the late-stopping Antonio Giovinazzi's Alfa Romeo. He therefore finished 12th when he could have been at least ninth. Sainz was an early retiree with an engine fire in Australia, and a gearbox problem eliminated him in Bahrain, but thereafter he was a regular top-10 finisher. He was fifth in Germany and Hungary, sixth in Monaco, France and Britain, seventh in Azerbaijan, and eighth in Spain and Austria. Norris scored his first points with sixth in Bahrain, then took another sixth in Austria, eighth in Azerbaijan,

ninths in France and Hungary, and 10th in Italy. But there was heartbreak in Belgium, when his engine stopped just as he started his final lap while he was running in fifth.

The MCL34 was still draggy in a straight line, but it was a strong all-rounder that was often able to qualify in the top 10 and contend for a decent helping of points in each race. Much of the time it was faster than Renault's RS19, and the fact that it continued to hold its own as the season continued was another major fillip to a team that were once more in the ascendant.

Behind the scenes there was more good news, as Key worked on his first car for the Woking team - the MCL35 — and Seidl secured board authority to initiate the building of a brand new wind tunnel, to come on stream for 2021.

MODEL	MCL-34	TRANSMISSION	McLaren seamless shift hand-operated 8-speed	TYRES F/R	Pirelli
TYPE/FORMULA	Formula 1	CHASSIS	Moulded carbon-fibre composite; driver controls and fuel cell	LENGTH	223.5in - 5677mm
YEAR OF PRODUCTION	2019	BODY	Carbon-fibre composite engine cover, sidepods, floor, nose, wings	WIDTH	78.7in - 1998mm
DESIGNER	McLaren Racing	FRONT SUSPENSION	Carbon-fibre wishbone and pushrod suspension	HEIGHT	37.3in - 948mm
EXAMPLES BUILT	4		elements operating inboard torsion bar and damper system	WHEELBASE	143.4in - 3643mm
ENGINE	Renault RE19 V6 hybrid	REAR SUSPENSION	Carbon-fibre wishbone and pushrod suspension	TRACK F/R	65.1/61.3in - 1653/1558mm
CUBIC CAPACITY	1598cc		elements operating inboard torsion bar and damper system	WEIGHT	1473lb - 668kg
ELECTRONICS	McLaren Applied Technologies (MAT)	BRAKES F/R	Outboard carbon-fibre discs, pads, Akebono calipers	PRINCIPAL DRIVERS	Sainz, Norris
POWER OUTPUT	910bhp	WHEELS DIAMETER x WIDTH F/R	13x13.7/13x16.9in	IDENTIFYING COLOURS	Papaya

2019 600LT SPIDER ROADCAR

Available to order in early 2019, the new 600LT Spider fully embodied the McLaren Longtail philosophy of increased power, reduced weight, optimized aerodynamics, track-focused dynamics and limited availability. In addition, it brought a new dimension of excitement over the 600LT Coupé, without compromise to the dynamic purity of the most performance-focused car in the Sports Series line-up: a retractable hardtop to give the choice of open-air driving.

Like the 600LT Coupé, the Spider recorded a significant weight saving over the model on which it was based, with McLaren's engineers achieving a reduction of 219.1lb over the 570S Spider the car it replaced. The result is a weight penalty of only 110.2lb over the Coupé, which contributes to a lightest dry weight for the Spider of just 2,859lb. This is at least 176.4lb less than any direct competitor and the resulting power-to-weight ratio of 457bhp-per-ton underpins astonishing levels of performance and dynamic prowess.

Enhancing the Sports Series Longtail experience with open-air motoring on the 600LT Spider was as easy as pushing a button to lower or raise the three-piece, powered retractable hardtop roof. An electrically-operated, glazed wind deflector could also be activated independently of the hardtop with the roof raised or lowered to reduce buffeting or increase ventilation – or simply to provide more of the aural and visual drama provided by the top-exit exhausts. When lowered, the roof stowed elegantly with the assistance of soft-close technology beneath a tonneau cover located behind the

seats; with the roof raised, this tonneau storage area provided an additional 1.8 cubic feet of luggage space.

"In creating the 600LT Coupé we took a radical decision to incorporate the top-exit exhausts, but it was an even greater challenge to make these work with the added complication of a retractable hardtop designed to operate whilst the car is in motion. It was certainly worth the effort; not only have we retained the 600LT's unique feature but we've also enhanced the visual and aural experience with the excitement and drama that only a spider can deliver," commented Rob Melville, Design Director, McLaren Automotive.

The same enhanced 592bhp powertrain as the 600LT Coupé enabled the driver to exploit the new Spider's dynamic abilities to the full, aided by a dual-clutch, Seamless Shift seven-speed Gearbox (SSG) featuring Ignition Cut and Inertia Push technology. The 600LT Spider could reach 60mph from a standstill in 2.8 (0-62mph in 2.9 seconds), with 124mph achieved in just 8.4 seconds – a near-indistinguishable 0.2 seconds slower than the Coupé. The maximum speed with the roof raised was 201mph; and with it lowered 196mph.

Performance was further enhanced by the lightweight carbon-fibre bodywork that created the Longtail silhouette and the same design of fixed rear wing as the Coupé, which – despite the aerodynamic challenges posed by a convertible body – generated the same 220.5lb of downforce at 155mph. The track-focused handling was assisted by a forged aluminium double-wishbone suspension system with recalibrated dampers, firmer engine mounts and a

lightweight braking system, and the Spider was fitted with bespoke 600LT Pirelli P ZERO™ Trofeo R tires.

The interior, featured lightweight Alcantara trim and carbon-fibre Racing Seats taken from the McLaren P1 as standard. The Super-Lightweight carbon-fibre Racing Seats that were designed for the McLaren Senna were also available as an option, either on their own or within the MSO Clubsport Pack. Other weight-saving options and measures – including deletion of the audio and climate control systems – are available to buyers determined to shave off every pound possible.

MODEL	600LT Spider		TRANSMISSION	7 Speed Seamless-Shift Gearbox (SSG)		TYRES F/R	Pirelli P ZERO Trofeo R: 225-35 R19/285-35 R20
TYPE/FORMULA	Roadcar		CHASSIS	Carbon-fibre monocoque, aluminium front/rear crash structures		LENGTH	181.3in - 4605mm
YEAR OF PRODUCTION	2019		BODY	Carbon-fibre over aluminium front and rear frames		WIDTH	76in - 1930mm
DESIGNER	McLaren Automotive design team		FRONT SUSPENSION	Independent adaptive dampers,		HEIGHT	47in - 1194mm
EXAMPLES BUILT	Currently in production			aluminium dual wishbones		WHEELBASE	105in - 2670mm
ENGINE	McLaren M838TE V8		REAR SUSPENSION	Independent adaptive dampers,		TRACK F/R	66.1/62.6in - 1679/1590mm
CUBIC CAPACITY	3799cc			aluminium dual wishbones		WEIGHT	2859lb - 1297kg
INDUCTION	Twin turbocharged		BRAKES F/R	Carbon Ceramic Discs		PRINCIPAL DRIVERS	n/a
POWER OUTPUT	592bhp		WHEELS DIAMETER x WIDTH F/R	19x8/20x11in		IDENTIFYING COLOURS	n/a

2019 720S SPIDER ROADCAR

Well over a year after the McLaren 720S Coupé redefined expectations in the supercar class when it was introduced in 2017, in February of 2019 McLaren automotive announced the release of the 720S Spider. The revised, patented electrically actuated roof system now delivered the fastest operating time in the supercar class, lowering or raising in 11 seconds at vehicle speeds of up to 31mph.

The design foundations of the new McLaren 720S Spider were of course shared with the 720S Coupé, the organic shapes that comprised the second-generation McLaren Super Series combining to maximize downforce, minimize drag, enhance powertrain cooling and optimize aerodynamic balance.

For the new Spider, a new, electrically actuated Retractable Hard Top (RHT) design and new buttresses were seamlessly integrated into the design. Like all McLaren cars, the 720S Spider has a carbon-fibre core, in this case with a new designation, Monocage II-S. The strength, rigidity and light weight of the structure was the base for the dynamic excellence for which McLarens are well renowned; the Monocage II-S was a logical development of the Coupé's Monocage II, without the central 'spine' running front to rear above the cabin and with the rearmost section of the upper structure also unique, to accommodate the Retractable Hard Top. The header rail across the top of the windscreen has also been revised, to suit the RHT sealing.

Comfortably the lightest car in its competitive set, with a weight of 2,937lb – 194lb less than the 3,131lb weight of its closest rival – the new 720S Spider was also lighter by 20lb

than the first-generation Super Series 650S Spider. The new Spider weighed in just 108lb above the 720S Coupé, the difference primarily associated with the RHT and tonneau system. The low weight offered a stunning power-to-weight ratio of 533bhp-per-ton (in comparison to 478bhp for the 650S Spider).

The 4.0-liter twin-turbocharged McLaren V8 engine that powered the 720S Spider was unchanged from the Coupé. The mid-mounted power unit produced 710bhp and 568lb.ft. of torque – outputs that support extreme performance. Acceleration subsequently was nothing short of phenomenal, with 0-60mph achieved in 2.8 seconds.

The standing quarter mile sprint could be dispatched in 10.4 seconds — only 0.1 seconds slower than the Coupé — and where conditions allowed, the 720S Spider could continue onwards to match the Coupé's top speed of 212mph (with the roof raised). Even with the roof lowered, maximum speed remained an extraordinary 202mph.

Owners who wanted to experience the open-air nature of the 720S Spider even with the roof closed could specify a carbon-fibre-framed, glazed RHT option that allowed even more light into the cabin. The glass on this option is electrochromic and could switch rapidly between a transparent or tinted state at the touch of a button. When the ignition is off, the glass reverted to its tinted setting, helping keep the cabin of the 720S Spider cool during hot days, and even has a memory function that recalls the previous setting selected when the vehicle is next started.

Andreas Bareis, Vehicle Line Director of the Super Series, who was heavily involved in the design work on the Spider commented, "The 720S Spider marks a revolutionary step forward in our pioneering use of carbon-fibre technology. Every McLaren built since 1981 has had a carbon core, but this is the first time a convertible has featured a carbon fibre upper structure. The windscreen surround, the rollover protection system and the architecture above the powertrain — in fact all integral parts of the new Monocage II-S — are constructed of carbon-fibre, as is the new Retractable Hard Top (RHT), including the frame and exterior panel."

MODEL	720S Spider	TRANSMISSION	7 Speed Seamless-Shift Gearbox (SSG)	TYRES F/R	Pirelli P ZERO
TYPE/FORMULA	Roadcar	CHASSIS	Carbon-fibre monocoque, aluminium front/rear crash structures	LENGTH	179in - 4543mm
YEAR OF PRODUCTION	2019	BODY	Carbon-fibre over aluminium front and rear frames	WIDTH	76in - 1930mm
DESIGNER	McLaren Automotive design team	FRONT SUSPENSION	Independent adaptive dampers,	HEIGHT	47in - 1196mm
EXAMPLES BUILT	Currently in production		dual aluminium wishbones, Proactive Chassis Control II (PCC II)	WHEELBASE	105in - 2670mm
ENGINE	McLaren M840T V8	REAR SUSPENSION	Independent adaptive dampers,	TRACK F/R	65.9/64.2in - 1674/1629mm
CUBIC CAPACITY	3994cc		dual aluminium wishbones, Proactive Chassis Control II (PCC II)	WEIGHT	2937lb - 1332kg
ELECTRONICS	Twin turbocharged	BRAKES F/R	Carbon Ceramic Discs	PRINCIPAL DRIVERS	n/a
POWER OUTPUT	710bhp	WHEELS DIAMETER x WIDTH F/R	19x9/20x11in	IDENTIFYING COLOURS	n/a

2019 GT
ROADCAR

2019 saw McLaren Automotive reveal its unique interpretation of a modern Grand Tourer. Positioned alongside the established Sports, Super and Ultimate Series families, the GT was a new McLaren for a new audience and provided an alternative to existing products in an expanding market segment. In re-imagining the spirit of traditional Grand Touring – long distance driving in comfort, at higher speeds and with room for luggage – McLaren redefined the modern GT ownership experience with a car that was lighter, faster and more engaging, a car with greater space, comfort and usability.

The bespoke MonoCell II-T monocoque – the T denoting 'Touring' – incorporated a carbon-fibre rear upper structure that added minimal weight but allowed the creation of 14.8 cubic feet of luggage area below the front-hinged, full-length glazed tailgate. The tailgate had a soft-close function as standard and could be optioned as electrically powered.

The low height of the engine and positioning of the exhaust system allowed the volume, shape and usability of the luggage bay to be optimized. A golf bag or two pairs of 185cm skis and boots, as well as luggage could be carried with ease, while a further 5.3 cubic feet of storage at the front meant the GT a total capacity of 20.1 cubic feet..

"The GT combines competition levels of performance with continent-crossing capability wrapped in a beautiful body and stays true to McLaren's ethos of designing superlight cars with a clear weight advantage over rivals. Designed for distance, it provides the comfort and space expected of a Grand Tourer, but with a level of agility never experienced before in this segment. In short, this is a car that redefines the notion of a Grand Tourer in a way that only a McLaren could." said Mike Flewitt, CEO at McLaren Automotive.

At a little more than 4-inches over 15 feet, the new McLaren was longer than any of the cars in the McLaren Sports or Super Series. The front and rear overhangs extended further than was traditional for McLaren of the modern era, but the 10-degree approach angle at the front (13-degree with vehicle lift engaged) meant that the GT could cope with the most aggressive sleeping-policemen (traffic calming measures!). This combination, with underbody clearance of 4.3in (5.1in with vehicle lift), ensured the car was eminently usable in all urban situations and in that 'lift' mode it was the equal of mainstream sedans.

The source of that performance on the GT was a new, 612bhp 4.0-litre, twin-turbocharged engine, designated M840TE. Further expanding the family of McLaren V8 engines, it was bespoke to the GT and has the immense power and torque and superior exhaust sound quality that are the hallmarks of a true Grand Tourer. Torque of 465lb ft was produced

between 5,500rpm and 6,500rpm, with more than 95% of this available from 3,000rpm to 7,250rpm. The new engine was of course mated to the now familiar 7-speed SSG McLaren transmission that was pretty much used across the full McLaren Automotive range.

The driving precision of the GT was enhanced by a new hydraulic steering configuration which used a single software 'map' across Comfort, Sport and Track modes to deliver optimal feel and response. Reflecting the requirements of a GT car, it also provided increased assistance at low speeds to aid urban driving and parking, without loss of rewarding feedback at higher speeds.

Ahead of the driver and providing key vehicle information was a 12.3-inch TFT screen. The instrument graphics were not dissimilar to those seen on aircraft, the aeronautical influences delivering clear, crisp displays that were easy to read. In addition to vehicle speed, gear selection and engine revs, the instrument cluster could also display turn-by-turn navigation, phone calls, chosen audio output and tyre temperatures and pressures. When a reversing camera was specified, the image behind the vehicle was displayed when reverse gear was selected, keeping the driver's eyeline as high as possible.

The infotainment system developed for the GT was the company's most sophisticated to date. Among the fastest-operating in any car on the road, it also featured industry-standard 'HERE' navigation mapping and real-time traffic

information. The driver interface operated in a similar way to a smartphone and the seven-inch central touchscreen could be used to select from vehicle functions such as satellite navigation, Bluetooth telephony, media streaming and voice activation. DAB digital radio (or Sirius satellite radio in North America) was standard. Heating and ventilation controls were also incorporated into the touchscreen system, ensuring ease of use and reducing the overall number of switches and controls in the cockpit.

MODEL	GT	TRANSMISSION	7-Speed Seamless-Shift Gearbox (SSG)	TYRES F/R		Pirelli
TYPE/FORMULA	Roadcar	CHASSIS	Carbon-fibre monocoque, aluminium front/rear crash structures	LENGTH		184.4in - 4684mm
YEAR OF PRODUCTION	2019	BODY	Carbon-fibre monocell II-T monocoque	WIDTH		79.5in - 2019mm
DESIGNER	McLaren Automotive design team	FRONT SUSPENSION	Double aluminium wishbone;	HEIGHT		47.8in - 1214mm
EXAMPLES BUILT	Currently in production		independent adaptive dampers with Proactive Damping Control	WHEELBASE		105.3in - 2675mm
ENGINE	McLaren M840TE V8	REAR SUSPENSION	Double aluminium wishbone;	TRACK F/R		65.8/65.5in - 1671/1664mm
CUBIC CAPACITY	3994cc		independent adaptive dampers with Proactive Damping Control	WEIGHT		3232lb - 1466kg
INDUCTION	Twin turbocharged	BRAKES F/R	Cast iron discs	PRINCIPAL DRIVERS		n/a
POWER OUTPUT	612bhp	WHEELS DIAMETER x WIDTH F/R	8x20/10.5x21in	IDENTIFYING COLOURS		n/a

2020 SPEEDTAIL ROADCAR

First announced in October of 2018 and set to use the first production petrol-electric hybrid drivetrain to come out of the Woking factory, the next chapter in McLaren's Ultimate Series, the unique three-seat cockpit (with central driving position) Speedtail, was set to be the first 'Hyper-GT' from the pioneering British company.

Just 106 examples of the Speedtail were set to be built and all were pre-sold at a price of £1.75 million plus taxes, to eager customers (whose first glimpse of the car was at a private reveal in central London), before the car made its first public appearance at the 2019 Geneva Motorshow in March.

At that October announcement Mike Flewitt, CEO of McLaren Automotive was understandably excited, "McLaren has never built a vehicle like the Speedtail before. As our first 'Hyper-GT', the Speedtail is the ultimate McLaren road car; a fusion of art and science that combines an astonishing maximum speed with an iconic central-driving position and a truly pioneering approach to bespoke personalization. A ground-breaking hybrid powertrain sits within a lightweight carbon-fibre body reminiscent of sleek 'streamliners' that once set world speed records, while the luxurious three-seat cockpit offers a sublime combination of an incredible driving experience, unmatched individualism and innovative materials never seen before in a road-going vehicle."

Every element and every aspect of the McLaren Speedtail was considered in the mission to reduce drag and maximize top speed. The car was narrower than a McLaren P1, but more than 1.6ft longer, measuring nearly 17 feet (5,137mm) from nose to tail. The purity of form was remarkable when viewed from above. Essentially a teardrop — the fastest shape in nature — the sculpted form created the smoothest initial contact with the air at the front splitter, while the dramatically elongated tail bled off the flow to reduce turbulence. Not only was the overall shape a teardrop, but so too was the cockpit glasshouse set within the body, once again benefitting aerodynamic drag efficiency. The seamless silhouette was enhanced by a reduction in the number of

shutlines – including a one-piece rear clamshell, and carbon-fibre front-wheel static aero covers helped reduce air turbulence around the wheelarch area.

The teardrop-shaped cockpit and aerodynamic body were the foundation for the exceptional aerodynamic drag efficiency, with innovative features such as retractable digital rear-view cameras (in lieu of mirrors) and patented active rear ailerons contributing to the ultra-low drag achieved.

The Speedtail was built around a bespoke version of the McLaren Monocage carbon-fibre structure and benefitted from lightweight engineering throughout, including an all-carbon-fibre body, aluminium active suspension and carbon ceramic brakes. The Pioneering petrol-electric hybrid powertrain delivered a combined 1,035bhp (1,070PS) and a relentless increase in vehicle speed regardless of engine rpm, for acceleration figures of 0-186mph in 12.8 seconds and a top speed of 250mph (403km/h).

This speed of 250mph was achieved in a unique 'Velocity Mode', which was developed specifically for the Speedtail. Velocity mode optimised the hybrid powertrain for high-speed running while also tailoring the angle of the active rear ailerons. Additionally, the digital rear-view cameras could be retracted to further improve drag. Furthermore, the Velocity Active Chassis Control lowered the Speedtail by 1.4-inches, leaving the highest point of the vehicle just 3.7ft (1,120mm) from the road surface.

As with the 1995 McLaren F1, the driver in the Speedtail was positioned centrally in the perfectly symmetrical luxurious cockpit, with seating for two additional passengers set slightly rearwards. The double-skinned, power-operated dihedral doors fitted with lightweight glazing and the advanced electrochromic glass that darkened top of the windscreen at the touch of a button, (removing the need for sunvisors) helped offer an unparalleled view of the inevitably fast approaching road.

MODEL	Speedtail
TYPE/FORMULA	Roadcar
YEAR OF PRODUCTION	2020
DESIGNER	McLaren Automotive design team
EXAMPLES BUILT	106
ENGINE	McLaren M840TQ IPAS (V8 + electric)
CUBIC CAPACITY	3994cc
ELECTRONICS	Twin turbocharged
POWER OUTPUT	1035bhp (746bhp +309bhp)

TRANSMISSION	7-speed
CHASSIS	Carbon-fibre monocell
BODY	Carbon-fibre monocage body structure
FRONT SUSPENSION	Velocity Active Control
REAR SUSPENSION	Velocity Active Control
BRAKES F/R	Carbon Ceramic Discs
WHEELS DIAMETER x WIDTH F/R	21x9/21x13.7in

TYRES F/R	Bespoke Pirelli P-ZERO
LENGTH	202.2in - 5137mm
WIDTH	76.3in - 1938mm
HEIGHT	46.5in - 1181mm
WHEELBASE	107.4in - 2728mm
TRACK F/R	66.3/64.0in - 1683/1627mm
WEIGHT	3153lb - 1430kg
PRINCIPAL DRIVERS	n/a
IDENTIFYING COLOURS	n/a

Model	Type/Formula	Year	Built	Engine	Capacity	Designer(s)	Comments
M1A	Group 7 Sports	1964/65	2	Oldsmobile V8	3900	McLaren	Automatic transmission used in 1965
McLaren-Elva M1A (MkI)	Group 7 Sports	1965	24	Oldsmobile/Ford V8	3900-5000	McLaren	First Elva built customer McLaren
M1B	Group 7 Sports	1965/66	4*	Oldsmobile/Chevrolet V8	4700-5400	Herd/McLaren	Body designed by Michael Turner
McLaren-Elva M1B (MkII)	Group 7/Can-Am	1966	28	Oldsmobile/Chevrolet/Ford V8	4700-5400	Herd/McLaren	Elva built M1B
McLaren-Elva M1C (MkIII)	Can-Am	1967	25	Chevrolet/Ford/Oldsmobile V8	4500-6000	Herd	Last car built by Elva
M2A	Prototype single seater	1965	1	Oldsmobile/Ford V8	4500/6000	McLaren/Herd	First single seater McLaren
M2B	Formula 1	1966	2	Ford/Serenissima V8	3000	McLaren/Herd	First Grand Prix car
M3A	Formula Libre/Hillclimb	1966	3	Oldsmobile/Ford/Chevrolet V8	4700-5400	McLaren/Herd	'Woosh-bonk' spaceframe car
M4A	Formula 2	1967	2	Ford Cosworth FVA 4cyl	1598	Herd	First Formula 2 car
McLaren-Trojan M4A/B	Formula 2/Formula B	1967	25	Ford Cosworth FVA 4cyl	1598	Herd	First Trojan built model
M4B	Formula 1	1967	1	BRM V8	2070	Herd	Interim 1967 Formula 1 car, destroyed in fire
M5A	Formula 1	1967	1	BRM V12	2998	Herd	Chassis M5A-1 ran first BRM V12 engine built
M6A	Can-Am	1967	3	Chevrolet V8	5900	Herd/Coppuck	Can-Am Championship winning 1967 team cars
McLaren-Trojan M6B	Can-Am	1968	26	Chevrolet V8	5900	Herd/Coppuck	Trojan built version of M6A
M6GT	Roadcar	1969	1	Chevrolet LT1 V8	5740	McLaren/Coppuck	Only M6GT built at McLaren, Bruce's roadcar
McLaren-Trojan M6GT	Roadcar	1969	3	Chevrolet LT1 V8	5740	McLaren/Coppuck	Trojan customer version of M6GT
M7A	Formula 1	1968/69	3	Ford Cosworth DFV V8	2993	Herd/Coppuck	First Cosworth DFV engined McLaren
M7B	Formula 1	1969	1*	Ford Cosworth DFV V8	2993	Coppuck	Pannier tank version of M7A
M7C	Formula 1	1969	1	Ford Cosworth DFV V8	2993	Coppuck	One off with modified M7A monocoque
M7D	Formula 1	1970	1	Alfa Romeo T33 V8	2995	Coppuck	One off Alfa engined M7A
M8A	Can-Am	1968	3	Chevrolet V8	6997	Coppuck/Marquart	1968 Can-Am Championship winner
M8B	Can-Am	1969	3*	Chevrolet V8	6997	Coppuck/Marquart	Unbeaten 1969 Can-Am Championship winner
McLaren-Trojan M8C	Can-Am	1970	15	Chevrolet/Ford V8	7000-7500	Coppuck/Marquart	Trojan built customer version of M8A
M8D	Can-Am	1970	4	Chevrolet V8	7100-7600	Marquart	1970 Can-Am Championship winner - 'Batmobile'
McLaren-Trojan M8E	Can-Am	1971	15-18	Chevrolet V8	7000-8095	Marquart	Trojan built customer version of M8D
M8F	Can-Am	1971	3*	Chevrolet V8	7900-8400	Coppuck	Works car for 1971
McLaren-Trojan M8F/P	Can-Am	1972	10	Chevrolet V8	8093	Coppuck	Trojan built customer version of M8F
M9A	Formula 1	1969	1	Ford Cosworth DFV V8	2993	Marquart	Experimental four-wheel drive Formula 1 car
McLaren-Trojan M10A	Formula 5000/A	1969	20	Chevrolet V8	5000	Coppuck	First F5000 car from McLaren
McLaren-Trojan M10B	Formula 5000/A	1970	21	Chevrolet V8	5000	Coppuck	Revised M10A for 1970 season
M11	-	-	-	-	-	-	Number not used - possible confusion with M1B Mk.II
McLaren-Trojan M12	Can-Am/Group 7	1969	15	Chevrolet V8	6997	Coppuck	1969 Trojan production Can-Am car on M6 tub
M12GT	Roadcar	1970	1?	Chevrolet V8	7000	McLaren/Coppuck	Rumoured coupe built on M12 chassis
M13	-	-	-	-	-	-	Number not used - superstition
M14A	Formula 1	1970/71	3	Ford Cosworth DFV V8	2993	Coppuck/Marquart	Last Formula 1 model driven by Bruce McLaren
M14D	Formula 1	1970	1	Alfa Romeo V8	2995	Coppuck/Marquart	Alfa engined version of M14A
M15	Indianapolis/USAC	1970	3	Offenhauser (turbo) 4cyl	2600	Coppuck	McLaren's first 'Indy 500' USAC/Indianapolis car
M16	Indianapolis/USAC	1971	3	Offenhauser (turbo) 4cyl	2600	Coppuck	Classic wedge shaped Indy car
M16B	Indianapolis/USAC	1972	4	Offenhauser (turbo) 4cyl	2600	Coppuck	First 'Indy 500' winner for a (Donohue)
M16C	Indianapolis/USAC	1973	6	Offenhauser (turbo) 4cyl	2600	Coppuck	Heavily revised M16B
M16C/D	Indianapolis/USAC	1974	3*	Offenhauser (turbo) 4cyl	2600	Coppuck	1974 'Indy 500' winnner (Rutherford)
M16E	Indianapolis/USAC	1975	2	Offenhauser (turbo) 4cyl	2600	Barnard	John Barnard re-worked M16D
M16E	Indianapolis/USAC	1976	2*	Offenhauser (turbo) 4cyl	2600	Barnard	1976 'Indy 500' winnner (Rutherford)
M17	Sports Prototype	1971	-	Ford Cosworth DFV V8	2993	Bellamy	Project cancelled
McLaren-Trojan M18	Formula 5000/A	1971	8	Chevrolet V8	5000	Bellamy	Production F5000 car for 1971
M19	Formula 1	1971/72	2	Ford Cosworth DFV V8	2993	Bellamy	Bellamy's 'Coke bottle' shaped Formula 1 car
M19C	Formula 1	1972/73	2	Ford Cosworth DFV V8	2993	Bellamy	Heavily revised car for 1972 & 1973
M20	Can-Am	1972	3	Chevrolet V8	8095	Coppuck	Final Can-Am car from McLaren
M21	Formula 2	1972	1	Ford Cosworth BDA/BDF 4cyl	1899/1998	Bellamy	F2 car designed for proposed Trojan production
McLaren-Trojan M22	Formula 5000	1972	3	Chevrolet V8	4950	Coppuck	Trojan production F5000 car for 1972
M23	Formula 1	1973	4	Ford Cosworth DFV V8	2993	Coppuck	One of the most long-lived & successful Formula 1 cars
M23	Formula 1	1974	4	Ford Cosworth DFV V8	2993	Coppuck	Double World Championship winner (Fittipaldi)
M23	Formula 1	1975	2	Ford Cosworth DFV V8	2993	Coppuck	3 GP wins in 1975
M23	Formula 1	1976	4*	Ford Cosworth DFV V8	2993	Coppuck	Drivers' Championship in 1976 (Hunt)
M23	Formula 1	1977	3	Ford Cosworth DFV V8	2993	Coppuck	3 Grand Prix wins in fifth season
M24	Indianapolis/USAC	1977	6	Ford Cosworth DFX (turbo) V8	2650	Coppuck	1977 Indycar based on M23
M24B	Indianapolis/USAC	1978	3	Ford Cosworth DFX (turbo) V8	2650	Coppuck	Revised M24 for 1978 & 1979. Still running in 1982

Model	Type/Formula	Year	Built	Engine	Capacity	Designer(s)	Comments
M25	Formula 5000	1974-78	1	Chevrolet/Ford Cosworth DFV V8	5000/2993	Barnard	One-off and final F5000 car
M26	Formula 1	1976-78	7	Ford Cosworth DFV V8	2993	Coppuck	M23 replacement used from 1976 to 1978
M27	Formula 1	-	-	-	-	-	Project cancelled - superceeded by M28
M28	Formula 1	1979	3	Ford Cosworth DFV V8	2993	Coppuck	McLaren's first 'ground-effects' car
M28C	Formula 1	1979	1*	Ford Cosworth DFV V8	2993	Coppuck	Heavily revised M28
M29	Formula 1	1979-80	5	Ford Cosworth DFV V8	2993	Coppuck	Hastily produced Williams copy 'ground-effects' car
M29C	Formula 1	1980-81	2*	Ford Cosworth DFV V8	2993	Coppuck	Revised M29 for 1980
M30	Formula 1	1980	1	Ford Cosworth DFV V8	2993	Coppuck	Further developed 'ground-effects' car
MP4/1	Formula 1	1981	4	Ford Cosworth DFV V8	2993	Barnard	First carbon fibre chassis Formula 1 car
MP4/1B	Formula 1	1982	5*	Ford Cosworth DFV V8	2993	Barnard	Updated MP4/1 for 1982
MP4/1C	Formula 1	1983	4*	Ford Cosworth DFV/DFY V8	2993	Barnard	Updated MP4/1 for 1983
MP4/1D	Formula 1 Test Car	1983	1*	TAG Turbo (turbo) V6	1496	Barnard	First TAG Turbo engined Formula 1 test car
MP4/1E	Formula 1	1983	3*	TAG Turbo (turbo) V6	1496	Barnard	Late 1983 interim race car
MP4/2	Formula 1	1984	5	TAG Turbo (turbo) V6	1496	Barnard	Double Championship winning car with revised engine
MP4/2B	Formula 1	1985	5*	TAG Turbo (turbo) V6	1496	Barnard	Revised MP4/2 wins another Championship
MP4/2C	Formula 1	1986	5	TAG Turbo (turbo) V6	1496	Barnard	Revised MP4/2B gives 3rd Drivers' title in a row
MP4/3	Formula 1	1987	6	TAG Turbo (turbo) V6	1496	Nichols	First 'low-line' Formula 1 car
MP4/3B	Formula 1 Test Car	1987	2*	Honda RA108E (turbo) V6	1496	Nichols	Test version of MP4/3 with new Honda V6 engine
MP4/3C	Formula 1 Test Car	1988	1	Honda RA109E V10	3490	Nichols/Oatley	Honda V10 version of MP4/3 - never completed
MP4/4	Formula 1	1988	6	Honda RA168E (turbo) V6	1494	Nichols/Murray	Record breaking first season with Honda engine
MP4/4B	Formula 1 Test Car	1988	3	Honda RA109E V10	3490	Nichols	Late 1988 test car with Honda V10 engine
MP4/5	Formula 1	1989	8	Honda RA109E V10	3490	Oatley	First season with normally aspirated engine
MP4/5B	Formula 1	1990	7	Honda RA100E V10	3490	Oatley	Third Drivers' & Constructors' titles in a row
MP4/5C	Formula 1 Test Car	1990	2	Honda RA121E V12	3493	Oatley	Mid 1990 test version of MP4/5B with new Honda V12
MP4/6	Formula 1	1991	11	Honda RA121E V12	3493	Oatley	Honda V12 power brings another double championship
MP4/6B	Formula 1	1992	2*	Honda RA122E V12	3493	Oatley	Revised MP4/6 used in first Grand Prix of 1992
MP4/6Y	Formula 1	1991	1*	Honda RA122E V12	3493	Oatley	MP4/6 with semi-auto transmission practiced in Hungary
MP4/6C	Formula 1	1992	1*	Honda RA122E V12	3493	Oatley	Modified MP4/6 run in early 1992
MP4/7	Formula 1	1992	10	Honda RA122E/B V12	3493	Oatley	New 1992 car with Honda pneumatic valve engine
MP4/7B	Formula 1 Test Car	1992	1*	Honda RA122E/B V12	3493	Oatley	Honda active ride with 2nd generation 'fly by wire' system
MP4/8	Formula 1	1993	8	Ford HBE V8	3494	Oatley	Senna wins sensational European GP at Donington
MP4/8Z	Formula 1	1993	1*	Ford HBE V8	3494	Oatley	Experimental MP4/8 with developed engine
MP4/8B	Formula 1 Test Car	1993	1*	Chrysler Lamborghini V12	3498	Oatley	One off Chrysler powered test car
McLaren F1	Roadcar	1993	64	BMW V12	6064	Murray/Stevens	World's fastest roadcar
MP4/9	Formula 1	1994	8	Peugeot A4/A6 V10	3498	Oatley	Single season with Peugeot engine
MP4/10A	Formula 1	1995	5	Mercedes-Benz FO 110D V10	2997	Oatley	First season with Mercedes-Benz, first 'high nose' car
MP4/10B	Formula 1	1995	6	Mercedes-Benz FO 110D V10	2997	Oatley	Widened chassis MP4/10 for Nigel Mansell
MP4/10C	Formula 1	1995	3*	Mercedes-Benz FO 110D V10	2997	Oatley	MP4/10B with lowered centre of gravity
MP4/10D	Formula 1	1995	2*	Mercedes-Benz FO 110D V10	2997	Oatley	MP4/10C with revised rear suspension
F1 GTR 1995	Racecar	1995	9	BMW V12	6064	Murray/Stevens	Le Mans winner at first attempt
MP4/11A	Formula 1	1996	6	Mercedes-Benz FO 110E V10	2997	Oatley	Last year with longtime sponsor Marlboro
MP4/11B	Formula 1	1996	2	Mercedes-Benz FO 110E V10	2997	Oatley	Long wheelbase version of MP4/11A
MP4/11C	Formula 1 Test Car	1996	2*	Mercedes-Benz FO 110E V10	2997	Oatley	Revised MP4/11A-B to test narrow track regulations
McLaren F1 LM	Roadcar	1996	5	BMW V12	6064	Murray	Le Mans commemorative edition
F1 GTR 1996	Racecar	1996	9	BMW V12	6064	Murray	Japanese GT Championship winner
MP4-12	Formula 1	1997	7	Mercedes-Benz FO 110E/F V10	2997	Oatley	First Grand Prix win for West Mercedes
MP4-12W	Formula 1 Test Car	1997	1*	Mercedes-Benz FO 110F V10	2997	Oatley	MP4-12 with special gearbox and 'wet' clutch
McLaren F1 GT	Roadcar	1997	3	BMW V12	6046	Murray	Longtail homologation roadcar
McLaren F1 GTR 1997	Racecar	1997	10	BMW V12	5990	Murray	Longtail version of GTR, 2nd at Le Mans
MP4-98T	Two-Seat Formula 1 car	1998	1	Mercedes-Benz FO 110G V10	2997	Lett/Murray	Adrenaline programme, VIP Formula 1 experience
MP4-13	Formula 1	1998	7	Mercedes-Benz FO 110G V10	2997	Oatley/Newey	Championship double winning car
MP4-13S	Formula 1 Test Car	1998	1*	Mercedes-Benz FO 110G V10	2997	Newey/Oatley	MP4-13 test car with experimental transmission
MP4-14	Formula 1	1999	8	Mercedes-Benz FO 110H V10	2997	Newey/Oatley	Second Drivers' title for Häkkinen
MP4-14J	Formula 1 Test Car	1999	1*	Mercedes-Benz FO 110J V10	2997	Newey/Oatley	Development car for winter testing 1999-2000
MP4-14S	Formula 1 Test Car	1999	1*	Mercedes-Benz FO 110H V10	2997	Newey/Oatley	MP4-14 test car with MP4-13S experimental transmission
MP4-15	Formula 1	2000	7	Mercedes-Benz FO 110J V10	2997	Newey/Oatley	7 Grand Prix wins
MP4-15B	Formula 1 Test Car	2000	1*	Mercedes-Benz FO 110J V10	2997	Newey/Oatley	

Model	Type/Formula	Year	Built	Engine	Capacity	Designer(s)	Comments
MP4-15K	Formula 1 Test Car	2000	1*	Mercedes-Benz FO 110K V10	2997	Newey/Oatley	Development car to run Mercedes-Benz K spec engine
MP4-15S	Formula 1 Test Car	2000	1*	Mercedes-Benz FO 110J V10	2997	Newey/Oatley	MP4-15 test car with MP4-14S experimental transmission
MP4-16	Formula 1	2001	7	Mercedes-Benz FO 110K V10	2997	Newey/Oatley	4 Grand Prix wins
MP4-16B	Formula 1 Test Car	2001	1*	Mercedes-Benz FO 110K V10	2997	Newey/Oatley	MP4-16 with revised transmission
MP4-17A	Formula 1	2002	9	Mercedes-Benz FO 110M V10	2997	Newey/Oatley	David Coulthard Monaco win
MP4-17B	Formula 1 Test Car	2002	5*	Mercedes-Benz FO 110M V10	2997	Newey/Oatley	
MP4-17C	Formula 1 Test Car	2002	1*	Mercedes-Benz FO 110M V10	2997	Newey/Oatley	MP4-17A with experimental rear suspension & gearbox
MP4-T5	Gravity Racer/Soapbox	2002	1	n/a	n/a	Childs	Category record at the Goodwood Festival of Speed
MP4-17L	Formula 1	2003	0	Mercedes-Benz V10	n/a	Newey/Oatley	Cancelled 2002 car with innovative engine concept
MP4-17D	Formula 1	2003	6*	Mercedes-Benz FO 110M V10	2997	Newey/Oatley	Raced due to aborted MP4-18
MP4-18A	Formula 1	2003	3	Mercedes-Benz FO 110P V10	2997	Newey	Conceived with a composite cased, twin clutch gearbox
MP4-18B	Formula 1	2003	3*	Mercedes-Benz FO 110P V10	2997	Newey	MP4-18A with revised rear bodywork and exhaust outlets
MP4-18X	Formula 1 Test Car	2003	1*	Mercedes-Benz FO 110P V10	2997	Newey	MP4-18A with development carbon fibre gearbox
MP4-19A	Formula 1	2004	5	Mercedes-Benz FO 110Q V10	2997	Newey	
MP4-19B	Formula 1	2004	4	Mercedes-Benz FO 110Q V10	2997	McLaren Racing	
MP4-20A	Formula 1	2005	7	Mercedes-Benz FO 110R V10	2997	McLaren Racing	10 Grand Prix wins
MP4-20B	Formula 1 Test Car	2005	2*	Mercedes-Benz FO 108S V8	2400	McLaren Racing	MP4-20A with 2006 spec engine
MP4-21A	Formula 1	2006	7	Mercedes-Benz FO 108S V8	2400	McLaren Racing	
MP4-22	Formula 1	2007	6	Mercedes-Benz FO 108T V8	2398	McLaren Racing	8 Grand Prix wins
MP4-23	Formula 1	2008	6	Mercedes-Benz FO 108V V8	2398	McLaren Racing	Drivers' title for Hamilton, 6 Grand Prix wins
MP4-24	Formula 1	2009	5	Mercedes-Benz FO 108W V8	2398	McLaren Racing	2 Grand Prix wins
MP4-25	Formula 1	2010	4	Mercedes-Benz FO 108X V8	2398	McLaren Racing	5 Grand Prix wins
12C	Roadcar	2011	n/a	M838T V8 (Turbocharged)	3799	Automotive	
MP4-26	Formula 1	2011	4	Mercedes-Benz FO 108Y V8	2398	McLaren Racing	
12C GT3	Racecar	2011	25	M838T V8 (Turbocharged)	3799	Automotive	
MP4-27	Formula 1	2012	4	Mercedes-Benz FO 108Z V8	2398	McLaren Racing	
12C Spider	Roadcar	2012	n/a	M838T V8 (Turbocharged)	3799	Automotive	
MP4-28	Formula 1	2013	4	Mercedes-Benz FO 108F V8	2398	McLaren Racing	
P1	Roadcar	2013	375	M838TQ Turbo (V8 + electric)	3799	Automotive	
MP4-29	Formula 1	2014	4	Mercedes-Benz PU 106A V6 hybrid	1598	McLaren Racing	
650S	Roadcar	2014	n/a	M838T V8 (Turbocharged)	3799	Automotive	
650S Spider	Roadcar	2014	n/a	M838T V8 (Turbocharged)	3799	Automotive	
650S GT3	Racecar	2014	15	M838T V8 (Turbocharged)	3799	Automotive	
MP4-30	Formula 1	2015	4	Honda RA615H V6 hybrid	1598	McLaren Racing	
675LT	Roadcar	2015	500	M838T V8 (Turbocharged)	3799	Automotive	
570S	Roadcar	2015	n/a	M838TE V8 (Turbocharged)	3799	Automotive	
P1 GTR	Racecar	2015	58	M838TQ Turbo (V8 + electric)	3799	Automotive	
P1 LM	Racecar	2016	6	M838TQ Turbo (V8 + electric)	3799	Automotive	
MP4-31	Formula 1	2016	4	Honda RA616H V6 hybrid	1598	McLaren Racing	
540C	Roadcar	2016	n/a	M838TF V8 (Turbocharged)	3799	Automotive	
570GT	Roadcar	2016	n/a	M838TE V8 (Turbocharged)	3799	Automotive	
675LT Spider	Roadcar	2016	500	M838T V8 (Turbocharged)	3799	Automotive	
570S GT4	Racecar	2016	n/a	M838TE V8 (Turbocharged)	3799	Automotive	
MCL-32	Formula 1	2017	5	Honda RA617H V6 hybrid	1598	McLaren Racing	
720S	Roadcar	2017	n/a	M840T V8 (Turbocharged)	3994	Automotive	
570S Spider	Roadcar	2017	n/a	M838TE V8 (Turbocharged)	3799	Automotive	
MCL-33	Formula 1	2018	4	Renault RE18 V6 Hybrid	1598	McLaren Racing	
600LT	Roadcar	2018	n/a	M838TE V8 (Turbocharged)	3799	Automotive	
McLaren Senna	Roadcar	2018	500	M840TR V8 (Turbocharged)	3994	Automotive	
720S GT3	Racecar	2019	n/a	M840T V8 (Turbocharged)	3994	Automotive	
McLaren Senna GTR	Racecar	2019	75	M840TR V8 (Turbocharged)	3994	Automotive	
MCL-34	Formula 1	2019	4	Renault RE19 V6 Hybrid	1598	McLaren Racing	
600LT Spider	Roadcar	2019	n/a	M838TE V8 (Turbocharged)	3799	Automotive	
720S Spider	Roadcar	2019	n/a	M840T V8 (Turbocharged)	3994	Automotive	
GT	Roadcar	2019	n/a	M838TE V8 (Turbocharged)	3994	Automotive	
Speedtail	Roadcar	2020	106	M840TQ Turbo (V8 + electric)	3994	Automotive	

Notes: * Number of cars built on this model are included in the figure for the same model in the line (or lines) immediately above.

Car	Year	Championship Title	Type/Formula	Engine	Capacity	Wins	Poles	Races	Driver(s)
M23	1974	F1 World Constructors' Champions	Formula 1	Ford Cosworth DFV V8	2993	4	2	15	Emerson Fittipaldi, Denny Hulme
M23	1974	F1 World Drivers' Champion	Formula 1	Ford Cosworth DFV V8	2993	4	2	15	Emerson Fittipaldi
M23	1974	South African F1 Champion	Formula 1	Ford Cosworth DFV V8	2993	6	6	11	Dave Charlton
M23	1975	South African F1 Champion	Formula 1	Ford Cosworth DFV V8	2993	2	1	9	Dave Charlton
M23	1976	F1 World Drivers' Champion	Formula 1	Ford Cosworth DFV V8	2993	6	8	16	James Hunt
MP4/2	1984	F1 World Constructors' Champions	Formula 1	TAG Turbo (turbo) V6	1496	12	3	16	Alain Prost, Niki Lauda
MP4/2B	1985	F1 World Constructors' Champions	Formula 1	TAG Turbo (turbo) V6	1496	6	2	16	Alain Prost, Niki Lauda
MP4/2B	1985	F1 World Drivers' Champion	Formula 1	TAG Turbo (turbo) V6	1496	5	2	16	Alain Prost
MP4/2C	1986	F1 World Drivers' Champion	Formula 1	TAG Turbo (turbo) V6	1496	4	1	16	Alain Prost
MP4/4	1988	F1 World Constructors' Champions	Formula 1	Honda RA168E (turbo) V6	1494	15	15	16	Alain Prost, Ayrton Senna
MP4/5	1989	F1 World Constructors' Champions	Formula 1	Honda RA109E V10	3490	10	15	16	Alain Prost, Ayrton Senna
MP4/5	1989	F1 World Drivers' Champion	Formula 1	Honda RA109E V10	3490	4	2	16	Alain Prost
MP4/5B	1990	F1 World Constructors' Champions	Formula 1	Honda RA100E V10	3490	6	12	16	Ayrton Senna, Gerhard Berger
MP4/5B	1990	F1 World Drivers' Champion	Formula 1	Honda RA100E V10	3490	6	10	16	Ayrton Senna
MP4/6	1991	F1 World Constructors' Champions	Formula 1	Honda RA121E V12	3493	8	10	16	Ayrton Senna, Gerhard Berger
MP4/6	1991	F1 World Drivers' Champion	Formula 1	Honda RA121E V12	3493	7	8	16	Ayrton Senna
MP4-13	1998	F1 World Constructors' Champions	Formula 1	Mercedes-Benz FO 110G V10	2997	9	12	16	Mika Häkkinen, David Coulthard
MP4-13	1998	F1 World Drivers' Champion	Formula 1	Mercedes-Benz FO 110G V10	2997	8	9	16	Mika Häkkinen
MP4-14	1999	F1 World Drivers' Champion	Formula 1	Mercedes-Benz FO 110H V10	2997	5	11	16	Mika Häkkinen
MP4-23	2008	F1 World Drivers' Champion	Formula 1	Mercedes-Benz FO 108V V8	2398	5	7	18	Lewis Hamilton
McLaren	1966-2019	F1 World Championship Grand Prix Races	Formula 1	Ford, BRM, TAG, Honda, Peugeot, Mercedes-Benz, Renault	n/a	182	155	863	Grand Prix Winners see below: McLaren, Hulme, Revson, Fittipaldi, Mass, Hunt, Watson, Lauda, Prost, Senna, Berger, Coulthard, Häkkinen, Räikkonen, Montoya, Alonso, Hamilton, Kovalainen, Button
M10A	1969	Guards European F5000 Champion	Formula 5000	Chevrolet V8	5000	9	12	16	Peter Gethin
M10B	1970	Rothmans European F5000 Champion	Formula 5000	Chevrolet V8	5000	9	12	16	Peter Gethin
M10B	1970	Gulf Canadian Road Racing Champion	Formula 5000	Chevrolet V8	5000	5	3	7	Eppie Wietzes
M10B	1970	Continental Formula 5000 Champion	Formula A/5000	Chevrolet V8	5000	3	3	13	John Cannon
M10B	1971	Continental Formula 5000 Champion	Formula A/5000	Chevrolet V8	5000	5	5	8	David Hobbs
M10B	1971	Tasman Cup Champion	Formula 5000	Chevrolet V8	5000	3	2	7	Graham McRae
F1 GTR	1995	24-Hours of Le Mans, overall winners	Sportscar	BMW V12	6064	1	n/a	n/a	J.J. Lehto, Y. Dalmas, M. Sekiya
M6A	1967	Canadian American Challenge Cup	Can-Am	Chevrolet V8	5900	5	5	6	Bruce McLaren
M8A	1968	Canadian American Challenge Cup	Can-Am	Chevrolet V8	6997	4	6	6	Denny Hulme
M8B	1969	Canadian American Challenge Cup	Can-Am	Chevrolet V8	6997	11	11	11	Bruce McLaren
M8D	1970	Canadian American Challenge Cup	Can-Am	Chevrolet V8	7100-7600	7	11	10	Denny Hulme
M8F	1971	Canadian American Challenge Cup	Can-Am	Chevrolet V8	7900-8400	8	8	10	Peter Revson
M16B	1972	Indianapolis 500	Indycar	Offenhauser (turbo) 4cyl	2600	1	n/a	n/a	Mark Donohue
M16C/D	1974	Indianapolis 500	Indycar	Offenhauser (turbo) 4cyl	2600	1	n/a	n/a	Johnny Rutherford
M16E	1976	Indianapolis 500	Indycar	Offenhauser (turbo) 4cyl	2600	1	n/a	n/a	Johnny Rutherford